Against Academia

Against Academia:

The History of the
Popular Culture Association/
American Culture Association and
The Popular Culture Movement

1967—1988

Ray B. Browne

Bowling Green State University Popular Press
Bowling Green, Ohio 43403

Library of Congress Catalogue Card No.: 89-60324

ISBN: 0-87972-451-X clothbound
0-87972-452-8 paperback

Cover design by Gary Dumm

Dedicated to

Russel B. Nye

Carl Bode

and the memory of

Earl F. Bargainnier

and the thousands

of participants through

whose efforts the success

of the movement was guaranteed.

Contents

Background and Development of an Idea   1
Development of the Idea at
   Bowling Green State University   14
The Development of the Popular Culture Association   21
Birth and Development of the
   American Culture Association   57
History of the
   American Culture Association   61
Internationalizing the PCA/ACA   70
Development of the Center for the Study of Popular Culture,
   the Popular Press and the Popular Culture Library   78
The Popular Culture Library   87
Growth and Development of Regional Chapters   91
The Popular Culture Association of the South   95
Popular Culture Association of the Southwest
   and Texas   98
The Northeast PCA and Other Latecomers   101
History of the ACA Superior Chapter   103
Photos of PCA/ACA Officers   opposite 105
First PCA Program   105
First ACA Program   119
Index of Participants   143

Preface

The idea of a history of the Popular Culture Association/American Culture Association and the whole movement in the study of popular culture has lain in the back of my mind through the years. Occasionally I have gathered some data and thought about gathering much more on the background of the movement but never really put my mind and energy to it. Several people have suggested—even urged—me to write this history, and I have occasionally taped interviews with former and with present-day participants.

One day last year the importance of writing a history of the movement finally struck me with considerable and irresistible force. The history had to be written, I decided, and had to be written and published now. So I set about reconstructing the halcyon days of the past when everybody was young and many ideas were vital and vibrant. It was a pleasant occasion for me to reconstruct those far-gone days and to realize that although the original ideas were long past their descendants are still around, are still young and are still very vital. We are and can still be young. Halcyon days can be yesterday, today and tomorrow—not yesteryear.

In remembering and reliving the past I found many occasions when I simply could not bring history again to the fore. On those occasions I have called upon people who kept better records than I did, whose memory was sharper on particular points or who simply knew far more about some aspects—particularly the growth and development of regional chapters—than I did. For their contribution, which I have always acknowledged, I am grateful.

The trip for the past twenty years has been in many places rough. But the battle has been won. Perhaps no stronger testimony can be found than in an article recently published in the *New York Times* about the Department here at Bowling Green State University and the whole study of popular culture. When the reporter called several people who in the past would have been implacable opponents they no longer railed against it but instead merely commented on what they felt might be the short-comings—in so doing admitting tacitly that the movement is firmly based and here to stay! Indeed it is, and expanding every day. The day has been won.

As author of most of the following pages, I wish to thank all those who have written portions of the history, those who have participated in creating the history and those who have furthered the cause either formally or informally as they have worked in popular culture although not as members of the PCA or ACA or people whom we have known. Those workers have made large contributions.

Undoubtedly there are pages in the history that are missing, chapters ignored, people overlooked or forgotten. For those errors and omissions I take full responsibility and am sorry. Perhaps a revised edition will make some corrections. But it is difficult to get timely cooperation from some thousands of people I have known and worked with through the ages.

Background and Development of an Idea

The academic mind begins with almost unlimited capabilities but never utilizes all its potential.

Such a failing accounts for most of the lack of advancement—the freeing of humanity from the shackles of the past—in education. Instead of using knowledge as a basis on which to build, especially in the Humanities, human beings are generally content to stir around laterally in the cold ashes of today and yesterday rather than to build new outpost fires down the line into tomorrow. The cliched conventional wisdom of the day is that unless we know history we will be forced to relive it. The axiom should be that unless we *understand* history and build on our knowledge we will be tyrannized by its steel grip. We may know all about our past and still not be interested in moving forward. Or we can *understand* the past and build on our knowledge for improved political, social and cultural systems, can improve the conditions of spaceship earth and provide a richer technological-humanities enhancement for human existence in the global village or the global city.

Various academic individuals and groups in several ways have been building out-fires for years in efforts to explore the fringes of our knowledge, discover new fields of inquiry and new ways of looking at the familiar—with the hope and expectation that many new insights and conclusions can result which can be not only rewarding to the individuals immediately involved but also to society at large. They are trying to *understand* the past in order better to develop the present and the future. To a certain extent the problems these individuals face are monumental. America has jumped into a love affair with nostalgia, with folk culture, with the glories of the geologic and anthropological past for their own sake, and such feelings are hard to combat and overcome. But no task is too great for human achievement, so the efforts will continue. These tasks facing the Humanities should be overcome in precisely the same way the scientists overcome theirs—by building *on* the achievements of the past, not looking at the achievements of the past as the desired goal and end-all. Knowledge is to be used and developed, not to be learned, canonized and worshipped as the end in itself.

One of the most innovative, far-reaching and tradition-shattering of academic—and non-academic—movements in the Humanities and social sciences of the last half century has been the development of Popular Culture and its various spin-off areas as an academic discipline. This development has been a kind of class-action suit against conventional points of view and fields of study in the Humanities. It has been a call for scholars in

1

the Humanities to be less prone to constantly re-canonize the Classics, but instead to question their relevance and value in the academic program. In other words, the study of Popular Culture has been a call for academics to be more thoughtful and critical of the works they have been taught to accept as the canon and to exercise their rationalizing power more than their memory.

In the class-action suit that Popular Culture brought against the conventional Humanities, people with the new questioning frame of mind faced formidable obstacles and odds. Academics outside the Humanities did not understand the problems faced within the Humanities and therefore generally opposed the Popular Culture movement. Academics within the Humanities and social sciences could understand but would not admit the problems and the opportunities for advancement, and they therefore strongly, and at times savagely, opposed the introduction of the study of Popular Culture as the New and Practical Humanities—or the new Social Sciences or the Techno-Humanities, or anything else involving the use of Popular Culture in academia. Such individuals opposed radical change just for opposition's sake. They did not feel that new methods should be tried to alter old points of view and old methodologies because they were not needed. Old wine in old bottles was still the proper drink. The proponents of Popular Culture studies, thinking that the old wine had been in the old skins too long, did favor such radical changes.

Thus the lines were drawn in the Humanities for a classic battle between two sharply differing points of view. To overstate the case, it was a confrontation between the Past and the Present, the Old and the New, the Sleepers and the Wakers, the Knowers and the Learners. Although the tug-of-war might seem a tempest in a teapot to non-academics, actually it was and remains to a certain extent a radical revolution in the making. The conflict represents a dramatic shift in Academia's way of looking at the whole approach to the canon and the curriculum in such fields as literature, sociology, history, humanities, ethnic studies, women's studies, comparative literature, music, philosophy, environmental studies, and many others. More important, since intellectual interests usually follow, as well as direct, funding agencies, the impact of the new attitude toward the study of popular culture must win over the usually conservative funding agencies such as the National Endowment for the Humanities, the fifty-one state NEH chapters, such Funds as those of Ford, Rockefeller, Getty, Carnegie, and hundreds of others, nearly all of which are controlled by conservative minds who are reluctant to startle anybody or anything—especially their own training and biases—with innovative change. Such people seem eager to coin and use innovative and fine sounding names and titles but reluctant to alter content. The battle between the innovative and the conservative has not been won by popular culture, but it is very much joined.

To a large extent the introduction of the study of Popular Culture into academia has been the result of the efforts of hundreds—even thousands—of academics. Their reasons have been as varied as the personalities and experiences of the individuals concerned, but they consistently fit a broad pattern. The people are tired and bored, burned out, frustrated with their academic pursuits and want something new. Like their students, the professors are restive and think that there must be new fields to explore and to conquer. Much of the thrust has come from a smaller group of very dedicated individuals who led the fight because they felt that their goal was proper and justified and were prepared to suffer a good deal of criticism, contumely and savage attacks in order to demonstrate and prove their point. The course of this triumph has not been straight and uninterrupted, smooth and flower-strewn. Often the applause and appreciation that has greeted these people has been self-generated and self-contained. There has been a good deal of suffering, bleeding and self-examination along the way. But there has always been a lot of pleasure and satisfaction in the course of the fight—and a fierce determination to persevere and succeed. Success has not necessarily been achieved to date. But a lot of progress has been made. A foot, at least, has been inserted into Academia's door. Undoubtedly the whole body will eventually be admitted and welcomed!

This story of the introduction of Popular Culture into academia is then the saga of a gleam in some academics' eyes, an idea in protest and rebellion, the movement which resulted and the people who directed it and how they became engaged in it. Sometimes sad, often aggravating, the story is nevertheless always optimistic and pleasurable because it charts a movement which is pushing back some of the impediments to a proper American education, cracking some of the shells of the holy of holies about that education, and rewriting forever some of the myths and rituals about American academia. In *Moby Dick* Ishmael's voyage was always toward the democratic future. So has been ours. From the vortex of the sinking ship, Ishmael rose to a new and enlightened life. The hope is that a new force might rise from the scuttling of a few of the old beliefs in academia and a new force will rise from the suds.

My own background might serve as a kind of paradigm of one type of person and motivation propelling people in the Popular Culture movement. If not representative of a large number, it cannot be far off from the backgrounds and motivations of many.

I was born into a middle-class and upwardly mobile family in Millport, Alabama, January 15, 1922. My father, named Garfield after the President of the United States, was from Kentucky. He was a free-thinking intellectual banker who in years when it was not politically smart to do so in the South always addressed black people as Mr. and Mrs. My mother, Annie Nola Trull, was the daughter of a country squire living at Meadow Branch, near Kennedy, Alabama. We four children (Lydia Catherine, called Kay, some eight years older than I was; Annie Mevalene, called Joan, five years older than I was; Byron Hughes—how difficult it was for Southern kids to pronounce Byron as anything but "Barn"—three years older than I was) grew up sometimes deprived of many or most of the necessities of life. But we always had Pride. My mother, for example, knew that her father had known people who associated with the Bankhead political family from Jasper, Alabama, and she was proud of her heritage. My father, perhaps less proud of his social standing but pulling his stature of 5 ft. 6 inches straight and firm, always stood tall and undismayed in Bible-belt rhetoric with his intellectual and deeply learned agnosticism. I was profoundly influenced by his frame of mind and enthusiastic belief in the capabilities of the human mind when it is properly motivated and supported. From my father I developed a great—perhaps unrealistic—respect for knowledge and the capabilities of human intelligence.

My growing up was done in the small-town South. In his many jobs in banks, my father moved his family from town to town in such states as Tennessee, Arkansas, Mississippi, Florida and several towns in Alabama. In 1929, however, with the stock market crash his fortunes plummeted, and from 1932 to 1940 I grew up in Millport, a town in west central Alabama, in Lamar County, near the Mississippi state line.

Millport was a town of 730 people, in a dirt-poor section of the state, where nearly everybody but a few townspeople was deep in poverty and deprivation. Two merchants eventually came to own most of the southern part of the county through foreclosure of mortgages which the farmers could not pay off because they could not sell their crops.

It was a town and a people that Sam Clemens would have been at home in. Except for not having a mighty river flowing on our edge (we did have a small river, the Luxapallila—"Floating Turtle"—that could accommodate no ships but flooded annually) we had all other constituents of a typical Southern small town: hard-working citizens, drunks, thieves and many mischievous kids—Tom Sawyers and Huck Finns abounded. Kids regularly at Halloween would shoot out all street lights (after the town got electricity) or steal somebody's wagon and hoist it onto the top of a building—working all night just to release animal spirits. It was a town where acts were often violent and unshielded, and death was always close. For example, early one Saturday morning a farmer from out of town had his son drive him to Millport. On his way, the man stopped at a creek to get a drink of water and took a handful of strychnine. His son drove up to the funeral parlor just as his father died.

But it was a town and a way of life filled with more pleasure than sadness. People were generally optimistic despite their poverty and general hopelessness. They filled the streets on Saturdays just to socialize and to try to win prizes that the merchants offered to lure people into town in the hope that they could find a dime to spend. There were prizes given away by the merchants, such as the Yellow Front Store's (Sumter Farm & Stock Co.'s) gift of cheap dishes—dishes, incidentally, now considered collector's item, as "Depression dishes." Other merchants gave away much bally-hooed gifts of little intrinsic value but of immense symbolic importance. There were also hours of pleasure when entertainments came to town— an occasional circus, Saturday movies under a tent, "medicine shows," selling their ninety-proof whiskey under the name of some Indian Chief, and other frauds and phonies. There were regular summer "protracted meetings" held by all the churches in town and in the surrounding country. All provided relief from the tedium of small-town life.

I was generally in the midst of all activities. I helped the tent people raise and strike their tents. I worked once as a volunteer with a couple who were demonstrating their power to hypnotize; when they told me to act "hypnotized," I acted hypnotized. I was a great fisherman and could find the fish when others could not. I was considered the most promising baseball player in town, and people often encouraged me to think of playing as a professional. Also, in the early years there were always marbles to play with. I was the marbles king of the town, accumulating a gallon bucket full that I won from other kids in daily and especially Saturday sessions.

So growing up in small-town Alabama was difficult, humiliating and exhilirating and fun. But the knife of poverty cut so deep and left such a scar that I was never able to change the attitude etched in my soul about social injustice and the power of the human mind to develop and justify every kind of denial of justice and reason. Privilege, like power, corrupts, and when only slightly different, protects itself.

After high school I was in many ways lucky in getting a chance at so-called "higher education." I was having trouble getting the money to go to college. But I had friends who respected me and my potential. They wanted me to succeed and to begin that success by attending college. One day in the early summer of 1940, after I had graduated from high school, Elbert Coleman—my high school teacher and father of Theo, with whom I had more or less grown up—asked me if I had got a college to attend. When I told him that I was still having financial problems, he told me to get in the car and we would drive the fifty miles from Millport to Tuscaloosa, the site of the University of Alabama.

When we got to the University campus, where he had graduated, Elbert went around to see the Dean of Men and persuaded him to give me a National Youth Administration job at $.15 per hour for the coming school year. That job and all the other needed support supplied by my sister Joan was enough to keep me at the University. By cutting costs and going without things— for example an overcoat—I got through the University. The cost to me for fees, books, housing and food was $30. a month.

I was fortunate in another way at the University. As my Freshman English instructor, I had a graduate of the University of Alabama who had, incidentally, played on the football team that featured Johnny Mac Brown and went to the Rose Bowl. He had just come back to the University with a Ph.D. from the University of Chicago, and William P. Fidler was full of vinegar and self-assurance, determined that no administration was going to push him around. To my green and ignorant eyes, Fidler's behavior was proper and demonstrated the power of education. His statements put stars in the eyes of at least one undergraduate. Incidentally, Fidler went on to become Secretary-Treasurer of the American Association of University Professors, and at his retirement from that position I sent him a note about how great an influence he had been in my life, and I received a nice little note in return, congratulating me on what little "success" I had had in my career. The star in my eye seemed not to have been misplaced.

After graduating from college in 1943 I spent three years in the U.S. Army, two of which were spent in Europe. True to my upbringing, I never really fit into the Army mold. My existence was always in some jeopardy, not only from the nominal enemy but also from my officer corps. So precarious was my fortune, in fact, that I always congratulated myself every night when I got to sleep in my own barracks or pup tent and outside the stockade. Not that I broke any law or was threatened in that way. But I did not stand straight enough long enough, did not salute sharply enough and did not have enough "Sirs" in my vocabulary. One of my earliest changes in rank in the Army was being reduced from corporal to private for leaning on the Colonel's desk when he was chewing me out for some minor infraction.

But I did survive the Army, returned and decided that I would get a Masters degree at Columbia University in New York City. There I did a thesis on "H.G. Wells and the 'New Woman'." Was it a valuable experience? Yes. Was it a valuable thesis? Probably not. I have never looked at it since finishing it in 1947.

After Columbia I taught three years at the University of Nebraska in Lincoln. I loved the rolling plains, the occasional stretches of virgin sod, and even the bleak and harsh winters. While at the University, I saw colleagues who were interested in subjects that seemed to me narrowly specialized and arcane. Although I was a year or two late to be her colleague, I heard about Louise Pound, scholar and folklorist, who even in her last days would climb up and put a roof on her house. She was of the stock that Willa Cather had praised. To me such activity and such attitudes seemed proper for an academic who wanted to be thoroughly alive and properly committed.

In 1950 I left Nebraska, toured the West to select the graduate school of my choice, and after visiting numerous campuses decided on UCLA to do my Ph.D. work.

Again I was fortunate in my choice of university, or somehow I managed to bend the university to fit my needs. Perhaps there was some of both. UCLA was not really the place where square pegs would easily fit into round holes. Or at least it did not seem that kind of place. But maybe it was. The English Department at UCLA felt very inferior to that at Berkeley, and as a result tried to ape and outdo Berkeley on its own turf, that is in conventional English disciplines. The people representing this outlook were really splendid individuals. Majl Ewing, the Chairman of the Department, was perhaps a little precious for my money, but always gracious and helpful. James E. Phillips, who succeeded Ewing as Chair, was gracious, generous, understanding, helpful and always smiling. The success of his career in whatever he undertook was demonstrated by the fact that he continued to rise and succeed in the Administration at UCLA, to retire almost at the top.

But there were professors of a different stripe. Blake Nevius became a friend; he eventually became editor of *Nineteenth Century Fiction* and entertained a fresh, though cautious, and innovative approach to American literature. There was also Philip Durham, whose interests were radical— he was concerned with pulp fiction, and with Western and detective fiction. His academic future was tenuous and uncertain.

Then there was Leon Howard, looming head and shoulders above all the others. He had been brought out to UCLA at the unheard of and enviable salary of $10,000 to head the American literature program. The author of several books and already recognized as a leading Melville scholar, Leon was interested in any kind of intellectual (and social) activity that brought new knowledge, new attitudes and new appreciation, and new intellectual curiosity, to literature and life. Interestingly, although primarily concerned with American literature (and American scholars), Leon worried throughout his academic life over other literary and intellectual problems. For example, he was always mulling over John Milton's *Paradise Lost*, and the English and American thinkers who influenced and were influenced by Milton. At death, Leon was still worrying over the subject.

I got along well with Leon Howard. Soon after I got to UCLA I outlined my interests and goals to him and confessed that I was probably going to have trouble with the courses and requirements. I admitted that I might not be sufficiently house-broken and might not salute enough. He told me not to worry, he would smooth out the rough spots academically. And true to his word, he did. Several times he had to talk to the Chairman of the Department and explain why I really should not be required to take a particular course. Leon and I worked closely in my interests in Alabama folk culture. He was keenly interested in American Studies and nearly every year would give a program at the national meeting on some aspect of American music and culture, and I would help him prepare the tape of illustrative songs. Leon's attitude toward the American Studies Association and its activities is summed up in his pithy though sympathetic statement he made to me a dozen times: "The American Studies Association is a first-class railroad but the passengers are trying to get along on second-class tickets." Leon's attitude was that of the deeply probing mind trying to improve academia and life. In his attitude and in every way, Leon helped me. We remained friends throughout his life. Upon his death I personally felt the loss of a power in academia that would long be missed. The loyalty of his many graduate students after his death attested to this deep feeling he had generated wherever he was.

One other person at UCLA assisted me in every way possible, Wayland Hand, Professor of German and Folklore. Wayland was always a friend and helper, a counselor and confidante. He was always eager to advise me in my work in folklore. When my interests exfoliated into popular culture, Wayland did not understand or appreciate them, but until his death in 1986, at age 82, we remained friends. Typically, so dedicated was he to the study of folklore, Wayland died in the Pittsburgh airport, on his way to Baltimore to the annual meeting of the American Folklore Society. Wayland's death was like a closing of the book on the UCLA chapter of my life. Except for several graduate student friends, with whom I have remained in contact, most of my connections were severed.

In my first job after graduating from UCLA in 1956 I was again fortunate. I got a position in the English Department at the University of Maryland. Carl Bode was there. Carl had been Leon Howard's first Ph.D. and had remained in close contact with Leon (as nearly all his graduates always did) and was keenly interested in the same kind of things that constituted my interests. Carl had been one of the founders of the American Studies Association because he felt the need in academia for inter- and multi-disciplinary approaches to the study of the Humanities and culture. When I arrived at Maryland, Carl was still one of the movers and shakers in the American Studies movement.

Carl understood my interests and aided and abetted them all the time. Maryland's English Department had a modest thrust in American Studies headed by Otho Bell but he was not aggressively pushing the program. Carl seemed more interested in the national picture than the local program. He once told me that realizing that he could not devote energy to both the Maryland program and the national American Studies Association he had opted for the larger goal. And he was active on the national scene. He and I talked many an hour—often over ice cream at the University Dairy— about the problems of American Studies and how I might fit into the large program. Both he and I thought that the field was big enough to accommodate all my interests.

Had I remained at Maryland probably the American Studies program there could have contained my excursions into unfamiliar terrain. But unfortunately I did not remain. In my third year there, Carl went to England as Cultural Attache. I regretted his leaving for both personal and professional reasons. But I did not realize how much I would really need him. While he was away I came up for tenure in the Department. One Friday morning, the Chairman of the Department called me in and told me that he had decided to grant me tenure. On the basis of that announcement I went out on Saturday and bought a house and prepared to hunker down and become serious about the future. Unfortunately, the announcement about my tenure, like the announcement about Mark Twain's death, was premature. On Monday, the Chairman called me in for a second time and told me that he had been mistaken on Friday. Instead of granting me tenure, the Department was going to deny it, and I would have to leave. So my *modus operandi* had finally caught up with and tripped me. I had remained out of the stockade in the Army, and I had swiveled around obstacles at UCLA, but now my square peg had been pulled out of the round hole and I was free to find another position. If Carl Bode had been on campus I would have appealed to him; he has told me many times since the event that he was sorry that he had not been around to save my neck because he and I had so many dreams stored up for the future. But he was not around, my water had been turned off, and I looked around for green pastures that had not been seared where I wanted to graze. Perhaps my firing was justified and proper. I am convinced that everybody should be fired once. It blows some of the cobwebs out of the head.

The year was 1960; jobs were plentiful, and without much difficulty I settled in the English Department at Purdue University. Purdue was a beehive of opportunity for a person like myself. Barriss Mills's, the Chairman's, philosophy was in effect to do anything one wanted as long as that person was doing something. Barriss was himself a poet. He had a fine literary magazine, *Modern Fiction Studies,* with accomplished editors, and various professors were turning out fine research in various fields. There were many faculty members just rusticating, to be sure, but several were feverishly working on valuable material. A Masters degree was offered in American Studies, with Chester E. Eisinger in charge of the program. There was already one professor, Virgil Lokke, standing in the aisle ready to fill in any needs in the American Studies program. But there were many opportunities in other closely-allied fields, and Purdue had sufficient money to aid the enterprising young scholar. I wanted to move into the national American Studies scene and to develop new approaches to the whole area.

When I got to Purdue it was really a department and university that was interested in promoting any kind of scholarly activity that redounded to the benefit of the students and/or the faculty. I had stirred around among my colleagues for several years and had discovered that several of us would like to hold a conference on American culture, loosely defined, and that the Administration would be pleased to help out in our efforts.

There was also strong support off-campus, especially in the person of one individual. Russel B. Nye, of Michigan State University, had been coming down to Purdue at least since 1962, when I first met him, lecturing on children's literature, his interest at the moment, and various other aspects of American Culture. On one of his several trips to Purdue, I discussed with Russ the advantages to be gained from a conference in Popular Culture, a field that he and I had been discussing for several years. He and I were convinced that the time was ripe to hold just such a conference. We therefore were determined to hold it. Preparatory to forming this conference I met another person who has worked with me through the years in pushing the study of Popular Culture, Marshall Fishwick. (More about both these individuals later in this study.)

In order to give the Conference I was planning as broad a base as possible, I got in touch with the national office of the American Studies Association and asked if they would support the Conference in spirit if not in money. The answer from the national office was that they would be delighted to help in any way possible. I then consulted with several of my colleagues. I convinced Allen Hayman, on the staff, and Donald Winkelman, who had been at Purdue but who had moved on to Bowling Green State University, to join me.

The result was a Midwest Conference on Literature, History, Popular Culture and Folklore held at Purdue in the spring of 1965. Some fifty people attended the various papers and discussions, including many from the Purdue faculty. The participants were indeed a sterling group and their papers interesting and seminal. Leo Stoller, from Wayne State University, who tragically died soon afterwards, spoke on "American Radicals and Literary Works of the Mid-Nineteenth Century"; Louis J. Budd, of Duke University, spoke on "Mark Twain and the Upward Mobility of Taste"; Louis Filler, of Antioch College, read a paper on "A Tale of Two Authors: Theodore Dreiser and David Graham Phillips"; David Sanders, of Harvey Mudd College, spoke on "John Hersey: War Correspondent into Novelist"; Edwin H. Cady, of Indiana University, " 'The Strenuous Life' as a Theme in American Cultural History"; Russel B. Nye, "The Juvenile Approach to American Culture, 1870-1930; Ray Browne, "Popular Theater in *Moby-Dick*"; Tristram P. Coffin, University of Pennsylvania, "Real Use and Abuse of Folklore in the Writer's Subconscious: F. Scott Fitzgerald"; Americo Paredes, University of Texas, "The Anglo-American in Mexican Folklore"; Bruno Nettl, University of Illinois, "Some Influences of Western Civilization on North American Indian Music"; C.E. Nelson, Purdue, "The Origin and Tradition of the Ballad of 'Thomas Rhymer' "; and Donald Winkelman, Bowling Green State University, "Some Rhythmic Aspects of the Child Ballad."

The conference was a complete success. I felt that the subjects and the thrust of the speakers' messages were sufficiently important to warrant their publication. So in 1966 Purdue University Studies brought out the papers. In a short introduction to the volume I placed emphasis on what I thought was a new way of looking at American Studies and the potential for a great deal of good that might be achieved through a broadened approach. Under the title "The Proper Study for American Studies," I tried to make two or three points.

Through the years the various scholarly fields loosely associated with "American Studies" have developed into a coherent discipline with momentum. This discipline has made a determined effort to achieve comprehensiveness, to cover all aspects of American culture (or cultures). For an even longer period, scholars in American folklore have grown in number and in seriousness about their subject. Unfortunately for both disciplines, there has been little association between the two.

But new thinking, new energies, new movements are at work. Revised logic in American Studies urges that the isolated regional chapters grow into larger, more productive loose federations. Scholars in this discipline are recognizing that much is to be gained from (relative) bigness, from the larger communities in which people who are interested in the same fields or related areas get to know one another personally and professionally.

I expressed my belief that the whole scholarly community would benefit by American Studies scholars recognizing their need to incorporate both folklore and popular culture. It would not be my last statement and effort.

In fact it was only the beginning of a campaign that was to take years to succeed.

But the first Purdue conference spurred us to call another another as quickly as we could. This time the planners included Richard H. Crowder, Virgil L. Lokke and William T. Stafford, all of the Purdue English Faculty. We also received a great deal of assistance from various other persons: Frederick Eckman (Bowling Green State University), John Jacobus (Indiana University); Barnet Kottler, Martin Light, Barriss Mills, Mark Rowan, Henry Salerno, Raney Stanford, Walter Staton, Felix Stefanile, Tom H. Towers, Dean Doner and the Office of the Dean of Humanities, Social Science and Education. Of this group most would not stick with the study of popular culture. But Tom Towers was valuable as a colleague at Purdue and has remained invaluable ever since (more of him later). The first Purdue conference had been an effort to broaden the scope of American Studies interests. This second Purdue conference was openly concentrated on popular culture, as an excerpt from the Introduction of the published papers points out:

> Conferences on American culture, or civilization, or studies, are usually free to pursue many organizing approaches—thematic studies, period investigations, examination of methodological problems which beset interdisciplinary studies, and, optimistically, research into areas not yet explored or sufficiently developed. The title of this volume, *Frontiers of American Culture,* will suggest the gentle blurring of focus. The persons responsible for arranging the second Conference on American Culture at Purdue University had as a loosely controlling intention the investigation of unexamined aspects of popular culture. Toward this end outstanding scholars were chosen to discuss aspects of the field which, it was felt, needed closer attention. The result was, and is as expected, a series of papers which are valuable in themselves. They employ a wide spectrum of moods and approaches— speculative, descriptive, provocative, cautious, analytic, and polemical—with intersections of thesis and argument which are perhaps fortunately more a matter of accident than of disciplined intention.

The range of the topics was even wider than they had been in the earlier conference: "Symbols of the United States: From Indian Queen to Uncle Sam," E. McClung Fleming; " 'Cheap Books': And the Public Interest: Paperbound Book Publishing in Two Centuries," C. Hugh Holman; "An American in Rome: The Experiments of W. W. Story," Herbert M. Schueller; "The Cure of 'Nothing': Frederick J. Hoffman (Hoffman in fact did not attend because of death); "*Israel Potter*: Metamorphosis of Superman," Ray Browne; "Charlie, a Little Fellow," James Sandoe; "The New Western: or, The Return of the Vanishing American," Leslie A. Fiedler; "The American Utopian Anti-Novel," Virgil L. Lokke; "Economics and Race in Jazz," Leslie B. Rout; "Electronic Music: Past Present and Future," Walter Robert; "Folklore in Relation to American Studies," Richard M. Dorson; "Even if, by all the Oxen in the world (a polemic)," William H. Gass.

At least two incidents occurred at this conference which further convinced me that there was real need for integration of the folklorists with the American culturists and the popular culturists, and that the elitists of academia were driving education, their business, and intelligence to the wall.

The first occurred when Richard Dorson, one of America's and the world's leading folklorists of the day, was giving his paper, and was trying to make a point, one that has been pretty much proven wrong subsequently, that folk culture and popular culture are distinct entities though tied at times by common sources and even common media of dissemination; it was an attitude that Dorson was going to solidify in later presentations into a detestation of the study of popular culture. But his later blind-spot was not apparent in his paper at Purdue. Yet an eminent American Studies scholar sitting behind me was uttering unrepeatable phrases putting Dorson down for every statement. It seemed to me that common courtesy demanded a better hearing than Dorson was getting, at least from this one individual.

The second incident was more amusing and more revealing of the attitude of the audience and participants at the conference. I had talked with my colleague at Purdue, William Gass, about whether he really wanted to participate in the conference since his attitude would be so contrary and so antithetical to the people in the audience. He said that he would and that he intended to be provocative and controversial. Well he was. In Gass's mind, popular culture, like Marx's religion, is an opiate: "It is the principal function of popular culture—though hardly its avowed purpose—to keep men from understanding what is happening to them, for social unrest would surely follow, and who knows what outbursts of revenge and rage." According to his statement in another place: "This muck cripples consciousness. Therefore no concessions should be made to it; and those who take their pleasure there should not be permitted to appear to lift those tastes to something higher with scholarly hypocrisy and philosophical pretense." With his paper, pretense and pretentiousness hit the fan. Although Gass defended his position with good grace, the audience, without good grace, was ready to show him the esthetic value of a good riding on a rail. The kindest thing said to Gass was that he should get the wax of pretentiousness out of his ears. His position, incidentally, is one that he has held ever since and has been echoed in the statements of various other elite scholars and critics. Fortunately for American academia it is a position which is fading away rapidly if it is not already gone.

Concurrently with these Purdue conferences I had been active in the national meetings of the Modern Language Association and especially of the national meetings of the American Studies Association. On two or three occasions I had organized sessions for the national ASA or had developed parallel sessions. These meetings revealed to me frequently not only the conservative nature of academics but their dissimulation and pettiness also. An excellent case in point springs to mind.

During the 'Sixties and 'Seventies the Modern Language Association had, as it has now, the policy of giving small amounts of money—$100-$200—to speakers of national prominence whose presence on a session would enhance it and who could not or would not otherwise attend. On several occasions I called on the MLA for this assistance. All academics were eager to receive this financial assistance—but some were not eager to have it known that they were so petty in the financial desires as to demand it. Some went to considerable lengths to avoid having their names tied in with this kind of subsidzation. One example sticks closely to my mind.

I had arranged a session of the American Studies Association for a Chicago MLA meeting and particularly wanted a well-known critic from one of the Eastern schools because I felt he would attract a crowd and might have something important to say. I asked him if he would go to Chicago, and he said he would if we paid him $150. I then went to the national office of the Modern Language Association, explained my needs, and was awarded the $150. I then told this leading scholar that I would have the money. He stated explicitly and carefully that I was to fold the check and slip it to him when we shook hands at the meeting, and that I was not to tell anyone about the money.

I did as I was told, palmed the check and slipped it to him. He gave his usual talk—rather effectively. But apparently I had not paid him enough for his services or his conscience began to hurt. For in his next column in one of the leading academic journals this critic roundly scored those academics who had to be paid for participating in academic meetings! Thus the power of the academic mind to justify its actions!

The success of my several national sessions and the two Purdue conferences convinced me and several of my colleagues at Purdue that there was a great need for popular culture studies in academia. I searched around trying to find the next needed implementation of this academic thrust and decided that I should start some kind of publication in popular culture that would develop the notion and keep it constantly before the academic community. Without any money and with only a general notion of what I wanted to do and perhaps even less of an idea of how I wanted to do it, I decided I would start some kind of newsletter. Luckily, however, at this time there arose the possibility of a sizeable and visible thrust.

Development of the Idea at
Bowling Green State University

While Donald M. Winkelman had been on the faculty at Purdue, he had been very active in folklore studies and in the American Folklore Society. I had joined him because I was interested in what he was doing and in promoting the study of folklore as I could. Winkelman had started a very worthy publication called *Abstracts of Folklore,* in which he planned to abstract every folklore article and publication available. It was a big undertaking. I wanted to help him. Although Purdue assisted him modestly in his endeavors, the project did not prosper as much as it should have, and Don got discouraged. When he was offered the position of folklorist at Bowling Green State University he accepted it gladly, hoping there to establish a folklore program that would reach national importance. He was at his new post only a year and a half when another job offer came through that he felt he could not refuse; it would give him even greater opportunities for developing folklore studies on a state-wide and perhaps national scale. Since his position at Bowling Green State University was going to become vacant, he proposed to the English Department there that I be hired to fill his shoes and carry on his work.

I was interested. Perhaps I had approached the mid-life crisis and needed new territory, but in fact there were compelling personal reasons why I should try new ground. In 1952 I had married fellow-student at UCLA Olwyn Orde. We had lived together for thirteen years, had a family of three sons named Glenn, Kevin and Rowan and married life seemed perfect for me. But tragedy struck through that pretense. On Christmas Day 1964 while driving my family home from a visit to my sister Joan's home in Alabama, I was struck by a fifteen year school drop-out who had stolen a car in Huntsville and was fleeing south on a joy-ride. Olwyn, who was pregnant, and our youngest son, Rowan, were killed. I was stove up for months, finally to emerge with many mended bones and scars. But, as poet Emily Dickinson said about her life, my life had closed at least once before its close. Having grown up something of a fatalist, I still felt that this blow was a little cruel and gratuitous. I was left with two young children who needed a mother, so when I remet a lady who was the sister-in-law of one of my colleagues at Purdue and found her compatible I married her in August of 1965. Alice, "Pat," Matthews, about whom I will speak more in another section, has been both strong right arm and whole body muscle in the popular culture movement.

So when the opportunity came in 1967 to move to Bowling Green State University I considered it seriously. I wanted to know, of course, about my personal fortunes at the new school, but more important I wanted to know how the new school would let me develop my interests in popular culture. Well, there was no better way to learn than to ask. With the Department of English I expressed my interest in broadening the study of folklore into popular culture. At that time there seemed to be no opposition, at least no expressed opposition; mine was, however, a misreading of the departmental climate, as I was to learn very concretely in subsequent years. For financing, I went to the President of the University, William T. Jerome, and told him that if I were to come over I would want a guarantee from him of an annual subsidy of $4000 to publish an academic quarterly to be called *Journal of Popular Culture*. He seemed to think it was a good idea and said that he would provide the subsidy. I thought I could get by on such a small amount. I shall discuss the publications of the Popular Culture movement in a later section.

In the folklore courses I started teaching, I immediately added popular culture segments, and within two semesters had in fact converted the courses to folklore and popular culture, with a strong shot of the new material. The students responded very favorably. Contrary to what my colleagues were to think later on, the students understood immediately the connection between the two and the need to include the popular culture with the folklore.

If I had remained unnoticeable in the Department I could have got along with no trouble. But in my zeal to legitimize the study of popular culture I did not remain invisible. The Chairman of the English Department, Stanley T. Coffman, was very much in my camp. He was so eager to have his department publish widely that he would have very likely approved of any topic. But, more important, he really felt that the study of popular culture was a legitimate area of scholarship and teaching, and so he was very much in favor of my enterprise. So, too, were the various deans and vice-presidents. President Jerome, a patrician who might have been very much opposed, backed my enterprise all the way. So too did the Board of Trustees.

President Jerome, perhaps for want of other examples, tried to star my undertakings, and put me out in the forefront of visibility whenever he could. One Wednesday, for example, he called me up and said that the Board of Trustees would be meeting on Friday and I should talk with them about what I intended to do here with the study of popular culture. Well, to tell the truth, I was at that moment trying to settle in with the new *Journal of Popular Culture* and did not have many new schemes. But I felt I should not let the world know that I was a man with one stone in his sling, so I announced to the Trustees on Friday that I was going to open a Center for the Study of Popular Culture and then filled in the various activities that the Center would engage in, such as becoming a depository of research materials and a publishing arm for my activities other than the *Journal*.

At various other subsequent public meetings, such as the University Senate, for example, my activities and plans were showcased. At one meeting of the Senate, when someone remarked that I had the President's ear for anything I wanted to do, Stanley Coffman remarked that it was one thing to have the Prsident's ear but I was in a much more fortunate position because I had the ear of the President's wife! Indeed I did. And it was a comfortable feeling to know that these two individuals, Bill and his charming wife Jean, were informed and enthusiastic backers of all that I was trying to do. They included me and my wife in various activities. Once, for example, Bob Hope was coming to the University to get an honorary degree, and I was designated to sit by him at lunch. I presumed my role for the lunch was to inform him of what I was doing here and ask for his cooperation and financial help. Unfortunately, that was one coup that was aborted by a higher power. Hope had to skip the luncheon because he had just been informed that his brother had died that morning in Cleveland and he had to fly there to take care of details.

In order to pack as much philosophy and symbolism as possible into the *Journal of Popular Culture*, I searched around for an appropriate symbol. Finally I settled on a picture of incompletely developed mankind in a world that was far from perfect and complete. I hired a Peruvian artist who was on campus as the wife of a graduate student in philosophy to execute the logo. I have used it ever since; and I should admit that generally speaking I am the only person who knows what it symbolizes or seems to care. But there was care on other fronts. As the *Journal of Popular Culture* gained  in notoriety and importance the English Department began to react more and more strongly against it. I had strong friends in John Gross, who knew exactly what I was about and heartily approved of it and Richard Carpenter, whose interests were eclectic and who approved of any material that would provide more effective and lasting teaching methods and materials. I also had an intellectual friend in Robert Bashore, but Bob was less inclined to fight for my cause than he was to silently agree that what I was doing was all right. Soon after I got to Bowling Green State University John Gross died in 1970 and Richard Carpenter was forced to assume various duties on campus which took him out of English and dissipated his influence on a broader palette. I was then, as it were, left to the tender mercies of the department. At times they were not very tender. But I always maintained contact and close cooperation and assistance with and from several members of the department, Edgar Daniels and Ralph Wolfe, for example. Both were very helpful in encouraging me in my activities. Since Ed retired from the University I have always found Ralph more interested and more helpful. He has been the kind of friend who has actively sought to improve the stature of Bowling Green State University and has encouraged me in numerous ways to work for that end also. Others have been great allies. Tom Wymer, for example, has always worked with me with his knowledge of science fiction. Lately, Art Neal, of the sociology department, has been immensely helpful in my work. A colleague with whom I have worked very closely and undoubtedly our symbiotic relationship has been very helpful to both is Alvar Carlson, a cultural geographer. At the suggestion of myself and my wife, Al began editing and publishing through the Popular Press his *Journal of Cultural Geography,* a publication that has become one of the leading publications of its kind in the world. His assistance in every way has always been unstinting. And there are many others. Although the number of my friends could not be counted on the fingers of two hands (R. Serge Denisoff, for example, more of whom later), they were definitely in a minority on campus. And my sentiment was not without foundation. Former Secretary of State Henry Kissinger quite properly observed once that paranoids do have enemies.

Increasingly the sentiment seemed to be running strongly against my action in trying to promote the study of popular culture. I had founded the Popular Culture Association in 1970, the Popular Press published its first book the same year, the whole movement was getting a lot of press coverage. So I think that by 1970-71 the Department saw the whole popular culture movement as much more of a threat than they had anticipated, and they were prepared to work against it. And they did. Some of the more conservative and conventional members of the Department began to beat the bushes for allies on campus—which were not hard to find—to demonstrate to the Adminstration that what I was doing was not casting a good light on the University. Somehow, my campus colleagues thought that the Center was either wealthy or was siphoning off vast sums of money from the administration, money that they could more usefully spend on their own projects. Nothing, of course, could be farther from the truth. The only money I was getting from the Administration was the $4000 subsidy for publication of the *Journal of Popular Culture.* But rumors run much faster than facts.

Sentiment mushroomed and soon I was hoisted on the three-pronged petard that my activities were 1) a misspending of the tax-payers money, 2) a disservice to the students, and 3) I personally was disgracing the University in the eyes of the public and academics. Against such charges reason obviously would have no effect, so I simply ignored the charges, getting some amusement at the heat with which they were spread. But they did continue to boil, and at one time came to a head. The English Department announced to the Provost that they were tired of my disgracing them and I could no longer be a member of the Department. They would not try to contravene my University tenure, but they did not want me in the Department any longer. The Provost was Stanley Coffman, now moved up from heading the English Department, and he was amused by the whole cause celebre, or cause macabre. He simply informed the English Department that nobody else on campus would take me, so they were stuck with me! It was a decision that did not raise much laughter in the Department. They were serious. My distinguished

colleagues did not want me around blotting their scutcheon. I was amused—
and only vaguely insulted. But I did read the handwriting on the blackboard
and knew that perhaps I should look to my interests.

In 1971 I started agitating for a Department of Popular Culture. which
would consist of a faculty of two, myself and one Ph.D. whose work I had
directed in the English Department, Michael T. Marsden. I anticipated
offering a Masters degree, which I always did in the Center, and an
undergraduate program. Numerous arguments were of course raised as to
why I should be content with less than a department of my own, it would
cost too much, would continue to disgrace the campus, and a dozen other
arguments. But finally, after much lobbying and much debate, the appropriate
council voted approval, after Karl Vogt, the Dean of Business Administration,
had shouted that he was tired of the whole business and the council should
approve the Department and then get on with important business. So with
backhanded approval and blessings, the only Department of Popular Culture
in the world was created!

We did not go forth into the world with empty cradle and no food.
For two years the Center had been offering a Masters degree in Popular
Culture through the English Department. We had graduated several people
and we had a comfortable group of half a dozen students, with numerous
others applying for admittance. The frame of mind of the late 60s was still
in the air, and many students wanted to continue their training in fields
and methodologies that they thought "relevant" and "useful." Parenthetically
I should say in all candor that some of these early students were unusual.
At times as their interests ran all over the board I had the feeling that what
we were really conducting was an out-patient clinic. But in truth our students
were just a little more unusual, if at all, than most of the other graduate
students on our campus or anybody else's. They were just sensitized with
unusual abrasives and responded to different stimuli. Their drummers were
somewhat off the conventional beat. But they were fun and stimulating to
teach. They could bring to class in a day more insights and questions than
another generation of students would discover in a year. Truth wore many
faces and disguises.

After being established did the Department prosper? Indeed! Almost
beyond our wildest dreams. At one time with a faculty of seven we were
teaching one-half of the BGSU student body of 15,000 over a four-year period.
In other words, during the tenure of one generation of students, four years,
we taught one half of them. At first we did not have a large number of
majors and minors, and for a while that fact worried us. But we understood
that students were taking courses in which they could make a living, not
so-called Humanities courses, and in the business world the concept and
name of popular culture was so new that it was not fully understood. The
few majors we did turn out, however, did extremely well. They had been
unusual students to begin with and therefore wound up as unusual graduates.
In graduate students we have always done extremely well. We have attracted
the student with unusual talents and unconventional interests. And we have

never lacked for applicants. Our graduates have gone on to all kinds of activities. Many, indeed most, have gone on to do Ph.D. work, mostly in American Studies programs. Others have gone into the media. We have our share of people who are doing well in Hollywood and New York. Others have gone into owning and working in radio stations, and two or three are self-employed entertainers. Only one or two have disappeared into the dark and uncharted deserts of obscurity. We are proud of our graduates, as indeed we have every reason for being. They have done their instructors and school proud.

But that is really not the end of the campus story of the Department of Popular Culture. It has continued to be a thorn in the side of local academia. Although it has achieved an international reputation and reflected much of that reputation onto the campus, it has not been appreciated for that reason. Through the years there has come to be more acceptance—perhaps even appreciation— of the Department. But with that gradual acceptance there has smoldered a resentment that has remained acerbic. It has worked its will in many ways. Various faculty members have bad-mouthed the Department in private and in public. The Chair of one department was so flagrant in his activities that he was probably guilty of libel; I told him that if he did not cease his libelous ways, I would have him in court. He stopped writing his slander but never stopped voicing it. Other colleagues across campus continued their drum beat. But such activities were bearable. Perhaps the most insidious and costly were those rumors poured into the ears of new administrators as they were brought to campus. Apparently, people of some seeming stature got to such persons as the new Graduate Dean, the new Dean of the College of Arts and Sciences, and even the new presidents, as they came to their jobs, and told them that Browne was a pariah and should be ignored and squelched. One Graduate Dean, one Dean of the College of Arts and Sciences told me that they had been warned to beware of me and my activities. One President, Paul J. Olscamp, once announced publicly that he had been told when he arrived on campus that he must beware of Browne. All three, to begin with, did indeed beware of Browne and kept him at arms length and with no special favors. In all three cases, it took the administrator up to two years to discover that the cause of the warnings was personal vitriol and spite. President Olscamp admitted when he told about having been warned to beware of Browne that his informant had tried to cut my throat because he was a person whose only triumph in life was doing nothing. But such underhand and insidious work by my colleagues at the university cut deep into the progress of the Popular Culture movement and prevented all kinds of growth. One other example will bear this out. Once I proposed an honorary degree for the popular novelist Irving Wallace. Knowing that he was a research scholar for the information he needed for his many books, and that he was a very successful author, I proposed that he be given an honorary degree. The proposal went through the various committees and was approved. When it came time for it to be approved by the University Senate, however, one of these do-nothing colleagues in the English Department conducted a weekend telephone smear campaign and got the Senate to vote against confirming Wallace's degree. I will always be convinced that the turndown was a mistake of monumental proportions. My long-time friend in the Sociology Department, Joseph Kivlin, always assured me that my adversities on campus have all sprung up and grown with green eyes, that everybody was simply jealous of my success. Such sage observations from Kivlin made life more amusing and more bearable. He was always a reliable friend who was able to read his colleagues with a sure eye. He was always a great personal friend and a friend to the advancement of the study of popular culture. Indeed, jealousy is a vicious monster, and its largest lair is the university and college campus. Many academics in so-called "higher education" seem primarily concerned with important issues, such as salary, promotion, parking and office space, not with the development of ideas. Academia is generally as dry and inhospitable to the nurturing of ideas as the Australian Outback is to the growth of rich gardens. There are green spots, but there are far more arid tracts.

As these pages are written there are two new developments in the study of popular culture on campus that I should report. One is a change in status of our participation in the American Culture Ph.D. program here. In the past we were a member of the program but not an "area of concentration" on a par with the Ph.D. granting departments. Now our status has been changed and we are equal in participation to those departments which give Ph.D.s in their disciplines.

The second development is more portentous. For over a year now I have been working on a proposal for a Ph.D. program in popular culture at this university. At first the idea was received with frigid distaste. In pursuing the desired goal, however, I have gathered my data. I have evidence of need in academia and in business; I have letters from academics on other campuses who approve of the proposal and make suggestions for improvement. I am pursuing the due course of the process in the various channels.

The Development of the Popular Culture Association

With the success of the *Journal of Popular Culture* assured, I began casting around for what should be done next to develop the study of popular culture. I had recently published a book on the American revolutionary Tom Paine, so I knew that in order to effect a revolution one must control not only the press but must have an army also. My army, in this case, I recognized must be a national association. Having had experience for many years in the American Studies Association, I knew that the "Army" would not be hard to develop if I had a viable project to engage their imagination and energies.

Throughout our association Russ Nye and I had talked about developing a Popular Culture Association to go along with the *Journal;* so we now began to investigate the idea.

I had been active for several years in the American Studies Association, and I had used their imprimatur for the two conferences I had held at Purdue, so I felt that I could get their cooperation in another, and larger, venture. I, therefore, proposed that I should sponsor the 1969 national meeting of the ASA with the explicit understanding that I would use the occasion to propose the establishment of a Popular Culture Association. I received no obstruction from the national office of the ASA. I went ahead with the national meeting concept, then, the meeting to be held in Toledo.

In preparation for the meeting three of the most interested and concerned persons, Russel B. Nye and Marshall Fishwick and I, decided that we needed to have an organizational conference; so we met in the Detroit Metro Airport for a Saturday of planning. Russ was of course at Michigan State University. Marshall was Director of the Wemyss Foundation, Wilmington, Delaware. Marshall was hoping to get financial support from the Wemyss Foundation but never did. He also hoped to get money from the Coe Foundation which had set up major programs at Yale and Wyoming; again, no success.

At this meeting we spent a great deal of time debating what the name should be. We wanted to break away from the American Studies Association and knew that we wanted the name to reflect the break but not to indicate hostility. Marshall favored "Contemporary Culture," saying that "Popular Culture" would be seen as light-weight. Russ liked "Comparative Culture," and wanted to include Canada in our field. I held out for "Popular Culture," the other two—perhaps with genuine misgivings—allowed me to have my way. Through the years their apprehension proved prophetic, but I would like to think that history has proved that my name was after all the proper one.

At this meeting Marshall volunteered to publish a series of small brochures outlining our program and philosopohies. The first was Russel Nye's *Rationale for Popular Culture,* I published *Notes on a Definition of Popular Culture* and Marshall wrote and published several during the next few years, among which were *Black Popular Culture* and *Confessions of an Ex-Elitist* (both while he was at Lincoln University); through the years he has continued to publish these "probes" into new areas of interest and importance. With this background we were ready for the new "probe" that was to come with our establishing the Popular Culture Association.

On a certain afternoon at the ASA meeting some 200 interested persons assembled with the purpose of establishing a national Popular Culture Association. We had three speakers to begin the session: Abraham Kaplan, of the Philosophy Department of the University of Michigan, who spoke on the importance of studying popular culture though it might be different and even qualitatively inferior to elite culture; John Cawelti, of the English Department, University of Chicago, who spoke on convention and invention in popular literature; and Robert Meyers, of the English Department of Bowling Green State University, whom I had induced to talk because I felt he would bring an interesting and different perspective to the discussion.

After the scholarly activities had vindicated our presence, we rather quickly established the notion that there should be a national Popular Culture Association, and that it should begin activities immediately.

Not all the people who were in attendance at the organizational meeting, however, seemed to agree. For example, I talked with Chester Eisinger from Purdue after the meeting and jokingly congratulated ourselves on the success of the meeting; I discovered that Chet thought the organization misguided and likely to do mischief—to the American Studies Association, I gathered. Such was a feeling that Chet and many others in the ASA continued to hold for years. Despite every argument we raised, saying that we were not out to undermine or compete with the ASA but to supplement its activites, Chet and others would not agree. They continued to look upon us as a deliberate threat. Gradually through the years the feeling of threat seemed to subside but never to disappear.

Russ Nye and I for our parts were very enthusiastic and delighted, though filled with some trepidation over the magnitude of the possibilities. Just before the organizational meeting, Russ and I had been having a cup of coffee in the coffee shop of the hotel when he said to me that it seemed a little presumptuous for two old goats like us to be trying to revolutionize the whole concept of the Humanities in American schools. I assured him that, on the contrary, two old goats might indeed change the whole concept of the Humanities and education in America. My optimism has been proved more prophetic than Russ' half-serious demur.

The question of officers came up, as it always does, though not with the urgency of a need for an iron-clad bureaucracy. Russ was made president. There were three vice-presidents: John G. Cawelti (University of Chicago); Philip G. Durham (UCLA); Marshall Fishwick (Lincoln University). Of the vice-presidents Durham had worked longest in popular culture, having for years been interested in pulp magazines, but being at UCLA in a traditional department he never really managed to push from his angle and he gradually faded away and died before his time and prospects lived up to their potential. Cawelti and Fishwick both worked long and hard to develop the study of popular culture. I was made secretary-treasurer, a position I have held and worked in since the beginning. I have always found this office filled with many duties and obligations but also with numerous opportunities and potentials. We did not need a constitution and worked without one until David Madden became president, as we will see in discussing his administration.

The first national meeting of the Popular Culture Association was held at Michigan State University, in April 1971. We had all the trappings of the *bon voyage*. The program was prefaced by an enthusiastic greeting from Hollis A. Moore, Jr., President of Bowling Green State University, which because of its prophetic nature, needs to be quoted in its entirety. (I had written it, but he had endorsed it):

In these unusually trying times when students, faculty, administration, and citizens, feel thwarted in trying to achieve their goals, the activities of the Popular Culture Association, and the thrust of the various activities in Popular Culture on the many campuses represented on this program, are meritorious. There is a drive here toward what seems to me are worthwhile new dimensions in education on both the undergraduate and the graduate levels. The key to this new thrust is not so much the clichéd word *relevancy*, though it is still a worthwhile term, as *sensitivity*—an awareness of the needs and hopes of education in the broadest sense—and humaneness in a world that is becoming increasingly dehumanized, with the resulting frustration, anxiety, even terror, that stalk the world today.

As observers—academic and non-academic—increasingly are commenting, much of the chaos on campuses results from lack of communication. When people understand the goals of the new movement in Popular Culture, resistance will largely melt away. It is becoming increasingly manifest that the goals of the PCA, as revealed in this program, are to bridge gaps, to bring about new understandings on one plane (between students and their world off campus) and on another plane among students, faculty, administrators.

As President of one of the sponsoring schools, I look upon the first national meeting of the Popular Culture Association with great enthusiasm and hope.

President Moore's enthusiasm was mirrored in the faces and behavior of many of the attenders. We had a large number of graduate students, as we were going to continue to have for years. They came from far and wide, and at times with considerable hardship. They expected a cordial welcome from faculty members, and they got it. One group from Boston drove their rattly old car out, with no money and no food other than a head of cheese and a dozen loaves of bread that one of the wives had baked. They got into Bowling Green one day before the conference was to start and called me up saying that they hoped I could put them up for the night. I put them up all right, or rather down, because I put their bedrolls on the living-room floor and had them sleep there. This group was joined by many other graduate students, most of whom, naturally, came from Michigan State University and Bowling Green State University.

We had all the trappings of a legitimate on-going conference. Our keynote speaker was David Madden, writer in residence at Louisiana State University, a dynamic person who was to add a great deal to the PCA through the next few years. We covered such areas as Psychological Approaches to Popular Culture, Black Stereotypes, Underground Popular Culture, the Motion Picture, Radical Teaching, Pulp Fiction, Photos, Popular Religion, Science Fiction, Popular Literature, Folklore, Mark Twain, Images of the City, Television, Sociology and Popular Culture, the Musical, Theater, American Humor, Sexuality, the Western, Protest Music and Television. (As a historical document of considerable interest, the program for this first meeting is included in the appendix of this book.) All the movers and shakers in the movement were present: Marshall Fishwick, Carl Bode, John Cawelti, David Madden, Larry Mintz, Tom Towers, Serge Denisoff, Tom Clareson, Henry Glassie, Mike Nevins, Hamlin Hill, Allen Hubin, Philip Durham, Fred E.H. Schroeder. It was indeed a stellar assemblage. And an auspicious beginning. Some of the people who attended the first meeting have for one reason or another dropped out of the PCA through the years, but most at that first meeting were at the second and have been at virtually every one ever since. The tenacity of some of our members is almost unbelievable.

It was immediately apparent that we needed a philosophical and theoretical definition of popular culture for our own good and for those who had similar ideas about the Humanities and social sciences but who might not know that they were interested in popular culture. All of us in these early days had our own definition, but generally speaking we could all agree that we were talking about all elements of the culture around us except the narrowly elite and narrowly elitely creative. Popular Culture to us was the everyday, the vernacular, the heritage and ways of life that we inherited from our predecessors, used and passed on to our descendants. It was the cultural environment we lived in. Popular culture is mainly disseminated by the mass media (word of mouth, print, radio, pictures, movies, television) but not necessarily limited to such media of dissemination. Popular culture probably should not include some ten per cent of so-called elite culture but it should include all folk culture. It is by definition international and comparative in scope, with no time limit; it is not restricted to the present.

After the success of the first meeting, we looked forward eagerly to the second, which was held in Toledo the following April. The hundred fifty who had attended the East Lansing meeting had more than doubled for this second meeting. Again, we had the trappings of the viable association. For our main beginning presentation we had "Fifty Years of Vaudeville," with John Di Meglio (Mankato State University) as master of ceremonies, and the redoubtable Hollywood actor of silent and talkie movies, Benny Rubin, as our main speaker. After that successful beginning, we branched out into all kinds of sessions, more in number and broader in approach than we had had in East Lansing the year before. Again we were successful in attracting many graduate students because we initiated a practice which we kept up for some years, that of paying the housing costs of graduate students, until the economics of the situation drove us, against our will, to give up this splendid underwriting of graduate student development.

After Toledo, Russ had served two years as President of the PCA, and like George Washington who after two terms as President of the United States felt that in order to set the right precedent he should not stand for a third term, Nye felt that two years was the proper length of office for the president. So he urged us to select a successor.

It is proper that Russ' role in the development of the study of popular culture and the Popular Culture Association be assessed. There is no doubt that his contribution in all areas cannot be overemphasized. At the time of the initiation of the whole Popular Culture movement, Russ had been working in it for years, long before we even conceived of the idea. One of the earliest of the current publications was his monumental *The Unembarrassed Muse: The Popular Arts in America* (1970). In his introduction, Russ, speaking of the popular arts only, pretty much set up proper explanations, analyses, and definitions, concerning these arts. Some scholars would differ with him on his feeling that the popular arts can exist only with the presence of media of mass communication (first the rapid printing press), and with his feeling that the "popular art confirms the experience of the majority." Again, some people see in the popular arts and, more broadly, in popular culture certain subversive forces which constantly push back the borders of popular culture and through threatening those borders constantly bring change to itself and to society. But everybody recognizes that this book was a constitution in the study of popular culture. As such it will be amended but will not be replaced. It is and will remain a classic.

But this volume was only one of hundreds of contributions to the study of popular culture that Nye made. As president of the association, he was always ready to travel anywhere at his own cost to talk to anybody about the study of popular culture. He attended virtually every regional meeting and every special conference he knew of. He spoke at numerous meetings of allied scholarly groups, such as the American Historical Association. He assisted the editor of the *Journal of Popular Culture* in defining and maintaining editorial policy against consistent and heavy pressure. He read thousands of manuscripts for the journals and the Popular Press. He allowed his considerable reputation to be put on the line by allowing his name to be used in publications for which he had very little responsibility, for instance in the Popular Press publication *Crises on Campus* (1971). He never missed a meeting of the PCA or one of its rare executive meetings. He never failed to give counsel with the greatest good grace. He spent thousands of dollars in telephone calls, discussing various problems and possibilities of popular culture development and studies. On the National Humanities

Council he argued, generally unsuccessfully, for the subsidizing of projects in popular culture.

Russ Nye did all these things, and many more, always with good grace and great dignity and wisdom. On his shoulders stand all people who study popular culture. We are all in his debt.

Nye was succeeded by Marshall Fishwick. I had got to know Marshall Fishwick in about 1963 when at Purdue I was trying to drum up moral and financial support for the first of my Conferences to be held on that campus. Marshall was long on the first and short on the second. He was enthusiastic about my enterprise and wished me well—with no financial assistance from his end; he was temporarily out of cash. But Marshall had worked hard in the PCA from the very beginning. He was tireless and never short of ideas and suggestions for actions and improvements. We felt sure that he would serve the PCA well. He did not let us down.

Experience had proved that we could hold a successful yearly meeting, and such was our plan. Our 1973 meeting was held in Indianapolis, sponsored by the Indianapolis campuses of Indiana University-Purdue Universiy. Our program chair was the indefatigable Warren French.

For this meeting we had an unusually heavy barrage from the heavy guns of academia. We had a discussion of a project entitled "Republishing a 40-volume Popular Culture Library" with the editors, David Manning White, Russel Nye, Marshall Fishwick, and Ray Browne; the library was subsequently published by the New York *Times*. We had a panel on "Popular Art and Historic Artifacts: Principles for the Study of Universal History," by Alan Gowans, Chair of the Department of History in Art, University of Victoria, who was then Visiting Professor at Harvard. Because the subject was a running sore with American Studies people, we had a discussion of "The Relationship Between American Studies and Popular Culture Studies," with such participants as Daniel Aaron, John Hague, James McLachlan, Russel Nye, Marshall Fishwick, Carl Bode, Bruce Lohof, Allen Davis, and Patricia Averill. Another subject, "Esthetics and Popular Culture," was a burning issue, so we had a session on that subject, chaired by Ray Browne, with participants John Seelye, David Madden, and Leslie Fiedler.

After such a heavy diet, we turned to a lighter touch, to a group who called themselves the Tollson Institute. So fresh and daring, so outrageously humorous was this group that everyone present thought them the star of the day. They set a high precedent, and we were, therefore, very sorry when they could no longer participate in our conferences. One other very significant event occurred at Indianapolis, which was the establishment of regional chapters of the Popular Culture Association, a needed and highly successful move, which will be discussed at length later.

Indianapolis was a hard act to follow. The 350 participants had had a thoroughly pleasurable and educational experience. But even greater plans were in store for the 1974 meeting, to be held in Milwaukee. Over 700 people attended this meeting, which was sponsored by the Center for 20th Century Studies, Robert F. Roeming, Director, and the University of Wisconsin

Extension Center. My old friend Melvin Friedman, whom I had known from my days at the University of Maryland, was in charge of local arrangements.

With twice as many participants we naturally had more sessions in familiar topics and new topics introduced. We carried on with the precedent instituted at Indianapolis, having starred participants in plenary sessions. In a welcoming keynote speech, Hayden White, Director of the Center for the Humanities, Wesleyan University, spoke on "Structuralism and Popular Culture." The speech was later published in the *Journal of Popular Culture* and was considered something of a success. From that plenary session we went to another, an exercise in obscurantism, as usual, with Ihab Hassan discussing "Culture and the Prophetic Imagination." Three discussants, Leslie Fiedler, Hans Mayer and Hayden White, tried to direct some light onto the subject, but that exercise gave us all pause. There were, of course, several other luminaries at the meeting. Stan Lee, of Marvel Comics, was in attendance, as was Virginia Carter, of Norman Lear Enterprises.

But most important of all, there was a comaraderie, a good-fellowship, experienced by all which reached a new high. It may have been the water served in the restaurants that was so appealing. Regardless of the cause the meeting was universally adjudged a great success.

Milwaukee marked the end of Marshall Fiskwick's tenure in office as President of the PCA. His had been a fruitful term. When we had first started the PCA, Russel Nye and I had agreed that in general we would be inclined to say yes to proposals for presentations and papers at the annual meetings. We would supplement proposals with suggestions, and we would gladly assist anyone in clarifying some project or straightening out some proposed route, but wherever possible we would say yes. We wanted to be inclusive rather than selective. We wanted to welcome rather than turn the haughty shoulder. Our plan had worked and had accounted for the phenomenal growth of the PCA. Fishwick had agreed wholeheartedly with our thinking. His seminal mind was ready to reflect a dozen projects for every one fed into it. And he was ready to work on the projects, not just talk about them. Marshall had been an informal student of Marshall McLuhan, and like his Canadian colleague, Marshall was deep in exploratory probings. Like Nye and me, Fishwick was eager to see how something would work, if it would work, and what would be the conclusions reached from this working.

For example, during Fishwick's tenure in office, he and I envisioned a Popular Culture Association Advisory Faculty who would have great impact on the promotion of Popular Culture studies. The group was founded and started on their way. According to the information supplied on the advertising brochure the individuals were always ready and able:

The Popular Culture Association Advisory Faculty is a group of people who have made themselves available to assist any university, college, junior college or public school in improving its curriculum by introducing or developing courses in Popular Culture.

Members of the PCAAF have for years been concerned with American education: its strengths, weaknesses, potentials. They are eager to contribute their knowledge and experience to implementing any program in Popular Culture, from a single course to a whole program, with a major and/or minor. Because they represent various disciplines, they can be especially effective in explaining the need for new courses and in broadening the interdisciplinary approach.

Five years ago P.C.A. was founded to study thoroughly and seriously those productions, both artistic and commercial, designed for mass consumption. The founders were convinced, as first president Russel B. Nye put it, that this vast body of material encompassed in print, film, television, comics, advertising and graphics "reflects the values, conviction, and patterns of thought and feeling generally dispersed through and approved by American society." Their work has grown in scope, depth and influence. They believe that it can be helpful in many different ways. That is why they are launching the PCAAF.

The vast library and archival holdings of the Center for the Study of Popular Culture at Bowling Green State University, will also be made available insofar as practicable.

We advised individuals seeking assistance from the PCAAF that applications would be judged by a board and wherever possible services would be provided free of charge.

To a considerable extent this notion of the PCAAF succeeded. Russ Nye was invited to numerous schools for talks and consultation. Ray Browne visited dozens, as did Marshall Fishwick and John Cawelti. Interestingly, as I write this history of the PCA in 1988 the concept, though vastly muted from its early assertions is still alive. Prof. Fred Geib, in the Sociology Department of Colby College, Waterville, Maine, tells me that he is about ready to retire from the College and is more than ready to become a roving ambassador to aid in promoting popular culture studies in any way possible. Thus, old ideas never die; they just sometimes take a long time in their growth.

Under Fishwick's able leadership, the PCA reached out in various directions. We had an active group of vice-presidents during those years: Carol Bagley, Univ. of Idaho; Carl Bode, Univ. of Maryland; Leslie Fiedler, SUNY, Buffalo; Marshall McLuhan, Toronto University; David M. White, Boston University.

We also had an impressive Advisory Council: Howard Adams, National Gallery, Washington, D.C.; Joseph Arpad, UCLA; Arthur Berger, San Francisco State University; Seymour Betsky, University of Utrecht; C.W.E. Bigsby, East Anglia University, U.K.; Craighill Burks, Everglade School for Girls, Miami, Fla.; John Cawelti, Univ. of Chicago; Robert Corrigan, Univ. of Iowa; Kenneth Davison, Heidelberg College; Mollie Davis, West Georgia State College; Harriet Deer, Univ. of South Florida; Iriving Deer, Univ. of South Florida; Elio H. Del Sette, Saratoga Springs, New York; Anne Falke, Michigan State University; Marvin Felheim, Univ. of Michigan; Warren French, IU-UP, Indianapolis; John Hague, Stetson University; Akira Fujitake, Tokyo University; Stuart Hall, Univ. of Birmingham, England; David Madden, LSU; Roger Mudd, CBS; Russel B. Nye, Michigan State University; Charles Peavey, Univ. of Houston; John Seeley, Univ. of

Connecticut; William Stafford, Purdue University; Kay Weibel, Michigan State University.

We also had a growing and effective group of Regional Presidents: Gerard O'Connor, New England; Lawrence Mintz, Middle Atlantic; Henry Marks, South; Joel Jones, Southwest; Fred Schroeder, John DiMeglio, Midwest; Carol Bagley, Dick Etulain, Bill McReynolds, Rocky Mountains; Arthur Berger, West Coast.

Throughout his career with the PCA, Marshall has maintained his enthusiasm, his vision, his willingness—nay, his eagerness and determination—to work, to make new probes into undisclosed realities, to try anything twice. An enthusiastic scholar, Marshall has excelled most other people in the PCA with the range and number of his scholarly publications. His contribution to the overall success of the PCA movement was almost immeasurable.

John Cawelti succeeded Fishwick as President. He was eminently fitted for the position. John had published with the Popular Press in 1970 his classic study *The Six-Gun Mystique*, had done dozens of other theoretical and pragmatic studies of areas of popular literature and culture, was of a frame of mind like mine and Russ' and was, therefore, guaranteed to succeed in his role.

The 1975, that is the fifth, national convention was held downriver from Milwaukee, in Sam Clemens country, in St. Louis. The Chair of the local arrangements committee was Carol Miller, of Meramec Junior College, St. Louis. For this meeting we had instituted a new instrument which was in fact going to revolutionize the growth of the PCA—installation of Area Chairs for various areas which we were familiar with and with others with which we were unfamiliar. It was an obvious recruiting device and very successful.

In the past the PCA had used various recruiting devices to guide us in mailing out our posters announcing the annual meetings. We had bought labels from similar groups, such as the ASA, and sent out the posters. But we were convinced that other methods would be more profitable. I had argued for some time that what we needed was state chairs, that is, people acting as heads of the states in which they lived. Their purpose would be to try to get in touch with as many people as possible from their local address. I was convinced that material mailed out from a state address often carried more weight and received more attention than material mailed out from a faceless person in another state. I was convinced that the idea of the state chair should be refined to the individual campus level. That is, every campus in the U.S. should have a PCA chair who would recruit by sending out posters and reminders through the campus mail and making local campus calls asking people if they did not want to participate in the PCA meetings. That idea never flew, perhaps from the sheer enormity of the undertaking.

The first list of area chairs consisted of most of the people and most of the areas that we could think of at the time. Still the coverage demonstrated how seriously we were trying to be inclusive: Architecture: J.M. Neil, Boise,

Idaho; Automobiles and Racing: David Neuman, Bowling Green State University; Bibliography: Larry Landrum, Michigan State University; Blacks: Ronald C. Foreman, Jr., Gainesville, Fla.; Children's Literature: W.B. Tyrrell, Michigan State University; Comics: William Young, Lynchburg College; Country & Western Music: William Ivey, Country Music Foundation; Detective Fiction: George Grella, University of Rochester and Agate Krouse, University of Wisconsin; English Literature: Earl Bargainnier, Wesleyan College; Ethnic Groups and PC: Frank Pino, University of Texas; Folklore, Joseph Arpad, UCLA; Forums and Works-in-Progress Sessions: Larry Mintz, University of Maryland; German & Russian: Hedda Martens, SUNY, Brockport; History: William Cohn: Carnegie-Mellon; Magazines and Print: Bruce Lohof, University of Miami, Fla.; Movies: Peter Rollins, Oklahoma State University; Music: Joseph Mussulman, University of Montana; Musicals and Popular Theater: Timothy Donovan, University of Arkansas; Occult: Marcello Truzzi, Eastern Michigan University; Politics: Brownlee Corrin, Goucher College; Popular Culture and Curricula: Sam Grogg, American Film Institute; Popular Literature: Tom H. Towers, University of Rhode Island; Popular Music Trends and Content of the Industry, R.S. Denisoff, Bowling Green State University; Popular Religion: Elmer Suderman, Gustavus Adolphus University; Pornography: Wayne Losano, Rensselaer Poly. Institute; Romance Languages: H.A. Bouraoui, York University, Toronto; Science Fiction: Thomas Wymer, Bowling Green State University & Thomas Clareson, Wooster College; Sociology: Terry Furst, CUNY, Staten Island CC; Soviet Europe & Asia: Frederick Kaplan, Michigan State University; Sports: Eldon Snyder, Bowling Green State University; TV and Radio: Fred E.H. Schroeder, University of Minnesota & Joan M. Grumman, Santa Barbara City College; Visual Vernacular: Parks, Battlefields, etc.: Richard Martin, Fashion Institute of Technology; Westerns: William Stafford, Purdue University & Michael T. Marsden, Bowling Green State University; Women & Popular Culture: Barbara Desmarais, University of Arkansas & Barbara Sullivan, Gaston College.

Another innovation worked out for the PCA by the time of the St. Louis meeting was an enlargement of the number of officers. Now in addition to the President, the Association had six vice-presidents: Mollie Davis Abernathy, Queens College, Charlotte, N.C.; Carl Bode, University of Maryland; Pat Browne, Bowling Green State University; Leslie Fiedler, SUNY, Buffalo; Michael Marsden, Bowling Green State University; Marshall McLuhan, University of Toronto. In addition we had two new offices: Education Programs Coordinator, Sam Grogg, Jr., AFI, Washington, D.C.; and Bibliographer: Larry N. Landrum, Michigan State University.

In addition the PCA had an Advisory Council consisting of twenty-four members: Howard Adams, National Gallery, Washington, D.C.; Joseph Arpad, UCLA; Arthur Berger, San Francisco State College; Seymour Betsky, University of Utrecht; C.W.E. Bigsby, East Anglia University, U.K.; Craighill Burks, Everglade School for Girls, Miami, Florida; Robert Corrigan, University of Maryland; Kenneth Davison, Heidelberg College; Harriet Deer,

University of South Florida; Irving Deer, University of South Florida; Anne Falke, Michigan State University; Marvin Felheim, University of Michigan; Marshall Fishwick, Lincoln University; Warren French, IU-PUI, Indianapolis; John Hague, Stetson University; Akira Fujitake, NHK Theoretical Research Center, Tokyo; Stuart Hall, University of Birmingham, U.K.; David Madden, Louisiana State University; Henry Marks, Huntsville, Alabama; Russel B. Nye, Michigan State University; Charles Peavy, University of Houston; John Seelye, University of North Carolina; Willian Stafford, Purdue University; Kay Weibel, Michigan State University. The interesting thing about this list is that it reveals not only how well known the PCA had become in just four years but also how widely our interests had ranged and how international our membership had become.

We had also developed the concept of Regional Presidents to cover most of the areas of the country: Middle Atlantic, Chesapeake: William H. Young, Lynchburg College; Middle Atlantic, Metropolitan: Ruth Prigozy, Hofstra University; Midwest: Fred Schroeder, University of Minnesota, Duluth; New England, Gerard O'Connor, Lowell Technological College; Northern California, Arthur Berger, California State University, San Francisco; Rocky Mountains, Richard Etulain, Idaho State University, Pocatello; South: Earl Bargainnier, Wesleyan College, Macon, Ga.; Southern California: Joseph Arpad, UCLA; Southwest: Joel Jones, University of New Mexico; Texas: Joseph Hilfer, University of Texas at Austin; Washington: Mary Land, Washington State University; Wyoming: Robert Barthell, Northwest Community College, Powell.

During the first few years the PCA was very conscious of the newness of the subject matter in popular culture and the need to assist teachers as much as possible in the art of teaching the subject. Therefore we had numerous "How-To" sessions at our meetings which were dedicated not only to how to teach popular culture but also to what materials were available and how they could be obtained. Locating the materials was the province of bibliographer Larry N. Landrum. By the time of the St. Louis meeting, Larry Mintz, University of Maryland, was in charge of informal sessions and workshops. Although varying in degree of success, everyone, particularly those who dropped by for assistance, thought that they were worth the time and effort. Sometimes for a session there would be thirty people in the audience; at other hours there would be one or two teachers in talking with the director. But everybody thought they should be continued.

At St. Louis, following in the footsteps of our practice in Milwaukee, and in the precedent set by nearly all other academic associations, we again had a Keynote Speaker in a plenary session. This time the speaker was Walter J. Ong, S.J. We made the event as ceremonious and dignified as possible. After some welcoming remarks by Ray Browne, we had more welcoming remarks by Glynn Clark, Meramec Community College, Edwin G. Eigel, St. Louis University; John Atkins, Southern Illinois University; and Richard W. Davis, Washington University. John Cawelti then introduced the keynote speaker, Father Ong, whose title for his remarks was "African Drum Talk:

Quintessence of Oral Communication." Several hundred people filled the Chase Club in the Chase-Park Plaza, and Father Ong's remarks were theoretical, deep and enlightening. But the consensus was that perhaps we should think of discontinuing the Keynote Speech. Russel Nye and I had worried over the practice of having a Keynote Speaker and the St. Louis reaction convinced us that the members of the Popular Culture Association, fitting the remark by Dr. Samuel Johnson, were an unclubbable group. One of the reasons for being a member of the PCA was apparently to get away from some of the rituals and routines of other academic organizations. So Russ and I were sure that our evaluation of the unclubbability of the PCA members was correct.

Despite such minor misreadings of the membership and what they wanted in the program, however, the meeting went very well. Five groups had co-sponsored the meeting, with financial assistance: Bowling Green State University, St. Louis-St. Louis County Junior College District, St. Louis University, University of Southern Illinois, Edwardsville, and Washington University. The Local Arrangements Committee, headed by Carol Miller, Meramec Community College, had done a superb job. So everyone in attendance left the meeting filled with enthusiasm for the next yearly meeting.

In searching for the most strategically located city for the conference we always tried to locate a place close to or in the heart of our strength in membership. Since Chicago was obviously strategically located, a fine convention city and the home of President John Cawelti, we chose Chicago for our sixth annual meeting. As we had in St. Louis, we received excellent co-sponsoring cooperation from the schools in the neighborhood. Again Bowling Green State University, University of Chicago, and Northeastern Illinois University sponsored our meeting, and we received a financial contribution from the Alumni Association, Northeastern Illinois University.

We had an especially effective local arrangements committee for the Chicago meeting: Ralph Carnes, Roosevelt University, Valerie Carnes, Roosevelt University, John Cawelti, University of Chicago, Bethe Hagens, Governors State University, J. Fred MacDonald, Northeastern Ilinois University, Carol Williams, Roosevelt University and Gary Wolfe, Roosevelt University. The meeting was especially notable for the efficient way Ralph Carnes organized and conducted the business of meetings and conflicts. He carried a walkie-talkie radio with him all the time and could summons assistance to any spot at any time within minutes. His was the most efficiently run meeting that the PCA has ever had.

One of the obligations, and pleasures, of the Secretary-Treasurer through the year was the enlargement of the Area Chairs. My technique was to go through the program and see if I could find areas which would not fall under the categories represented by the Area Chairs, and to try to think of other areas that we should have represented but did not. By this technique, I had nearly doubled the areas by the time of the sixth meeting in Chicago. Though there is some repetition in the Area Chairs of the sixth and the fifth meetings, it will perhaps be useful to repeat them all for the later meeting in order to demonstrate how the device succeeded: Advertising, Marketing, Image-making and Public Relations: Ralph Carnes and Valerie Carnes, Roosevelt University; Afro-American Studies: Ronald C. Foreman, Jr., University of Florida; Art and Architecture: Jan Cohn, Carnegie-Mellon University; Asian Studies: Surjit S. Dulai, Michigan State University; Bibliography: Robert Galbreath, University of Wisconsin, Milwaukee; British Popular Culture: Earl F. Bargainnier, Wesleyan College, Macon, Ga.; Children's Literature and Youth Culture: Sarah J. Schwartz, Ohio University; Comics and Cartoons: William H. Young, Lynchburg College; Country and Western Music: Charles Wolfe, Middle Tennessee University & Bill Malone, Tulane University; Culture of the American West: William T. Stafford, Purdue University & Michael T. Marsden, Bowling Green State University; Detective/Mystery/Suspense/Gothic Fiction: Agate N. Krouse, University of Wisconsin, Whitewater; Entertainment and Leisure-Time Activities, Ray Browne, University of Maryland (I was at Maryland for the year); Ethnic Studies (including Afro-American Studies): Frank Pino, University of Texas, San Antonio; Folklore: Kenneth Thigpen, Pennsylvania State University; Forums and Works-In-Progress Sessions: John W. English, University of Georgia; Germanic Languages: Robert Brooks, University of South Florida; Heroes, Heroines and Super-People: Richard Gid Powers, Richmond College, SUNY, Staten Island; High School Curricula: J. Fred MacDonald, Northeastern Illinois University, Chicago; History, Historical Events & Development (since 1776): William H. Cohn, Carnegie-Mellon University; Libraries and Library Culture: Jan Schroeder, Duluth Public Library; Movies: Peter Rollins, Oklahoma State University; New Journalism: Marshall Fishwick, Temple University; The Occult, ESP, Parapsychology and Astrology: Marcello Truzzi, Eastern Michigan University; Popular Music, Musicals and Musical Theater: Joseph A. Mussulman, University of Montana; Popular Culture Before 1776: Fred E.H. Schroeder, University of Minnesota, Duluth; Popular Culture and Curricula: Sam Grogg, Jr., American Film Institute; Popular Language and Dialect: Henry Sustakoski, State Univ. College, Buffalo; Popular Literature (including poetry): Tom H. Towers, University of Rhode Island; Popular and Folk Medical Practices: Arthur Wrobel, University of Kentucky; Popular Music: Trends and Social Commentary: R. Serge Denisoff, Bowling Green State University; Popular Religion: Elmer Suderman, Gustavus Adolphus College; Pornography: Frank Hoffman, State University College, Buffalo; Print Media (including newspapers and magazines): Richard A. Kallan, Univ. of Nevada, Las Vegas; Psychology and Popular Culture: Gary Fine, Harvard University; Rites of Passage: James Hughes, Wright State University; Romance Language Studies: Georges Joyaux, Michigan State University; Science Fiction and Fantasy: Tom Clareson, Wooster College & Tom Wymer, Bowling Green State University; Sex and Marriage (including the liberation movement): Emily Toth, Univ. of North Dakota; Science and Technology: David Wright, Michigan State University; Slavic Languages and Soviet Europe: Frederick Kaplan, Michigan State University; Sociological Theory and Mass Culture:

Terry Furst, Staten Island Community College; Sports: David Voigt, Albright College; UFO'S and Flying Saucers: David Stupple, Eastern Michigan University; Television and Radio: Michael R. Real, University of California, San Diego & Dan Johnson, University of Minnesota, Duluth; Visual Vernacular: Richard Martin, Fashion Institute of Technology, New York; Wedding Customs as Cultural Phenomenon: Joseph Kivlin, Bowling Green State University; Women in Popular Culture: Barbara Desmarais, University of Arkansas & Barbara Sullivan, Central Piedmont Community College; Cultural Geography: Alvar Carlson, Bowling Green State University. The concept of the usefulness of the Area Chairs was demonstrably viable, so we continued to expand it year by year.

Amid a host of innovations and new presentations (especially in films) two other programs at this meeting were notable. One was the presence and presentation of a representative of the National Endowment for the Humanities. Through the years I personally and Russel Nye especially had gone to the NEH for official recognition and financial assistance. When I had started the Center for the Study of Popular Culture at Bowling Green State University I had applied for a sizable grant from the NEH. Apparently the idea was favorably read in Washington and an inspection team had been sent out to look over my enterprise. At the last moment, the request was turned down. I sought out an explanation, and talked with two of the three inspectors, who assured me that they had written favorable reports. The third member, a faculty member from Hampshire College, had voted no on my proposal because, as I learned through the grapevine, he felt that he "had a better Center for the Study of Popular Culture," than we had at Bowling Green. If he said so, it obviously represented envy on his part and a desire to keep important whatever he did have at Hampshire. This determination to put down and keep down all efforts to develop popular culture studies was epidemic in the early years of the movement, and that spirit, aided and abetted by the NEH's reluctance to fund anything so inimical to their traditional interests kept money away from the movement.

Russel Nye regularly reported to me that he had had the same problems with the NEH. He could not get his projects funded. He also served for some years on the National Humanities Council, the supergroup that made final recommentations to the Chairman of the NEH for funding. On that committee Russ was always voted down whenever he suggested funding for some popular culture projects that came in. Ironically, apparently the one individual who always led the fight to keep funding away from the popular culture applications was Henry Nash Smith, whose career had been built on popular literature and who even while he voted against other people's projects was himself editing a book on popular culture and writing one on Henry James' use of popular culture. Perhaps the whole affair was a matter of definition and clarity in proposals.

Anyway, that is what the representative of the NEH was to tell us in a lengthy and stormy session that went on for two hours when he tried to explain what the NEH was up to and how it wanted to carry out its mission. The audience was filled with disappointed and frustrated people who had asked for funding from the NEH and had been turned down. So it was not a pleasant session we had with the NEH. The representative kept insisting that the NEH wanted to fund projects in popular culture but we had to apply for funding for projects that they wanted to fund. It seemed a closed circle (a Catch-22 situation) that we could not understand and could not break. The impasse has not been broken since that memorable explanation and invitation.

In fact the disagreement with the NEH was long-standing and explosive. All along we had felt that we were working in the Humanities and deserved at least a level field to play on in competing for NEH money. But we had not received, in our estimation, a free and open competition. We had tried to do something about it.

When I was at the University of Maryland as Visiting Professor in 1975-76 I had called Ronald Berman, Chairman of the NEH, who had been Spiro Agnew's speech writer, and asked for an appointment, telling him that we would like to discuss the NEH and the PCA association. Berman refused to give me the appointment, saying that as far as he was concerned there was to be no relationship. I, however, refused to accept his attitude. I told him that as a tax-paying citizen I demanded that he meet with us. So reluctantly he arranged for the meeting. Three of us attended, Carl Bode, Robert Corrigan (Provost of Arts and Sciences, University of Maryland) and I. We found an entirely alien and hostile atmosphere at the meeting. No matter how we argued our case, Berman remained adamant. We lost the round but did not leave with no points. Carl Bode told Berman in a tone of coolness and firmness, a tone that only Carl can assume, that it would be to his benefit if he took our arguments seriously. Unfortunately, however, all we got from our interview was the satisfaction of having scored a point or two. For nothing ever came of Bode's arguments.   The sore with the NEH continued to fester. As the time came for Berman to be reappointed under the new Administration in Washington or be replaced, only Senator Claiborne Pell (D. Rhode Island) stood up against the reappointment. In his opposition, Pell became the whipping boy of most of the press, and virtually all of the Establishment. But he stood firm. Thinking that this was an opportunity to exert some imfluence, I got in touch with Senator Pell, told him how much we in the PCA approved of his stance and suggested that we would like to have some voice in the choice of the next Chairman of the NEH. The situation seemed much improved and to hold some promise. Senator Pell put me in touch with his Administrative Assistant and promised that I would be consulted before and during the hearings for the next Chairman. As it turned out, perhaps because of administrative snafu or because of the way things are done in Washington, I was not brought into the confirmation hearings, but I was brought to Washington for an interview with the new Chairman, Joe Duffey, after he was confirmed. I explained the difficulty the PCA people had had with the NEH and hoped that we could have less biased access to the NEH resources under his chairmanship.

Mr. Duffey was very sympathetic and acceded to my request to provide the PCA with enough money to hold a conference at the NEH headquarters in Washington.

The meeting was arranged and I invited some twelve persons to spend a Saturday with the NEH people explaining our situation and attitude. Our attitude almost exactly paralleled the remarks Duffey had made at his Confirmation hearings before the Senate. The people who attended the Saturday meeting for the PCA included Carl Bode, Tom Inge, Tom Towers, Bill and Jan Cohn, Ray Browne, Harriet and Irving Deer, Larry Mintz, Russel Nye and J. Fred MacDonald. But although the meeting brought the PCA closer to the NEH in philosophy and understanding, there is some question whether it ever brought any tangible results. There seem to have been more projects submitted in the name of popular culture accepted. But with Joe Duffey's departure from the NEH, if there had been any tangible improvement, this softening seemed to have hardened under William Bennett, the new Chairman. As to the fate of popular culture projects under the new Chairman, Lynn Cheney, after William Bennett became Secretary of Education, the jury is still out. We hope that popular culture will be recognized as the New Humanities and its practical and pragmatic value accepted as being real and tangible.

But at least one other pleasant benefit was introduced at the Chicago meeting. For some time I had been thinking that the PCA should make some kind of recognition for those excellent people in popular culture who are extraordinarily successful. We should have our own "Oscar" and "Emmy" Awards, giving our acknowledgement of excellence to individuals who had excelled in general or within the preceding year. So we developed our "Popular Culture Association Award of Excellence for Distinguished Achievements in the Popular Arts." The first presentations were made at the Chicago meeting to three individuals who were as meritorious as could be: Agatha Christie, Studs Terkel and Ross Macdonald.

Agatha Christie could not come from England, but she wrote a cute and delightful refusal as would have been voiced by Hercule Poirot and by Miss Marple. Studs Terkel was present and made a revealing and amusing acceptance speech. In many ways, however, the highlight of the evening was in the speech by Ross Macdonald, who stopped by on his way to Toronto to supervise the filming of a movie being made from one of his Lew Archer novels. Macdonald said that in his eyes the history of civilization and history was tied to entertainment. Of the Arts, Entertainment was perhaps Queen. He felt that study of popular culture was right and proper, should be continued, and should not be criticized by other academics and non-academics. Macdonald, who in addition to his skill as serious entertainer in fiction was also a Ph.D. in English from the University of Michigan, with a dissertation on Samuel Taylor Coleridge, was speaking from knowledge, experience, and, we felt, considerable wisdom. He surely reinforced our attitude, which really needed no reinforcement.

All in all the Chicago meeting had been one of the most successful of our brief history. It had been efficiently engineered, the speakers were first-class and we all had learned a great deal, from exploiting the offerings of the city outside the hotel and from hearing one another speak both formally and informally. We all looked forward to the next meeting in Baltimore.

The seventh national convention, 1977, was held in Baltimore. This was the first time we had met on the East Coast and we expected a large turn-out. As events would dictate, we had about 700, more than we had had, perhaps, the year before, but surely no more than we had had in Milwaukee.

Some things had remained virtually the same, and some had changed. The Regional Presidents were practically the same: William H. Young, Middle Atlantic, Chesapeake; Ruth Prigozy, Middle Atlantic, Metropolitan; Carol Miller, Midwest; Marie Ahearn, New England; Arthur Berger, Northern California; Richard Etulain, Rocky Mountains; Gary Harmon, Southeastern; Joseph Arpad, UCLA; Frank Pino, Texas; Robert Barthell, Wyoming. The number of Vice-Presidents had been reduced to three: William Cohn, Tom H. Towers, Emily Toth. The Education Program Coordinator was now David Feldman. The Council Members at Large were Michael Real, Peter Rollins and Gerard O'Connor.

The new President was David Madden, LSU, who had worked hard in other positions and merited this new office. As for the events of the meeting, they were pretty much parallel to those of the preceding year at St. Louis. We had invited Stan Lee, of Marvel Comics, to be with us again. Stan always loved these bits of exposure and associating with academics. So he accepted invitations whenever he could. We also carried through our practice of granting the PCA Award of Excellence. This time it went to Louis L'Amour, western writer whose total sales at that time had exceeded 70,000,000. L'Amour made a poignant speech about his work, saying how he crafted his works and what he was trying to do with them. L'Amour felt then, and before and after, that American history of the West was fallacious, and he was determined to write novels until he set the record straight. His speech was well received. One other innovation was created for the Baltimore meeting— presentation of the Russel B. Nye Award for the best article published in the *Journal of Popular Culture* for the preceding year. This was a practice which was to continue and to grow as the PCA realized more and more vividly how many meritorious "firsts" we were having. So, with the minor exception of some unpleasant episodes with the personnel of the hotel, the meeting was a success, though perhaps not as widely attended as we had expected.

There were actually several changes in the PCA brewing in the mind of David Madden. David was a powerhouse of energy and ideas. Often he felt that change was beneficial just for change's sake. He generally wanted to improve the machine even if there was nothing broken about it. His purpose was to bring more democracy to the PCA, as he felt it needed it, and to broaden the base of membership and participation. After the Baltimore meeting he began to work hard for these "needed" changes.

In the past, for example, we had never had formal meetings of the various officers except at the national convention. We had observed other academic groups, such as the ASA, and had seen them spend a lot of time and money getting the various officers together for a day-long meeting, and in our opinion the only thing that resulted from such a meeting, with its long officers' reports, was confusion and mischief. So we had determined not to have them. President Madden, however, felt that the meetings were necessary, for short-term and long-term planning of the PCA. So, at the invitation of vice-president William Cohn and his wife, Jan, we met at their home in Pittsburgh to make plans. The first thing on the agenda was the writing of a constitution. Using those constitutions of other academic groups, President Madden hammered out one for the PCA, and after much talk and debate finally worked out one that would not cause too much damage. In effect the Constitution merely formalized the existing practices. It was, however, pretty much the cautionary work of Carl Bode and Larry Mintz that caused the document to be no more mischievous than it was. It was a Constitution that the organization could live with. A copy is given in the Appendix. It was to be modified later, as people began to see that it created at times more problems than it solved.

The eighth meeting, in 1978, was held in Cincinnati. We had chosen that city for the site because it was centrally located, was a clean and safe city for those who wanted to take advantage of local offerings, and because the people at the hotel seemed so pleasant. After our experience with surly and uncooperative hotel personnel in Baltimore, we were grateful that the personnel in Cincinnati were as pleasant and cooperative as possible. In addition, the hotel, the Netherland Hilton (now refurbished and renamed) was delightful.

Although the official personnel were essentially unchanged from the preceding year, we had many new participants in the sessions, and we instituted a new and delightful "first." Emily Toth and Susan Koppelman-Cornillon proposed that we have an "Elvis Presley Memorial Sock Hop," which would at the same time be lively enough to suit a group of academics but not so strenuous that it would strain backs and ligaments. Emily Toth acted as the disc jockey in charge, and William Schurk, of the Bowling Green Popular Culture Library and Sound Archives provided the platters to be spun. It was a tame event, at best, but the teachers did a lot of watching and their children, and a few of the youngest among themselves, did some dancing. But it did not matter. Everybody judged the sock hop a smashing success. Bill Randle, a former radio personality at radio station WERE Cleveland, later in the program gave an "Evaluation and Tribute to Elvis." He was indeed well qualified for the program, for Bill had been one of the most influential radio personalities in the rise of the Presley star. The Author's Forum: Mystery and Detective Fiction, featured Robert B. Parker, author of the Spenser series of detective novels, including *The Godwulf*

Manuscripts, Mortal Stakes and *The Promised Land* and winner of the 1977 Best Novel Award of the Mystery Writers of America, who discussed mystery and detective fiction. Again the presentation of the Russel B. Nye award for the strongest paper in the *Journal of Popular Culture* was made.

The consensus was that this meeting, with the possible exception of the one held in Milwaukee, was the strongest to date. The papers and presentations were of continued high quality, and everyone left with a feeling of genuinely having learned a lot about his interests.

For the ninth meeting, 1979, at the William Penn Hotel, in Pittsburgh, considerable changes had been made, at least in the official corps of the PCA. Carl Bode, University of Maryland, was President. The number of Vice-Presidents had been reduced to two: Harriet Deer, University of South Florida, St. Petersburg; and Earl Bargainnier, Wesleyan College, Macon, Ga. Jack Nachbar, Bowling Green State University, was now Education Programs Coordinator; and Michael Marsden had been elected as editor of PCAN, our much needed newsletter intended to keep the society informed about goings-on in allied fields, and to form a bond of comradeship among the members of the PCA by publishing material of interest to all. The Council Members at Large had changed: J. Fred MacDonald, Northeastern Illinois University; Gary Harmon, University of North Florida; Janice Radway, University of Pennsylvania; George Belden, Maple Heights Senior High School. There were also several changes in the Regional Presidents: Middle Atlantic, Chesapeake: Suzanne Ellery Greene, Morgan State University; Middle Atlantic, Metropolitan: Ruth Prigozy, Hofstra University; Midwest, Robert Brake, Illinois State University; New England: Josie Campbell, University of Rhode Island; Northern California: Arthur Berger, San Francisco State University; Rocky Mountains: Richard Etulain, Idaho State University, Pocatello; South: Thomas Hood, University of Tennessee; Southern California: Michael Real, University of California, San Diego; Southwest: Joel Jones, University of New Mexico; Texas: Frank Pino, University of Texas, San Antonio; Wyoming: Robert Barthell, Northwest Community College, Powell.

Participants at this meeting will remember that although there were about the usual number and kind of particpants, there was at least one event that nearly threw us. It was the result of our success. In choosing the hotel in Pittsburgh Pat and I had been very careful to choose one that we thought would be large enough. Every facility looked adequate. But nothing is stable and sure—and safe from renovation—in the hotel business. We had faced the inconvenience of renovation before. When we had chosen the Mark Plaza in Milwaukee, we were told that before we got back for the meeting the hotel would be renovated. We were not sent any plans and names for the new renovated rooms. So when we made out the program we used the names of the rooms before they had been changed. When we got there, however, we found that not a single room existed as we had them listed. But that was really a simple process of making signs with the new names on them. Despite some little confusion, the whole procedure had gone off well. But the William Penn was a different story altogether. In renovating the hotel, the architects had in fact done away with several rooms. So we had assigned rooms that did not exist, and we were desperately short of space. The solution for the problem was no solution at all. It only created chaos. We took the ballroom and divided it into some eight little pods for eight sessions to be run concurrently. The hotel promised us large and tall screens to encircle each little session-pod, but of course they could not be found. In rearranging the sessions for the ballroom we chose those that did not involve any kind of PA equipment, but the results were potentially disastrous nevertheless. But, so good was the spirit of the participants of the PCA, disaster did not occur. We merely shrugged our shoulders, agreed that life is full of imperfections, and concurred that despite the physical discomforts we all had had a pleasant time. We had had mystery writer Robert Parker again, and his presentation was successful. We had also had a marvelously amusing session of the Sock Hop that had been initiated in Cincinnati. Here we called it "Night of the Living Dead Sock Hop," which featured a miraculous achievement, "Taped music, mostly by dead people." Disc jockeys in charge were Susan Koppelman-Cornillon and Emily Toth. It was, despite all, a very lively session.

The most notable aspect of this meeting in Pittsburgh was the first formal get-together of the American Culture Association, an event and a history which will be discussed independently.

Women's study reached a kind of crossroad at the Pittsburgh meeting. The Popular Culture Association had almost from its inception been a natural and receptive academic field for Women's Studies. The field of study as well as the philosophy of the people concerned dictated that the PCA be a leader in this field. Almost from the beginning, therefore, Women's Studies had flowered. At the Indianapolis meeting, for example, there had been six sessions which touched directly or peripherally on women's studies. Since that meeting in 1973 the field had continued to grow. At Pittsburgh it in effect came to a head. Although there was no real need or cause, certain individuals assumed a more militant stance and determined to force women's studies in the PCA to take on a distinctive political posture. The move caused considerable consternation. It was the feeling of the officials, and my own, that the field was large enough for both the militants and the non-militants, and that those who wanted to be more "radical" in their approach should not infringe on the rights of others. But, the PCA being an open and democratic organization, the affirmative feminists carried the day. There now seemed to be two well identified groups within the PCA, those in favor of a more affirmative stance in women's studies, and those more inclined to traditional approaches to the openly-approved field of women's studies. The immediate result of the new militancy was an overwhelming vote to boycott meetings in all states that had not approved the proposed Equal Rights Amendment.

The joint meeting of the PCA/ACA in Detroit in 1980, the tenth of the PCA and the second of the ACA, was an all-round success. Attendance bore out my feeling that a large number of people would come to an ACA meeting who would not attend one named the Popular Culture Association. For the first time we had 900 people in attendance; this was, of course, consistent with the PCA's natural growth rate, but I am sure some of the attendees were present because of the new thrust; they were names I had not seen on our rosters before and they represented schools that had not been represented before.

Physically as far as the city went, everyone had a surprisingly good time. There had naturally been some apprehension about the safety of Detroit and even its desirability, but we had chosen it because of its proximity to Canada (just across the river), which we felt many of our people would enjoy visiting. Those people who visited Greek Town in Detroit were amazed and delighted. I still hear murmurs of our needing to go back to Detroit so that we can have access to Greek Town.

Within the hotel, the Radisson Cadillac, matters were somewhat different. The Cadillac was an old hotel that had been scheduled for demolition, and I sometimes think the owners had postponed demolition only so that we could hold our meeting there! Anyway, the physical conditions left much to be desired. Again, we had to place various sessions in little pods within the ballroom, with the consequent babble of intermixed voices; in many ways the ballroom sounded like an old-time blab school. But though the conditions were hardly maximal, everyone seemed to enjoy himself/herself.

Again we had something old and something new. We continued the Sock Hop, this time concentrating on the Motown Sound, with records from the Bowling Green University Sound Archive, and records spun by William Schurk, director of that Center. Our something new was arranged by J. Fred MacDonald, and was in the finest tradition of our trying to present new material which capitalized on the local conditions. At the PCA/ACA luncheon (which we dared to attempt because of the nature of the associated program) we had as guests of honor many of the WXYZ Detroit radio people connected with the production of the three most famous radio shows that originated on WXYZ, Detroit, and were carried on Mutual and ABC radio networks: *The Lone Ranger, Sergeant Preston of the Yukon* and *The Green Hornet.* After lunch these guests discussed their participation in these shows. The participants included Paul Hughes, actor; Rube Weiss, actor; Liz Weiss, actress; White Vernon, actor; Elaine Albert Stern, actress; Richard Osgood, actor; Harry Goldstein, actor; Tony Caminita, sound effects; Fred Flowersday, director; Bill Hengstebeck, sound effects; Dan Beattie, writer. It was the ripest kind of nostalgia, bringing back all those wonderful programs from our childhood and seeing in the flesh the sounds that made the Lone Ranger and the Green Hornet so effective. Incidentally, as is often the case, we established a lasting contact with Richard Osgood, and eventually the Popular Press published his history of WXYZ radio, *Wyxie Wonderland.*

There were other firsts. In keeping with trying to make learning as pleasant and pragmatic as possible, under the title "Will There be Mogen David in Heaven? The Oenologist's Dilemma," we had our first demonstration session in which the art of wine tasting was explained, theoretically and practically. As the invitation to the session stated, "Audience participation will be invited." Needless to say, it was a well-attended and highly appreciated session.

We also expanded our dimensions in another area. Almost from the beginning we had been having sessions on how to teach popular culture in colleges and universities and in public schools. Those were always well attended, for the belief was persistent that popular culture as a curriculum or as a means of promoting other curricula would be effective. So we were delighted at the Detroit meeting when Stanley Asher, Department of English, CEGP/John Abbott College, Kirkland, Quebec, offered a seminar in "Teaching Canadian Popular Culture." His was the only course, at least as far as he knew, in popular culture being taught in Canada.

One other area of concern was becoming manifest. Patricia Carlson, Rose-Hulman Institute of Technology, Terre Haute, Indiana, had been pushing "Literature and Lore of the Sea," and her efforts were bearing fruit. The Area has continued to grow, and now constitutes one of the major areas in both the PCA and the ACA. Another Area we were particularly proud of was that being chaired by Harold E. Hinds, Jr. and Charles M. Tatum, Latin American popular culture. After chairing sections at the PCA for a few years, they broke off from the PCA and founded the annual journal, *Studies in Popular Culture*, organized international meetings of scholars devoted to studying the popular culture of Latin America (1980-   ), and have begun to explore the possibility of founding an international organization devoted to this Area. Another interesting tongue-in-cheek session was one created by Edward J. Whetmore, San Francisco State University, called "Bret Maverick Memorial Poker Seminar," a session that lasted most of the night. It was billed poker, with emphasis upon social, cultural and economic conditions." Some people thoroughly enjoyed it.

For the eleventh annual PCA/third annual ACA meeting we went back to Cincinnati. The consensus was that we had so thoroughly enjoyed ourselves there two years earlier, and since it was a centrally located city, we should go back again. The success of the program was equal to our memories.

We had always listed the PCA and ACA sessions separately, in our effort to give identity to each organization. Sometimes we had sessions under the joint sponsorship of both. Our Keynote session at Cincinnati this time was one of those joint presentations: Regionalism as academic and Organizational Focus. The participants represented various shades of academic bias: Ray Browne, Russel Nye, Marshall Fishwick, Helen Bannan (Univ. of New Mexico), Dorothy Schmidt (Pan American University), Alvar Carlson (Bowling Green State University), William Grant (Bowling Green State University) and Fred Schroeder.

This new thinking was consistent with that of the new President, J. Fred MacDonald, who had been elected at Detroit for a two-year term. Fred was to become an effective president. He was always filled with ideas, and had an immense collection of movies at his Center for Popular Culture, at Northeastern Illinois University. We knew that he would bring about improvements. He had worked hard at expanding the concept of the Area Chairs, trying to find new ideas and to implement them. In Cincinnati we were testing some of his ideas. The other officers of the PCA at the time were: Vice-Presidents Gary Harmon (University of North Florida), Peter C. Rollins (Oklahoma State University) and Carol T. Williams (Roosevelt University, Chicago). The Council Members-at-Large were Liahna Babener (Grinnell College), Suzanne Ellery Greene (Morgan State University), Emily Toth (Pennsylvania State University) and Edward Jay Whetmore (University of San Francisco).

One of our more innovative and fascinating sessions was produced by the personnel at Gallaudet College, Washington, D.C. Called "The Deaf Character in Popular Culture," its purpose was, according to the program, definite: "This panel proposes to analyze characterizations of deaf people in the media and compare them with deaf characters created by deaf writers for their own theater. The participants are deaf. Their presentations will be reverse-interpreted by Catherine Kalbacher, who will deliver her commentary in 'Simultaneous Communication' (sign and voice)." It was a fascinating and informative session. One other fascinating innovation was forwarded by the feminists. It was a session called "Preparing the Feminist Cookbook." The discussants were Susan Koppelman (St. Louis), Helen Eisen (New Rochelle, N.Y.) and Barbara Ann Caruso (Earlham College). Their purpose was to use this session as the beginning of an effort to compile a feminist cookbook to benefit the National Women's Studies Association. Another interesting session was "An Afternoon with Stuart Kaminsky," author of the Toby Peters detective novels, *Murder on the Yellowbrick Road*, *The Howard Hughes Affair*, *Never Cross a Vampire*, *Bullet for a Star* and others, both before and afterwards. Kaminsky was a faithful member of the PCA and this afternoon spent with him discussing his works was fruitful.

Two other incidents at the Cincinnati meeting might be of some interest. The range of subjects in our sessions always tended to amaze non-members. We had been enjoying a good press for years; reporters came to our sessions and wrote up interesting reports of the range of our interests. It is true the reporters were generally condescending and contemptuous, but they are always condescending toward any academic organization. At this particular meeting in Cincinnati I happened to be riding down the elevator with a reporter from *Newsweek*. He told me that he was amazed at the diverᴊity of our presentations and could there possibly be any area within popular culture that was not represented and that I wish was there. I immediately mentioned that there were no sessions on wall coverings (such as tapestry, wallpaper, paintings, etc.). The reporter was amazed. And of course my remark received central billing in his article. Incidentally, I continued to search for somebody to do a paper on wall coverings, and eventually found just such a person. But there are still areas not yet covered in our comprehensive range.

One other small episode at our meeting reveals just how conservative the city of Cincinnati was and is. A week or two before our meeting, a reporter from a Cincinnati paper called up and said he had looked at our program and seen that we had a couple of sections of pornography and he wondered if we would have illustrations at this session. At the moment I forgot what he was probably probing for and naively answered of course we like to have illustrations for our presentations. Well, the reporter and the city had other things in mind. At the session a man from the morals squad came in, without permission and without paying his registration fee, to see just how far we were going with our illustrative material. Well, the man obviously knew nothing about academics and how far they go, for after ten minutes of the first paper he stalked out in a huff, saying, "If that's all they do they are harmless." Indeed!

The PCA Award of Merit was given to Henry C. Rogers, President of Rogers & Cowan, Inc. Public Relations, in Beverly Hills, California. Rogers was also author of the then popular book *Walking the Tightrope*. Rogers gave a nice speech outlining the business of selling authors to the public, as he did with the famous Irving Wallace, who one might think needed very little selling.

For this meeting we had the largest turn-out of our history, nearly a thousand people.

President J. Fred MacDonald made some significant changes in the early months of his presidency. For example he created the "Caucus," a meeting of the interest areas to discuss their plans for their area, election or appointment of Area Chair and/or other officers, and he strengthened the concept of the Area Chairs and their coverage. For the 1982 meeting, the twelfth for the PCA and the fourth for the ACA, to be in Louisville, Kentucky, Peter Rollins, Oklahoma State University, had been appointed Program Chairman, in charge of the whole program, and he came up with another innovation which was to bear fruit. Peter arranged for "Open Forums," a series of presentations which clustered around a particular topic but which for one reason or another did not get on the regular program. Another interesting concept was introduced by Peter, with Michael K. Schoenecke, Texas Tech University, in charge. It was arranged for a student to get one or two graduate or undergraduate hours credit for attending the PCA/ACA sessions, after having read a suitable text and then taking exams after the conference. Few people availed themselves of this golden opportunity. The PCA Award of Excellence was given to Frederik Pohl, distinguished author of numerous works in science fiction.

Louisville being a compact city, it provided many opportunities for the participants to enjoy themselves outside the hotel. Many went to Churchill Downs, of course. But perhaps the highlight of "off-campus" activity was the voyage of the *Belle of Louisville* up the Ohio with the participants chatting and commenting on the views. The climax came when the *Belle* tried to turn around for the return cruise only to discover that the wind was so strong that she could not turn around. I believe that difficulty does not occur on Mark Twain's Mississippi. Having to bear north until the ship could be sheltered behind an island and thus enabled to turn comprised a real adventure to the fresh-water sailors, many of whom had been no closer before to real sailing than the bathtub. Over nine hundred attended the meeting in Louisville, and a good seven hundred were on the ship. The cry as everybody left Louisville was "When do we come back?" The answer was not for some years. The PCA had prospered greatly under Fred MacDonald's leadership. He had been happy and quick to make suggestions for change, had effected them. But mainly he had been willing to work hard, to expend energy and time in developing the PCA. Growth and development had been assured under his stewardship.

New forces, initiated by MacDonald, asserted themselves and tended to take over at Louisville. One of the new forces was the election of Peter Rollins, of Oklahoma State University, as President. Peter had in fact been with the PCA from its inception. He had turned up at the second meeting in Toledo as a graduate student, and had declared himself totally committed to working physically and intellectually in the popular culture framework and Association. And he had indeed labored diligently and hard in every field and in every way. He had served as general program chair for the Louisville meeting, had thought up a dozen innovations, and had proved many of them feasible. He was ready to do more. He was elected President of the PCA.

He was to have his metal tested immediate'y. Before the Louisville meeting, the Convention Bureau at Wichita, Kansas, had asked if they could come to Louisville and make a presentation for Wichita as the meeting place for the PCA. Knowing perfectly well that their trip would be wasted, I assured them that they would be welcome. Well, they appeared, made a very effective presentation about why the PCA should hold its next meeting in Wichita, and convinced the committee to try it. There were, of course, the usual arguments against Wichita, some valid and some invalid, some snobbish and some very practical. But such matters as airlines and air costs aside, although they were very important, the problem arose with the delegation from the Southwest as to how they could do a creditable showing in the city of Wichita.

The challenge put Rollins and the other representatives of the Southwest into a stimulated flurry of activity. They were determined to make such a good showing in attendance that nobody could ever question the intellectual activity of the Southwest or the leaders' role in being able to stir it up and deliver it to Wichita. Peter had got to know many people in his role as Program Chair. He had also been busy in the Southwest Popular Culture Association, and had strength there to call upon. He and his colleagues, however, were strengthened by their iron will of determination, and they got to work. They called upon all the states and schools of the Southwest, tested their regional pride, their intellectual strength— possibly their sense of patriotism. The result was that the meeting at Wichita, which the cassandras of the PCA had declared already misbegotten and stunted if not dead, turned out to be one of the most interesting, and surely the largest, we had ever had.

The new Vice Presidents were Liahna Babener, Earl Bargainnier, Edward Jay Whetmore and Tom H. Towers. The Council Members-at-Large were Kathleen Klein, Indiana University-Purdue University, Indianapolis; Marty Knepper, Augustana College; Richard Gid Powers, University of Staten Island; Roger B. Rollin, Clemson University. Our new International Representative was Gary Nederman, York University. All worked hard to make the Wichita meeting a success. The meeting was sponsored by Bowling Green State University, Oklahoma State University and Wichita State University.

Dressed up in its western garb and prose, the Wichita meeting was a complete success. We had a special 10 kilometer run sponsored by the Holiday Inn—Downtown, we had a special sculpture tour of Wichita State Campus and coincidentally we met at the same time the Wichita Jazz Festival was meeting. All the great jazzists were in attendance. There was also a remarkable presentation which was almost unprecedented in "Wargames II: Extended Percussion and Professional Wrestling." People who saw these events conducted together reported that it was, to say the least, unusual. One of the highlights of the Wichita meeting was, indeed, a High Tea with Ruth Rendell, noted British author of crime fiction, as the honored guest.

But mainly there was the museum walk. The copy for the announcement of this event speaks for itself:

The cultural and historical legacy of Wichita, Kansas, will be ours to savor on Monday afternoon as part of a local museum experience. FIRST STOP: At the Mid-American Indian Center, we will hear Indian music, watch ninety dancers perform, and see the excellent collection of Amerindian art and artifacts. After a taste of squaw bread and a quick look at the museum shop, we will move on. SECOND STOP. The Wichita Art Museum is a modern structure which specializes in Southwestern art, to include the traditional contributions of Remington and Russell, but also more recent interpretations of the landscape by Murdock and Alvar. The sun will be setting as we leave the museum; not that the "unreal" colors of the Western painters are actually part of the daily crepusoule. THIRD STOP: Wichita's Historic Cowtown will be open to PCA/ACA museum walkers. The Cowtown is a serious effort to reconstruct the first settlement circa 1865-1880: crafts such as soap making, wood carving, cider pressing, and blacksmithing are recreated; activities such as water witching, the selling of patent medicine, and barroom dancing are displayed; drug stores, tailor shops—even the local jail—are open for inspection. Historical guides will provide background for interpretation to the physical culture on display and a barbecue dinner will provide a final spice to the afternoon's immersion in Western culture. Cowboy Koolaid (beer) and other liquid refreshments will be available with dinner.

Like the *Belle of Louisville* trip last year, this delightful and edifying day is designed to allow informal interaction among professionals of PCA/ACA, reminding us all that we are members of a community of learning, a community which develops more cohesion with each passing year....Please bring a Western outfit for the occasion.

The local arrangements committee had, as we say, done themselves proud. We all were delighted to express our gratitude to them all: to Gayle Davis, for museum and statuary walks; Jim Erickson for film efforts; William Nelson for a bit of everything, including good sense and good companionship; Martin Reif for moral support; Jacqueline Snyder for the restaurant guide; Gregory Sojka for a bit of everything; and Jim Thomas "for comic relief."

One other development in the PCA was announced in the Program for Wichita. For years the PCA had voted to boycott any state that had not approved the ERA. We had, for example, voted against going to Atlanta because Georgia had not ratified the ERA. The sharpness of debate over this question had sharply resonated among the members at the Pittsburgh meeting and had caused some hard feelings. By 1983, it was felt that perhaps the ERA, since it had failed to be ratified, was a dead or at least a moribund issue, forced to remain so until it was reintroduced into the Congress of the United States. Otherwise it could not really be a live issue. So as Secretary-Treasurer I conducted a poll among the members of the PCA/ACA about recalling our boycott of the offending states. Among the members voting, the ballots ran 179 to suspend the boycott of states not approving the ERA; 90 to continue the boycott; 14 to suspend for Chicago alone. The ballot seemed to be a clear mandate to suspend the boycott and to feel free to choose a site that fitted our needs regardless of the state's feeling about the ERA. Before leaving the subject of Wichita another fortunate coincidence should be cited. We happened to meet in the Hotel Broadview at the same time that a national Identical Twins Annual Meeting was being held. Although there was no public announcement of this meeting in the lobby of the hotel, it immediately became apparent that something was different when all PCA people began seeing double. When we had the elevator stop at a floor, instead of one person getting on there would be two—and they were always exactly alike. Identical twins by the hundreds were everywhere. If you think that is not a disturbing sight for sore eyes who have just come from a deeply thoughtful session late at night, just give it a try. There were identical twins everywhere, big ones, little ones; old ones, young ones; all dressed identically, and having the same body measurements after many years even if they did live far removed from each other and saw each other only once a year. Such is the power of genetic influence. Such is also the disturbing and charming impact of an Identical Twins Conference. Many of us, seeing double, accounted Wichita, despite the apprehension of many members as the announcement was made in Louisville the year before, a roaring success. This success also supported my long-held thesis that the academic world is ready for the study of popular culture and will flock to the banner and practice if they are only informed of its possibilities. The people who poured out for the Wichita meeting have, generally, stuck with the PCA. They do not want to give it up.

The fourteenth PCA national meeting and sixth ACA meeting, 1984, provided yet more reason for not giving up the ACA. This meeting, for the first time, was to be held outside the United States, though in close proximity, in Toronto, Canada. It was expected that there would be a larger than usual turn-out because of the natural growth pattern of the organizations energized by the attraction of Toronto, a delightful city. We thought the city would provide an inexpensive trip "overseas" for many of our members. Such proved to be the case. The registration for this meeting was 1500. The meeting was co-sponsored by Bowling Green State University; Centre for Culture and Technology, Univ. of Toronto; Innis College, University of Toronto; and the University of Toronto.

Barrie Hayne, a faithful member of the PCA since the beginning, was the Chairman of the Local Arrangements Committee and general Program Chairman. He worked hard to provide unusual attractions. There were many: "History of Jazz Through 1920: Concert Lecture"; "An Evening with the National Film Board"; "An Oratorio Performance of *The Song of Songs*"; "*Women in Production: The Chorus Line 1932-1980*"; "*Carnival in Canada*"; "Lecture Recital: Judith Cohen: Canadian ethnomusicologist"; a Ken Maynard movie, *His Fighting Blood*; "An Evening with Mary Pickford," who as Gladys Smith was born in Toronto in 1893 and went on to become America's Sweetheart; "An Evening with Walter Huston," who was born in Toronto in 1884; "*Seeing Things*, a CBC mystery series"; a discussion of the MSU Voice Library. The keynote speaker was Josef Skvorecky, expatriate Czech Novelist, author of *The Cowards, Miss Silver's Past,* and nominee for the Nobel Prize for Literature. He was given the PCA Award of Excellence. There was also a tour of old Fort York, which was enjoyed by all who went.

The whole meeting was dedicated to the memory of Ross Macdonald, who had recently died. The general feeling among the members of the mystery writers caucus was that Macdonald was one of the giants of crime fiction and that his contributions for the future would be missed.

In general the whole meeting was a great success. There were many new topics and fields not theretofore represented. The speakers were of unusually high quality, and the Special Events were exceptionally rich and varied. A special word should be said here about the contributions of Netta Gilboa. Netta had joined the PCA and taken over the Eros and Sexuality area while still a graduate student at Northwestern University. She worked tirelessly and imaginatively to produce the finest programs and speakers for her sections. She had done a brilliant job at the Wichita meeting, getting as a featured speaker Annette Haven, Adult Film Actress who had made dozens of adult films and who had been called by *Home Video* "a clear-headed, cagey, straight-shooting liberal who describes herself as a 'feminist,' a 'perfectionist' and, most of all a 'professional'." In Toronto, Netta outdid herself again, and produced interesting and informative sessions. The Eros caucus owes a great debt to Netta.

The next meeting was to be held in Louisville again. It was most fitting then that the new President be Earl Bargainnier, from Wesleyan College, Macon, Georgia, and a leading figure in the PCA of the South. As Peter Rollins turned over the gavel to Earl it is fitting that we round out Peter's contribution to the growth and development of the PCA.

He had worked hard, imaginatively and energetically, as general Program Chairman before he was President, and as President. We have already seen how he opened new territories in the Southwest, and throughout the country, for the Wichita meeting. In addition to the several changes he made for that meeting, we should also register that he introduced another improvement among the participants and in the printed program. He suggested that we invite every participant to send in a fifty-word abstract for inclusion in the printed program. Although there was some initial hesitation about the value of this added cost of production, it has turned out to be a welcome addition; it has doubled the size of the program, and would enlarge it even more if more people sent in their abstracts, but in general it provides a useful service.

Peter had another very useful idea. He had always felt that the more closely the members of the PCA associate one with another the better for us as individuals and for the PCA as a learned society. Toward providing keys for the closer association he proposed some years earlier that we should have a "National Finding List" of members which would include names and addresses, areas of interest, previous publications (optional) and other useful information about all members. Despite his pleas to the membership for cooperation in the project, his first efforts were only partially successful. However, with more talk and another mailing effort, we were able to get some fifty per cent of the members of the PCA to provide this information. It was published in the Fall 1984 issue of the *Journal,* and has proved immensely useful at least at the office of the Secretary-Treasurer as a finding list and a telephone directory when it is useful or necessary to get in touch with members. Throughout all his efforts, Peter has remained good-spirited, energetic and willing to help. His help has been immense.

The officers for the Louisville meeting, the fifteenth for the PCA and the seventh for the ACA, 1985, were Earl Bargainnier, President; Liahna Babener, Grinnell College, Barrie Hayne, University of Toronto, and Gregory Sojka, Wichita State University, Vice-Presidents; Netta Gilboa, Northwestern University, Peter Lennon, Chicago, Michael T. Marsden, Bowling Green State University and Nancy Ellen Talburt. University of Arkansas, Council Members. President Bargainnier had worked imaginatively and energetically toward making the second Louisville meeting a success, and it was. We had about the same number of participants that we had had the year before in Toronto, despite the fact that several persons did not want to return a second time to Louisville. The nature and range of paper presentations were extensive. Again, more and more new areas and subjects were being proposed and accepted.

In addition to the usual city-wide activities, we had planned again to have our delightful trip on the Ohio River aboard the *Belle of Louisville*. But early April in Louisville is subject to various whims of Mother Nature, and we got whimmed out on this trip. We boarded the *Belle* with some trepidation because the weather looked somewhat ominous. We waited for nearly an hour and then were informed that there was a threatening weather front approaching and it would be impossible for the boat to be taken out on the river. Most of us piled off disappointed but understanding. A hardy bunch, however, remained on the boat for the rest of the afternoon, listening to the Blue Grass band that had been obtained for the occasion by Prof. Michael Zalampas, Jefferson County Community College, and volunteered their services for the occasion and talking. Reports came back to headquarters, in fact, that the afternoon was probably more enjoyable with the *Belle* tied up at the mooring than it would have been out on the river. Such are the unintended fruits of a moody nature.

The PCA Award of Excellence for Dist inguished Achievements in the Popular Arts was granted to the Renfro Valley Folks, of Renfro Valley, Kentucky. The Renfro Valley Folks have been one of the most important stimuli in the development and promulgation of country music. The Renfro Sunday Gatherin' has been on the air since 1939, with John Lair its creator and proponent. Although Mr. Lair was ill and could not attend the session, at the luncheon we played portions of one of his programs, and a grand time was had by an appreciative and enthusiastic group of 100.

The 1986 meeting, the sixteenth of the PCA and the eighth of the ACA, was scheduled for Atlanta. Since Atlanta was deep in the heart of Dixie, we expected a large participation in regional and Southern materials. We were not disappointed. We had created areas and area chairs in various fields of Southern history and culture, and numerous people participated in those new areas. Generally speaking the morale among the members of both associations was high. There were about 1500 people present. This showed very little rise in participation over the Toronto and Louisville meetings, but there were perhaps two or three explanations. One was an unusually high hotel room rent. Another was that numerous people who otherwise would have been at the meeting had to bow out because of financial constraints. Although we regretted the absence of numerous old friends and new participants, we felt that the Atlanta meeting was successful.

The Atlanta meeting, however, served in a way to remind us that the PCA was after all sixteen years old and subject not only to the growth of years but also to man's frailty with increasing age. The printed Program was dedicated to Russel B. Nye, who had suffered a stroke the summer before and was recovering very slowly. Many people spoke about the tremendous and unpayable debt that the PCA/ACA owed Professor Nye. And all wished him a speedy recovery.

Another great tragedy hit the Associations after the Atlanta meeting. In early January, 1987 Earl Bargainnier, a bachelor, was found dead in his apartment, the victim of a massive heart attack. The verbal memorial here to Earl must be lengthy. He had joined the PCA at the meeting in St. Louis. He said that he had come from his small college in Missouri to the meeting of the PCA with real trepidation because he was sure he would be a nobody and therefore alienated. But he found just the opposite atmosphere. He was immediately welcomed and his interests encouraged.

A man of very wide interests and energy, Earl began making significant contributions to the PCA/ACA, to the various journals associated with the Associations and the Popular Press, and especially to the genre of crime fiction. He was one of the several innovators in this genre who were always thinking of new ways to enhance their interests and the field. He was one of the most active editors of crime fiction for the Popular Press, and one of the forces behind the establishment of the Dove Award, an honor to be bestowed on someone in the PCA/ACA each year for his/her achievements in the field of crime fiction. His contributions to the establishment and development of the Popular Culture Association of the South and its various enterprises were almost unlimited and unparalleled. Often running contrary to the opinions of several important members of the PCAS, Earl was always gracious in his suggestions and innovative in his approach. His contributions to this particular thrust of the PCAS were indeed considerable.

As President of the PCA Earl began with energy and suggestions, and continued through his two year term with unabated contributions. Repeatedly he said to the Secretary-Treasurer that he was really sorry to give up the office because he had so many ideas yet untried and untested. His term in office was one of very cordial relations with all members of the PCA. Earl's imprint on the Popular Culture/American Culture Association is written large and boldly. He will be sorely missed and not soon forgotten.

The sixteenth annual meeting of the PCA and the Ninth annual meeting of the ACA was held March 25-29, 1987, in Montreal, Canada. The officers were Liahna Babener, Montana State University, president; Christopher D. Geist, Bowling Green State University; Barrie Hayne, University of Toronto, and Gregory Sojka, Wichita State University, vice-presidents; Jeanne Bedell, on leave at the University of Prague, Nancy Ellen Talburt, University of Arkansas, and Michael Zalampas, Jefferson County Community College, Council Members-at-Large. It was by far the largest meeting to that point in number of people in attendance, some 1700. The meeting was also noteworthy in that in addition to the PCA/ACA joint meeting, we met with another academic group, The Society for the Study of Play, which had over a hundred members present.

As was to be expected, the range of sessions and of topics under discussion was unusually large. There were some 475 different sessions, all spread out from Wednesday morning to Saturday at noon. As usual we were strong in fiction, in literature of the sea, in music, in Black culture, comics, film, and dozens of others. One notable session was that organized by Anne Cheney, under her general topic "Imagination in the South." In this session she had as her special guest the noted writer of Southern novels Gail Godwin, who spoke on "Evolution of a Novelist." In addition she had "Barry Hannah:

Southern Writer," Don Noble, University of Alabama; and "Political Activism at the University of North Carolina, 1960-1985," Laura D. Birg, Xavier College, Chicago.

One notable event occurred at the meeting in Montreal which has many ramifications. At the Toronto meeting in 1984 I had tried to arrange for the establishment of a Popular Culture Association of Canada, with the results that I have already enumerated, no success. Some fifty people had attended the meeting at which the establishment had been discussed. At the Montreal meeting there were some 150 Canadians on the program, and there was a different kind of atmosphere around about the establishment of a PCAC. The feeling was that one should be established, though it was modest, and that it would grow. So the PCAC was in fact established. But for reasons known only to the would-be Canadian participants the PCAC never met, never got started. Now in the middle of 1988, after talking with some Canadians about the fate of a possible PCAC I can only be pessimistic and wait for the Canadians in their own time to move on the idea.

One other innovation in the structure of the officers of the PCA/ACA should be recounted here. Through the years we have prided ourselves on the innovations we use in making public presentations, and we have been particularly strong in the use of audio-visual equipment. Generally we have been rather informal in the method used to help distribute these materials to the proper room at the proper time. The Secretary-Treasurer has toted the equipment himself and has called on local arrangement people to help provide it and to see that it is properly situated for its use. In the first meeting, Larry Landrum had provided it from the holdings of Michigan State University. In Indianapolis, Warren French had provided it under the auspices of IU-PUI. At times we have had to pay rather large sums for use, as at Wichita, when for one reason or another arrangements committees have not been able to obtain the equipment gratis. Generally people have been unstinting in their willingness to provide the muscle and legwork required for this purely physical labor. An excellent example was provided by Thomas Crippo, Morgan State University, when we met in Baltimore. Tom was so busy seeing after the care of the A-V equipment, delivering most of it himself to the various rooms, that he could not get to any of the sessions. At Montreal the PCA/ACA finally recognized the dire need for some official to operate in the capacity of A-V Expeditor, and Michael Zalampas, Jefferson County Community College, was appointed to the post. Michael immediately took the issue to heart and made some valuable suggestions. For example, despite our realization through the years that the requests for A-V equipment were getting out of hand and that the costs for this equipment, where it was not provided by the local sponsoring college or university, were getting out of hand. Michael pointed out at the business meeting that the equipment was costing the organizations some $11,000 and that the costs could be reduced. Finally the membership at large realized the heavy outlay of cash for the luxury of A-V equipment, and we decided that all of us would try to discourage the frivolous and free use of A-V equipment except where it formed a substantive portion of the presention and was integral and genuinely necessary. Zalampas drew up a new set of suggested rules for requesting A-V equipment. These rules were promulgaged for the meeting to be held in New Orleans in 1988, and Michael was officially put in charge of this branch of the operation. At this writing it remains to be seen how willing the membership is to accept the leaner and less lavish use of A-V equipment, but Zalampas has recognized the full extent of the program and has determined to stanch the flow of financial resources.

The 1988 meeting was held in New Orleans, March 23-26. Again, as had been the case in Montreal, we had to meet in two hotels because of the size of the turnout. We chose the Clarion and the Pallas Suite hotels. In general the arrangement was satisfactory. The Clarion hotel, the recently renovated Jung Hotel, was more than pleasant. The personnel were gracious and helpful. Although the two hotels are some five minutes walking time apart, there seems to have been very little trouble in the "commute" between the two hostels. But although there was little grumbling about the accommodations, the Secretary-Treasurer continues to feel that using two hotels for the meetings is satisfactory only when the need is great. It seems that the need may continue. The PCA/ACA are somewhat unusual organizations in their needs for meetings. Most organizations use a minimum of meeting rooms, as most people who attend come to be a part of the audience, with particular "stars" being the ones to deliver the papers and presentations. But the PCA/ACA has always insisted that people who attend should also participate. Therefore when we have 2000 people in attendance, as we had in New Orleans, some 1850 will be participants. Such arrangements are difficult for hotels to supply. Therefore we must search for hotels or pairs of hotels that can supply some 32 meeting rooms at all times for a three-day period, and such accommodations are hard to find. So we probably must continue in the foreseeable future to use the double-hotel accommodations. Again, except in dire and adverse weather participants seem to understand the need and not feel imposed upon greatly.

The meeting in New Orleans, as suggested by the attendance and participant figures given above, was by far the most successful we have had to date. Perhaps the reasons, or some of them, are obvious. Everybody wanted to go to New Orleans (the city seems to be a state of mind, the American Land of Oz, where everybody wants to go). So we had the largest turnout in participants we have ever had. Many participants brought their spouses and family, making the trip to New Orleans something of a vacation.

Further, however, there was a new strength and headiness in the air and in the minds and demeanor of the participants. An observer could sense immediately that there was a new sense of dedication, of self-confidence, of standing-tall among the participants. They all felt that they had in fact "arrived" academically and scholastically. They all felt sure of themselves and of their areas of study and investigation. They were encouraged also at the attention paid the meeting by the national press, which included the *New York Times, Wall Street Journal, USA Today, Manchester Guardian,*

Mother Jones, and others. The write-up in the *Times* stirred up at least half a dozen letters and phone calls from people interested in what the PCA is doing. Further, subsequent to the New Orleans meeting, two articles, one in *Rolling Stone* and another possible one in *Harper's* will almost certainly be published. So as far as the media were concerned the New Orleans meeting was a resounding success.

It was successful in yet another way, that of participation by non-academics. We arranged for participation in the various sessions on crime fiction several authors, notably Chris Wiltz, James Lee Burke, and Nikki Giavonni. These authors were gracious in appearing and talking. But we also arranged to have their books sold in the lounge area and for them to autograph copies. Many copies were sold at these signings. Surely one of the highlights was the appearance of Rev. Andrew Greeley, who attended two sessions devoted to his works and commented on the papers. He was given the Popular Culture Association Award of Excellence for Distinguished Achievements in the Popular Arts. No one could have been more appreciative or more gracious in accepting it. Greeley had been ill all week and his appearance was threatened. Yet he literally got up from his sick bed, flew to New Orleans, attended his sessions, made his fine speech of acceptance, autographed books, talked with people, then got on his plane and flew back to his sick bed in Chicago. One could hardly expect greater selflessness, and all of us in the PCA/ACA appreciate his dedication to what he considers his obligations and opportunities.

Certain other events with great potential occurred at the New Orleans meeting. I had spent a good time of time pondering what should be done at this time by the two organizations to strengthen their present activities and to open up new possibilities. It occurred to me that one would be to return to our former commitment to students' participation in the PCA/ACA meetings that we used to have but had to suspend because of lack of money. Now, however, the two organizations had enough money in their treasuries to finance on a modest scale student participation. So I proposed that each regional chapter be given $1000 to help subsidize the participation of students, both graduate and undergraduate, by underwriting such expenses as housing, travel and food. The two advisory committees of the organizations approved of this expenditure, with the explicit understanding that the money be used exclusively for students. A parenthetical development along the same lines was a proposal by Carl Kell, Western Kentucky University, that $300 be granted for his use in developing strictly undergraduate participation. The motion was approved, I am glad to say, and the sum raised to $1000. Carl, who is experienced in this endeavor and dedicated to its success, will undoubtedly spend the money fruitfully. Both efforts to encourage student particpation will undoubtedly pay off in high returns for the money spent.

Another, allied, suggestion that was approved was a motion by Roger Rollin, of the ACA, that $100 be granted each officer of the two organizations to help defray their costs in attending the national meetings. This suggestion was apt and timely, and undoubtedly will be appreciated and fruitful. I have already received several letters and telephone calls, only weeks after the meeting, responding favorably to the motion.

Perhaps the motion with the greatest implications approved by the two organizations was my proposal that each Association fund a Fellowship for Ph.D. graduate study in Popular Culture at a college or university offering such a degree. My proposal was that a full Fellowship be funded by each Association to be used exclusively for Ph.D. study (not that for a Masters degree) and that the two be awarded to a school offering that Ph.D. in Popular Culture. After some clarification as to purpose and goal and means of administration, the advisory committees of each Association approved the proposal. I think the ramifications of this legislation will be far-reaching, especially in the nurturing of a Ph.D. program in Popular Culture somewhere.

For years I have dreamed of a Ph.D. in Popular Culture and have begun work on a proposal for such a degree program at Bowling Green State University, where I am located. The history of the development of Ph.D. degrees has always been that some school, or several schools, offer such a degree as soon as it is needed. I have gathered data from colleges and universities throughout the United States demonstrating that the demand for courses in popular culture is increasing rapidly, that faculty feel the need for specific training in popular culture areas, and that administrators are prepared to hire faculty with Ph.D.s in the discipline. Data also indicate that there is considerable need outside academia (for example, in museums, halls of fame, even in business) and that such a degree would be marketable. Surveys from potential students also reveal a real desire for such a degree. So the background for a request for such a degree is manifest. I have begun the process at Bowling Green State University for the implementation of this degree. Although there may be some temporary set-backs, success seems assured. It is perfectly obvious that the time is right for this degree and that it will be started at one college or university or another. The only question is which school will be bold and innovative enough to be the first.

Bowling Green State University already has what is called an "Area of Concentration" in Popular Culture in its American Culture Ph.D. program. That means that a candidate can "major" in Popular Culture in his/her work in the American Culture program. Such a "major" is highly desirable because of the importance of popular culture in any American Culture Ph.D. program. But no one should mistakenly assume that such a "major" is all that is needed at this time in the development of graduate work in Popular Culture. The discipline, the study, the need have developed sufficiently at this time so that it is imperative that the degree be developed. And it will be developed soon. The only question is which school will be the first to reap the rewards.

As much as anything else the realization of the maturity of the study of popular culture is evidenced in the notice that the world at large and academia specifically is currently paying the whole discipline. The presence of five or six newspapers and magazines at the New Orleans meeting is only one sign. I personally get up to ten calls from the media weekly; the other members of the faculty at Bowling Green State University receive a like number. I have appeared on all the major network shows: CBS, NBC, ABC, 20/20, and scores of local shows. Someone from *Newsweek* once said that I am the most quoted academic in the United States. Appearances in the media reveal and develop interest in the whole field. Publications of all kinds, especially books, are mushrooming around the country. When the Popular Press, and the *Journal of Popular Culture* first began operations, we were alone. Now, however, there are at least a dozen presses (major and minor) which are specializing in popular culture materials. The number is bound to grow. Acceptance of the legitimacy of the discipline as a field of study is now resisted mainly by entrenched areas within academia and by some funding Endowments which do not understand or who cannot see beyond the perimeters of their historical approaches. But their defenses are melting away and their cooperation is only a matter of time.

So what is the future of Popular Culture studies as we review it here in April 1988? The future is bright and promising. Development in the past has pretty much paralleled any kind of innovation in academia which seems to threaten the establishment and introduce material which is not completely understood in a manner which seems radical. Such was the history of the American Studies Association and the American Folklore Society. Difficulties are inevitable. But success is also inevitable if strong and respectable academics back strong and respectable areas and disciplines. There can be no doubt that Popular Culture Studies represents a strong and respectable area. There can be no doubt that it will prevail. As Secretary-Treasurer I have nothing but confidence as I write this history of the PCA/ACA at this time. It is a history which must be continued in the future, since a program as dynamic as ours cannot be concluded at a point. But what I have tried to do in this brief account of the development of the PCA/ACA is to chart the course to date, leaving the second chapter of the history to other hands.

Birth and Development of the
American Culture Association

The birth and development of the American Culture Association was in many ways a more deliberate effort, and responded to a more precise need than that associated with the Popular Culture Association. Its genesis and growth will be instructively recounted.

During the early years of the Popular Culture Association we who had founded the PCA and worked for its continued growth were sharply criticized, as I have recounted in the section on the PCA, for lowering standards of scholarly achievement and involvement. We did not entertain for a moment such criticism as having any validity. Yet, although we thought it was short-sighted in view, elitist in philosophy and negative in accomplishment, the point of view several of us realized was real at least as far as those people who held it were concerned. Although after five years we felt we had suffered about all the slings and arrows outraged academics could throw at us, and had given up accounting to that edge of our academic constituency, I at least was still conscious of the problem. And wondered what could be done about it.

I still had my argument with what was being done to the American Studies Association and through it to the study of American culture and humanities. I still felt that the focus of the ASA was too narrow, too elitist and not sufficiently relevant. Again, the problem was what I could do now that the Popular Culture Association was having great impact on the ASA.

One cold February Sunday morning in 1978 as I sat before a roaring fire the solution to the problem came to me, I would like to think as a bolt from on high. What we needed was a *Journal of American Culture,* with an American Culture Association. Both would fill the gap between the Popular Culture Association and the *Journal of Popular Culture* and the American Studies Association and its *American Quarterly.* I was sure that such an organization and journal would be more acceptable to a certain percentage of academia and to the Administrative type and therefore would enrich the study of American Culture and the humanities in a needed and valuable way.

I have always liked to cover my tracks, to hedge my bets, and to see what the world felt about my ideas, so I decided I would talk to Russel Nye, at Michigan State, and to Carl Bode, at the University of Maryland. I called Russ and outlined my ideas and plans and asked his opinion. As usual, he concurred with my ideas, reminding me that there were still many people out there who although basically interested in our approach to the study of culture could not or would not associate their interests with popular culture and the *Journal of Popular Culture*. I next called Carl, outlined my plans and asked for his reaction. I was somewhat surprised to hear that Carl thought it was an unworkable and unnecessary idea. He suggested that since the PCA was going well it would be a mistake to hazard a parallel association which might drain some of the vitality from it. His was an objection that was to be voiced numerous times throughout the years. It is interesting that six years after I had established the ACA, Carl graciously told me that he wanted to congratulate me on having pulled off a very worthwhile and timely idea. It was a success.

But at the time I thought I had a good idea and I had a mandate of 66% of my survey, which was all I needed. to go ahead. So I went ahead.

With me my plans were perfectly clear. The American Culture Association and the *Journal of American Culture* would dedicate themselves to studying American Culture, present and past, with influences on it and with its influence on other cultures. They would include but not be limited to any aspect of mass media. They might include but surely would not be limited to popular culture. Vis-a-vis popular culture, they would try to be more "serious," and surely would include studies that were hardly appropriate in the study of popular culture. As I saw the difference, an essay on the impact of the *New York Times* on American culture would belong to JAC, whereas an essay in the *New York Times* on some aspect of American culture might well go in JPC. An essay on Edward R. Murrow as conscience of America would belong to JAC, whereas a paper on Murrow's success with the media would appropriately go in JPC. A paper on the influence of Puritanism in the printing trade would belong to JAC, but one on the effect of Puritan hymnals on Protestant songs would properly belong in JPC. To me the difference was very clear and consistent with an enlargement of the study of the humanities and American culture. As it developed, the differences were not so clear to many others who thoroughly agreed that such an association and such a journal were needed.

The establishment of the new area certainly found positive reception in some circles. John Cawelti, for example, told me that as soon as the announcement reached his building at the University of Chicago, several anthropologists rushed up to him and said that finally there was an association and a journal that they could work with and publish in. Such congratulations went up on various other campuses in this country and abroad. It was snobbery-defense, to be sure, but it was practical and therefore had to be catered to. I had properly read my potential constituency.

Since I had so much experience with the PCA and JPC, I had my path clearly laid out before me. Just as Russ and I had done with the establishment of the PCA, he and I started out again with a new organization and a new plan for improving American education. I asked him if he would be President of the American Culture Association, and I appointed myself as Secretary-Treasurer. Again, two slightly older old goats out to change the world!

The two immediate needed steps were clear. We needed to round-up some participants for the first national meeting of the American Culture Association, and we needed to bring out the first number of the *Journal of American Culture*. Each was in fact easily done. For JAC I looked carefully through the files of papers accepted for JPC and chose those most nearly like the ones I ideally would like and decided to publish them. In that procedure there was, of course, a built-in weakness and danger. Since the papers were appropriate for JPC they might not be ideal for the new JAC. But I felt that it was more important to get JAC out than to search around for a year commissioning papers and trying to set the new tone immediately. To a certain extent, of course, some of the consequent failure to see clearly the parameters of JAC were inherent in the procedure by which I chose papers for the first JAC. Through the years, however, I have been able to "correct" and adjust my course, at least to my own satisfaction.

For the first issue, Spring 1978, I ran up my masthead and declared that the *Journal of American Culture* was dedicated "to promote and facilitate the study of American Culture in the broadest sense of the term, from 'elite' to popular and folk culture as a continuum." Manuscripts were invited "on any aspect of American culture, its antecedents and impact on other cultures." I chose to include the remarks that Joe Duffey, newly appointed Chairman of the National Endowment for the Humanities, made at his confirmation hearings before the U.S. Senate. Aside from the political thrust, his remarks, at least in part, coincided with my purpose in JAC: to "promote learning in areas related to the understanding of our heritage as a people, our potential as men and women, and our purpose as a nation." Duffey declared as his purpose to support "the contributions made to our society by scholars and teachers in these disciplines, which probe the meaning and the purpose of human experience." His declared mandate could almost have been mine.

For other articles for this first issue I chose "The Democratization of Travel: The Travel Agent in American History," Hugh De Santis; "Music in the Washington Household," Nicholas E. Tawa; " 'It's Not Nice to Fool Mother Nature': The Disaster Movie and Technological Guilt," Harold Schechter and Charles Molesworth; "The Portrait of Hiram Powers: Practicality, Physiognomy and the American Ideal," Charles Thomas Walters; "The Natural Health Food Movement: A Study of Revitalization and Conversion," Dennis Brisset and Lionel S. Lewis. In addition I had an In-Depth section of twelve essays, edited by Henry F. Salerno, on "The Popular Theater": "Introduction," Henry Salerno; "Post-Tragedy and the Public Arts," H. L. Nieburg; "Radio City Music Hall," Harry Goldman; "Integration of Elements as a Viable Standard for Judging Musical Theatre," Margaret M. Knapp; "The Musical Goes Ironic: The Evolution of Genres," Richard Hasbany; "The Theater of Stylized Amateurism," Philippe R. Perebinossoff; "An Alternate Irony: Film on Film," Harold H. Watts; "Russian Formalist Theories of Melodrama," Daniel Gerould; "Workers' Theater in America: A Survey, 1913-1978"; "The French Theater: For and Against the People," Vera Lee; "Politics, the Media and the Drama," Henry

F. Salerno; "recent Trends in American Drama; Michael Cristofer, David Mamet and Albert Innaurato," Peter James Ventimiglia; "Afro-American Popular Drama," Chester J. Fontenot, Jr. I topped the issue off with a large picture of the Radio City Music Hall Rockettes dancing behind the openings in the headpiece of the Statue of Liberty! Hardly strict "serious" American culture? Perhaps not the paradigm for the desired issues to come. But at least the journal was out. And it was a journal and a direction that the co-editors, Ray Browne and Russel Nye, could work with.

We had a distinguished Advisory Board: Steve Allen, Hollywood; Robert Coles, Harvard University; Thomas Cripps, Morgan State University; Melvin Friedman, University of Wisconsin—-Milwaukee; C. Hugh Holman, University of North Carolina; M. Thomas Inge, Virginia Commonwealth University; Roderick Nash, University of California, Santa Barbara; David Noble, University of Minnesota; Henry Salerno, SUC, Fredonia; Henry Nash Smith, University of California, Berkeley; William C. Spengemann, Claremont Graduate College; Milton R. Stern, University of Connecticut, Storrs; Irving Wallace, Hollywood, California. Pat Browne was book review editor for JAC as she was for JPC.

Hammering out the first national meeting for the American Culture Association required a little more work. We had the large field of popular culture to seek recruits in, but we wanted to appeal to a different constituency and in fields more narrowly limited than those covered in the PCA. So we had our first national program in 1979. Our brief history and purpose as stated in the program should be presented here.

History of the
American Culture Association

Working with the Popular Culture Association and, especially, the *Journal of Popular Culture* convinced some people that the PCA perforce was having to cover certain areas which only loosely speaking could be classified as popular culture. For example, JPC has been receiving through the years excellent articles which the editor had to refuse simply because they were not sufficiently *popular* culture to warrant inclusion. To correct this situation, the *Journal of American Culture* began publication at the beginning of 1978. As creation of JAC justified itself, the creation of a national association that would parallel the purposes of the magazine seemed warranted.

The JAC and the American Culture Association center on those areas in American culture which are American, although comparative studies, backgrounds and impacts are included, and which are not, in the strict sense of the term *popular*. Discussions of so-called elite culture are also included. The officers of the ACA and the editors of the JAC feel that these parallel associations and publications, along with those that already exist, cover the areas of American and international culture in a complementary way. Together they provide the framework and boundaries—as well as the directions—for a comprehensive study.

In order to make the ACA as closely related as possible to the PCA, at the suggestion of Tom Towers, we bound the two programs together— we would later integrate them into one program, with proper identification PCA and ACA assigned to each session. One hundred eighty persons presented papers or talks at the first meeting. Two sessions were devoted to hammering out philosophy and definition. I chaired one, which included such eminent scholars as Milton Stern, University of Connecticut, Storrs; Daniel Walden, Pennsylvania State University; Bernard Sternsher, Bowling Green State University; and Carl Bode, University of Maryland. Russel Nye chaired the second session, which included the speakers: Tom Cripps, Morgan State University; Edmund J. Danziger, Jr., Bowling Green State University; Henry Salerno, SUC, Fredonia; and Alan Gowans, University of Victoria. A glance at the first program of the ACA (in Appendix 2) demonstrates the drift of the ACA away from the PCA. Interestingly of the 203 separate sessions at the whole meeting, 49 were with the ACA. A sample of the titles will be instructive: "Art and Democracy," "America's Melting Pot," "The American Dream," "Regionalism and American Cultural Studies," "Architecture and Sense of History," "Blacks in America," "The Success Ethic," "Forms of Religious Expression," "Conflicts Between Cultures: The Police and the

Public," "The Concept of the Hero," "The Threat of Apocalypticism," "The West: Real and Feigned." Of course there were a few sessions suspiciously close to others that were being held in the PCA. But a powerful start had been made.

The second ACA national meeting was held with the PCA meeting in Detroit, 1980. The officers were the same. But the attendance and number and variety of sessions showed a dramatic growth pattern. We had integrated the ACA and PCA sessions so that there would be greater facility for attendees to pick and choose among the sessions they wanted to attend. Of the 376 total sessions 109 were with the ACA. In other words, of the thousand plus people in attendance, some 400 were presenting papers in American culture. The strength of this second effort symbolizes roughly the track and the strength the ACA has taken and held through the years.

At the second meeting, as at the first, there were few officers: Nye was President, I was Secretary-Treasurer, and the Advisory Council consisted of Tom Cripps, Morgan State University; Henry Salerno, SUC, Fredonia; Milton Stern, University of Connecticut; and Daniel Walden, Pennsylvania State University.

After the second national meeting, Russ Nye, again reflecting his feeling about the importance of involving as many people as possible as officers in the ACA, refused to continue as President. In the position Russ had shown the same wisdom and gentle effectiveness that he had demonstrated as President of the PCA. Under his leadership the ACA had developed from nothing to a large segment of the total Popular Culture thrust. As with the PCA, the ACA development and movement is forever indebted to the capable leadership of one of the grand people of scholarship, Russel B. Nye. During his second year, I had of course been searching for a potentially effective person to fill that position. David Wright, of Michigan State University, was a potential candidate. He had been active for the preceding two years, especially in technology, a field we wanted to develop. Furthermore he was energetic. He happened to be from Michigan State University, as Russ was, but we felt that nobody would object to the seeming dynasty at MSU if the people involved were effective. David seemed to hold much promise. Consequently he became President of the ACA.

David did indeed show leadership qualities and vision. He immediately started to bring in people from other disciplines, especially those in technology. He quite properly realized that there was a great potential in people and scholarly activity among these people, and quite properly he knew that the development of American culture is inseparably connected to technology and science. He set about immediately to include many of these people in our activities.

During the next few years the ACA and *JAC* would become particularly strong in photography, in architecture and in various forms of study of technology. In architecture, for example, in the able hands of the highly imaginative Dennis Mann, University of Cincinnati, we would have numerous panels on some form of architecture, for example this one at

Detroit: "Route 66: Main Street of America," Robert D. Perl, Texas Tech University; "The Many Faces of Queen Anne: A Sculpltural Analysis of Late 19th Century American Domestic Architecture," H. Jeffrey J. Bayer, University of Alabama in Huntsville; "Two Houses: One Contextual and One Transcendent," Dennis Mann. The area in which Wright was particularly effective was technology. Through the years we have had many sessions, as this one at Detroit: Philosophy and Technology: "Attitudes Toward Technology in Mid-19th Moral Philosophy Textbooks: Francis Wayland's 'Moral Science'," Carol Ann Smith, University of Missouri, Rolla; "Nineteenth Century Marxist Attitudes Toward Technology," Bernard Gendron, University of Wisconsin-Milwaukee; "Herbert Hoover's Engineer and Technology," Thomas Long, University of Cincinnati.

By the time of the fourth ACA national meeting, we had enlarged the Advisory Council to include ten people: Alvar Carlson, Bowling Green Univerisity; Maureen Honey, University of Nebraska; William Jackson, Bowling Green University; Dennis Mann, University of Cincinnati; Edith Mayo, Smithsonian Institution; Jay Mechling, University of California, Davis; Jack B. Moore, University of South Florida; Grace Reed, Library of Congress; Dorothy Schmidt, Pan-American University; and Daniel Walden, Penn State University. Otherwise the officers were the same.

But the areas included in the ACA were bringing new dimensions to the overall thrust of the PCA/ACA. We now had numerous new areas brought to the national meetings of the combined Associations. Some of these were somewhat transient but most were permanent. For example, Fred Schroeder, who was to become as much a key force in the ACA as he had been in the PCA, constantly pushed the study of the city, as in this session at the fourth ACA, in Louisville, a session that he chaired: The City in History: "St. Patrick's Day in Kansas City: When Public Drunks are OK," Larry Rochelle, Johnson County Community College, Overland Park, Ks; "The Boat People and the City," Mary Anne Norman, El Centro College; "The Persistence of History in Small Town Life Styles," Fred Schroeder. Carl Bode chaired a session in American politics, an area that was to develop in the ACA: American Politics in the 20th Century: "William Randolph Hearst and Pro-Germanism During WWI," Yuvaraj D. Prasad, University of Maryland; "Politics and Conceptual Reconstruction," James Campbell, Univ. of Kentucky. Wilderness Studies also began to flower somewhat at this meeting, and have continued, though sometimes under different names and in different directions: Americans in the Wilderness was chaired by George Ward, Bowling Green State University: "Crevecouer's Romantic Religion of the American Landscape," John Oopie, editor, *The Environmental Review,* Duquesne University; "The Romantic Traveller in the Wilderness," Philip Terrie, Bowling Green State University; "Buckskin and Velvet: Images of the 19th Century Sport Hunter," George Ward, Bowling Green State University. There was continued interest in art, as in this session chaired by Nancy H. Pogel, Michigan State University: The Artist's Response to the Midwestern Experience: "Emma Goldman's Response to American

Dramatists," Marilyn Judith Atlas, Ohio University; "Jim Tully: A Hobo in Hollywood," David D. Anderson, Michigan State University; "Bill Mauldin: The Midwestern Experience," Nancy Pogel and Paul Somers, Jr., Michigan State University. And David Wright's continued work in recruiting papers in technology continued to pay off, as in this session Public Perception of 20th Century Science and Technology, chaired by Edmund Byrne, IU-PUI, Indianapolis: "Public Perceptions of Science and Technology in the 20s and 30s," David Wright, Michigan State University; "Recombinant DNA Research: New Strains from New Strains," Leonard N. Isaacs, Michigan State University; "The Curing of Computer Cholera," Tom Trout, Coastal Carolina College. And in a second such session, Science, Technology & Cultural Studies, chaired by Kristin Shrader-Frechette, University of Louisville: "Alternative Technologies," Kristin Shrader; "Five Bases for Evaluating Technology," Carl Mitcham, St. Catharine's College; "Alternative Technology and the Norm of Efficiency," Stanley Carpenter, Georgia Tech University. One other area was becoming increasingly important. In many ways one of the most energetic individuals behind this thrust was Lee L. Schreiber, History, Temple University, who was also instrumental in the development of the fields of outside markets and antiques. Schreiber read a paper in the session called Studies in Regional Culture, chaired by the very able and hard-working Mary Johnson, East Tennessee State University: "Tradition and Innovation in Pennsylvania German Furniture and Design," Lee Schreiber; "Nineteenth Century Domesticity in the Brandywine Valley," Mary Johnson; "Philadelphia Architectural Regionalism, A Socio-Architectural Consideration," Edward Teitleman, Camden, N.J.

For the fourteenth annual PCA meeting, in Wichita, the ACA had about the same percentage of participants of the whole meeting as it had had in the past. This year there were sixty four sessions out of a total of 313. We still had not developed all the area chairs that we wanted, but we had twenty-five, and David Wright was the General Program Chair. The officers of the preceding year still held place. Although we still had some programs that closely shaded similar ones in the PCA, the ACA was continuing to chart its own course. For example, there was now a rather strongly established section on Gay Fiction, chaired by John Leo, University of Rhode Island, and for this meeting included the papers "Reading Maupin: Life in a Post-Hippy Heartbreak Rooming House," Michael H. Palmer, Louisville College, Louisville, NC; "Nomadic Desire: Reflections on Kerouac and Cassady," John R. Leo. The section on City Culture continued to thrive, as in this year's presentation: "San Antonio's Battle of the Flowers Parade: An Evolving History," Judith Berg Sobre and Mark Farber, University of Texas, San Antonio; "An Aural Appeal and Visual Impact: The Sound and Image of The Supremes," Anthony T. Rauche, University of Hartford; "Discovering Italy in the City: Play-Frames in an Italian-American Food Market," Richard Raspa, Wayne State University. There were also shadings of PCA topics to fit the more narrow definition of American Culture, as in The Documentary Film as American Culture, chaired by Gary Edgerton, Bowling Green State

University: "Reading *The River* (1937): Film as a Social-Cultural Artifact,"
Gary Edgerton; "*The Real West* as The Reel West," Patrick McCarthy,
Bowling Green State University; "*Middletown* (1982): Direct Cinema as a
Document of Socio-Cultural Reality," Esther Yau, Bowling Green State
University. One fine series was started by Marie Campbell, Mt. St. Mary's
College, Emmitsburg, Md., on Challenges in the Humanities and Curricula.
She had two sessions at Wichita: "Intersections—Large Controversy and
Limited Success," Leo J. Hertzel, University of Wisconsin, Superior;
"Meeting Freshmen Needs Through Interdisciplinary Programs," Joan P.
Krieg, Hofstra University; "How Do You Start and Finish a Quest? Recruiting
and Retaining Students," Irene Sample, Westminster College, New
Wilmington, Pa.: "Team Teaching: Proceed with Care," Ingrid Shafer,
University of Science and Arts College, Chickasha, Oklahoma. Campbell's
second section was entitled Programs in the Humanities: Overviews: "Twigs
in Search of Their Roots," Irene Sample, Westminster College; "The
Concentration: American Culture for the Small College," Marie Campbell;
"Interdisciplinary Studies: Daring to Dream," Ingrid H. Shafer, University
of Science and Arts of Oklahoma, Chickasha, Ok.

For the sixth meeting, in Toronto in 1984, there was a larger number
of ACA sessions, 79, but then there was a larger number of total sessions,
419. So the percentage of ACA sessions to PCA remained about the same,
perhaps declined a little. Some sessions were continuations of the older
traditions. Some developed the ACA's new thrusts. One, The Camera and
American Culture, continued to place the ACA and JAC in the forefront
of study of the camera and photography. This session was chaired by Russel
Nye and developed some new angles: "The Socio-video Wisdom of Abby
and Ann: Toward an Etiquette of Home Made Photography," Richard
Chalfen, Temple University; "Turn of the Century Midwestern Women's
Photograph Albums as Social Commentary," Marilyn F. Motz, Bowling
Green State University; "Photographing in Public Places," Lisa Henderson,
University of Pennsylvania. Another session, chaired by Andrew Gulliford,
Bowling Green State University, concerned Schoolhouse Architecture: "Early
20th Century Rural Schools in Eastern Washington," William G. Williams,
Cheney, Washington; "'Vernacular Architecture as it Moved Westward,"
Richard Bennett, The Libraries University of Manitoba; "The Regulation
of Creativity in Architecture," Gaylord Richardson, University of Kansas;
"Country School Legacy: Humanities on the Frontier," Andrew Gulliford,
Bowling Green State University.

For the Seventh Annual Meeting, in Louisville, 1985, we had a largely
new cast of characters. The President was Fred E. H. Schroeder, University
of Minnesota, Duluth; the Vice-Presidents, Gayle Davis, Wichita State
University, and Maureen Honey, University of Nebraska. The Advisory
Council: Marilyn Atlas, Ohio University; David Bertolotti, General Motors
Institute, Flint, Mi.; Gary Burns, Northwestern University; Marie Campbell,
Mt. St. Mary's College; Donna Casella, Gustavus Adolphus College; Gary
Edgerton, Bowling Green State University; Sara Faulds, Santa Monica, Ca.:

Dennis Mann, University of Cincinnati; James B. McClintock, Michigan State University; Jack B. Moore, University of South Florida; Amy Skillman, Topanga, Ca.; Dan Walden, Penn State University. And the editor of the newsletter, ACAN, was David Bertolotti, General Motors Institute.

The percentage of ACA papers to PCA papers was a little higher in Louisville than it had been in Toronto, 78 to 395. Again, there were those sessions that were getting to be standard, and there were some new ones: Viewing the Past, Present and Future, chaired by Susan E. Allen, University of Kentucky: "Reinterpreting the '50s: Changing Views of a Dull Decade," Todd Postol, Chicago, Il.: "From Humanism and Existentialism to Biological Naturalism: Some Shiftings in Elite and Popular Culture, 1945-1984," Hughson F. Mooney, Central State University; "Anticipating the Past; Recalling the Future; Pursuing the 4th Dimension in Oral Testimony," Susan E. Allen. We continued our development in photography, in a session called Photography and American Popular Culture, chaired by Larry Rudner, North Carolina State University: "Images of Middletown," Dwight W. Hoover, Ball State University; "Photographic Images of Washington, D.C. During the Eisenhower Years," Clifford Norse, Radford University; "Technology and Leisure: Innovations in the Camera and Some Consequencers for the Tourist," T. David Botteril, Texas A & M. There was another interesting and expanding session, Expressive Behavior in Small Groups, chaired by Patricia A. Hall, American Association for State and Local History, Nashville, Tn.: "The 'Poor Lad': How Miners Remember Accidents and the Company Safety Program," Linnie Thuma, Michigan Technological University; "Four Corners of Earth: Seminole Women Within the Tribe," Peggy A. Bulger and Merri Belland, Florida Folklife Program, White Springs, Fl.; "Are All Groups as Together as We Are? The Expressive Behavior of Seminar and Workshop Participants," Patricia A. Hall. There was a session on Herman Melville, chaired by Gail Coffler, University of Kansas: "*Moby-Dick*: Its Higgledy-piggledy' Transformation in Contemporary American Fiction," Elizabeth Schultz, University of Kansas; "A Savage Dandy. Herman Melville's Portrait of John Paul Jones in *Israel Potter*," James J. Schramer, Hamline University; "Land and Sea: The Duality of Melville's *White Jacket*," Gail Coffler.

The number of ACA sessions compared to PCA sessions was down noticeably for the Eighth Annual meeting in Atlanta, 1986. The drop-off may have been purely coincidental. There were 58 sessions for ACA out of a total of 432. Nevertheless there were some new and promising sessions. One, for example, Art and Culture in the South, was chaired by David M. Sokol, University of Illinois: "Rbt. Guathmey: The Social/Historical Context of a Southerner's Art," Charles K. Piehl, Mankato State University; "Regionalism, Style and Reality in the Works of Rbt. Gordy, James Stteven & Linda McCune," Sandra Laner, University of South Carolina. Another new session, Borderland Cultures, chaired by Art Neal, Bowling Green State University, opens up all kinds of possibilities: "Movement of Hutterite Colonies Over the US-Canadian Border," Max E. Stanton, Brigham Young

University; "The American Image of Canada: The Role of Canadian Tourism Advertising," Douglas C. Nord, University of Minnesota, Duluth; "A Boundary Ignored: Interaction Between French-Canadians and Franco-Americans, 1870-1930," Robert G. LeBlanc, University of New Hampshire; "The Leisure Dimension in the United States and Canada," Larry Neal and Christopher R. Edginton, University of Oregon. Another session, Imagination in the South, chaired by Anne Cheney, VA. Tech, Blacksburg, Va., is pregnant with possibilities: "Architecture in the South," Charles Steger, Va. Tech.; "Attention K-Mart Customer, or Notes for an Unmade Southern Film," Charles Rose, Auburn University; "Evolution of a Southern Writer," Jesse Hill Ford, Bellevue, Tn.: "An Atlanta Footnote: Jesse Hill Ford and Southern Voices," Anne Cheney; "The South: A Sociologist Responds," Laura Birg, St. Xavier College, Chicago.

The patterns for the 1987 meeting, in Montreal, remained essentially the same as for the preceding year. Of a total of 477 sessions of both PCA and ACA, 88 were in ACA. Again the subjects of the papers were about what they had been in the past, but there were some new areas, for example: Everyday Life in American History, chaired by Patricia Bentley, Benjamin Feinberg Library, SUNY, Plattsburg, N.Y.: "Daniel Rea, Eighteenth Century Craftsman in Boston," John H. Cary, Cleveland State University; "An American Music: The Search for an American Musical Identity," Barbara L. Tischler, Bernard College, New York; "Forward Into Light: The Use of Pageants as Tribute and History," Patricia Bentley. Also: Labor in the Robotic Age, chaired by Frank Henninger, University of Dayton: "Robots, Industry and Labor: An Overview with Recommendations," James R. Koelsch, Production Engineering, Cleveland, Oh.; "Robotics: The Organizational Implications," Roger Anderson, Montana State University; "New Technologies, New Environments...and New Organization?" Robert J. Miller, University of Wisconsin, Madison; "Some Effects of Automatic Production Processes on People at Work," Henry F. Stark, Rutgers University; "The Robotic Age, Labor and the Meaning of Work," Fredric C. Young, University of Dayton. "There were two sections on Art in Canada and the U.S.A.: Interaction and/or Regionalism, both chaired by David M. Sokol, University of Illinois, Chicago: "Robert S. Duncanson and Landscape Painting in Canada," Joseph D. Ketner II, Washington University; "Marsden Hartley in Nova Scotia," Abraham Davidson, Temple University; "Emily Carr's Modernist Affiliations and Inspirations: The Landscape Painting of 1927-1940," Ruth S. Appelhof, Birmingham Museum of Art, Birmingham, Al.; "Goodridge Roberts and the Importance of New York," Sandra Paikowsky, Concordia Art Gallery, Concordia University; "Two Non-Canadian 'Canadian' Artists & Their American Reception," Robert J. Belton, Queens' University, Kingston, Canada; "Frances Loring and Florence Wyle: Expatriate American Sculptors in Canada," Christine Boyanoski, Art Gallery of Ontario, Toronto, Canada; "The Eastern Seaboard as a Region of Art History: The View from Halifax," Patrick C. Laurette, Art Gallery of Nova Scotia, Halifax; "The Role of Spiritualism in North American Abstraction,

1910-1940," Ann Davis, Brescia College, London, Ont. Canada; "Geography, I-Site and (Post) Modernism: Canadian and American Painting," Gaile McGregor, Toronto, Canada; "Canadian Cultural Nationalism and Expo '67: A Case Study," David B. Howard, Vancouver, Canada. There was also an interesting session on Art and Social Change, chaired by Gayle Davis, Wichita State University: "Altered States: Classroom Experiments With Religion, Film and Social Religion," Jacquelin J. Snyder and Gregory A. Robbins, Wichita State University; "Utopia, Social Change and Artistic Creation," Diane Pacom, University of Ottawa, Ottawa, Canada;" Among Narrative Textiles: An Analysis of a Memory Art," Marsha MacDowell, Michigan State University; "Quilts & The Fine Arts Arena: Changing Values in the 70s, 80s," Gayle R. Davis. Two other sessions moved into a new area for our proceedings: Law, Legal Theory and Ideology, chaired by John Cole, Mercer University: "Natural Rights, Rational Beings, and The Declaration of Independence," John Deigh, Northwestern University; "The Triangulation of Critical Legal Studies and Legal Realism: The Revival of Policy Science," J. Allen Smith, Mississippi College, Jackson, Ms.:" The Cultural Presuppositions of William Blackston," George Anastaplo, Loyola University, Chicago; "Ideology, Textbooks and Law," Stephen E. Gottlieb, Union University, Albany, New York. The second session, Law as Cultural Symptom, was chaired by William Wiethoff, Indiana University: "Libel and the Changing American Character," Rodney A. Smolla, University of Arkansas; "An Aging Population: Medical Technology and Law," Robert A. Seltzer, Seltzer and Seltzer, Philadelphia; "Debt Enforcement in Frontier Michigan," Richard P. Cole; "The Law Between the Sexes: Changing Perceptions," William Braithwaite, Loyola University, Chicago; the respondent was William Withoff.

After nine years of activity, perhaps it is time we glanced for a moment at the accomplishments of the American Culture Association as distinguished from the Popular Culture Association. True they feed in the same field, but they eat essentially on different flora. Some of the interests of the two groups are the same. Often the same people belong to both Associations. That is not to say, however, that the two interests of the same people are the same. The Popular Culture Association is a philosophical statement. The American Culture Association is to a certain extent a political statement; it was created to satisfy and to appeal to a particular group of people. So far it has succeeded. There are still many areas of scholarly interest and research which either do not fall within the provenance of the Popular Culture Association or which can be better accommodated in the American Culture Association.

At this moment in 1988 there is considerable talk among the members of the American Culture Association toward trying to establish a definition, and even methodology, for the American Culture Association. So far, ACAN, the official newsletter of the ACA, edited by Carlton Jackson, Western Kentucky University, has carried several provocative and probing essays outlining the authors' points of view about what constitutes and what should constitute the philosphy of the ACA. Perhaps Tom H. Towers has come closest to the mark in outlining that the ACA is a political organization. It covers those aspects of American culture which for one reason or another do not fit into the PCA. It also accommodates those academics who for one reason or another do not fit or do not want to fit into the PCA. Such laudable ends justify the existence of the ACA and the work it does. Perhaps there need be no other purposes. The history of academic associations seems to demonstrate that organizations, like its members, grow old and conservative; when they do they search for methodologies and philosphies to replace the free-wheeling self-contained reasons for existence which fed on *joie de vivre* and required nothing more. Free and open inquiry using all the means at hand, without the paralyzing grip of methodology and philosophy still seems to constitute the best route for the American Culture Association and its members to pursue. Nothing can or should replace open inquiry openly pursued.

Internationalizing the PCA/ACA

Since the beginning it has been understood that the study of popular culture, properly pursued, should be international. I tried immediately to place the *Journal of Popular Culture* and the *Journal of American Culture*, as well as the various other journals the Popular Press publishes, in libraries around the world. I also sought to get essays from scholars in various countries. The rate of success in both enterprises has varied from country to country and from part of the world to part of the world. Essentially the reasons are financial and political. Obviously many libraries in Third-World Countries do not have the financial resources to subscribe to the various publications. Obviously, too, for many other reasons many scholars in various countries do not know about the organization, though an astonishing number of scholars throughout the world—from the largest country to the smallest—know about the *Journal of Popular Culture* and our other publications.

I have also wanted to have conferences in other countries, and to set up Popular Culture Associations in various countries around the world. I have felt that conferences were a right step toward internationalizing the Associations and should lead to establishment of PCA chapters in other countries. I have always felt that the chapters in other countries should concentrate on their own popular culture, and not on that of the United States. But that is a rather difficult point of view to inculcate overseas.

I have made many efforts to develop these Popular Culture Associations overseas. The first effort was in Chichester, England, in 1978, when I held an international conference there. There were at least 150 people from the U.S. and abroad in attendance. The country with the largest representation was of course America, with some fifty persons. But there were people from all over Europe, from France, Italy, Scandinavia, Holland, and England. All agreed that the conference had gone well indeed and all agreed that there should be Associations in the countries represented there. But somehow nothing ever came of the suggestions. We should all realize, as it took me a long time to realize, that the academic structure is different in other countries than in the United States and that it takes a long time for scholars to overcome inertia and get things moving. There is, also, the question of cost. Academics outside the United States get paid in different comparative ranges than those in the U.S., and they are unable or unwilling to commit their time and resources to academic organizations.

The second international PCA meeting was held in Winchester, England, in 1980. Again, the attendance was excellent. A large number of Americans were on hand, of course, and scholars from France, Italy, Scandinavia, Holland, and many from England. We all talked at considerable length about establishing some kind of Popular Culture Association in the respective countries represented, and there was considerable hesitation about commitment. We all agreed, however, that there was a desperate need for some kind of international newsletter that would keep us all informed about what was going on in the various countries in the way of scholarship, meetings, and informal get-togethers. Willy Dahl, of the Department of Scandinavian Studies, University of Bergen, undertook the considerable task of editing and publishing the newsletter. At first the newsletter was published with considerable enthusiasm, with contributions from various people. It was building toward a real success. Then enthusiasm and contributions dropped, and the newsletter lay addled on the drawing boards. Prof. Dahl suggested that it was time that some other editor from some other country took over the editorial duties. Prof. David Bertolotti, of General Motors Institute, Flint, Michigan, volunteered to assume the responsibilities. Under his expert editorship the publication managed two numbers, then for want of copy it languished and apparently expired. So, at least for the moment, was the fate of at least one thrust at internationalism.

But others were kept up. My determination to establish the Associations never waned. In 1980, just after the conference in Winchester, England, I was sent around the world by the USIA to speak on Popular Culture in South Korea, Japan, Indonesia, and various places in India. In all these countries I found real enthusiasm. At first, of course, there was considerable confusion about what I was talking about, and some resistance, as there had been and continued to be in the United States. But once people got to understand the drift of my suggestions, generally they were receptive.

Perhaps the greatest resistance came in South Korea, where I talked to a rather conservative group of academics but who were very radical in their political views. Perhaps I would have had more success had the professors not been under fire politically. Anyway, nothing ever came of my suggestions that somebody establish a Popular Culture Association of South Korea.

I had much better luck in Japan. There the Japanese were quite open in their feeling that the study of popular culture would be stimulating to the professors and to the students and would open up many new ways for the Japanese academics to cooperate among themselves and with their counterparts in the United States. They were, naturally, cautious. The feeling among nearly all the academics was that the study of popular culture placed demands on themselves in range of interests and competence that they were not sure they could meet. I assured them that the demands are only those that the academics admit and approve. I suggested that those people who prefer to remain basically in the original field of their interests, in literature for example, could easily expand those interests to include popular literature, and in so doing introduce much new popular material.

The suggestions obviously took root, for a good two dozen academics in fact formed the Popular Culture Association of Japan, have had two national meetings, now publish a newsletter and plan other publications. The group, though small, is enthusiastic, energetic and dedicated. As a result of my trip to Japan, the *Journal of Popular Culture* has published one "In-Depth" section on Japanese popular culture, and plans another. Also, and this is a kind of fringe benefit from stirring around trying to establish PCA associations in foreign countries, we have discovered new interests among Japanese scholars and American scholars in Japanese culture who are working in the Popular Culture Association. All such associations are mutually beneficial. The important individual in Japan was and remains Kazuo Yoshida, at Kyoto Sangyo University. He is a very successful individual who knows precisely how to work in popular culture.

My success in Japan was not duplicated in Indonesia. There the interest was strong in certain individuals, but the academic coherence seemed to be too loose and chaotic to result in anything definite.

The situation in India seemed somewhat, or definitely, different. I talked to various groups in New Delhi, Bombay and Hyderabad. At first there was open skepticism or hostility. In New Delhi, especially, there was the feeling that the old English, or at best conservative American, ways were the best, the canon had been set, or at least the level of the canon was established, and there was considerable suspicion of efforts to test the canon. But there was some openness in some areas. There was, for example, considerable feeling among several academics in Bombay, especially those who had worked with Marshall Fishwick in the past, that there was room for change.

The most open-minded approach was at the U.S. Library at Hyderabad. Isaac Sequira, professor at Osmania University, who has a Ph.D. from the University of Utah and has spent several years in the U.S., knows precisely the value of popular culture studies culturally. He insists that in a country like India, which has some 450 languages and dialects, the cultural interests and means of communication are so disparate that any kind of nationalism is virtually impossible. The only thing the Indians have in common is their popular culture. Sequira therefore quite properly sees Indian popular culture as the one *lingua franca* in the country, the only cultural experience that the nation can build on and cohere around. As he lectures around the country his point of view is being more and more recognized.

In India, however, an American at times thinks that movements develop slowly. And one gets somewhat impatient. Sequira still thinks that there will be an Indian Popular Culture Association but it will be some time in coming. Meanwhile, some progress is being made. The *Journal of Popular Culture* has published an "In-Depth" section on India, as well as random essays strewn through other issues, which auger well for popular culture studies in the country. Several Indian scholars have visited the Center for the Study of Popular Culture at Bowling Green State University, and more are expected. So the wheels turn slowly, but they turn.

I made another trip around the world in 1986, again under the auspices of the USIA.

I visited Japan again and found there that the PCAJ was prospering. I talked with the members and found their morale high, their expectations great, and their hopes very concrete.

I had much less success in Australia, but there the failure was essentially one of timing. I had written to the various people there who subscribe to the *Journal of Popular Culture* or who have sent papers in for consideration or otherwise shown interest in the field. I know that there is considerable interest in Australia on the subject. Our own Dan Walden spent some time there on a Fulbright lecturing in American literature some years earlier. Further, I received numerous invitations from schools to come and talk to them. But the budget of the American Embassy in Australia had been used up, and I could not get an invitation to lecture to the various schools. So Australia was not tested as it should have been. I still feel that the prospects are very ripe there.

New Zealand, which I did visit, I found to be an atmosphere somewhat different. I spoke to various groups in Wellington, Christchurch, Dunedin and Palmerston North. At the time, anti-American feelings, though not intense, were running nevertheless. I had just published an "In-Depth" section in JPC on New Zealand, so the model of what routes I suggested were at hand. There was a great deal of interest in the study of popular culture. But, according to the academics I talked with, the obstacles are nearly insurmountable. In New Zealand they are distance and small number of academics. The likeliest prospects for some action in New Zealand reside with Jock Phillips, Director of the Stout Research Centre, Victoria University, Wellington. He was interested in establishing a PCA Association of New Zealand and has the resources.

In many ways the most interesting week on this tour was spent in Russia, in Leningrad and Moscow. In both cities I talked with numerous intellectual leaders and groups. For example, in Moscow I spoke to the Library of Foreign Literature, to the personnel of the publishing house "MIR," the leading scientific publishers, to the Union of Writers, to IMLI (Institute of World Literature of the Academy of Sciences of the USSR), and the Institute for the USA and Canada Studies. At every one of these groups the people were keenly interested in the study of popular culture. They wanted some explanation of how popular culture differs from mass culture, and they were insistent that there is a difference. Interestingly, they were much more concerned about studying American popular culture than their own, popular or mass. They were not in a position to talk about the establishment of a Popular Culture Association of the USSR because that would be a decision that would have to be arrived at on a different level. But many of the persons I spoke to were interested in the whole movement, and would like to come to the U.S. for our national conference, and would especially like to gather a group of essays for an "In-Depth" section in the *Journal of Popular Culture*.

In all the countries I visited there was keen interest in the journals that we publish at Bowling Green State University. In many instances various groups do not have the money to subscribe or the means to transfer the subscription price. So the Popular Press arranged to send gratis subscriptions of all our journals, with complete runs from number one, to various groups. They will have the Journals to consult and read even if they cannot start their own associations or otherwise participate in the activities we are engaged in in the U.S.

Of all the foreign countries that have expressed interest in the study of popular culture the foremost is the People's Republic of China. With the change in the official political stance in China from one of a closed door to one of an open door, and with the numerous students and professors coming to the United States to learn about American culture, the interest in popular culture is being discovered. Most of the academics in the humanities come to the United States to study what they assume will be American Studies, and they generally enroll in such programs. They soon discover, however, that what they are most vitally interested in is popular culture. That is what explains America most to the Chinese, what they most easily and fruitfully understand and what they want to take back with them when they return to China.

I had hoped to spend some time during the summer of 1986 in China. The plans had been for me to visit Xi-an, make arrangements for an international conference to be held there in the summer of 1987. Things did not work out. But as a compromise, and in an effort to promote the study of popular culture anyway, I sent three complete sets of the various journals we publish to China, two to Xi-an and one to the University of Peking, in Beijing, as well as one to the Embassy in Washington. Perhaps in the future some plan can be made to visit China and to work toward establishing a Popular Culture Association of China.

One other effort toward the establishment of a popular culture association in another country has met with frustration. I have always assumed that a PCA of Canada is so logical that it is self evident. In the *Journal of Popular Culture* I have published two "In-Depth" sections. I have read scores of papers submitted by Canadians. So in 1984 when the PCA/ACA met in Toronto, I had on the agenda the establishment of a PCAC. It was not that easy, however. First, there was the usual resentment against a Yank trying to tell the Canadian academics how they should run their show. Second, I discovered that there was less desire to establish a national organization than I, with my experience in the United States, had expected. When I suggested, for instance, that a PCAC could be a group that would bring interested academics more closely together, several people questioned my thesis that they would like to be drawn more closely together. Provincialism, in the true sense of the word, was rife, and many people wondered if there could be any future in a national organization. There seemed to be little. The most that the Canadians would commit themselves to was a promise that they would investigate and talk it over. In 1987 at the national meeting of the PCA/ACA in Montreal, there was a considerably changed attitude on the part of the Canadians. At a meeting specifically designed to take up the subject of a Canadian Popular Culture Association some ten people discussed the concept at great length. The leading power behind the effort this time was Prof. Stan Asher, English Department, John Abbott College, St. Anne de Bellevue, Quebec, who has been working in the PCA almost from its beginning and has always held out hope that a Canadian Association can be developed. Under his careful and skillful guidance, the talk at Montreal finally turned a corner and agreement was reached that a Canadian Association does in fact exist and the first meeting would be held in the fall or winter of 1987. But the modest beginning never materialized. Prof. Asher found that there simply was not enough interest to warrant continued effort.

It should not be assumed that my efforts are unique or that others in the United States interested in popular culture studies have not worked hard in other countries. Dan Walden was one who tried in Australia. Richard Gid Powers, of CUNY, Staten Island, is another. He spent some time in the Philippines and traveled around the world speaking on popular culture. He became so interested that he, with the assistance of Marshall Fishwick, established the journal *Popular Culture International*.

Marshall Fishwick had traveled widely around the world, especially in Third World countries and had talked extensively about the study of popular culture. In many countries he stirred up papers that were submitted to my journals. And in many instances I sent gratis copies of books the Popular Press had published and of the journals to libraries and USIA reading rooms. His efforts, like mine, seem to have been more ground-breaking procedures than reaping of the harvests. But whatever else they do these efforts reveal the great desire of academics in various countries to study popular culture, their own or that of the United States.

A very similar experience was reported by M. Thomas Inge, who during the years 1984-85 was Scholar in Residence at the Smithsonian Institution and as such made numerous trips to foreign countries lecturing on various aspects of American culture. He reported that wherever he went and whatever other topics he talked about, his lecture on comic strips and comic books was by far the most appreciated. The topic was a burning issue to the people in nearly every audience he talked to. Everybody knows the importance of the comic book in the teaching and learning culture of other countries, especially the Third World, and Japanese cultures. The importance of this medium in other cultures is not so well known. But it should be recognized for its value.

My latest investment in foreign travel and effort to establish a Popular Culture Chapter was to Mexico in November 1987. At the invitation of Marta Turok, Directora General de Cultural Populares, in Mexico City, I spent two weeks touring the various state chapters of this government agency. I found that the government backed study of popular culture is generally different from our own but the views and hopes of the many people parallels our own. I spoke to half a dozen different chapters in that many cities, found out what the people are doing. The Mexicans met and founded the Mexican Popular Culture Association. I have sent the various offices in Mexico 10 complete sets of all my journals and will continue to send them. Knowing the people, having only the highest respect for them and their undertaking, I am confident that they will continue to read and cherish the publications and the MPCA will continue to grow.

One other major effort has been on-going for some years in the international study of popular culture; that of Harold Hinds, University of Minnesota, Morris, and Charles Tatum, University of Arizona. After beginning in the Popular Culture Association with a major interest in Latin American Popular Culture, these two scholars have developed their own Latin American Popular Culture interests and regularly publish a journal that develops the areas of their, and our, interest. Such publications are of the greatest importance.

In an effort to capitalize on the importance of the study of popular culture internationally, in 1987 I got in touch with the USIA in Washington and suggested that I would provide free copies of all my journal publications for overseas distribution if the government would pay the freight. Not surprisingly my offer was accepted. I have shipped over 100 complete sets of all our journals to various outposts around the world. Some have gone into the USIS libraries, some in college and university libraries, and probably some in museums. I assume without knowing for sure that these journals are being scanned eagerly. I was told by the public library in Leningrad that the people in charge would keep an eye on the readers of the journals and would let me know the number of readers and their reactions. But it is difficult to keep a tab on such a long sightline. I have not received any word but do not necessarily feel deprived or shortchanged. This is an investment in long-range goals. I will continue to send these journals to the overseas posts and hope that the seeds planted will receive water and will eventually flower.

What the experiences of these various people demonstrate is the value of popular culture studies as the one international language that all people share. The flexibility of the studies guarantees that all academics no matter what their degree of advancement in cultural studies have a point of beginning and a rather rapid acceleration of advancement. American popular culture, for better or worse, for good or bad, is omnipresent, is everywhere. Without any degree of imperialism, no matter if at times the suspicion of others might be understood, American popular culture can be used and suggested for introduction into this *lingua franca*. But it can also be used as a showcase for the study of other popular cultures. There is no doubt that popular culture is an international language. American popular culture scholars should be interested in and should study those cultures of other countries. In so doing we can remove some of the provincialism that seems to permeate our culture and especially our students' lives. Popular Culture studies can and should be a two-way street with mutual education experienced along the way and reaped at the end. International understanding is too important not to be sought in every possible way.

Development of the Center for the Study of Popular Culture, the Popular Press and the Popular Culture Library

Two parts of the development of popular culture both locally at Bowling Green State University and nationally and internationally have been the Center for the Study of Popular Culture and the Popular Culture Library. Both are fingers of the same hand, and as such have developed at the same time both independently and collectively.

The Center for the Study of Popular Culture is a kind of parent grouping which houses and nurtures several other enterprises. The Center was in fact a kind of from-the-hip inspiration which I created to cover the publication of the *Journal of Popular Culture* and other publications and activities, some of which I foresaw in 1968 and some of which I did not foresee.

One of the things I foresaw was the publication of various journals and books. I assumed from the first that the *Journal of Popular Culture* might develop into other journals, though I did not know what or in what directions. But I wanted to keep my options open.

The first opportunity for extended publications came in 1969 with the publication of one book. Bowling Green State University was still not providing any subsidy for the publishing ventures of the Center, but Stanley C. Coffman, Jr., then Provost, arranged for the income from the *Journal of Popular Culture* to become a revolving account, and we could use the income for whatever purposes we desired. This freed us somewhat and gave greater potential. We immediately began thinking of suitable manuscripts for book publication.

With no typesetting equipment and not enough money to have the type set off-campus, we bought an IBM Executive typewriter and determined to set the type ourselves. Our first book was by one of the brightest graduate students in the English Department, Arnold Rampersad, *Melville's Israel Potter*. Rampersad was the outstanding Masters candidate of my colleague John Gross. John alerted me to the quality of this Masters thesis, and we published it. Gross' high evaluation of this student's promise has been borne out through the years. Professor Rampersad is today an outstanding scholar in American literature. The second book was by a more established scholar, John Cawelti, Professor of Humanities at the University of Chicago.

Cawelti had been with the Popular Culture movement from the very beginning. He had been one of the persons I first went to when I planned the *Journal*. He was one of the three original speakers at the establishment of the Popular Culture Association in Toledo in 1969. He was a prime mover. We were therefore delighted when he said that he had finished a primary study of formula, convention and invention, in popular literature, especially the Western. With publication of this volume, called *The Six-Gun Mystique,* we really launched the Center's publishing career. *The Six-Gun Mystique,* revised in 1984, through the years has been the Popular Press' best seller. Widely adopted for classroom use, *The Six-Gun Mystique* has been one of the most influential books that the Popular Press has published and one of the most influential in the whole field of popular culture.

The Press' third book, also in 1970, was also by established authors, and it too proved to be a very influential book, *Folksongs and Their Makers,* by Henry Glassie, Edward D. Ives and John F. Szwed. This book studied three folksong makers as well as their songs. The book proved to be something of a classic and even after all these years still sells as a textbook and as a model in scholarship about makers of folksongs.

With these successes on our shelves, the future of the Popular Press was looking up. We were beginning to carve out a niche in the publishing business that nobody else recognized or wanted and which we could modestly fill as we generated manuscripts and located authors. Marshall Fishwick and I began at this time an association in editing books that has persisted through the years and borne a lot of ripe fruit for the Popular Press. Our first venture was into a field that both he and I liked and thought popular, that of icons. In 1970, we edited and published *Icons of Popular Culture.* Called a "Probing in Popular Culture," it contained many interesting and seminal essays: "Pop Iconology: Looking at the Coke Bottle," Craig Gilborn; "Soft Drinks and Hard Icons," Arthur A. Berger; "Further Thoughts on Icons," Marshall McLuhan; "Pop Icons," Nicolas Calas; "Icon on Wheels: Supericon of Popular Culture," B.A. Botkin; "The Image in American Life: Volkswagen," Harry Hammond; "Semi-Annual Installment on the American Dream: The Wish Book as Popular Icon," Fred E.H. Schroeder; "The Missing Image," Sam Rosenberg; "Christ, Icons and Mass Media," Spencer C. Bennett; "Artifacts: Folk, Popular, Imaginary and Real," Henry Glassie, and a concluding essay by Ray Browne, called "Exit." Naturally the cover used the coke as artwork. This book became so popular and was so widely used as a text that we brought out a revised edition.

1971 saw another publication of considerable importance not only for the Press but also for the study of popular culture in general. We had got to know Francis M., "Mike," Nevins and knew of his interest in detective fiction. So when he asked to edit and us to publish a volume of essays on detective fiction we were pleased. The volume, *Mystery Writer's Art,* was reviewed favorably in the *New York Times Sunday Review* and was instrumental in getting detective fiction taught in the classrooms and in pushing the popularization of detective fiction in general. It was a volume that stood up well through the years.

Published the same year was another book that has stood up well during the years, *The Other Side of Realism,* edited by Tom D. Clareson, a collection of essays on science fiction. *Analog Science Fiction* said of the volume, "You're going to find this a prescribed book in colleges for a long time to come," and indeed we did. It was a leading text for years, selling well, and confirming Professor Clareson's position as one of the leading authorities in science fiction.

Being a trail-blazer with Nevins' and Clareson's books, we also blazed a trail and opened up entirely new, and controversial, territory with our publication of *Images of Women in Fiction,* 1972, edited by Susan Koppelman- Cornillon, discussing fiction as conditioning agent, art as propaganda, and all aspects of life useful in women's studies. This book, too, set the trend, and sold well indeed for years as one of the first in its field, in a subject that was to become more heated as time went by.

Two other books in the earliest years of the Popular Press deserve mention. One was edited by Russel B. Nye, *New Dimensions in Popular Culture,* 1972, and consisted of essays that Nye's graduate students at Michigan State University had written in a year-long class. Because it was an eye-opener to students and instructor alike, portions of the Introduction, written by Prof. Nye, should be quoted:

[These essays] are offered here not so much as models as examples of what may occur when the traditional techniques of literary study and analysis are applied, at this level, to popular culture materials. Collectively, (as the students and their instructor hope) they may make modest contributions toward an increased knowledge of the popular arts, and to serve to elicit interest in similar projects among students and instructors elsewhere. The gap that exists today between society and the academy is far too obvious and far too wide to need comment here; as others have suggested, the study of popular culture— seriously, with care and understanding—may assist in throwing one small bridge, at least, across it.

While it would be presumptuous to claim importance for this particular experimental foray into the uses of popular culture, two things emerged from the experience with great clarity. First, since six of the papers are now in the process of becoming doctoral dissertations, it appears that the study of popular culture opens up a whole new, fresh and exciting field for exploration and exploitation. Some members of the seminar, after its conclusion, drew up a list of thirty possible dissertation topics, using only materials available at Michigan State University or from other easily-reached sources. Second, since all of the members of the seminar were involved in teaching either literature or history in one fashion or another, it is significant that all agreed that they had found, in the study of popular culture, not only new materials but new ways that might be used in their own classrooms. The study of popular literature and the popular arts helped us all, students and instructor alike, to add an extra dimension to our understanding of *all* literature and the arts; exploring popular culture helped to give depth to our comprehension of our total society and its broad, multi-levelled culture. Here, I think, the future of the study of popular culture lies. My overwhelming impression, after teaching this course, is that we have merely opened the door a crack. I think these students, and many others like them at other institutions, will push it open wide within the next decade.

Little wonder that the volume was called "indispensable" by *Choice*. In 1972 another volume, this one a reprint of *Popular Culture and Curricula*, which with Ronald Ambrosetti I had first edited in 1970, also contains some remarks which tend to parallel Nye's statements and perhaps need to be restated for historical purposes. In the Introduction, we said:

The study of popular culture offers something new to the students, the faculty, scholars and critics—new materials, new approaches, new understandings—and all are excited about it.

Recognition of the deep-felt need for examination of the curricula in public schools and institutions of "higher" learning is not new. The gap between schools and the rest of society is well known. In today's complex society the academic community is wielding greater and greater influence, but usually off campus rather than on. Academics are solving many of the world's greatest problems but failing to solve one of their own or even to address themselves to it—sometimes even refusing to admit that it exists: That is the growing gap between life on the campus and that facing the student when he is away from school. As a result of this failure students feel disenchanted with campus life and their professors, that life on campus is unreal, that this kind of life does not prepare them for life off campus.

Harold Howe, then Commissioner of the United States Office of Education, in speaking to the Fifty-fourth Annual Meeting of the American Association of University Professors in Washington, D.C. on April 27-28, 1968, challenged the professors by saying that although they are instrumental in altering the world outside they neglect to do anything about changing campus life to make it more meaningful. As a result, he said, many students are becoming disaffected and disgruntled: "They are disaffected and disgruntled with what is going on in the universities; and they cannot understand why university professors who are responsible for the reach into space, for splitting the atom, and for the interpretation of man's journey on earth seem unable to find a way to make the university pertinent to their lives." Mr. Howe said that young people are justly demanding that their education prepare them for "an incredibly complex world that makes tremendous new demands on the citizenry of a democracy." "Poverty, integration, defense, transportation, space exploration, economic development, and deterioration of the cities cry out for creative, interdisciplinary thinking," he affirmed. There is, he insisted, a great need for a radical change in university departmental structure and sometimes anachronistic curricula, for interdisciplinary courses, to bring them up to modern life and its challenges, to face the crisis.

The *Library Journal* said in its review of this volume: "This thoughtfully prepared collection should be of great value to universities." And indeed its thrust was immense and the tidal wave it created is still sweeping across the campuses of academia.

With the success of these several books, the future of the Popular Press seemed assured. What the Press needed to insure its success was published titles. For a time, naturally we had some trouble in having manuscripts voluntarily submitted to the Press, and we had to generate our own. But by the mid-1970s the picture had changed. Authors were seeking out the Popular Press because of its reputation, and the publishing schedule was full up to our capabilities.

By 1988, at the time of writing this history, the Popular Press had a list of 200 titles and was publishing in addition to the various journals some 20 titles a year.

With the urging of the university Administration, the Press borrowed $50,000 and installed some new state-of-the art typesetting equipment. With that new capability our production increased radically. By the end of the decade, and the start of the 1980s the Popular Press was publishing, in addition to its many journals, some twelve books a year. The range of titles was immense. We published books on theory, on literature, a textbook used widely in the popular culture classroom, on music, on architecture, on sports, and virtually every other topic imaginable. Some of the authors were repeaters many times over. LeRoy L. Panek, for example, became almost our house-voice on detective fiction. The late Earl Bargainnier, sometimes working with others like George Dove, authored and edited at least half a dozen books on crime fiction of various kinds. Robert Sampson authored several volumes about characters from the pulps. I authored and edited a baker's dozen books on all kinds of subjects ranging from Alabama folk culture to icons, heroes, fetishes, the U.S. Constitution to the leading Australian writer of crime fiction, Arthur Upfield. Marshall Fishwick, sometimes working with me and sometimes on his own, edited and authored a dozen books for the Press. Fishwick and I, at least, were so interested in the welfare and future of the Popular Press that we did not take royalties for our work.

There was through the years always a genuine feeling among the people in the Popular Culture movement that the Popular Press should be supported. And support it they did. During the years when the Press was short of cash, people from around the country gladly and quickly read article-length and book-length manuscripts free of charge. Members of the fraternity referred to the Popular Press as "our" press and indeed felt that it belonged to the Popular Culture Association although it was repeated thousands of times that the Popular Press belonged to us at Bowling Green State University. But many, including Marshall Fishwick, Tom H. Towers, M. Thomas Inge, Earl Bargainnier, Russ Nye (hardest of all, of course), Larry N. Landrum, Henry Salerno, Ronald Ambrosetti, Peter Rollins, Tom Clareson, Gary Hoppenstand, Garyn Roberts, George Dove, Roger Rollin, Jane Bakerman, Mary Jean DeMarr, and dozens of others worked hard to make sure the Press was successful. The members of the Popular Culture Department through the years —Michael Marsden, Jack Nachbar, Christopher Geist, Susan Arpad, George Ward, Marilyn Motz, Jack Santino, and R. Serge Denisoff, in Sociology, Alvar Carlson in Geography and Tom Wymer in English—have worked tirelessly to assist in every possible way.

But in many ways the main force in the progress and development of the Popular Press, the energy that kept the presses moving, has been Alice "Pat" Browne, my wife. Her story is one of complete dedication and selfless labor.

When I started at Bowling Green State University editing the *Journal*, she was my unpaid assistant. Being interested in the study of popular culture and having untiring energy, Pat began assisting. She would work half a day, a whole day, or a day and half a night without hesitation when the crunch time came and the work had to be done. After three years of this unpaid labor, she demanded that she start getting paid, at least enough to make up for the baby-sitter's fees that we were paying. At that time she was put on hourly wage, at a minimum of course, and worked that way for three years. Finally she was put on regular contract with the University, but she would have continued her work had she remained unpaid.

Her duties escalated as I discovered more and more how easy it was to put the burden on her shoulders. She was soon taking care of the business end of the *Journal*, the production of the *Journal*, and everything else but the editorial work. With the development of the Popular Press her duties increased dramatically. Through the years her title has been everything from Business Manager to Editor. But throughout, her duties have consisted of virtually everything. With the journals she has never got interested in the editorial policy or the editorial work. With the Press book manufacturing, however, her duties have grown from Business Manager to virtual control of the manuscripts and to complete supervision of manufacturing, advertising and selling the finished books. Under her expert supervision the Press has flourished; without it the Press would have floundered. The whole movement in Popular Culture is deeply indebted to Pat for whatever success it has now and whatever it achieves in the future.

In addition she created a journal of her own, *Clues: A Journal of Detection*. The creation of this journal is rather amusing, as it reveals how simply something like this can be done, given the energy and facilities. One day as we drove home for lunch Pat suggested that we really needed among our many other journals a magazine on detective fiction. It sounded good to me. So I asked her what we should call it. We toyed with the name of *Sleuth* and did not like that, then with a couple of other names and did not like those, finally settling on *Clues* as being most appropriate because Pat suggested that the publication should not limit itself to detective and crime fiction but should publish in any area in which some kind of detective work, some kind of induction was involved. Thus she hoped that *Clues* might publish essays of forays in deduction in geology, archeology, medicine, anthropology, etc., as well as in literature.

Clues was an immediate success. It called forth new essays from old acquaintances in detective fiction and spurred new ones to get interested and to write significant essays. Pat has always handled every aspect of publication, making it soon into the most significant academic publication in the field of crime fiction.

This publication illustrates yet again how important Pat's contribution to the study of popular culture has been.

But it in no way comprehends her full contribution to the movement. Pat has been indispensable in the Popular Culture Association. As soon as I began with the PCA, Pat began helping. She would help stuff envelopes, mail them out, do all the drudgery connected with running an organization. But her forte has been in arranging the program. Almost from the first she demonstrated an uncanny ability to remember every participant's name, face, desires, abilities and inabilities, and to put those facts into order. She helped me choose the city for the national meeting which would be most accessible and appropriate, she generally chose the most workable hotel so that the program could go off with few hitches, and she then put together the program, remembering what each participant requested in matters of time, equipment, whimsies and other preferences. Generally Pat did this as a kind of unseen and unnamed force. Everybody knew she worked hard for the PCA but few realized just how heroically she labored, for her position was unnamed. Finally, however, she was officially named as "Program Coordinator," the position she had been filling for at least fifteen years. Again, however, the named position does not cover all the duties, the triumphs, the fizzles, the pleasure of working for the PCA. Without her the development and growth of the Popular Culture Association would undoubtedly have been quite different. She has always been without peer.

And she has accomplished her successes under great duress, for always through the years she has suffered from devastating migraine headaches which can at times lay her up for a week. She has always felt, however, that under almost all circumstances she would get up from her sick bed, even under the direst circumstances, and work for the PCA. Like a good soldier, she has fought the good fight.

Two other journals which we have published through the years also illustrate how dedicated she has been to her work. When R. Serge Denisoff was hired in 1970 in the Sociology Department at Bowling Green State University, he and I almost immediately began talking about the need for a scholarly journal and his willingness to edit it. Thus *Popular Music and Society* was born. Through the years it has published some of the leading essays in the country under Denisoff's editorship. The other publication which has had a great impact and of which we are proud is *Journal of Cultural Geography,* edited by Alvar Carlson, of the Geography Department at Bowling Green State University. Again this journal was born in a casual way. Pat and I one Friday were talking about what areas in the study of popular culture should be covered that were not being covered. Both decided that cultural geography was a ripe field, and that we had a potential perfect editor on campus, Carlson. I called him that night, suggested that we have lunch the next day, we proposed the publication to Al, and he accepted. Such was born one of the two most prestigious publications in cultural geography in the United States. Carlson is the perfect man for the job, and the job is well worth doing. Again, our success with Carlson and his publication illustrates how easily things can be done if one really gets after doing them.

But in fact not all things that could be done—with ease or with difficulty—with the Popular Press, or with the Association was guaranteed success. Several worthwhile ideas died soon after borning. For example, in 1975 while Visiting Professor at the University of Maryland I developed the idea that the study of popular culture need a publication of *Abstracts* in order to bring some order and indexes to the vast store of publications which thunder on us every week and month. I had in mind something like *Folklore Abstracts*, then being published, and other such scholarly associations. In order to facilitate the fullest study of popular culture, I proposed at first that all publications worldwide be abstracted. I had long entertained the notion that an international popular culture retrieval system would be the best possible assistance to the popular culture scholar, and I thought that the *Abstracts* notion was the first step toward that popular culture information bank.

I sought financial assistance from Washington, but of course the request was turned down—mainly because the people who reviewed the application felt that it was too comprehensive; I have always discovered in my relationship with Washington that applications should demonstrate laziness, uncertainty and a certain amount of graft on the part of the persons writing up the grant proposals. Nevertheless, without the grant from Washington, we went ahead with *Abstracts of Popular Culture*. We hired one person to work full-time, sought out hundreds of publications, reduced the scope of the abstracting to selected publications in the U.S. and published *Abstracts* for four years. We enlisted the volunteer work of scores of abstracters, whose work was exactly on target, or which could be easily redirected to be on target. Despite the great amount of work produced, however, subscriptions to *Abstracts* did not nearly pay for the enormous cost of producing it, and the Popular Press had to reluctantly terminate publication. Is it possible that Washington could have been right?

Another great idea that the Press carried on for a time was a new journal called *Journal of Regional Cultures* (with emphasis on the multiplicity of regions). One day, after years of thinking about it, I decided that the academic community was ready for a journal that studied exclusively the many aspects of regionalism in the U.S. So I started the publication. Peter Rollins, of Oklahoma State University, and others had just completed a meeting of the Southwest and Texas chapters of the PCA. Since the theme of the meeting had been the Southwest, I turned to Peter and published some of the papers of that meeting. It was very successful, and I then centered on getting collections of papers on other regions of the U.S. Sometimes I could call on papers already written. At other times I sought out individuals and asked them to make collections. After Rollins' contribution, however, it became increasingly difficult to get collections of papers on regions of the country. I shrank my definition of "region" from large or natural expanses of terrain or culture to smaller ones, finally ending up with a state as "region." I assumed that with states as regions *JRC* would get copy for at least fifty future issues. In this, however, again I was incorrect. Copy came to be impossible to get on time, even to get at any time. So the publication had to be suspended. Perhaps until another day. People who with me lamented the demise of *JRC* seemed to agree that although the interest in the study of various aspects of popular culture continues to expand, the simple financing of various journals, as long as they depend on the same group of people, cannot be expanded and sustained. Although the subject of popular culture seems to be infinite, clearly scholarly probings into the subject must be considered finite.

The lifespan of the *Journal of Canadian Culture* paralleled that of the *Journal of Regional Cultures*. We had expected great things from this journal.

Russel B. Nye, with virtually a lifetime of association with Canadians and with Canadian Studies, realized precisely the ingredients needed to make a journal on Canada edited by Americans flourish, namely it must be co-edited by a Canadian. He chose Ronald Sutherland, professor of comparative literature, University of Sherbrooke, Quebec. Then these two, joined by Victor Howard, Michigan State University, another veteran Canadian Studies man, worked slowly toward bringing out the *Journal of Canadian Culture*. To accommodate French speaking Canadians *JCC* was published in both English and French. The journal, though the cover was draped in a beautiful maple leaf, was not to prosper. It was published twice annually, but never did receive the subscriptions needed to pay for itself. After Professor Nye received a disabling stroke, it was decided that JCC probably should expire. Regrettably the Popular Press ministered over the death of a great idea and a fine journal.

So the Popular Press, despite countless scores of hours of unpaid and paid work, has experimented with publications that did not succeed. Such failures, lamentable as they are, are more the results of outside and uncontrollable forces than internal problems. Maybe they are ideas whose time have not yet come and might surface in the future in their first incarnation or in a different guise in subsequent reincarnations.

The Popular Culture Library

The development of the Popular Culture Library at Bowling Green State University has been a joint effort by several people. Its history is another excellent example of what dedicated individuals can do with a little money, a little time and a lot of determination.

When Pat and I first came to Bowling Green State University it seemed logical to build up a library along with the *Journal of Popular Culture* and whatever else we did with the whole notion of studying popular culture.

There was a willing ally in the person of William Schurk, who was just then beginning his notion of building a large collection of recorded popular music. He was more than eager to work with us.

We had no opposition from the central Administration and but little in the library administration. But there was also very little assistance. But Schurk, Pat and I had all kinds of interests and energy. So we set about collecting the books and records for the Library. We began with a major thrust. There was a radio personality by the name of Bill Randle, at station WERE in Cleveland, who had been on the air for many years, and had been a most influential personality in the area. He had been one of the first, for example, to recognize and plug Elvis Presley. In addition to being a radio personality, Randle was also an academic. He had a Ph.D. from Case-Western in American Studies, and was therefore keenly interested in assisting any kind of academic effort in the medium that he had been gracing for many years. I got in touch with Randle on a different matter, and he asked if I would be interested in his collection of recordings and books. I of course said yes, and Bill Schurk and I rented a truck one Saturday and went over and loaded it with Randle's contribution. Eventually the material he gave was valued at $75,000 and constituted the core of the collection of the Popular Culture Library.

With this large core to build on the collecting seemed easy. Sometimes in varying combinations, Pat and Bill and I merely went to flea markets, to second-hand book stores and stocked up. Sashays into adjacent Toledo were, naturally, easy. We visited various kinds of book sales and bought books by the ton, generally at ten cents apiece. Trips into the larger potential of Detroit were not much more difficult. Pat and I used to spend nearly every Saturday blowing dust from the books in the stores in Detroit. We would take our infant daughter, Alicia, with us, park the portable crib in the middle of the floor, and generally ignore her while we searched for books. Often, of course, the owners of the bookstores were intrigued by the presence of our daughter and would take care of her while we shopped, often feeding her in the process.

Often, Pat and my sons, Glenn and Kevin, served as our pick-up agents. They were prepared to drive for hundreds of miles in any direction to look over or pick up books for the collection; they collected untold numbers.

Our range of acquiring radiated out from Bowling Green in a much larger radius than Detroit. Pat and I once drove to Iowa to look in the barn of a potential contributor to see what we could find, and found a whole cache of glass transcriptions of a very popular radio program in the midwest. She and I on our many drives to Alabama would make a point of visiting second-hand book stores in all the cities and towns, and along the highway, between Bowling Green and south Alabama. We made special trips to Dayton, Cincinnati, Louisville, Chicago, Philadelphia, Upstate New York, New York City, Providence, Rhode Island, everywhere within the touch of the wheel, to buy books.

Often Bill Schurk and I undertook even more strenuous enterprises. Once, for example, we heard of a warehouse in Fort Wayne, Indiana, full of old pamphlets and numerous publications. Nothing would suffice but that we drive over one Saturday, load up Schurk's station wagon and drive back. On another occasion we were told by the owner of a book warehouse in Cleveland that we could have any or all of his supply of 20,000 books if we would clear them out during a weekend. So Bill and I loaded into his station wagon, drove to Cleveland and worked all day Saturday loading his wagon with books to be transported to his parents' house and there stored until we could get them transported to Bowling Green. We chose most of the books in the warehouse.

Other large collections came our way. In 1976, for example, I was visiting professor of American Studies at the University of Maryland. One of my Ph.D. graduates from Bowling Green University, Sam Grogg Jr., was head of the Education Division of the American Film Institute in D.C., and he was constantly on the look-out for materials for me. One day he said that the AFI had a large supply of old film posters that they could no longer store and I could have them if I would truck them out. Again, the challenge was great but the problem small. I rented a U-Haul truck, Christopher Geist, a graduate student of mine at Bowling Green State University who had gone with me to Maryland for his Ph.D. work, and I loaded the posters one Saturday, and he and I drove them the thirteen hours to Bowling Green. The collection was, of course, very valuable, and constituted the core of our holdings in film posters at the Popular Culture Library.

As Schurk and I continued to gather material for the library, he was made Popular Culture Librarian. We had considerable material to be called popular culture but no real physically identifiable location where it could be housed. Finally, under pressure, the Administration granted us space if I could find the money to put up walls. So, I found in the budget of the Center for the Study of Popular Culture $4000 to buy wall boarding to enclose a space in the main library to become the Popular Culture Library.

The space was immediately filled with our holdings, and with the students who came to the library to use the materials. We had long since developed an academic program in popular culture, and the students poured into the Popular Culture Library to use the material for their classes, and those in class and out of class spent many hours a week poring over the interesting material to be found in the library.

Increasingly the growth of the Popular Culture Library and Bill Schurk's collection of albums and singles of popular music began to nudge each other. Finally, for administrative purposes, Bill's collection was separated and placed in the Sound Recording Archives, with him as head, and the Popular Culture Library became an entity by itself, with its own librarian. The Popular Culture Library has had several librarians through the years. Nancy Lee has worked with us for years. Evron Collins worked with us for a too-short period, during which the PC Library grew well. Jean Geist now works full-time in the PC Library, where her assistance and knowledge are indispensable. Now the Head of the Popular Culture Library is Brenda McCallum, who joined the staff in 1986, bringing with her great experience and a skill as popular culture librarian and archivist which promises to make this collection one of the major ones in the world. Both, however, have continued to grow with the twin thrusts and energies of Shurk and the Brownes, all three continuing to work for the benefit of the other without stint of time, energy or resources. Schurk's collection has grown into the largest one of its kind in the world, with at least 500,000 albums and singles, running all the way from Edison cylinders to yesterday's latest album. The Popular Culture Library cannot claim to be the largest in the world, obviously. The Library of Congress has a much larger holding, as do such public libraries as the New York Public, the Los Angeles Public, and others. But the Popular Culture Library has never aspired to be the largest in the world, just the most convenient and useful single collection of popular culture of all kinds, one in which the student and scholar can have access to all kinds of popular culture, many of which he might not otherwise recognize and consult. For example, the Library is making a determined effort to acquire the manuscripts of popular writers, and already we have collected those of over a hundred authors. The development and use of the word-processor and computer might, of course, eliminate many such manuscripts, as authors do their composing on the computer. But the manuscrips are still available and are very valuable. And we are collecting them. At the moment, under the newly acquired Popular Culture Librarian, Brenda McCallum, it looks very much like we will achieve our goal. We have this dedicated and skillful popular culture librarian, and she works in what can now only be called the ideal adminstration, the kind we have hoped for and dreamed about since the Popular Culture Library was founded. The Dean of the Library and Library Resources is Rush G. Miller. No Librarian could be more knowledgeable and cooperative than he is for our purposes. He knows the value of the collection, as does the President of the University, Paul J. Olscamp, and the other people in the Administration, particularly the Dean of the College of Arts and Sciences, Kendall Baker. Although large sums of money are not being poured into the collection, we who are working to develop the library know that at least the Administration is sympathetic. Poor but sympathetic.

One other evidence of the sympathy of the Administration was recently demonstrated. On November 5, 1986 the popular culture holdings of the Bowling Green State University William T. Jerome Library were named and dedicated as the Ray and Pat Browne Popular Culture Research Collections. The guest speaker for the occasion was Ruth Rendell, leading English author of bestselling crime fiction. Rendell was awarded an honorary degree of Humane Letters. During her remarks, Rendell pointed out how the growth of crime fiction has matured from what used to be called detective fiction and how it has affected and continues to affect literature in general. She pointed out how appropriate it was that she as author of widely-selling books should speak at the dedication of this special library which is committed to preserving and making academically useful the kind of literature that she represents.

Dedication of the Ray and Pat Browne Popular Culture Research Collection was not casual or impromptu. Prof. Michael Marsden, of the Bowling Green State University Department of Popular Culture, with whom I founded the Department in 1972, had worked hard and long on it. Under his imaginative care and guidance, members of the Popular Culture Association were asked to contribute money to the Collection toward purchasing more materials and with the purpose of making a significant collection even more significant. Many members of the PCA very generously contributed their money toward the goal; many made sizable contributions and others made notable pledges. The money has come in and the pledges continue to arrive. The money raised points out how much the members of the Popular Culture Association, and others, appreciate the work that has gone into making the collection and the hope they hold out for its future. It is a kind of trust that brings out the best in people and the kind that cannot be betrayed. The future of the Browne Collection is assured. It will continue to grow and become significant.

For our part in our collecting, Pat and I have decided to concentrate as much as possible on the genre of crime fiction and to work toward building up one of the finest collections possible. We therefore acquire all the books we can in that widely-expanding genre, including periodic trips to Canada to pick up titles and imprints not available in the U.S. and to order as many books as possible from overseas markets, such as Europe, Russia and Asia. These books will eventually be given to the Ray and Pat Browne Collection of the Library and will be used to enrich its holdings. We assume it will become one of the significant collections in the library.

Growth and Development of Regional Chapters

The Midwest Popular Culture Association

The growth and development of regional chapters of the PCA has been an integral part of the thrust of the national chapter; for some reason the development of regional chapters of the ACA has not been as successful. The philosophy behind the regional chapters has been that demonstrated as imperative by all other academic organizations in the U.S., like the American Studies Association, the Modern Language Association, and numerous others. The thinking behind the regional associations is a kind of grass-roots, or near grass-roots approach. The regional chapters provide a kind of near-home meeting which gives easier and cheaper access to the association than does the national meeting. Further, there are many people who for any of a dozen reasons prefer the smallness, the intimacy, the homeyness of the regional meeting. There are also, unfortunately, many people who think that their level of experience and scholarship qualify them only for the regional meetings. I know from having talked with hundreds of participants at the regional meetings that if they are assured that they qualify for presenting papers and would be welcome at the national meeting they would be delighted to attend. I have assured all these people of their welcome at the national meetings, and have been delighted to see them attend and enjoy the national meeting. This is a kind of assurance that the participants of the national meetings should guarantee the new members of the PCA. Success in this guarantee has been instrumental in a large portion of the growth of the national association.

With these suppositions in mind, from the very beginning I began developing the regional chapters. I have always had in mind, as I have said elsewhere, that the most productive regional representation would be on a statewide basis. That is, each state in the Union should have a chapter of the PCA, and should have annual meetings. I have always felt sure that with a headquarters for the PCA in each state, with mailouts from that headquarters, the PCA regional meetings could be very successful. Experience has taught me that invitations from schools within the state are often taken more seriously than those from some distant national headquarters. Use of campus mail for a single campus is especially effective.

Despite the conviction of this approach, however, I have never been able to summon up enough volunteers to staff so many offices. Perhaps those dreams are still possible of fulfillment. What we have had instead is a series of regional chapters corresponding roughly to some kind of real or designated section of the U.S.: the South, the Midwest, the Southwest, the Northeast, the Northwest. Some of these chapters have existed enthusiastically from the very beginning, others have been desultory and patchy in their work. Several, however, have done outstanding work.

Of the two or three leading and most vigorous associations, that of the Midwest (the MPCA) has been very active. Perhaps it should have been a leader. The national headquarters of the PCA has always been at Bowling Green State University, Bowling Green, Ohio, the very heart of the Midwest. If there was to be any rub-off effect from the national Secretariat it should have been on the adjacent states.

Such has been the case. The MPCA has always been one of the more effective of the regional chapters. Its history has been direct and certain. The following pages of the history are verbatim from the report supplied for this volume by Fred E.H. Schroeder.

At Ray Browne's request, Fred Schroeder of the University of Minnesota-Duluth launched the Midwest Popular Culture Association on Columbus Day in 1973. With the assistance and venture funding of the university's Continuing Education division, this first conference attracted over seventy-five persons, including a number of people who have gone on to leadership roles in both the Popular Culture Association and the American Culture Association. J. Fred MacDonald, for example, presented "Civil Defense Propaganda Films," with their famous "duck-and-cover" exercises for school children, while Elmer Suderman of Gustavus Adolphus and the late and lamented David Stupple of Eastern Michigan shared in a session on "Popular Religion and Morals." Suderman has been a continuing leader in the study of popular religion in America (many PCA members have fond memories of the gospel sings and hellfire sermons conducted by Elmer, his wife and son at several national conventions), while David Stupple pursued flying saucers to his grave. At the Duluth conference, however, Stupple reported on "Ann Landers and Public Moral Advice." Three other stalwarts were Maureen Honey, then completing her doctorate at Michigan State, who started a career of feminist study with "Images of Women in the *Saturday Evening Post*," with Charles Nelson, who brought a team of his Michigan Tech students with their audio project on popular radio, and John DiMeglio, who provided a sparkling opening session with a lecture demonstration on the structure of a vaudeville show.

These last items reflect some of the liveliness of the early PCA meetings. In this first Midwest meeting, a panel on "Popular Fast Foods and the Quality of Life" included Bea Ojakangas, whose experience included being a staff-member of *Sunset* magazine's food section and being chief home economist for Jeno's Pizza, then manufactured in Duluth. At the time of the conference, she had embarked on a "gourmet hamburger" chain enterprise. Along with her was the editor of the trade journal *Snack Foods*, published in Duluth by Harcourt Brace. In the popular literature session, the editor of *Big Little Books* from Whitman Publishing discussed the business of popular literature, and made a formal presentation of the latest volumes to the curator of the University of Minnesota Special Collections (whose dime novels collection had served as resources for Henry Nash Smith's seminal *Virgin Land*.) At Fred Schroeder's suggestion, the Whitman publishing editor, William Larson, had loaned a collection of original paintings of *Zane Grey Magazine* covers for an exhibition at the Tweed Museum of Art in conjunction with this conference. The exhibit also included artifacts and publications from the "Krazy Kat Collection" of St. Andrews University in Scotland, and the first exhibit outside of Mississippi of the now famous folk artist of embroidery, "Granny" Mohamed. The Zane Grey paintings, incidentally, had been languishing in an attic in Racine, Wisconsin; the Krazy Kat collection loan was a by-product of the first International Popular Culture meeting in Norwich, England. Other non-academic participants included members of a panel from public libraries and museums who discussed the collecting of popular materials.

The second annual MPCA meeting was in much the same vein, under Fred MacDonald's energetic leadership. Held at Northeastern Illinois University, October 10-12, 1974, it included as panelists blues performer Eddie Taylor, the editors of *Living Blues Magazine* and a producer of commercial recordings, and the former and current "Sir Hugo" of The Chicago Baker Street Irregulars. Notable at this second MPCA meeting was the active representation of several secondary school programs in popular culture. These continued to be an important segment in the 1975 conference at Western Michigan University which was organized by Lew Carlson. Highlights of this third annual conference included an exhibit of original drawings by Stan Lee from *Marvel Comics* (these were donated to Western Michigan as a result of the popular emphasis that Beverly "Penny" David had introduced into a general humanities course); and a popular architecture tour of nearby Kalamazoo by Peter Schmitt. Ralph and Valerie Carnes of Roosevelt University illustrated their study of "Ideal Body Types" with examples from their own avocations as body-builder and fashion model.

In 1976 these same people organized a demonstration of cultists from a *Star Trek* convention, complete with costumes and revolting Klingons. This, the fourth Annual MPCA, was held at Bowling Green State University. By now it was clear that the Midwest regional was a going concern, and the 1976 program shows some expansion in areas of interest, especially into architecture and earlier historical studies. And, by this time, the number of names that were to become familiar is too extensive to list, but we should note people who later hosted conferences of both MPCA and PCA: Larry Landrum, of Michigan State University; Jane Bakerman, of Indiana State; Christopher Geist of Bowling Green; and William Schurk, also of Bowling Green. One easily forgotten aspect of the history of the MPCA cannot be overemphasized,and this is its generous function as a spawning pool for smaller organizations. At the 1981 Ninth Annual meeting, sponsored by Franklin University in Columbus, Ohio, organizer Timothy Scheurer combined programs of the National Association for Humanities Education with those of the Midwest American Culture Association and the MPCA. NAHE continued its "masterpiece and commonplace" theme at the MPCA meeting at Terre Haute, and the struggling national group of "elitists" was set on a course of independence.

Although Schroeder's report pretty well outlines the development of the MPCA, there are one or two meetings which should be mentioned. In 1983 a second meeting of the MPCA was held at Bowling Green, this time under the energetic and well-directed scrutiny of William Schurk, of the Sound Archives Library. At that meeting a session was dedicated to development of the Popular Culture Library at BGSU and an appeal for all members of the MPCA to contribute through donations. Although the idea was new, some members did respond with contributions. The next year the meeting was held at Indiana University, under the able direction of Ruth I. Meserve, of the Inner Asian and Uralic National Resource Center. Dr. Meserve had become interested in the international aspects of popular culture studies, especially those having to do with inner Asian and Uralic Culture, and she subsequently edited and we published in the *Journal of Popular Culture* an In-Depth section on the culture of those areas of the world. The MPCA meeting held at Indiana University was especially fruitful because it was opened to some people who had not been regular attendees of the meetings.

The 1985 MPCA meeting was held at Loyola University in Chicago, under the direction of Sammy Danna. Again this meeting attracted several persons who are not usual attendees and a sumptuous feast was spread for all. It was decided at the 1985 meet that the faithful would congregate the next year for the second time at Western Michigan University, with the program being arranged by Christine and James Ferreira. So it was, despite the fact that the two principals had to rush off to China to study the popular culture in that distant country. At the meeting in Chicago in 1985, live-wire Susan Koppelman was elected President of the MPCA and she immediately began enriching the program. For example, for the meeting in Western Michigan State University, Susan arranged for Cathy Davidson, of Michigan State University, to be the Keynote speaker, and for crime writer William X. Kienzle to be a featured speaker. Both spoke quite effectively and were highlights of the meeting. At Kalamazoo it was decided that the 1987 meeting would be at St. Louis Community College, Meramec Branch, under the joint sponsorship of Carol Miller and her colleagues. Koppelman exerted her tireless energy to bringing new aspects and persons to the meeting, and it was a smashing success.

Newsletters, as we have seen in connection with the national PCA, are a vital means of keeping a membership informed of the sentiments and actions of a body of people. Through the years the MPCA Newsletter was ably edited and distributed by Katherine Pavlik, Northern Michigan University. It is not an easy task to keep a newsletter alive, and the MPCA is indebted to Katherine for the fine job she did, until she resigned in 1984.

The Popular Culture Association of the South

Of the several regional popular culture associations, none has been more active and more productive than that of the South. There are probably several reasons for the productiveness of the PCAS. One is rather obvious. It is the one scholarly association in which the members can take a strong pride and in which they can be independent and productive. The PCAS is in the eyes of many of its members more important in their scholarly lives than the parent—or as some of them might say, the parallel—association. It has sometimes been said by members of the PCAS that if the PCA did not exist the PCAS could get along rather well on its own. Yet this thesis of semi-independence should not be overstated. Although a large number of people attend the PCAS and not the PCA, perhaps as large a percentage— perhaps even a larger percentage because of geographical proximity—of members of the PCAS go on to attend meetings of the PCA as from any other of the reginal chapters. There can be no doubt that the PCAS is a vital wheel in the PCA machinery.

The following brief history of the PCAS is supplied by Roger Rollin, of Clemson University.

The Popular Culture Association of the South (PCAS) is a regional affiliate of the Popular Culture Association. It draws its members mainly but not exclusively, from eleven Southeastern states: Alabama, Georgia, Kentucky, Louisiana, Mississippi, North Carolina, South Carolina, Tennessee and Virginia. PCAS is associated with the American Culture Association in the South (ACAS), itself a regional affiliate of the national American Culture Association.

PCAS was founded in 1971 and has held annual meetings since that time in such cities as Louisville, Ky., Jacksonville, Fl., Winston-Salem,N.C., Mobile, Al., and Atlanta, Ga. Attendance at meetings averages around 150 persons, although some meetings have drawn more than two hundred participants.

The purpose of PCAS is to foster the study of popular culture in the Southeastern United States by bringing together scholars from diverse academic disciplines as well as interested laypersons at its annual meetings and in the pages of its two publications, *Studies in Popular Culture* and *The PCAS Newsletter*. *Studies in Popular Culture* was begun as an annual journal in 1977, with semiannual publication beginning in 1985. Its current editor is Jerome Stern (Florida State University), with Gary Harmon (University of North Florida) as Assistant Editor. Previous editors were John English (University of Georgia) and the late Earl Bargainnier (Wesleyan College). *The PCAS Newsletter* is published 2-3 times per year, its present editor (1987) is Robert Doak (Wingate College, NC). PCAS members in good standing receive SIPC and PCASN with the payment of their annual dues. Growing numbers of college and university libraries subscribe to SIPC.

Commemorating a past PCAS President and loyal member during his lifetime, the George Whatley Award is presented annually to the best article published in SIPC in the judgment of the PCAS Executive Council.

The PCAS Executive Council is the governing body of the organization, responsible for overseeing the general operations of the association and for developing and implementing association policy. The Executive Council consists of the President, who serves a one-year term; the Vice-President/President-Elect, who is selected by the membership for a one-year term; the Executive Secretary, appointed by the Executive Council for a three-year term (once-renewable); the Program Chair and the Local Arrangements Chair, both appointed by the Executive Council for a one-year term; three Members-at-large and one ACAS representative, elected by the membership for staggered two-year terms; the editors of SIPC and PCAS, both named by the Executive Council for three-year terms (once renewable); and the Immediate Past President.

The PCAS President is responsible for overseeing all the operations of the Association, with primary duties in such areas as planning the annual meeting, supervising its implementation, chairing meetings of the Executive Council, and maintaining communications with the Council and the membership. The Vice President/President Elect assists the President and supervises the operations of the PCAS State Coordinators, one or two of whom are assigned to each of the eleven states; State Coordinators are responsible for recruiting members in their respective states and for publicizing the annual meeting. The Executive Secretary is the chief continuing officer of the Association, responsible for its day-to-day operations, especially fiscal matters and record-keeping. The current Executive Secretary is Maryhelen C. Harmon (University of South Florida); her predecessors were Gary Harmon (University of North Florida) and George Whatley (University of Alabama-Birmingham). The Program Chair is responsible for sending out calls for papers for the annual conference, receiving submissions for sessions and papers and evaluating their appropriateness, and for the final arrangement of the conference program. The Local Arrangements Chair is responsible for liaison between the association and the host institutions as well as with the hotel in which the meeting is to be held. Members-at-Large and the ACAS Representative serve in an advisory capacity and carry out such duties as the President or the Executive Secretary may assign them.

Members of the PCAS whose disciplines are English or Foreign Languages are also active in the Popular Culture Division of the South Atlantic Modern Language Association and the Popular Culture Division of the Modern Language Association. PCAS prides itself, however, on being a truly interdisciplinary organization, numbering among its members scholars from such fields as Anthropology, Architecture, Art, Business, Communications, Drama, Education, Folklore, Geography, History, Humanities, Philosophy, Psychology, Religious Studies, Speech and Sociology. Many, if not most, PCAS members belong to the PCA and/or ACA.

The annual conference typically lasts two days, beginning on a Thursday afternoon (usually in early October) and ending at noon on Saturday. The Executive Council normally convenes just before the conference begins, once during the conference, and for an evaluation session after the conference has ended. The conference itself typically features 3-5 90-minute sessions running concurrently during the regular meeting hours, a President's Reception social hour, a luncheon with a notable guest speaker, and special events such as showings of films and television programs, art exhibits, musical performances, etc.

PCAS has received substantial support from various Southeastern community and junior colleges, institutes, colleges and universities. Its operations, however, are chiefly financed by membership dues and conference registratation fees. No officer or other member is financially remunerated for his/her efforts on behalf of the Association. PCAS is academic volunteerism in action, and although volunteerism invariably causes problems, PCAS, in the more than fifteen years of its existence, has not only grown but evolved into a manageable and congenial, yet highly professional, organization. It has fulfilled its purpose of encouraging and advancing popular culture studies; moreover, it could be argued that it has made a significant contribution to the legitimization of those studies. (Roger Rollin, Clemson University; PCAS President, 1984-85.)

PCAS Past Presidents
1971-1973 Henry Marks
1973-1974 Molly Davis (Queens College)
1974-1975 Earl Bargainnier (Wesleyan College)
1975-1976 George Whatley (University of Alabama-Birmingham)
1976-1977 Duncan Jamieson (University of Alabama)
1978-1979 Ralph von Tresckow Napp (Winston-Salem State University)
1980-1981 Irving Deer (University of South Florida)
1981-1982 Ann Newman (University of North Carolina-Charlotte)
1982-1983 Patrick McLeod (Jacksonville University)
1983-1984 Dennis Hall (University of Louisville)
1984-1985 Roger Rollin (Clemson University)
1985-1986 John Scott Wilson (University of South Carolina)
1986-1987 Amos St. Germain (Southern Technical Institute)

Popular Culture Association of the Southwest
and Texas

The account of the Southwest and Texas chapters is another success story.

PCA Regional Meetings and the Organization

The Southwest and Texas Popular Culture Associations were founded to carry forward the efforts of the national. Early leadership was provided by Peter C. Rollins (English) of Oklahoma State University and by Fred Erisman (English) of Texas Christian University. Early meetings were held in Stillwater, Oklahoma and Wichita, Kansas, with the help of the faculty at Wichita State University like Greg Sojka, Jim Thomas, and others. Later, Jeanne Ellinger of Southwestern Oklahoma State University (Weatherford) propelled the organization in new directions as did Michael K. Schoenecke of Texas Tech University in Lubbock. Harold Hatt of Phillips University (Enid, OK) has been an important force in the organization, keeping officers entertained with outrageous puns.

Each year, Ray Browne or Mike Marsden of Bowling Green State University (OH) has made the trip to Oklahoma or Texas to give us the latest news on national developments. An important network of scholars has built up over the years, pooling resources in a region which easily isolates scholars with popular culture interests in towns many miles from one another. We are enriched as a discipline and as individuals by the meetings which the PCA brought to our doors.

1979 Stillwater, Oklahoma

The meeting was entitled "Popular Culture and the Southwest: A Will Rogers Centennial," and 129 people participated in the program. The meeting focused on the work of the great Oklahoman, to include papers on Will Rogers in connection with other humorists, with aviation, with his Indian heritage and with the film industry. Southwestern humor papers and presentations on Cowboy humor amplified the meeting's emphasis on the Oklahoma humorist.

Sessions also looked at Regional identity, sports in the Southwest, The Creation of the West as Myth, Images of Women in Modern Art, Western Music, Minorities, the Immigrant, the American Indian, Poetry, Western Film, Avenues for Future Research and LBJ as regional figure.

The spirit of the program was summarized in a Will Rogers quotation: "Take the 'popular' out of 'popular culture' and you've got no enjoyment."

Proceedings of the conference were microfilmed and placed on deposit at the libraries of OSU, The Oklahoma Historical Society, and PCA-National in Bowling Green, OH. Michael K. Schoenecke was the program chair.

1980 Stillwater, Oklahoma

The title for the program was "American Frontiers: Past, Present, and Future." The Southwest and Oklahoma chapters of the national PCA mounted panels on such subjects as Frontier Gothic, Women on the Frontier, Local History, Science Fiction, Native American Religion and Culture, and the Western Film Before 1929.

Greg Keeler of Bozeman State (MT) entertained the meeting at a mixer with original musical selections entitled "Cultural Contradictions of the West in Song."

Sessions on Literature and the Frontier, Wilderness and Civilization as Concepts of American Identity, Ideas about the Border, Motion Pictures of the West, and Minorities on the Frontier followed.

A Proceedings of the Conference was microfilmed and placed in the libraries of OSU, The Popular Culture Association—Bowling Green, and the Oklahoma Historical Society (OKC).

1983 Lubbock, Texas

The Lubbock meeting entitled "American Frontiers" brought the association south of the Oklahoma border, and 148 people were in attendance.

Texas Tech University's Museum and Ranching Heritage Center hosted the meeting with Michael K. Schoenecke as Program Chair.

Sessions examined Technical Writing and Technical Communicating, New Mexico Musicians, Evolution of the Western, Folklore and Culture, Science Fiction and Fantasy, The Eastern View of the Western Hero, Liberty and Popular Religion, 20th Century Personalities of the Southwest, Frontiers of Crime and Punishment, Popular Scientific Writing, 19th Century Heroes and Villains of the Southwest.

Texas Tech University proved to be a fruitful meeting. The Texas Tech University Graduate English Club provided transportation for the participants who attended the sessions as well as for those who attended the Cash Bar.

A Proceedings of the conference was microfilmed and placed in the libraries of OSU, Texas Tech University, The Popular Culture Association—Bowling Green, OH, and the Oklahoma Historical Society (OKC).

1985 Weatherford, Oklahoma

The Texas/Southwest Popular Culture Convention met on the campus of Southwestern Oklahoma State University from February 28-March 2. Participants came from a wide variety of backgrounds: stagecoach craftsmen to state legislators. Some of participants stomped their feet and clapped their hands to the tune of banjo pickers at a local oldtimer's barn, one of the few places left in this country where the public can enjoy an evening of good music at no cost.

Other features included a display of memorabilia ranging from a Hopalong Cassidy collection to a group of old milk bottles. One of the most interesting events was a video presentation of the history of Highway 66.

On the way back to the airport, Ray Browne and Jeanne Ellinger, an excellent program chair, stopped at Canton, OK, to take a peek at a collection of 2,000 old movie posters.

1986 Lubbock, Texas

The second Lubbock meeting focused on West As Frontier, and Kristine Fredricksson proved to be an inexhaustible program chair.

Sessions focused on Sports, Composition and Rhetoric in Popular Culture, Folk Dancing, Western Folk Literature, Science Fiction, Women on the Frontier, Western Music, and Crafts.

An evening program included drinking beer, dancing the Cotton-Eye Joe, and listening to several West Texas musicians perform.

A Proceedings of the conference was microfilmed and placed in the libraries of OSU, Texas Tech University, The Popular Culture Association—Bowling Green, OH, and the Oklahoma Historical Society (OKC).

1987 Lawton, Oklahoma

The Lawton meeting was entitled "The Fruited Plain" and combined a surprising amount of museum exposure with the usual papers.

Sally Jirik-Cook and others at the Leslie Powell Foundation were the hosts for the meeting.

Sessions focused on Personalities of the Southwest, Ethnic Groups of the Southwest, Main Street, Oklahoma (preservation), Religion, Indians, Contemporary Folk Groups, Theatre and Drama, Film and Photography, Mystery/Detective Fiction, Western Fiction, Sports, Local History, Heroes, Architecture, Humor, Music, and Bad Guys of the Southwest.

Lawton proved to be an exciting meeting; the city was truly hospitable, exemplifying some of the virtues of Southwestern culture the scholars were analyzing. The fellowship of the members made a cool weekend of rain a warm, indoor experience.

1988 Stillwater, Oklahoma

The meeting will take place on the Oklahoma State University campus from February 3-6, and the program will be supplemented by motion pictures of the West, plus a live performance of a Western drama of recent vintage. All day on February 3, there will be an intensive series of sessions on Folklore.

Students at Oklahoma State University will be attending for one hour of academic credit. Michael Schoenecke, English Department, Texas Tech University, Lubbock, TX.

The Northeast PCA
and Other Latecomers

The Northeast PCA has been a vigorous association because of the character and strength of its members. It began its meetings in 1974, convening at Southern Massachusetts University and holding a very successful meeting. Subsequently the Association met at Lowell University in 1975, at the University of Rhode Island in 1976, Westfield State College in 1977, University of Rhode Island in 1978, Clark University in 1979, University of Rhode Island in 1980, Connecticut College in 1981. The program was scheduled for the University of Connecticut in 1982 but had to be cancelled because of conflicts in scheduling. After 1981 there was a hiatus in meeings. But to that date they had been very successful. They usually lasted one day, attracted many scholars who have worked in the national PCA/ACA also. And they always arranged for informal hours during which people relaxed and pursued academic conversation in informal circumstances. The strength of the NEPCA has always been the character of its officers and participants. Two of the presidents have been Marie Ahearn (Southeastern Massachusetts University) and Josie Campbell (University of Rhode Island). Three of the powers behind the throne have been the diligent and enthusiastic workers Tom Towers (University of Rhode Island, Providence), Gerard O'Connor (Lowell University) and Richard Gid Powers (CUNY U. of Staten Island).

After the hiatus following the 1981 meeting, there was a vigorous revitalization of the NEPCA in 1986 under the strong leadership of David K. Vaughan (University of Maine, Orono) and generously supported by the Department of English, University of Maine, Burton Hatlen, Chair; and by the National Poetry Foundation, Carroll F. Terrell, Executive Director. It was held for two days and consisted of over fifty sessions, running three at a time. The meeting highlighted the works of Stephen King, a graduate of the University of Maine, and he was the keynote speaker on Thursday night before the conference opened. The next meeting of the NEPCA will be held in October, 1988, at Portland, Maine. The success of the 1987 meeting and the energy with which the 1988 meeting is being approached at the time of this writing (summer, 1987) bodes well for the uninterrupted continuation of the NEPCA.

Other groups have through the years held successful regional meetings, and then for one reason or another the meetings have not continued. Joe Arpad (UCLA) for example, held a very successful meeting of the Southern California PCA chapter in Las Vegas. Over one hundred people attended, and a grand and informative time was had by all.

Other areas are constantly generating interest and new chapters. For example, in January 1987 there was born, under the expert handling of Jack Estes (Peninsula College, Port Angeles, Washington) the Northern Pacific Popular Culture Association. The first meeting was held at Tacoma College. To a certain extent this first meeting was experimental. Jack Estes, the person in charge, wanted to see what direction and what strength might be generated and to see if the idea of a chapter of the PCA in the Pacific Northwest was viable. He found a vitality in the concept and the attendance that might have surprised him. Over a hundred participants turned out for the two days. All were enthusiastic about the program, all felt that it was a smashing success and that it should be made a permanent fixture on the academic landscape of the Pacific Northwest. Estes' wisdom in billing the association as the Northern Pacific PCA was borne out by the attendees. At least a dozen people came down from the University of British Columbia and were enthusiastic about the concept in general. The 1988 meeting of the NPPCA was held at the University of British Columbia, with more than a hundred—with about one third Canadian—in attendance. Again, great success. The 1989 meeting will be held at Tacoma, Washington. Success is anticipated.

The officers duly elected at the NPPCA 1988 meeting are the following: President, Don Wall, Eastern Washington University; Vice-President, Victoria Ballard, So. Puget Sound Community College; Board, Marilyn Ewing, Eastern Oregon St. College; Lotte Larsen, Western Oregon St. College; Michael Ames, University of British Columbia (Museum of Anthropology); Liahna Babener, Montana State University; Secretary-Treasurer, Jack Estes, Peninsula College, Port Angeles, Washington.

The latest effort at covering the entire United States with regional meetings comes with establishment of the Far West Popular Culture Association, with Felicia Campbell, University of Nevada, Las Vegas, President; and L. Arlen Collier, University of Nevada, Las Vegas, as Treasurer. They will hold their first meeting in January 1989, and success is almost guaranteed.

Regional meetings of the ACA on the whole have not been so successful as those of the PCA. Generally speaking the ACA regional meetings are held as part (often undramatized part) of the regional PCA. Thus we have ACA participants at the PCAS, the MPCA, the SPCA, and others, but infrequently are they held apart under their own flag. Now things are beginning to change in the PCAS. Michael Zalampas, program chair of the PCAS for 1988, made a special effort to enlist participants for the ACAS, and he was successful. Perhaps the movement will grow in that regional organization.

The one notable exception to my statement about the jointly-held nature of the ACA is that sponsored by Fred E.H. Schroeder, University of Minnesota-Duluth, which he very cleverly calls "The Superior Chapter." It is best that Schroeder give the history of this association in his own words.

History of the ACA Superior Chapter

The history of the Superior Regional Chapter of the American Culture Associaton reflected the times in 1980. A year or so earlier Ray Browne had discussed the formation of a midwestern regional association with Fred Schroeder of the University of Minnesota-Duluth (among others). Schroeder's view was that the times were wrong for a successful repetition of the Midwest PCA, which he had started in Duluth in 1973. Factor one was the energy "crisis." Factor two was airline de-regulation. Factor three was budgetary retrenchments in almost all institutions of higher education, and factor four was a conservative, even reactionary, attitude in most universities regarding tenure and promotion standards. The first two factors had produced more than general inflation in air travel costs, for any intra-regional travel was more expensive than long distance travel. It would be cheaper, Schroeder maintained, to have a midwest meeting in Las Vegas than in Bowling Green, Iowa City or Duluth. The answer to the cost problem was one-day drive-in conferences for a dozen or so participants rather than a sub-national regional convention.

The answer to the collegiate snobbery was to bill the Superior ACA as a conference on *research-in-progress*, thus making it possible for participants to share findings scheduled for major presentations and publications without engaging in heinous double-dipping. Enlisting the help of Charles Nelson of Michigan Technological University, who handled the annual call for proposals outside of the Duluth-Superior "Twin Ports" area, and Roger Fischer and David Smith of UMD who shared in the local hosting chores, Schroeder's analysis and tactics have been a local success, and a model that seems to have influenced no one else. In actuality, the "First Reading" conferences have extended over a 300-mile radius, drawing Michiganders from the Upper Peninsula and Wisconsinites from Green Bay, Oshkosh and Eau Claire and Minnesotans from Moorhead on the Dakota border. The 1987 conference brought one participant from Lakehead University in Thunder Bay, Ontario, a trend likely to increase because of a developing partnership between UMD and Lakehead.

The success of the Superior Chapter: in its first seven years it has entertained academics from fifteen institutions, researchers from four museums and several independent scholars; most presentations have gone on to publication and in many cases researchers attribute their work to the opportunity, challenge and friendly advice gained from First Reading; the UMD participants lobbied effectively for establishment of an American Studies Center— the success may be due to the academic geography of the Lake Superior region, which is fairly populous yet separated from metropoli to the south, containing no Ph.D.-granting university, and is generally unimpressed by their dominant counterparts in Minneapolis, Toronto, Detroit and Madison.

Schroeder, Nelson, Fischer and Smith have all been active in ACA, PCA and their publications, but other Superior scholars known in the national associations are Leonard Heldreth of Northern Michigan, Richard Goldstein of Michigan Tech, Elmer Suderman of Gustavus Adolphus and Douglas Nord, Robert Evans, Philip Campbell and Jerry K. Frye of UMD. (End of Schroeder's report.)

One other ACA regional chapter has prospered though it has not been as consistent in its meetings as some of the others. Marie Campbell, in English and American Culture at Mt. St. Mary's College, Emmitsburg, Maryland, has worked vigorously in the ACA in assisting participants in discussing the role of American Culture Studies in small colleges and universities. She has mounted several programs at virtually every national meeting. She has probed deeply into the area. As a means of assisting her in the field, she has established a Mid-Atlantic PCA/ACA chapter and held meetings which were very successful. She is determined that these meetings continue. They will. And under her leadership they will succeed.

Schroeder's report and the account of Marie's work serve as an excellent closing resume of the ways in which and the degree to which regional chapters and meetings have been successful in the PCA/ACA. Although some people for one reason or another have doubted the wisdom of starting regional or smaller meetings in their areas, experience has demonstrated that such reluctance is really unwarranted. Nearly all efforts toward initiating regional meetings have proved successful. In scholarly meetings, as in any other undertaking, the needed ingredients have been a little imagination and a little energy. No obstacles have proved insurmountable. And the rewards have always been rich and stimulating. The regional meetings constitute a very important part of the underpinning and vitality of the national associations.

The latest regional chapter formed is the Rocky Mountain Popular Culture Association. It has not had its first meeting yet, but it will have John C. Bromley as President and Susan Bromley as Secretary-Treasurer and we expect great results from a chapter so ideally located as this one is in Greeley, Colorado, at the University of Northern Colorado.

PCA Presidents and Helpers

Russel B. Nye

Marshall Fishwick

John Cawelti

David Madden

PCA Presidents and Helpers

Carl Bode

J. Fred MacDonald

Peter Rollins

Earl Bargainnier

PCA Presidents and Helpers

Liahna Babener

Ray B. Browne

Pat Browne

Michael T. Marsden
Editor PCAN

ACA Presidents and Helpers

Russel B. Nye

David Wright

Fred E.H. Schroeder

Maureen Honey

ACA Presidents and Helpers

Ray B. Browne

Pat Browne

David Bertolotti
1st editor ACAN
Editor International PC Newsletter

Carlton Jackson
2nd editor ACAN

FIRST NATIONAL MEETING

POPULAR CULTURE ASSOCIATION

LIBERTY   PROPERTY

MICHIGAN STATE UNIVERSITY
East Lansing, Michigan
April 8-10
1971

Kellogg Center, Michigan State University, April 8-10, 1971

PROGRAM

Thursday, April 8

2:00   REGISTRATION

3:00   KEYNOTE ADDRESS   Lincoln A   "Growth of an
Idea: from Novel to Film" David Madden (Writer-in Residence,
LSU)

4:00   EXHIBITS, TOURS, COCKTAILS & GOOD
         FELLOWSHIP

8:00   Auditorium   TIME OUT FOR MAN—THE NATIONAL
         HUMANITIES SERIES
         "The Jet Age Chautauqua" Marty Krasney, assistant to
         the Director (Princeton)

8:45   Program - Auditorium "The Popular Musician and
His Craft: Music and Commentary" Maury Crane and the New
Michigan Jazz Group

Friday, April 9

9:00

THE BLACKS AND THE JEWS, THE 1920's, THE 1930's.
Auditorium
Chairman: John Appel (Michigan State University)
"The Rise and Fall of the Harlem Renaissance: From Garvey to
     Hughes" Anna T. Robinson (University of Wisconsin)
"The Making of an American Jew: From Abraham Cahan to
     Clifford Odets" Daniel Walden (Penn State University)

CURRICULUM AND POPULAR CULTURE   Lincoln A
Chairman: Edward Dodson (Governors State University)
"Toward A Philosophy of Popular Culture Curriculum" Edward
     Dodson (Governors State University)
"Introductory Popular Culture Program in the Traditional
     Curriculum" John M. Solensten (Mankato State College).

3

"Popular Culture and the High School English Class" Jerry
   Hickerson (Kent State University)

PSYCHOLOGICAL APPROACHES TO POPULAR CULTURE
Lincoln B
Chairman: John Cawelti (University of Chicago)
"The Process of Psychological Inference in Accounting for
   Popular Taste" Harold Boris (Tufts University Medical Center)
"A Jungian Approach to Bergman's *Wild Strawberries*" Carlos C.
   Drake (Bowling Green University)

GENERAL Room 101 Chmn: F. Henninger (University of Dayton)
"Toys as Popular Culture" Luther Gore, (University of Virginia)
"Chairs and Their Owners: Show Me Where You Sit and I'll Tell
   You What You Are" Francis Henninger (University of Dayton)
"The Bigelow Chapel and Mount Auburn Cemetery: Monuments
   of a 'Cultivated Community' " Herbert Levine (Harvard)

FILMS Room 106
Chairman: Russell L. Merritt (University of Wisconsin)
"Charlie Kane and the Robber Barons' Fancy: A close reading of
   Citizen Kane" Russell L. Merritt (University of Wisconsin)
"Love's Scar: An Interpretation of Josef Von Sternberg's *The Blue
   Angel*" Gerry Molyneaux (University of Wisconsin)
"Early Busby Berkeley Musicals: An Interpretation of the New
   Deal" Clarice Roseen (University of Wisconsin)

10:00

NEW BLACK STEREOTYPES: TV MEETS THE CHALLENGE
OF YESTERYEAR Auditorium
Chairman: Herb Carson (Ferris State College)
"TV's Influence on Image Formation" Herb Carson (Ferris State)
"The Black Actor and the TV Industry: Is There Improvement?"
   Frederick O'Neal (Actors' Equity)
"The Image of the Black in TV Commercials" Father Paul Gopaul
   (St. John's University)
"TV and the Black Image" Singer Buchanan (Purdue University)
"Julia, Cosby, Haynes and Co." Max Dixon (Western Maryland College)

CULTURAL HISTORY Lincoln A
Chairman: Milton Plesur (SUNY at Buffalo)
"The Historian as Humanist" Archie Jones (Fort Lewis College)
"John Taylor and Jacobean Popular Culture" Frederick O. Waage
     (Northwestern University)
"John Clark Ridpath and Popular History-Neglected and Forgotten"
     Louis C. Smith (University of Illinois)
"The Uses of Popular Culture in Nineteenth Century Marxism"
     William H. Cohn (Hillel Academy)

THE VISION AND ART OF THE EDITORIAL CARTOON
Room 106
Chairman: H. James Clark (University of Wisconsin)
Panelists: Bill Sanders (Milwaukee *Journal*)
          John Fischetti (Chicago *Daily News*)
          Russ Myers (Creator of "Boom-Hilda")

THE UNDERGROUND ASPECTS OF POPULAR CULTURE
Room 101
Chairman: John L. Cotter (University of Penn. and National Park
     Service)
"An Archeological View of Popular Usage at Micholimackouac"
     Dave Armour (Dept. of Natural Resources)
"Popular Culture in a Frontier Garrison" Gene Peterson (Dept. of
     National Resources)
"Care and Analysis of Historic Sites and Artifacts" Lyle Stone
     (Dept. of Natural Resources)
"The Artifact and the Archeological Dig" George Miller and Arnold
     Pilling (Wayne State University)
"Techniques of Cultural Analysis in an Archeological Site" Charles
     Cleland (Wayne State University Museum)

THE ROLE OF THE MOTION PICTURE AS A SOCIALIZING
AGENT Lincoln A
Chairman: Garth Jowett (University of Penn.)
"The Film as Social and Intellectual History" Stuart Samuels
     (University of Penn.)
"Movies and Society" Ian Jarvie (University of Penn.)

5

11:00

POPULAR MUSIC Auditorium
Chairman: R. Serge Denisoff (Bowling Green University)
"From Swing to Bop" Robert D. Ilisevich (Alliance College)
"The Lingering South: Country Music in an Urban Society" Bill
    C. Malone (Wisconsin State University)
"The Old Religion's Better After All: Country Music as Reaction
    to Change in American Society" Jens Lund (Bowling Green U.)
"Rock and Roll: Right Wing of the Woodstock Nation" John van
    Deusen (University of Massachusetts)

POPULAR CULTURE AND RADICAL TEACHING Workshop-
Lincoln A
Chairman: George R. Adams (Wisconsin State University)
Co-chairman: William Reichert (Bowling Green University)

GENERAL Lincoln B Chmn: James Martin (BGU)
"Paul Goodman: The Asphyxiation of Alienation" Robert Schmuhl
    (Indiana University)
"Hills and Valleys of the Mind: The Phrenology Movement in Early
    Victorian England" T. M. Parsinnen (Temple University)
"Walt Disney's Wonderful World of Mythology" Margaret King
    (Bowling Green University)
"American Mentality A La Disneyland" Spencer Bennett (CRU)

PULP FICTION Room 101
Chairman: Frederick S. Cook (Jackson, Michigan)
"The Rise of Pulp Magazines 1920's, 1930's" Frederick S. Cook
"General Fiction Magazines: *Argosy* in particular" Lynn Hickman
"Weird Fiction Magazines: *Weird Tales* in particular" Peter Maurer

BOOKS AND PHOTOS Room 106
Chairman: Robert White (York University)
"Southern Places and Faces of the 1930's" Robert White (York U)
"Evans and Agee's *Let Us Now Praise Famous Men*" Rick Warch
    (Yale University)
"Wright Morris' *God's Country and My People*" Don Summerhayes
    (York University)

6

1:30

UNDERGROUND CULTURE Auditorium
Sachem: "Is the Underground. . .?" Warren French (IUPUI)
Shamen: "Underground Press" Mark Lapping (SUNY at Oswego)
           "Underground Theatre" Donald Pease (U. of Chicago)
           "Underground Film" H. Wayne Schuth (Ohio State U.)
Wizard: "The Underground is. . ." Marc Rosenberg (U. of Penn.)

RELIGION AS A CULTURAL PHENOMENON IN AMERICA
Lincoln A Chairman: Carl Bode (University of Maryland)
"American Culture and the Religious: A Study in Socialization"
     Barbara M. Sullivan (Sacred Heart College)
"RIOT: Religion in Our Time" W. J. McCutcheon (Beloit College)
"Benjamin L. Whorf: Transcendental Linguist" Peter C. Rollins
     (Harvard University)
"Big Massa: The Psychology of Slave Religion" Keith A. Winsell
     (IUPUI)
"United States Influence on Chilean Religious Movements" Peter
     J. Sehlinger (IUPUI)

POPULAR LITERATURE Lincoln B Chmn: Michael Marsden (BGU)
"American Popular Novels of Slum Life, 1890-1910" Charles Sheef
     (Michigan State University)
"Changing Attitudes Towards Class and Money in American Best
     Selling Novels, 1914-1945" Sue Ellery (Towson State College)
"Crime and Culture in Mrs. Rinehart's Fiction" Arnold R. Hoffman
     (Adrian College)
"An Analysis of Some Late Nineteenth-Century Children's
     Periodical Fiction" R. Gordon Kelly (U. of Penn.)
"Popular Literature and American Imperialism" Perry Gianokos
     (Michigan State University)

SCIENCE FICTION AND/OR FANTASY Room 101
Chairman: Tom Clareson (Wooster College)
"The Bibliography of Science Fiction" Tom Clareson (Wooster College)
"Science Fiction Comes to College" Jack Williamson (Eastern New
     Mexico University)

"The Relationship between Professional Writers and the Academy"
Gordon Dickson (President, S.F.W.A.)
"Six Reasons Why Tolkien should not be Popular Culture" Gerard
O'Connor (Lowell Technological Institute)

LECTURE AND SOUND TRACK CLIPS Room 106
"The Popularization of American Literary Works in Films" Herbert
Bergman (Michigan State University)

2:30

FOLKLORE Auditorium
Chairman: Henry Glassie (Indiana University)
"Folk Culture of the Hell's Angels" Michael Owen Jones (UCLA)
"Folk Culture and Professional Wrestling" John Gutowski (IU)
"Folklore in Black Novels" William Wiggins (IU)
"Modern Blues" Barry Lee Pearson (IU)
"Syncopated Slander: the 'Coon Songs' 1890-1900" W. K. McNeil
(Indiana University)
"Folklore's Use in Contemporary American Indian Programs" John
Brits (Indiana University)

COUNTER CULTURE Lincoln A
Chairman: Roy R. Wortman (Ohio State University)
"How Popular is the Counter Culture in Kingsville, Texas?" Harry
Russell Huebel (Texas A&I University)
"Do We Have a Drug Culture?" Richard Powers (U. of Mass.)
"Consciousness IV: The Counter Culture's New Morning?" Jerry
Griswold (University of Connecticut)
"Quest for a New Order: Ferment in Collegiate Culture, 1921-
1929" Mollie C. Davis (W. Georgia College)

MARK TWAIN AND POPULAR CULTURE Lincoln B
Chairman: Tom Towers (Wisconsin State University, Whitewater)
"*The Prince and the Pauper* or Popular Fiction" Roger Saloman
(Case Western Reserve)
"The Mark Twain Persona: Contribution to the Popular Novel"
Jan Cohn (Carnegie-Mellon)
"Mark Twain: High Art, Popular Artist" Paul Baender (U. of Iowa)
"Mark Twain: American Innocent" Howard Baetzhold (Butler U.)

POPULAR IMAGES OF THE CITY   Room 106
Co-chairman: Park Dixon Goist (Case Western Reserve) "The
    Automobile and the Blending of Urban and Rural Imagery"
Co-chairman: James M. Hughes (Wright State University) "A Tale
    of Two Games: An Image of the City"
"The City as Club: Edith Wharton's New York" James Gleason
    (Wright State University)
"Individualism, Community and Alienation: The American City
    in Recent Films" Orley Holton (Slippery Rock State College)
"Dreiser's Mystical City in *Sister Carrie*" Lawrence Hussman
    (Wright State University)

TELEVISION: RESHAPING THE MIND—OR THE MYTH Rm. 101
Chairman: Horace Newcomb (Saginaw Valley College)
"The Sound/Genre: Country Music on Television" John Scott
    Colley (Vanderbilt University)
"Kaptain Kronkite: The Myth of the Eternal Flame" Curt McCray
    (Saginaw Valley College)

3:30

SOCIOLOGY AND POPULAR CULTURE Auditorium
Chairman: R. Serge Denisoff (Bowling Green University)
"Contributions of Certain Sociological Theorists to the Study of
    Films" Jerry Lewis (Kent State University)
"The Current Status of the Sociology of Literature" Michael Gordon
    (University of Connecticut)
"Notes on Some Neglected Research in the Sociology of Art" David
    F. Gillespie (California State College at Los Angeles)
"Today Woodstock, Tomorrow The World: The Rock Festival
    Phenomenon" Richard A. Peterson (Vanderbilt University)

POPULAR CULTURE INTERNATIONAL Lincoln B
Chairman: Edward Harris (University of Cincinnati)
"Peter Handke: The Discovery of the Mundane" Joseph Scott
    (Columbia College)
"Influences of American English on German Periodical Advertising"
    Thomas Freeman (Columbia College)

"Spanish Scholarly Study of the American Popular Culture: The
    Comic Book" J. Eduard Mira (Bowling Green University)

THE MUSICAL SCENE: THE TERRITORY AHEAD Lincoln A
Chairman: Peter Nye (Eastern Michigan University)
Panelists: Bud Spangler, Program Director (WDET-FM, Detroit)
        Ron English, Guitarist (The Musical Orgone, Detroit)
        Charles Moore, Trumpet (The Contemporary Jazz Quartet,
            Detroit)
        Kenny Cox, Music Critic and Commentator (WDET-Detroit)
        Herb Boyd, Writer (Strata Music Corp., Detroit)

4:30

THE THEATRE OF POPULAR IMAGINATION Room 101
Chairman: Philip Bordinat (W. Virginia University)
Remarks on his production of Howie Richardson's *Dark of the Moon*
    Ronald C. Kern (Ashland College)
Remarks on his production of Brendan Behan's *The Hostage*
    Patrick Murphy (W. Virginia University)
Remarks on his adaptation and production of *Everyman* for Nigerian
    actors and audience, Peter Thomas (Lake Superior State College)

AMERICAN HUMOR AND POPULAR CULTURE Room 106
Chairman: Lawrence E. Mintz (University of Maryland)
"American Humor: Alive and Well in the Popular Culture"
    Lawrence E. Mintz (University of Maryland)
"The Americanization of Burlesque, 1840-1860" George Kummer
    (Case Western Reserve)
Hamlin Hill (University of Chicago)
Morris Yates (Iowa State University)

POPULAR CULTURE IN THE AMERICAN CIVILIZATION
PROGRAM Lincoln B
Chairman: Robert A. Corrigan (University of Iowa)
"Popular Music" Edward L. Donovan (Sacred Heart College)
"Popular Fiction" Mary McMurray (University of Iowa)
"Popular Radio Programs" Dale Ross (Iowa State University)
"Popular Films" Kay Mussell (University of Iowa)

8:45

"WE THE PEOPLE"—POPULAR DRAMA OF TODAY Auditorium
    Performing Troupe of the College of Lake County, Illinois

Saturday, April 10

9:00

SEXUALITY IN POPULAR CULTURE Auditorium
Chairman: Charles McCaghy (Bowling Green University)
"Fanny Hill and Masters and Johnson: Guides to Good Sex"
    Tom Kakonis and Ralph Desmarais (Wis. SU)
"The Sociology of Stripping" James K. Skipper (Western Ontario U.)
    and Charles McCaghy (Bowling Green University)
"The Etymology of 'Go-Go Girl' " A. Owen Aldridge (U. of Illinois)

SOCIAL & POLITICAL IMAGES IN AMERICAN MYSTERY
FICTION Lincoln A
Chairman: Francis M. Nevins (attorney and editor/critic)
Panelists: Philip Durham (UCLA)
        Robert E. Washer (editor and reviewer)
        Donald A. Yates (Michigan State University)
        Dan J. Marlowe (mystery writer)
        Allen J. Hubin (editor The Armchair Detective)

THE WESTERN Lincoln B
Chairman: John Cawelti (University of Chicago)
"Origins of the Western" Richard Etulain (Idaho State University)

11

"The Western Films of Anthony Mann" William Routt (Western
    Michigan State University)
"The Western Films of Richard Brooks" Charles Flynn (U. of Chicago)

PERFORMANCE: "TOWN HALL TONIGHT"—A Staged Anthology
of Popular Culture. Room 106
    Cooperative Extension Programs, University of Wisconsin

10:00

PROTEST MUSIC Auditorium
Chairman: Joe Glazer (United States Information Agency)
"The Impact of Woody Guthrie's Life and Songs on the Popular
    Mind" Richard A. Reuss (Wayne State University)
"TeenAngel: Resistance, Rebellion, and Death in Popular Music"
    R. Serge Denisoff (Bowling Green University)
"The Decline of Protest in Contemporary Popular Music" Jerome
    L. Rodnitzky (University of Texas at Arlington)
"So You Want to be a Rock and Roll Star" James Coffman
    (Bowling Green University)

ARCHIVING POPULAR CULTURE Lincoln B
Chairman: Bill Schurk (Bowling Green University)
"Starting From Scratch: A Practical Approach to Collecting Under-
    ground Materials for University Libraries" Dick Beards
    (Temple University)
"A User's Guide to Data Processing: A Summary of What Is Avail-
    able and Where to Find It" Keith Swigger (University of Iowa)

BLACK POPULAR CULTURE Room 106
Chairman: Marshall Fishwick (Lincoln University)
"Rural Healing Practices in the West Georgia Area" Carole E. Hill
    (West Georgia College)
"Responsibilities of Black Studies for the Treatment of Black
    Popular Culture" Robert Perry (Bowling Green University)
"Sambo: The Racial Stereotype in American Culture" Joseph
    Boskin (Boston University)

MYSTICISM, OCCULTISM AND THE SPIRITUAL QUEST Rm. 101
Chairman: Douglas Daye (Bowling Green University)
"Psi: Past, Present, Future" David Techter (Book Review Ed. of *Fate*)
"Modern Occultism: A Thematic Analysis" Robert Galbreath
    (Bowling Green University)
"Witchcraft" John J. Fritscher (Western Michigan State University)

THE PROBLEMS OF TEACHING INDIAN AND CHICANO
POPULAR CULTURE Room 106
Chairman: Joseph Arpad (UCLA)
Panelists: Richard Gonzales (University of South Dakota)
          Kenneth Lincoln (UCLA)
          Roger Buffalohead (University of Minnesota)
          Richard Vasquez (LA *Times*)

11:00

RATIONALE FOR AMERICAN VERNACULAR ARCHITECTURE
Room 106
Chairman: David Neuman (Bowling Green University)
Panelists: Denise Scott Brown (Yale; Venturi and Rauch Architects)
          Kingsbury Marzolf (University of Michigan)
          Harold Muschenheim (University of Michigan)
          Aida Tomeh (Bowling Green University)
          Thomas T. K. Zung (AIA; Architects Inc.)

JOURNALISM Lincoln B
Chairman: Annette Johnson (Bowling Green University)
"Out of the Vinyl Deep: Tom Wolfe and Popular Culture"
    Ronald Weber (University of Notre Dame)
"The Contemporary Appeal of Two Types of Women's Romantic
    Fiction: The Women's 'Gothic' Novel and the Historical Novel
    of Manners" Helen Blakely (John A. Logan College)

THE SOCIAL SIGNIFICANCE OF SOAP OPERA Room 101
Chairman: Anthony Linick (Michigan State University)
"Who Watches Television Soap Opera?" Natan I. Katzman (M.S.U.)

"The Irreality of Soap Opera Reality" Dorothy Linick (East
    Lansing, Michigan)
"The Image of Women in TV Soap Opera" Beth Cafagna (M.S.U.)
"Soap Opera and the Search for Intimacy" Frederick I. Kaplan
    (M.S.U.)
"Morality and Sponsors: A Soap Opera Writer's Perspective"
    Deborah Hardy (University of Wyoming)

1:00

NORMAN MAILER'S "MAIDSTONE" Auditorium

NOTE *** NOTE *** NOTE

There will be a number of informally scheduled film programs
throughout the Popular Culture Association meeting. Among the
films to be shown are *Madam Satan, Zoo In Budapest, Three,* and
Man of The West.

Cover design from *Catchpenny Prints. 166 Popular Engravings
from the Eighteenth Century*, originally published by Bowles and
Carver. Dover Publications, 1970.

* GREETINGS FROM BOWLING GREEN UNIVERSITY *

In these unusually trying times when students, faculty, administration and citizens feel thwarted in trying to achieve their goals, the activities of the Popular Culture Association, and the thrust of the various activities in Popular Culture on the many campuses represented on this program, are meritorious. There is a drive here toward what seems to me are worthwhile new dimensions in education on both the undergraduate and the graduate levels. The key to this new thrust is not so much the clichéd word relevancy, *though it is still a worthwhile term, as* sensitivity—*an awareness of the needs and hopes of education in the broadest sense—and humaneness in a world that is becoming increasingly dehumanized, with the resulting frustration, anxiety, even terror that stalk the world today.*

As observers—academic and non-academic—increasingly are commenting, much of the chaos on campuses results from lack of communication. When people understand the goals of the movement in Popular Culture resistance will largely melt away. It is becoming increasingly manifest that the goals of the PCA, as revealed in this program, are to bridge gaps, to bring about new understandings on one plane (between students and their world off campus) and on another plane among students, faculty, administrators.

As President of one of the sponsoring schools, I look upon this first national meeting of the Popular Culture Association with great enthusiasm and hope.

Hollis A. Moore, Jr. President
Bowling Green University

9TH ANNUAL CONVENTION

April 25-28, 1979

THE POPULAR CULTURE ASSOCIATION

AND

THE AMERICAN CULTURE ASSOCIATION

William Penn Hotel
Pittsburgh, Pennsylvania

AMERICAN CULTURE ASSOCIATION

OFFICERS

President   Russel B. Nye, Michigan State University
Secretary-Treasurer Ray B. Browne, Bowling Green State University

Advisory Council Tom Cripps, Morgan State University
       Henry Salerno, SUC-Fredonia
       Milton Stern, University of Connecticut
       Daniel Walden, Penn State University

Executive Committee Meeting
American Culture Association
Saturday
10:30-12:00
Sky Room

HISTORY

Working with the Popular Culture Association and, especially, the *Journal of Popular Culture* convinced some people that the PCA perforce was having to cover certain areas which only loosely speaking could be classified as popular culture. For example, JPC has been receiving through the years excellent articles which the editor had to refuse simply because they were not *popular* culture to warrant inclusion of those peripheral papers. To correct this situation the *Journal of American Culture* began publication at the beginning of 1978. As creation of JAC justified itself, the creation of a national association that would parallel the purposes of the magazine seemed warranted.

The JAC and the American Culture Association center on those areas in American culture which are American, although comparative studies, backgrounds and impacts are included, and which are not, in the strict sense of the term, *popular*. Discussions of so-called elite culture are also included. The officers of the ACA and the editors of the JAC feel that these parallel associations and publications, along with those that already exist, cover the areas of American and international culture in a complimentary way. Together they provide the framework and boundaries—as well as the directions—for a comprehensive studies.

MEMBERSHIP DUES

Annual dues are $15.00 for individual members, $20.00 for husband and wife, $10.00 for students and $25.00 for institutional support. Joint membership in both the ACA and the PCA is $25.00 for individuals. $17.50 for students, $50.00 for institutional support. The ACA invites support.

Thursday
8:30-10:00
Allegheny Room

ART AND DEMOCRACY

Chair: Dennis Alan Mann, Architecture Dept., University of Cincinnati, Cincinnati, OH 45221

Artist Walter Tittle: Friend of the Famous, Richard P. Veler, Art Dept., Wittenberg University, Springfield, OH 45501

Marrying Civilization to the Wilderness: Images of Fur Trappers in Nineteenth Century American Art, Dawn Glanz, School of Art, Bowling Green State University, Bowling Green, OH 43403

Towards Quality in Popular Art, Dennis Alan Mann, Architecture Dept., University of Cincinnati, Cincinnati, OH 45221
Learning to See: Historical Perspectives on Popular Commercial Art, Alan Gowans, University of Victoria, British Columbia, Canada V8W2Y2
Thursday
8:30-10:00
Parlor G

FOLKLORE AND REGIONAL DYNAMICS

Chair: John Moe, History Dept., Central Michigan University, Mt. Pleasant, MI 48858

Folk Dynamics of Women's Softball, Betsy Petersen, Folklore Institute, Indiana University, Bloomington, IN 47401

The Role of Storytellers in the Tales of the Southwest Humorists, Sonia Gernes, English Dept., Notre Dame University, Notre Dame, IN 46550

Cultural Landmark: Central Michigan Barn Decoration, John Moe, History Dept., Central Michigan University, Mt. Pleasant, MI 48858

Thursday
8:30-10:00
Urban Room 2

RUMOR AND REALITY ON TV

Chair: Frederick Koenig, Sociology Dept., Tulane University, New Orleans, LA

Gay Activists and Network Television: A Study of Protest, Pressure and Participation, Kathryn Montgomery, Speech Communication Dept., California State University, Los Angeles, Los Angeles, CA 90032

Come out of the Closet, Hutch Honey: Homosexual Implications in Starsky and Hutch, Carol M. Ward, English Dept., University of Tennessee, Knoxville, TN 37916

Television and the Rumor Process, Frederick Koenig, Sociology Dept., Tulane University, New Orleans, LA

Thursday
8:30-10:00
Urban Room 3

AMERICA'S MELTING POT

Chair: Dale Knobel, History Dept., Texas A & M University, College Station, TX 77843

Paddy and the Republic: The Antebellum Stage Irishman as Ethnic Stereotype, Dale Knobel, History Dept., Texas A & M University, College Station, TX 77843

The Importance of German Immigrant Culture in the Social History of Twentieth Century Chicago, Joseph Biesinger, Social Science Dept., Eastern Kentucky University, Richmond, KY 40475

Nineteenth-Century Ethnic Humor: The Music Hall Ridicules the Shakers, Helen Irvin, English Dept., Transylvania University, Lexington, KY 40508

Thursday
8:30-10:00
Urban Room 4

THE AMERICAN DREAM

Chair: James R. Huffman, English Dept., State University College, Fredonia, New York 13060

Phrenology: Getting Your Head Together in Nineteenth-Century America, Christian McHugh, University of South Carolina at Sumter, Sumter, SC 29150

A Jungian Approach to Norman Mailer's An American Dream, James R. Huffman, English Dept., State University College, Fredonia, NY 14063

An Analysis of the Acceptance and Rejection of the American Dream: 1960-1975, Daniel M. Dunn, Communication and Creative Arts Dept., Purdue University-Calumet Campus, Hammond, IN 46323

**Thursday
10:30-12:00
Allegheny Room**

THE DYNAMICS OF CHANGING ART FORMS

Chair: Ed Earle, Visual Studies Workshop, 4 Elton St., Rochester NY 14607

The Stereograph in America: Pictorial Antecedents and Cultural Perspectives, Ed Earle, Visual Studies Workshop, 31 Prince St., Rochester NY 14607

The Changing Image of Tatooing in American Culture, Alan B. Govenar, General Studies Dept., Columbus College of Art and Design, Columbus, OH 43215

Great Agitators and Demagogues: A Psychoanalysis, Howard Schwartz, Communications Dept., Rider College, PO Box 6400, Lawrenceville, NJ 08648

**Thursday
10:30-12:00
Parlor G**

SITCOM AND DAYTIME TELEVISION

Chair: Frederick Kaplan, Humanities Dept., Michigan State University, East Lansing, MI 48824

Was Anyone Afraid of Maude Findlay?, Philip Wander, Speech Communication Dept., San Jose State University, San Jose, CA 95162

The Relationship Between Normative Values and Eccentricity in the Situation Comedy, Richard Steiger, Murray State University, 2905 University Station, Murray, KY 42071

American Daytime Television Serial Drama, Frederick Kaplan, Humanities Dept., Michigan State University, East Lansing, MI, 48824

**Thursday
10:30-12:00
Urban Room 2**

REGIONALISM AND AMERICAN CULTURAL STUDIES

Chair: Thomas Anderson, Geography Dept., Bowling Green State University, Bowling Green, OH 43403

Sectionalism and Regionalism in American Political Culture: An Interpretation, Thomas D. Anderson, Geography Dept., Bowling Green State University, Bowling Green, OH 43403

Worcester Learns to Play, P. Bradley Nutting, History Dept., Framingham State College, Framingham, MA 01701

The Golden Age Clubs of Cleveland: Social Engineering Through the Small Group, William Graebner, History Dept., SUNY-Fredonia, Fredonia, NY 14063

Thursday
10:30-12:00
Urban Room 3

DREAMS AND DREAMERS IN AMERICAN CHANGE

Chair: Sheldon Hershinow, Humanities Dept., University of Hawaii, Kapioluni Community College, Honolulu, HA 96814

Alice Morse Earle as American Heroine, Adoracion F. Gonzalez, Arts and Sciences College, Youngstown State University, Youngstown, OH 44555

Exiles and Saints in the American Imagination, August Nigro, English Dept., Kutztown State College, Kutztown, PA 19530

Native American Literature: The Hawaiian Renaissance and the American Indian Movement: A Comparative View of Cultural Conflicts, Sheldon Hershinow, Humanities Dept., University of Hawaii, Kapioluni Community College, Honolulu, Hawaii 96814

Thursday
10:30-12:00
Urban Room 4

TEACHING PERSPECTIVES AND TECHNOLOGY

Chair: Amos St. Germain, English and Social Studies Dept., Southern Technical Institute, Marietta, GA 30060

Computing Sources of Media Preference of College Students: An Empirical Investigation, Michael Ohr & Robert Tournier, Sociology Dept., The College of Charleston, Charleston, SC 19401

Student of Pupil: Contrasts in the Educational Perspectives of Robert Pirsig and Sylvia Plath, Paul B. Beran, English and Philosophy Dept., Stephen F. Austin State University, Nacogdoches, TX 75962

Technology and Culture Studies: Interface in and out of the Classroom, Amos St. Germain, English and Social Studies, Southern Technical Institute, Marietta, GA 30060

Thursday
1:30-3:00
Allegheny Room

ARCHITECTURE AND SENSE OF HISTORY

Chair: James Barker, School of Architecture, Mississippi State University, Mississippi State, MS 39762

Designing for a Sense of Place in Southern Small Towns, James Barker, School of Architecture, Mississippi State University, Mississippi State, MS 39762

The Country Church and the Preservation of the Past, John Marsh, English Dept., Edinboro State College, Edinboro, PA 16444

Faith, Form and Identity: Episcopal Church Building in Dakota Territory, Ronald Lanier Ramsey, Architecture Dept., North Dakota State University, Fargo, ND 58105

Thursday
1:30-3:00
Parlor G

MAGAZINES IN AMERICAN CULTURE

Chair: Dorey Schmidt, American Culture Program, Bowling Green State University, Bowling Green, OH 43403

The Rise of Cultural Journalism, Thad Sitton, English Dept., Dominican College, 7214 St. Charles Avenue, New Orleans, LA 70118

The Brandywine School of Magazine Illustration: Harper's Scribner's and Century, *1906-1910,* James Best, Political Science Dept., Kent State University, Kent, OH 44242

The Germs are Everywhere: The Germ Threat as Seen in Magazine Articles 1820-1920, Andrew McClary, Natural Science Dept., Michigan State University, East Lansing, MI 48823

Thursday
1:30-3:00
Urban Room 2

URBAN REALITY VS. ARTISTIC PORTRAYAL

Chair: Robert Holmes, Legal Studies Dept., Bowling Green State University, Bowling Green, OH 43403

Correcting Quincy, John R. Feegel, MD, JD, 412 E. Madison, Tampa, FL 33602

Boredom in His Business: The Private Life of the Private Eye, Michael Barson, Popular Culture Dept., Bowling Green State University, Bowling Green, OH 43403

TV Lawyer, Myth and Reality, Robert Holmes, Legal Studies, Bowling Green State University, Bowling Green, OH 43403

Thursday
1:30-3:00
Urban Room 3

VARIETIES IN ENTERTAINMENT

Chair: H.T. Spetnagel, Communications Dept., University of Denver, Denver, CO 80208

Entertainment as a Sociological Enterprise, H.T. Spetnagel & Harold Mendelsohn, Communications Dept., University of Denver, Denver, CO 80208

Britten's Billy Bud *and Melville's Ambiquities,* Harold Farwell Jr., English Dept., Western Carolina University, Cullowhee, NC 28723

Rachel Crothers' Drama: The "Doll House" on Broadway, Jack Wallace, English Dept., Miami University, Oxford, OH 45056

Chaplin and the Critics, A. Anthony Oseguera, Radio-TV-Film, Valdosta State College, Valdosta, GA 31601

Thursday
1:30-3:00
Urban Room 4

CLASSROOM TEACHING

Chair: Donald R. Ballman, History Dept., Georgetown University, Washington, D.C. 20057

Pre-School Viewers: The Security of Sesame Street, Paul Borgman, Northwestern College, Orange City, Iowa 51041

Society/Culture/Media: an eclectic approach for teaching, Jerry Clavner, Cuyahoga Community College, Eastern Campus, Warrensville Township, OH 44122

Mental Hooks: Using Trivia to Teach History, Donald R. Ballman, History Dept., Georgetown University, Washington, D.C. 20057

Thursday
3:30-5:00
Allegheny Room

WHAT'S NEW WITH THE PAST: HISTORIC PRESERVATION IN OHIO

Chair: Ted Ligibel, Center for Archival Collections, University Library, Bowling Green State University, Bowling Green, OH 43403

What is New With the Past, David Brook, Director, Historic Preservation Program and the Ohio Historical Society, Columbus, OH

Ohio Historic Inventory Surveys: Barns, Folk Art, Log Houses and Main Streets, Ted Ligibel, Center for Archival Collections, University Library, Bowling Green State University, Bowling Green, OH 43403

A Geographical Perspective of Historic Preservation in the United States, Alvar Carlson, Geography Dept., Bowling Green State University, Bowling Green, OH 43403

Thursday
3:30-5:00
Parlor G

BLACKS IN AMERICA

Chair: Richard Liba, Michigan Technological University, Houghton, MI

The Negro: A Cultural Absurdity, Lanny Bowers, Morristown College, Morristown, TN 37814

Miscegenation in American Literature, Ken Bidle, English Dept., Elmhurst College, Elmhurst, IL 60126

Violence, Passion, and Sexual Racism: The Case of the Plantation Novel in the 1970s, Christopher Geist, Popular Culture Dept., Bowling Green State University, Bowling Green, OH 43403

Thursday
3:30-5:00
Urban Room 2

STUDIES IN REGIONALISM

Chair: Gary Harmon, Dept. of English, University of North Florida, Jacksonville, FL

Grants, New Mexico, The Uranium Capitol of the World, Don Webb, History Dept., New Mexico State University, Grants, NM 87020

Bowling Green's Center for Archival Collections' Role in Regional/Local Studies, Paul Yon, Center for Archival Collections, University Library, Bowling Green State University, Bowling Green, OH 43403

The Stuff of Myth: Florida in Fiction, Gary Harmon, Dept. of English, University of North Florida, Jacksonville, FL

Thursday
3:30-5:00
Urban Room 3

THE SUCCESS ETHIC

Chair: Gregg Franzwa, Philosophy Dept., Texas Christian University, Fort Worth, TX 76129

Popular Philosophy: The Self Helpers, Gregg Franzwa, Philosophy Dept., Texas Christian University, Fort Worth, TX 76219

The "Race for Riches:" Success Books in the 1930s, Robert David Habich, English Dept., Pennsylvania State University, University Park, PA 16802

Andrew Carnegie's Own Story for Boys and Girls, Jerry Griswold, English Dept., Northeastern University, Boston, MA 02115

Popular Culture and Political Consciousness: Ideologies of Self-Help, Old and New, Kim Ezra Shienbaum, Political Science Dept., Rutgers, Camden, NJ 08102

Thursday
3:30-5:00
Urban Room 4

FORMS OF RELIGIOUS EXPRESSION

Chair: Donald Winters, American Studies Program, University of Minnesota, Minneapolis, MN 55455

The New Gods: Religious Imagery in Comic Books, Harold Schechter, English Dept., Queens College, CUNY, Flushing, N.Y. 11367

American Revivalism and the Sacred Popular Tradition, James Downey, Box 198, William Carey College, Hattisbury, MS 39401

Sectarianism, Political and Religious: The Progressive Party Meets the Jehovah's Witnesses, Donald Winters, American Studies Program, University of Minnesota Minneapolis, MN 55455

Friday
8:30-10:00
Allegheny Room

AMERICA'S ETHNIC SYMPHONY

James Dale, American Studies, Youngstown State University, Youngstown, OH 44503

TV Documentary of 50 minutes narrated by Martin Balsam which dramatizes the issues involved in the rise of a new ethnicity in Contemporary America.

Friday
8:30-10:00
Parlor G

THE FOLK: PAST AND PRESENT

Chair: Nolan Porterfield, English Dept., Southeast Missouri State University, Cape Girardeau, MO 63701

American Gravestones and Culture (2 papers), Mac Nelson & Diana George, Division of Arts and Humanistic Studies, The Pennsylvania State University, The Behrend College, Erie, PA 16563

"Mr. Victor and Mr. Peer": The Role and Impact of the Victor Talking Machine Co. and Ralph Peer in the Country Music Industry of the 1920s, Nolan Porterfield, English Dept., Southeast Missouri State University, Cape Girardeau, MO 63701

American Culture as Falsehearted Lover in Folk-styled Music of the 1960s, Robert Gremore, American Studies Program, University of Minnesota, Minneapolis, MN 55455

Friday
8:30-10:00
Urban Room 2

SYMBOLS IN AMERICAN LITERATURE

Chair: Andrew L. Kelley, Languages and Literature, Shelby State Community College, Memphis, TN 38104

American Gothic: The Origins of Supernatural Fiction in America, Cathy Davidson, English Dept., Michigan State University, East Lansing, MI 48824

From A to V: The Paranoid Symbol in American Literature, Donald F. Larsson, English Dept., University of Wisconsin, Madison, WI 53706

Have Shakespeare's Bones Been Moved to America, Andrew L. Kelley, Languages and Literature, Shelby State Community College, Memphis, TN 38104

Friday
8:30-10:00
Urban Room 3

CHANGING PATTERNS IN CULTURE

Chair: Thomas B. Byers, English Dept., Calhoun Community College, Decautur, AL 35601

Flower Power: Pastoral in the '60s, P. Gila Reinstein, English Dept., Rhode Island College, Providence, R.I. 02908

Forgive the Father: A Memoir of Changing Generations, Howard Wolfe, English Dept., SUNY-Buffalo, Buffalo, NY 14260

Failure of Sensibility in the Counter-Culture, Thomas Byers, English Dept., Calhoun Community College, Decautur, AL 35601

Friday
8:30-10:00
Urban Room 4

THE THREAT OF APOCALYPTICISM

Chair: Saul Lerner, History and Political Science Dept., Purdue University-Calumet Campus, Hammond, IN 46323

Apocalypse and the American Imagination, Michael W. Sexson, English Dept., Montana State University, Bozeman, MO 59715

Environmental Apocalypticism, Saul Lerner, History and Political Science Dept., Purdue University-Calumet Campus, Hammond, IN 46323

Cultural Identities and Psychotic Behavior in the Mental Status Examination, John L. Caughey, American Studies Program, University of Maryland, College Park, MD 20742

Friday
10:30-12:00
Allegheny Room

CONCEPT OF THE HERO

Chair: Mark Siegel, English Dept., University of Wyoming, Laramie, WY 82071

The Messenger Boy Hero: An American Icon, Jules Zanger, English Dept., Southern Illinois University—Edwardsville, Edwardsville, IL 63026

The American Hero: Ringing the Changes, Daniel Walden, English Dept., The Pennsylvania State University, University Park, PA 16802

Heroes are Hard to Find: A Cultural Analysis of The Harder They Come, Mark Siegel, English Dept., University of Wyoming, Laramie, WY 82071

Friday
10:30-12:00
Parlor G

CONFLICTS BETWEEN CULTURES: THE POLICE AND THE PUBLIC

Chair: Patricia Weiser Remmington, Ethnic Studies and Sociology, Bowling Green State University, Bowling Green, OH 43403

Atlanta Police Officers—Their Behavior and Attitudes Towards the Public, Patricia Weiser Remmington, Ethnic Studies and Sociology, Bowling Green State University, Bowling Green, OH 43403

How the Police Administrative Structure Affects Police Reaction to the Public, Ian Rawson, Graduate School of Public Health, University of Pittsburgh, Pittsburgh, PA

How the Pittsburgh Public Forms its Attitudes Towards the Police, Richard Scaglion, Anthropology Dept., University of Pittsburgh, Pittsburgh, PA

Friday
10:30-12:00
Urban Room 2

NATIVE AMERICANS

Chair: Edmund Danziger, Jr., History Dept., Bowling Green State University, Bowling Green, OH 43403

Help for Native American Alcoholics: A History of Detroit's American Indian Services, Edmund Danziger, Jr., History Dept., Bowling Green State University, Bowling Green, OH 43403

The Navajo "Night Chant" and the Structure of Momaday's House Made of Dawn, Vishwanadha Hari Hara Nath, English Dept., Texas Tech University, Lubbock, TX 79409

Red, White and Blue: or "Lo, the Poor Indian", Patrick Lee, English, Foreign Language & Speech Communication, College of Great Falls, Great Falls, MT 59405

Friday
10:30-12:00
Urban Room 3

PORTRAITS IN AMERICAN LITERATURE

Chair: David Sanders, Harvey Mudd College (school affiliation) (on sabbatical), 65 E. Main St., Canton, NY 13617

Mark Twain's Roughing it: The Story Teller's Story, William Pett, English Dept., University of Rhode Island—Kingston, Kingston, RI

Mark Twain and Sherlock Holmes, David Wallace, Social Sciences and Humanities Dept., Morristown College, Morristown, TN 37814

Portrait of Ernest Hemingway a' Seen in John Dos Passos' Novels, David Sanders, Harvey Mudd College, Mailing Address, 65 E. Main St., Canton, NY 13617

Friday
10:30-12:00
Urban Room 4

WOMEN AND AMERICAN FICTION

Chair: Tom Towers, English Dept., Div. of University Extension, University of Rhode Island, Providence, R.I. 02908

The Published Works of American Women, 1776-1800, Gayle T. Pendleton, History Dept., Emory University, Atlanta, GA 30322

An Early Fictional Image of the Woman-Writer, Simone Vauthier, Institut d'Etudes Anglaises et Nord-Americaines, Universite des Sciences Humaines, 22 rue Descartes, 67000 Strasbourg, France

Frederic's Progressive Novel: The Lawton Girl, Tom Towers, English Dept., Division of University Extension, University of Rhode Island, Providence, RI 02908

Friday
1:30-3:00
Allegheny Room

LEISURE ACTIVITIES

Chair: David M. Johnson, Sociology and Social Science Dept., North Carolina A & T State University, Greensboro, NC 27411

The "Mouse House" as Urban Utopia: Disney World as Myth and Urban Message,
David M. Johnson, Sociology and Social Science Dept., North Carolina A & T
State University, Greensboro, NC 27411

"Goodness Gracious" Grady's Unprecendented Old Fashioned American Circus,
Ronald V. Ladwig, Speech and Theatre Dept., Ohio Northern University, Ada,
Ohio 45810

Magic and Divination at the Race Track, Lucy Jayne Kamau, Anthropology
Dept., Northeastern University, Chicago, IL 60625

Friday
1:30-3:00
Parlor G

AMERICAN CULTURE ASSOCIATION: PHILOSOPHY AND DEFINITION, I

Chair: Ray B. Browne, Secretary-Treasurer, American Culture Association,
Bowling Green State University, Bowling Green OH 43403

Discussants: Milton Stern, University of Connecticut, Storrs, Daniel Walden,
Penn. State University, University Park, Bernard Sternsher, Bowling Green
State University, Bowling Green, OH, Carl Bode, University of Maryland

Friday
1:30-3:00
Urban Room 2

SHAPING OUR CULTURE

Chair: David Eason, Mass Communication Dept., University of Wisconsin—
Milwaukee, Milwaukee, WI 53201

Potential Anthropoligica Contributions to the Study of American Culture,
Michael J. Intinoli, Burlington County College, Pemberton Browns Mills Road,
Pemberton, NJ 08068

Does SF Mirror our Cultural Ambivalences, Robert E. Myers, Philosophy Dept.,
Bethany College, Bethany, WV 26032

Journalism and the Construction of Public Time, David Eason, Mass
Communication Dept., University of Wisconsin—Milwaukee, Milwaukee, WI
53201

Friday
1:30-3:00
Urban Room 3

FROM BLUES TO ROCK

Chair: William P. Kelly, English Dept., Queens College, CUNY, Flushing, NY 11367

Home Sweet Chicago: The Formation of a Blues Tradition, William Barlow, Communications Dept., Mount Vernon College, Washington, D.C. 20007

Rock Music and the Record Industry, Arnold S. Wolfe, Fine Arts Dept., Triton College, River Grove, IL 60171

Running on Empty: Rock Nostalgia in the '70s, William P. Kelly, English Dept., Queens College, CUNY, Flushing, NY 11367

Friday
1:30-3:00
Urban Room 4

AMERICAN ETIQUETTE

Chair: Arthur Wrobel, English Dept., University of Kentucky, Lexington, KY 40506

Decorum, Manners and Primal Screams: Towards a New American Etiquette, Louis Gallo, English Dept., Columbia College, Columbia, SC 29203

Eating as a Social Institution, Pamela Malcolm Curry, Robert M. Jiobu, Sociology Dept., Ohio State University, Columbus, OH 43210

The "Americanness" of Chewing Gum, Arthur Wrobel, English Dept., University of Kentucky, Lexington, KY 40506

Friday
3:30-5:00
Allegheny Room

PORTRAYALS IN THE FILM AND TV INDUSTRY

Chair: Julian Smith, English Dept., University of Florida, Gainesville, FL 32611

Hollywood and Detroit—A Century of Witness, Julian Smith, English Dept., University of Florida, Gainesville, FL 32611

Television's Black Promise: Negroes on TV in the 1950s, J. Fred MacDonald, History Dept., Northeastern Illinois University, Chicago IL 60625

The Ethos of Inequality: Portraits in Pain Etched By Early Black American Film Makers, Gerald Lee Ratliff, Speech/Theatre Dept., Montclair State College, Upper Montclair, NJ 07043

**Friday
3:30-5:00
Parlor G**

AMERICAN CULTURE ASSOCIATION: PHILOSOPHY AND DEFINITION, II

Chair: Russel B. Nye, President, American Culture Association

Discussants: Tom Cripps, Morgan State University, Edmund J. Danziger, Jr., Bowling Green State University, Henry Salerno, SUC, Fredonia, NY, Alan Gowans, University of Victoria.

**Friday
3:30-5:00
Urban Room 2**

FORCES OF CHANGE IN AMERICAN CULTURE

Chair: Peter Levine, History Dept., Michigan State University, East Lansing, MI 48824

Labor in the Thirties: Social Democracy and Rank-and-File Democracy, Bernie Sternsher, History Dept., Bowling Green State University, Bowling Green, OH 43403

"For One Brief Shining Moment": Cultural Life in the Confederacy Janet E. Kaufman, 4 Pine Tree Lane, Worcester, MA 01609

The Promise of Sport in Ante Bellum America, Peter Levine, History Dept., Michigan State University, E. Lansing, MI 48824

Friday
3:30-5:00
Urban Room 3

MODERN AMERICAN WOMEN

Chair: Marcelle Thiebaux, English Dept., St. John University, New York, NY 11439

Images of Women During WW II, *or How we Lost Rosie the Riveter and Found Lucy Ricardo*, Maureen Honey, Lyman Briggs College, Michigan State University, E. Lansing, MI 48824

Popular Conceptions of Personality—Zelda Fitzgerald, Marleen Barr, English Dept., SUNY—Buffalo, Buffalo, NY 14260

Women, Learning, Literature and Libraries: Themes in the Early Prose of Julia C.R. Dorr, Marcelle Thiebaux, English Dept., St. John's University, New York, NY 11439

Friday
3:30-5:00
Urban Room 4

ENTERTAINMENT AND RITUAL

Chair: Irving Deer, English Dept., University of South Florida, Tampa, FL 33620

The Roast: American Ritual Humor and Satire, George A. Test, English Dept., SUNY-Oneonta, Oneonta, NY 13820

Travel as Play: Roads and Motels, Irving Deer, English Dept., University of South Florida, Tampa, FL 33720

Travel as Play: Motels and Fast Food Services, Harriet Deer, English Dept., University of South Florida, St. Petersburg, FL

Saturday
8:30-10:00
Allegheny Room

THE '60s: DOING THE INTERDISCIPLINARY TEAM-TAUGHT MULTI-MEDIA RAG

40 minute presentation by Bruce Atkins and Frank Burdick, English Dept., State University College at Cortland, Cortland, New York 13045

Saturday
8:30-10:00
Parlor G

MAGAZINES AS CULTURAL FORCES

Chair: Matthew Whalen, English and American Studies, Temple University, Philadelphia, Pa. 19122

To Hustle with the Rowdies: The Organization and Functions of the American Woman Suffrage Press, Lynne Masel-Walters, Journalism Dept., University of Alabama, University, AL 35486

Progressivism Incorporated: Everybody's, *William Hard and "Better Business," 1913-1914*, Ron Marmarelli, Journalism Dept., Central Michigan University, Mount Pleasant, MI 48859

Periodical Science and Newspaper Science: Versions and Visions of "New Knowledge" for the Public, Matthew Whalen, English and American Studies, Temple University, Philadelphia, PA 19122

Saturday
8:30-10:00
Urban Room 2

WOMEN IN AMERICAN PROFESSIONS

Chair: Sumiko Higashi, History Dept. and Women's Studies, SUC—Brockport, Brockport, NY 14420

Middle-aged Woman in Popular Drama, Audrey Dibble, Holland Library, Washington State University, Pullman, WA 99163

American Women as Foreign Correspondents, 1888-1918: Case Studies of Elizabeth Cochrane and Rheta Childe Dorr, Jennifer L. Tebbe, Political Science and American Studies, Massachusetts College of Pharmacy, Boston, MA 02115

Hold it! Women in Television Action Shows Sumiko Higashi, History Dept. and Women's Studies, SUC—Brockport, Brockport, NY 14420

Saturday
8:30-10:00
Urban Room 3

ELEMENTS IN LITERATURE

Chair: Felicia Campbell, English Dept., University of Nevada, Las Vegas, Las Vegas, NV 89154

Lies All Lies: Sufic Elements in Vonnegut's Cat Cradle, Felicia Campbell, English Dept., University of Nevada, Las Vegas, Las Vegas, NV 89154

"Richard Wright's 'Dozens'—More than a Game", Wilsonia E.D. Cherry, English Dept. Florida State University, Tallahassee, FL 32306

Kidsport: The Subversive Works of John R. Tunis, Adam Hammer, American Culture Program, Bowling Green State University, Bowling Green, OH 43403

Saturday
8:30-10:00
Urban Room 4

MACHO VALUES IN AMERICA

Chair: David G. Pugh, English Dept., Oregon State University, Corvallis, OR 97331

Running: An American Subculture or Social Movement?, Walter E. Clark, Sociology Dept., Cedar Crest College, Allentown, PA 18104

The American "Rites de Passage": Boys will be Boys—and so will Men, Robert L. McAndrew, Anthropology Dept., Pikes Peak Community College, Colorado Springs, CO 80906

The Manliness Ethos in Modern America, David G. Pugh, English Dept., Oregon State University, Corvallis, OR 97331

Saturday
10:30-12:00
Allegheny Room

IMAGERY IN FILM

Chair: Carol Williams, Continuing Education, Roosevelt University, Chicago, IL 60605

The Postwar Era in the Movies, Carol Williams, Continuing Education, Roosevelt University, Chicago, IL 60605

Portrayals of Communism in American Film, John Leary, American Studies Program, University of Maryland, College Park, MD 20742

Star Wars and the Christian Eschaton, D.W. Ingersoll, Jr., James M. Nickell & Douglas Lewis, Anthropology Dept., St. Mary's College of Maryland, St. Mary's City, MD 20686

The Image of Americans in Recent European Films, Gioacchino Balducci, Romance Languages Dept., Bowling Green State University, Bowling Green, OH 43403

Saturday
10:30-12:00
Parlor G

MAGAZINES AND SOCIETY

Chair: David A. Richards, History Dept., Lake City Community College, Lake City, FL 32055

America Conquers Britain: Anglo-American Conflict in the Popular Media During the 1920s, David A. Richards, History Dept., Lake City Community College, Lake City, FL 32055

The Dynamite World of Family Story Weeklies: or, How to be a Hip Publisher in 1879, Lydia S. Godfrey, Northern Virginia Community College, 3001 North Buregard St., Alexandria, VA 22311

Mass Communication as Cultural Form: Examination of the Comic Book Formula, Michael Cheney, Human Communication Dept., Rutgers University, New Brunswick, NJ 08903

Saturday
10:30-12:00
Urban Room 2

AMERICAN WOMEN AND SEX

Chair: Roberta Teague Roy, English Dept., East Tennessee State University, Johnson City, TN

The Myth of the True Woman and her Proper Sphere, Carol Kolmerton, English Dept., Hood College, Frederick, MD 21701

The "A" Stands for Adult, Carmen Cramer, English Dept., Texas Christian University, Fort Worth, TX 76129

Land and the Southern Woman: Sensual or Poetic, Roberta Teague Roy, English Dept., East Tennessee State University, Johnson City, TN

Saturday
10:30-12:00
Urban Room 3

THEMES IN AMERICAN LITERATURE

Chair: Charles R. Duke, English Dept., Murray State University, KY 42071

Cultural Guilt and the Child Criminal in Recent American Fiction, Ralph St. Louis, Languages and Literature Dept., University of Evansville, Evansville, IN 47702

A Visit to Landing zone Loon, on a Glance at Vietnam Novels, William Searle, English Dept., Eastern Illinois University, Charleston, IL 61920

Robert Frost, American: Reasons for his Popularity, Kathryn Gibbs, Harris, 2207 Yellowstone Rd., Bryan, TX 77801

Saturday
10:30-12:00
Urban Room 4

THE WEST: REAL AND FEIGNED

Chair: James R. Nicholl, English Dept., Western Carolina University, Cullowhee, NC 28723

The Frontier Era and the Rise of Religious Cults, Philip L. Berg, Sociology/Anthropology, University of Wisconsin-La Crosse, La Cross, WI 54601

The Mountain Man in Literature and Film, Joseph R. Millichap, College of Arts and Sciences, University of Tulsa, Tulsa, OK 74104

Dust in the Air: Narratives of Actual Versus Fictional Trail Drives, James R. Nicholl, English Dept., Western Carolina University, Cullowhee, NC 28723

JOURNAL OF POPULAR FILM AND TELEVISION

(formerly *The Journal of Popular Film*)

All historical eras of television and film are included.

Title and subject indexes are published annually.

One Year $7.00   Three Years $18.00   Students Per Year $6.00

The Journal of Popular Film And Television
Department of Popular Culture
Bowling Green State University
Bowling Green, Ohio 43403

Index of Participants

During the eighteen years that the Popular Culture Association has been holding its annual meetings, some ten thousand different people have participated in the program. A large number, though by no means a majority, of these participants are repeaters. But each year there is a sizable number of new people. In the early years this yearly increase could be by as much as twenty percent. In the later years it is something like fifteen percent. This yearly increase seems to be steady for the future, at least for the next decade, because of the continued expanding interest by people in academic departments which in the past did not participate and because of increased awareness by and participation by non-academics.

But for every fifteen percent of new people the PCA/ACA attracts every year a noticeable number—perhaps five percent—of participants drop out. Surveys have been taken of these drop-outs to try to determine their causes for discontinued participation. There seems to be no apparent pattern. Some participate only once because they have only one presentation that they want to make. Others get academic funding for once and once only. Others use the PCA/ACA for political and professional purposes and when they achieve tenure or promotion, or whatever, they no longer care to be scholars in the field. Such action is understandable.

Participation by members of certain schools is particularly enthusiastic and supportive. As one would expect the largest number of participants has always been from Bowling Green State University—some 230 different individuals through the eighteen years of the PCA's existence. Michigan State University has had some 150 participants during the same period. Oklahoma State University has been third in participants, with some sixty five. During the eighteen year period we have had thirty-five participants from countries other than the United States, excluding Canada. From Canada we have had nearly three hundred. The second largest representation has been from England. For one reason or another there have been virtually no representatives from Central or South American countries, a condition which must be rectified in the future.

In the listing below of participants effort has been made to keep abbreviations logical and as immediately identifiable as possible. The letters BGSU refer, of course, to Bowling Green State University. In other entries states have been identified generally with their most obvious abbreviations; universities and colleges have been identified with the letters U and C. Thus Michigan State University appears as Mich SU, Western Michigan University appears as W Mich U; Wayne State University appears as Wayne SU; always geographical directions appear as the first letter in the quadrant, W=West, SE=Southeast, etc.; obvious universities are not identified with a U or C, thus Harvard, Stanford, but when confusion might result by identification with a city, as in University of Chicago, the U or C is used, thus U Chicago; some people through the years have not been identified with colleges or universities, and for these people we have where possible given cities and towns of location. Finally, through the years some people have left our records incomplete by not having filled in all needed information. These people have been entered in the Index with whatever information we have available.

Index

Aaron, Daniel, Harvard, 1973
Abar, Edwin, Westfield St C, Mass 1988
Abbot, Frank W., U Houston, 1983
Abbott, Lawrence, U Pa 1982, 88
Abbott, Reginald, Lithonia, Ga
Abcarian, Gilbert, Fl St U
Abdelrasoul, Omer, King Faisal U,
   Saudi Arabia, 1984
Abel, Richard M., U Minn
Abicht, Monika, U Cin, 1973
Abinader, Elmaz, U Neb, 1983
Abolins, Ruta, BGSU, 1988
Abrahams, Etta, Mich SU, 1975,
   76, 77, 82, 84
Abramovich, Ilana, NYU, 1987
Abramowitz, Harold, Skidmore C, 1986
Abt, Vicki, Pa SU-Ogontz, 1981,
   82, 83, 84, 85, 86
Abubakar, Rashidah, SU New Jersey,
   Newark, 1985, 86, 87
Accaria-Zavala, Diane, U Puerto Rico, 1988
Ackerman, Kenneth J., U Del, 1973
Acton, Gary, E Mont U, 1983, 86, 88
Adams, Afesa, U Utah, 1984, 85, 86, 87, 88
Adams, Anthony, A. CSU-LA, 1976
Adams, Anthony, Richmond, Va 1986
Adams, Carol, Loyola U, Chicago, 1985
Adams, Charles, Whittier C, 1988
Adams, Charles H., U Ark
Adams, David P., Emory U, 1983
Adams, Gail, 1983
Adams, George R., Wisc SU, 1971,
   72, 73, 74; 77, U Wisc. Whitewater
Adams, Karen, Carson-Newman C, 1985,
   86
Adams, Kenneth, Jacksonville SU, Ala,
   1984, 85, 86
Adams, Mary Jo, Ann Arbor, Mi, 1978;
   82, Baylor U
Adams, Phil, Western Mich U, 1981
Adams, Richard, Lewis & Clark, 1981
Adams, Timothy Dow, Old Dom U,
   1975; 86, W VA U
Adams, Vicki, Kent SU, 1987
Adamson, Carl, Wichita SU, 1983
Adamson, Ginette, Wichita SU, 1983
Adkins, Philip, W. Liberty SC, 1975
Adler, Jacob, Purdue, 1983
Adler, Kerth, Mich SU, 1984
Adler, Philip, E Caro U, 1984, 86, 87, 88
Adler, Thomas, Purdue, 1981
Adrian, Lynn, Iowa City, Ia, 1984
Agis, Ayse, CUNY, 1986
Agnew, Jean-Christopher, Yale, 1982
Agnew, Priscilla, Saddleback C, 1988
Agosta, Lucien L., Kansas SU, 1981
Agte, Lloyd, Casper C, 1988

Ahearn, Marie, S Mass U, 1974,
   75, 76, 77, 78; 85, SE Mass U, 85, 87
Ahrens, John, Beer Can Collectors of Amer,
   73, 86, BGSU
Aiex, Nola Kortner, U Ill-Urbana, 1985
Aig, Dennis, Oh SU, 1978, 79
Airheart, Debra, E Texas SU, 1983,
   84, Wortham Independent school dist,
   Wortham, Tx, 85.
Aitken, Joan, U Mo, KC, 1988
Ajemian, Robert, CSU-Fresno, 1982
Aji, Aron, S Ill U, Carbondale, 1987
Akenson, James E. TN Tech U, 1979, 85
Akers, Stanley, U Akron, 1987, 88
Alarcon, Norma, Ind U, 1976
Albanese, Alex, Northwestern, 1985
Albanese, Catherine L., PA S, 1977,
   78, Wright S
Alberghene, Janice M, BGSU, 1980, 1984
Albertine, Susan, U N FL, 1986
Albinski, Nan, Penn SU, 1985
Albright, Alex, E Carolina U, 1986, 87, 88
Albritton, Tom, Tallahassee, Fl, 1986
Alcoze, Thom, U Sudbury, 1984
Alden, Sondra, Martin & Osa Johnson
   Safari Museum, Chanute, KS, 1983
Alderson, Martha, McGraw-Hill, 1982,
   83, 84, 85, 86, 87
Aldrich, Pearl, Frostburg SC, 1977, 78, 79
Aldrich, Ruth I, U Wisc-Milw, 1974
Aldridge, Alexandra, U Mich, 1977, 80, 81
Aldridge, A. Owen, U Il, 1971, 73
Aldridge, Henry B., East Mich U, 1982,
   83, 84, 85
Aldridge, Lionel, WTMJ Radio/TV,
   San Diego, CA, 1974
Alex, Nola, U Il-Urbana, 1984
Alexander, Alex, Hunter C, 1984
Alexander, James, U Al-Birmingham, 1988
Alexander, John A., U VA, 1982
Alexander, Lynn, Upper Ia U,
   Fayette, 1988
Alexander, Robert, Point Park C, 1984
Alford, Finnegan, Earlham C, 1981
Alford, Richard, Earlham C, 1981
Ali, Ahmed, Sou Il U, 1979
Allain, Matthew, U Sou La, 1988
Allegro, Anthony, U Miami, Fl, 1983
Allen, Gloria, DAR Museum, Washington,
   1986
Allen, Jack, Bemidji SU, 1988
Allen, Jennifer, Northwestern, 1986
Allen, Joan, York U, Downsview, Ont,
   1987
Allen, E. John B, Plymouth SC, 1983
Allen, Margaret, W Il U, 1984
Allen, Margaret, Pa SU, 1976

Allen, Richard, U Tx, 1983, 84
Allen, Roger, Ga SC, 1988
Allen, Susan, U Ky, 1985
Allen, Zita, NYU, 1985
Allensworth, Margaret, U Cin, 1986
Alley, Robert, U Richmond, Va, 1977, 1980
Alliband, Terry, St. Cloud U, 1983
Allison, Peggy, BGSU, 1973
Allshouse, Robert, Gannon U, 1987
Allsup, Carl Northeastern Il U, 1985
Allums, Chris, Mobile C, Al, 1988
Allums, Larry, Mobile C, Al, 1988
Alter, Nora, U Pa, 1988
Altherr, Thomas, Metro SU, Denver, Co,
   1986
Al-Maryati, Abid, U Tol, 1983
Alotta, Robert, Temple, 1981
Alperson, Philip, U Louisville, 1981
Alsop, James, McMaster U, Hamilton,
   Ont, 1985
Altemase, J.J., Lamar U, 1984
   Silver Spring, Md
Alter, Jason, U Hawaii, Manoa, 1983
Alter, Judy, TCU, 1975
Alterman, Peter S, Denver, Co, 1978; 79,
Altman, Andy, BGSU, 1981
Altshuler, Glenn, Ithaca C, 1981
Alvey, R.K Gerald, U Penn, 1973
Alvey, Richard, U Ky, 1975
Alward, Emily, Purdue, 1982, 83, 84
Amador, Victori, Denver, Co, 1985
Ambrogio, Anthony, Wayne SU, 1983, 84,
   85
Ambrosetti, Ronald, SUNY-Fredonia,
   1977, 78, 79, 80, 88
Amelio, Ralph, Willowbrook HS, 1976
Ames, Kenneth L., Winterthur Mus, 1978,
   79
Amesley, C.E., U Ia, 1987
Ameter, Bronda, Ind SU, 1987, 88
Amidon, Rick, Mich SU, 1984; 87, Baker
   C
Amladij, Parag, NYU, 1987, 88
Amour, Robert, VA Com U, 1978
Amram, Carolina, U Miami, Fl, 1985
Anania, Michael, U Il, 1973
Anastaplo, George, Loyola U, Chicago,
   1987, 88
Ancelet, Barry, U SW La, 1988
Anctil, Pierre, U Montreal, 1987
Anderberg, Mary, UC San Fran, 1987
Anders, Mary A, Ok SU, 1984, 85
Anderson, Barbara, Pa SU, 1987, 88
Anderson, Carolyn, U Mass, 1984
Anderson, Clarita, U Md, 1985, 86, 87
Anderson, David, U Nor Colo, 1985, 87,
   88

Anderson, David D, Mich SU, 1974,
  75, 76, 77, 78, 79, 80, 81, 82, 83, 84,
  85, 86, 87, 88
Anderson, Dawn, BGSU, 1973
Anderson, Dennis, BGSU, 1978
Anderson, Donald, U Louisville, 1985
Anderson, Duncan, Carleton U, 1984
Anderson, Erland, U Hawaii-Manoa, 1978
Anderson, James, U Louisville, 1982
Anderson, Jay, West Ky U, 1985
Anderson, Karen, Midway C, 1985
Anderson, Larry, BGSU, 1973, 74
Anderson, Lyle, U San Diego, 1987
Anderson, Mary C, Mich SU, 1982
Anderson, Marylland, Notre Dame U, 1978
Anderson, Maynard C, Warthburg C,
  1983, 86
Anderson, Norman, West Il U, 1976
Anderson, Patricia, Pleasant View School;
  75, Public schools, Lansing, Mi
Anderson, Patrick, Colby-Sawyer C, 1980
Anderson, Robert, Southwest Mo SU,
  1979, 80
Anderson, Roger, Mont SU, 1987
Anderson, Simon V, U Cin, 1975
Anderson, Sue, 1984
Anderson, Thomas, BGSU, 1979
Anderson, Thomas, Mich SU, 1987, 88
Andres, Deborah, Swarthmore, 1983
Andrew, Alicia G, Middlebury C, 1978
Andrew, John, Franklin-Marshall C,
  1983, 84, 85
Andrews, David, Middlebury C, 1987
Andrews, Nathalie, Portland Mus,
  Louisville, Ky, 1985
Andrysiak, Elain, Chicago, Il, 1987
Angress, Ruth, U Cin, 1973
Anisfield, Nancy, Champlain C, 1986, 87
Anker, Roy M., Northwestern C,
  Orange City, Ia, 1978, 80, 84, 87
Annas, Pamela, U Mass Boston, 1985
Annis, Linda F, Ball SU, 1981
Antelyes, Peter, Vassar, 1986
Anthony, Lillian, Towson SU, 1985, 86
Antonelli, George, UNC, Chapel Hill, 1979
Antrim, Harry, Fl Int U, 1973
Antshel, Debbie, UNC-Charlotte, 1980
Antush, John, Fordham, 1987, 88
Aponiuk, Natalia, St. Andrews C,
  U Manitoba, 1984
Appel, John, Mich SU, 1971
Appel, Charles, Nor Ky U, 1982
Appelhof, Ruth, B'ham Mus Art, Ala, 1987
Appleton, Thomas, Ky Hist Soc, Frankfort,
  1985
Aquila, Richard, Ball SU, 1981
Arbuckle, Don, U Pa, 1974
Arbuckle, Nan, Oh SU, Lima, 1987, 88
Arcana, Judith, Loyola U, Chicago, 1986
Armitage, Kay, Innis C, U Toronto, 1984
Armitage, Shelley, Tarrant Co JC, Tx,
  1976, 78, 79
Armour, Dave, Dept. Natural Resources,
  1971
Armour, Robert A, VA Comm U, 1979
Arms, Valerie, Drexel, 1982
Arner, Robert D., U Cin, 1979, 84, 85
Arnold, Allan A, US Merchant Marine
  Acad, 1980

Arnold, Edwin, Appal SU, 1985
Arnold, James, Marquette, 1974, 78, 79,
  81, 82, 83, 84, 85, 86, 87, 88
Arnold, Joseph, U Md, 1976, 77
Arnold, Sam, Fort Restaurant,
  Denver, 1987, 88
Arnold, St. George Tucker, Flint U, 1980,
  87, 88
Arpad, Joseph, 1971, 73, 74, 75; 76,
  BGSU; 77, UCLA; 84, BGSU
Arpad, Susan S, BGSU 1975, 76, 77, 78,
  79, 84, 85, BGSU, 88, CSU-Fresno
Arrington, Mary E, Ok SU, 1982
Arroyo, Beth, SUNY-Fredonia, 1973, 74
Arscott, William, Stephen F. Austin SU,
  1985
Arsooni, O.G.J., Ben Gurion U, 1984
Arthur, Kathleen, G, James Madison U,
  1980
Arthur, Tom, James Madison U, 1979, 80,
  81, 82, 88
Asam, Richard, R Is C, 1984; 86, Athens,
  Ga.
Asani, Ali, Va Tech, 1978
Aschenbrenner, Joyce, Sou Il U,
  Edwardsville, 1985
Ashby, Clifford, Tx Tech, 1982, 84
Ashby, LeRoy, Wash SU, 1976
Ashdown, Paul, U Tol, 1972, 87, U Tenn
Asher, Stanley, John Abbot C, Kirland,
  Que, 1978, 80; 84, 87, 88, John
  Abbott C,
  St. Anne de Bellevue, Que.
Ashinger, Phyllis, Wayne SU, 1981
Ashley, Leonard, Brooklyn C, 1981, 82,
  85, 86, 87
Ashliman, D. L. U Pitt, 1973, 74
Ashton, Dianne, Temple, 1985
Askeland, Richard, Syracuse, 1977
Askins, Justin, Radford U, 1987
Asquith, Peter, Mich SU, 1980
Astilla, Carmelo, Sou U, New Orleans,
  1988
Astro, Richard, Ore SU, 1975
Atamian, Sarkis, U Alaska, 1988
Atkin, David, Mich SU, 1985, 86
Atkins, Bruce, SUCY-Cortland, 1979
Atkins, John, Sou Il U, 1975
Atkins, Thomas A., Hollins C, 1974, 75
Atkinson, Danny, Ok SU, 1985
Atkinson, Michael, U Cin, 1981, 86, 87, 88
Atlas, Marilyn, 1973, 74, 75, Mich SU,
  1980, 81, 82, 85, 86, Oh U
Attig, Thomas, BGSU, 1976
Atwater, Tony, Mich SU, 1983
Atwell, Dick, Western MU, 1980
Atwell, Mary W., Hollins C, 1983, 84, 85,
  86, 87
Atwood, Erwin, Sou Il U, 1976
Atwood, Roy, U Id, 1988
Auburn, Mark, Ark SU, 1985
Aucoin, Michelle, U Vict, B.C.
Aufterhaar, Eugene, BGSU, 1982
Aulestia, Gorko, U Nev-Reno, 1988
Auster, Albert, Brooklyn C, 1983, 87
Austern, Nat, 1983
Austin, Bruce A, Temple, 1979, 1980,
  Rochester Inst Tech, 1984
Austin, James, Sou Il U, Edwardsville,

1974
Austin, William, Cornell, 1975
Avarez-Altman, Grace, SUNY-Brockport,
  1975
Aveni, Adrian, Jackson SU, Al, 1984
Averill, Patricia, U Pa, 1972, 73,
  Heidelberg C, 74 Sycamore, O
Averill, Tom, Washburn U, 1983
Avis, Harry H., Antioch C/West, San Fran,
  1979, 1980
Avisar, Ilan, Oh SU, 1988
Axelrod, Mark, U Minn, 1987
Axler, David M, U Pa, 1978
Axt, Richard, Smithsonian I, 1984
Aycock, D. Alan, U Lethbridge, 1984

Babener, Liahna, Grinnell C, 1979, 80, 81,
  82, 83, 84, 85, 86; 87, 88, Mont SU
Babington, Doug, Queens U, Kingston,
  Ont., 1983, 84
Babior, Sharmon, UCLA, 1988
Bacher, Lutz, Wayne SU, 1980
Bachscheider, Paula, Purdue, 1973
Backstrom, James, Nat'l Aca Sci, 1977
Bacon-Smith, Camille, U Pa, 1987
Badami, Mary Kenny, Northwestern, 1976
Badessa, Richard, U Louisville, 1981
Badger, Reid, U Al, 1976, 87, 88
Badley, Linda, Mid Tn SU, 1985, 88
Badley, William, Mid Tn SU, 1988
Baender, Paul, U Ia, 1971
Baer, Janine, UC Berkeley, 1984
Baetzhold, Howard, Butler, 1971
Bagert, Judith, Pa SU, 1982
Bagley, Carol, Ida SU, 1972
Bagnell, Norma, Tx A&M, 1980
Bailey, Bruce F, Dawson C, 1975
Bailey, Donald, U Winnipeg, 1988
Bailey, Jennifer, Towson SU, 1985
Bailey, Leigh, Kalamazoo Track Club,
  Mi, 1981
Bailey, Melanie, E Il U, 1985, 86, 87
Bailey, Sean, Oh SU, 1985
Bailey, Tom, Western MU, 1981, 84, 87
Baillie, W. M., Bloomsburg U, 1986, 887
Baird, Alexander, W Ky U, 1986
Baird, Nancy, W Ky U, 1981, 82, 85
Baird, Reed, Mich SU, 1975, 76, 78, 80,87
Baird-Lange, Lorraykne, Youngstown SU,
  1986
Baker, Anita, Baylor, 1985
Baker, Bruce, U Neb, 1984
Baker, Christopher, Lamar SU, 1985
Baker, David Jr., Ind U, 1973, 74
Baker, Donald, Southampton C, LI U,
  1973
Baker, Evan, Astoria, NY, 1988
Baker, Gary, Saucerian Press,
  Clarksburg, WV
Baker. Marilyn, Loyola Marymount U,
  LA, 1987
Baker, Pam, NYC, 1986
Baker, Ronald, Ind U, 1981
Baker, Thomas, Pittsburgh U, 1973, 74
Baker, Tod, Citadel, 1987
Baker, Zachary, Jewish Pub Lib,
  Montreal, 1987
Bakerman, Jane, Ind SU, 1975, 76, 77, 78,
  79, 80, 81, 82, 83, 84, 85, 86, 87, 88

Bakke, John, Memphis SU, 1982

Bakker, Jan, Godja Mada U, Indonesia, 1981; 83, 85, 86, Utah SU

Baldarsaro, Lawrence, U Wisc-Milw, 1981

Balducci, Giaocchino, BGSU, 1972, 79

Baldwin, Helena, Frostburg SC, 1985

Bales, Jack, Eureka C, 1976

Ballinger, Franchot, U Cin., 1988

Ballman, Donald R, Georgetown U, 1979

Ballone, James, Bellarmine C, 1982

Balof, Gene, Valdosta SC, 1979; U N Al, 1988

Baltensperger, Bradley H, Mich Tech, 1979

Banchich, Thomas, BGSU, 1974

Bandy-White, Linda, NYU, 1982, Brooklyn,NY, 87

Banes, Ruth, U S Fl, 1981, 82, 83, 84, 85, 86, 87, 88

Banks, Jennifer, Mich SU, 1975, 87

Banks, R. Jeff, Steven Austen SU, 1975, 77, 78, 79

Banks, Robert D., Ok SU, 1976, 77

Banks, Rosemarie, Kent SU, 1986

Bannan, Helen, U New Mex, 1981

Bannon, Barbara, U Ut, 1973

Baralto, Luigina, U Laval, 1980

Barbatsis, Gretchen S., U Neb-Omaha, 1978, 79; 80, Mich SU, 85

Barber, Bruce, Nova Scotia C Art & Design, Halifax, 1986

Barber, Susanna, BGSU, 1981; 82, 83, 87, 87, Emerson C

Barclay, Daniel, Kalamazoo C., 1976

Bardonner, Randy, Purdue, 1988

Barefield, Paul, U Southestern La, 1984, 85, 88

Barendse, Michael, Pa SU, Scranton, 1980, 82

Baresich, Michael J. Old Dom U, 1979

Barfield, Rayford, Clemson, 1984, 85, 86, 87, 88

Bargainnier, Earl F., Ga. Wesleyan C, 1976, 77, 78, 79, 80, 81, 82, 83, 84, 85, 86, 87

Barkan, Steve, U Me, 1980

Barker, Debra, Ball SU, 1986, 87

Barker, Ellen, E Ore SC, 1987; 1988, W Ga C

Barker, James, Miss SU, 1979

Barker, Ken, John Abbat C, Quebec, 1977

Barker, Peter, Memphis SU, 1979

Barker, Thomas, Tx Tech, 1983, 88

Barker, Walter, U RI, 1982

Barkin, Steve, U Md, 1981, 85

Barksdale, Richard, U Il, 1979, 81

Barlow, Aaron, U Ia, 1983, 84

Barlow, Jeffrey, Lewis & Clark C, 1988

Barlow, William, Mt. Vernon C, 1979, 85, 86, 87, 88

Barnard, Warren, Ind SU, 1986, 88

Barncson, Pat, BGSU, 1988

Barnes, Willie, Chicago, Il, 1981

Barnet, Randy, Harvard, 1975

Barnett, David, C Wooster, 1986, 87

Barnett, Louise K, Rutgers, 1979

Barnett, Marianne, U Ut, 1988

Barnum, Carol, So Tech Inst, 1982

Baron, Ava, Rider C, 1979

Barr, Brooke, New Haven, Ct, 1988

Barr, Cyrilla, Cath U, 1986

Barr, Marleen, SUNY-Buffalo, 1976, 77, 78; 79, 80 81, 82, Va Tech

Barr, Terry, U Tenn, 1982, 86; 88, Presbyterian C, Clinton, SC

Barraza, Isabel, Yale, 1979

Barresi, Dorothy, UNC-Charlotte

Barrett, C. L., 1978, Bellefountaine, Oh

Barrett, Daniel, Ia SU, 1982, 83

Barrett, James R, U Pitt, 1976

Barrett, Phyllis, Springfield C, 1979, 80, 84

Barrier, Michael, Ed. Funnyworld Mag, 1979

Barron, Craig, U Tn-Chattanooga, 1986

Barry, A. David, U SW-La, 1988

Barry, Michael, SUNY-Buffalo, 1988

Barshay, Robert, Prince George's Comm C., 1973, 75, 76, 77, 79

Barson, Michael, BGSU, 1976, 79, 80

Bartecchi, Carl, Puebelo C, 1985

Bartell, Gerald, NYC, 1986, 87, 88

Bartels, Andrew, Johns Hopkins, 1977

Barth, Melissa, Appal. SU, 1985, 88

Barthell, Robert, Northwest Comm C. Powell, Wy, 1978

Barthle, Damian, Jefferson Comm C, Louisville, Ky, 1982

Bartis, Peter T., U Pa, 1976

Bartkowski, Frances, Carnegie-Mellon, 1988

Bartlett, David, Morehead SU, 1982

Barton, Nicholas, Primal Inst, LA, 1982

Barton, Robert, Rutgers, 1976

Bartoni, Doreen, Northwestern, 1982

Bartsch, Donna, U Ct, 1986

Bartter, Martha, U Rochester, 1980, 84

Bartz, Fredrica, U Mi-Flint, 1981, 84

Basalla, George, U De, 1972, 75, 76, 77, 80, 82

Basinger, David, U Tol, 1985

Basinger, Jeannine, Wesleyan C, 1974

Basirico, Lawrence, Elon C, 1985, 86

Baskett, Sam, Mich SU, 1986

Baskin, Ken, U Md, 1977

Bass, George, Brown U, 1980

Bass, Jeff, Baylor, 1983

Bassett, John, NC SU-Raleigh, 1985

Bassett, Mark, Ia SU, 1988

Bassett, Sharon, Carnegie-Mellon, 1979

Bassford, H.A., York U, Toronto, 1987

Bassham, Ben, Kent SU, 1981

Bassman, Michael, E Caro U, 1984, 87, 88

Bast, Elaine M., BGSU, 1983, 84, 85, 86

Bastiampillai, Bertram, U Colomba, Sri Lanka, 1982, 83

Basye, Robert C., Ok SU, 1978

Bataille, Gretchen, Ia SU, 1973, 79

Bates, Margaret, Marymount Manhattan C, NYC, 1982

Bates, Paul, Colo SU, 1988

Battista, Guiseppa, Pa SU, 1980

Battle, Jennifer, Cornell, 1984

Bauer, Paul, Duke, 1988

Bauerle, Diane, Ind. U, 1985

Baugh, Susan, Pitt SU, Ks, 1983

Baukus, Robert, Emerson C, 1987

Baum, Bob, U Fl, 1985

Baum, Rosalie, U Fl, 1985, 86, 87

Baum, Werner, U Western Mi, 1974

Baumann, Ellen, Ore SU, 1987

Baumgartner, Jorg, Albion, Mi, 1988

Baxandall, Lee, Ed-Critic at large, NYC, 1974, 85

Baxter, Dave, U Guelph, 1986

Bayer, Jeffrey, U Al, 1976, 84

Bayha, Richard, Washburn U, 1986

Bayles, Michael, Westminster C, London, Can. 1984

Bazin, Nancy Topping, Old Dom U, 1985

Beach, Richard, SUNY-Plattsburgh, 1987

Beal, M.F. CSU-Fresno, 1974

Bealmear, David, U SFl, 1988

Beam, Jackie, W Ky U, 1986

Bear, Andrew, Flinders U, S Australia, 1980

Beard, John, Wayne SU, 1987

Beard, W., U Alberta, 1984

Beards, Dick, Temple, 1971, 73, 74, 75, 86, 87, 88

Beards, Virgina, Pa SU-Lima, 1987

Beatic, Bruce, Cleveland SU, 1987

Beattie, Don, 1980, 85

Beatty, John, Cornell, 1986; 87, SUNY-Cortland

Beatty, Sharon S., U Nev-Las Vegas, 1977

Beatty, Virginia, Evanston, Il, 1988

Beaty, Don, Stephen Austin SU, 1984

Beauchamp, Gorman, U Mich, 1980, 82

Beauchamp, William, S Meth U, 1987, 88

Beaudin-Ross, Jacqueline, McCord Mus, Montreal, 1987

Beaudry, Mary, Boston U, 1984

Beaumont, Stephen, Toronto, 1988

Beaver, Frank, U Mich, 1982, 84

Bechtel, Judith, Nor Ky U, 1985

Beck, Hamilton, Ok SU, 1986

Beck, James P., U Wisc-Whitewater, 1974

Becker, Mary Helen, Madison, Wi, 1975

Becker, Muriel, Caldwell, NJ, 1987

Beckham, Richard, U Wisc-River Falls, 1985, 86,87, 88

Beckham, Sue, U Wisc-Menomonie, 1985, 86, 87, 88

Beckman, Sue, U RI, 1977, 84

Beckman, Thomas, NJ St. Musuem, Trenton, 1984

Beckow, Stephen M, Nat. Mus. of Man, Ottawa, 1975

Bedell, Jeanne F., Va Commonwealth U, 1978, 79, 80, 81; 82, U Mo-Rolla; 84, 85, 86, 87, Va Commonwealth U

Bednarowski, Mary Farrell, U Wisc-Milw, 1976

Beeby, Ellen, Ok SU, 1983

Beerman, Jill, Antioch, 1985

Beezley, William, NC SU-Raleigh, 1988

Begnal, Kate, Ut SU, 1981, 82, 83, 86, 87

Begus, Sarah W., Baltimore, 1977

Behar, Joseph, Dowling C., 1988

Behiels, Michel, U d'Ottawa, 1987

Behling, Dorothy, BGSU, 1984, 85, 86, 87

Behm, Edward, Glassboro SU, 1984

Behr-Sylvestre, David, U Minn,1985

Beiswenger, Nora, Clarkson C Tech, 1974

Beitter, Ursula, Loyola C Baltimore, 1987, 88

Beker, Marilyn, Loyola Marymount U, LA,

1988
Belasco, Warren J., U Md, 1980, 82
Belden, George, Maple Hts Sen HS, Oh, 1977, 78, 79
Belins, Nadya, Auburn U, 1986
Belk, Russell, U Ut, 1987, 88
Bell, Brenda H., E Tx St U, 1979
Bell, Elizabeth, U S Caro, 1985, 86
Bell, Michael, Wayne SU, 1984
Bell, Thomas, U Tn, 1981
Bellamy, Bob, U Ark, 1988
Bellamy, Mike, C St. Thomas, 1987, 88
Belland, Merri, Fl Folklore Program, White Springs, 1985
Bellis, Peter, U Miami, Fl, 1986
Bellman, Samuel L., Cal S Poly-Pomona, 1975, 77
Bell-Meterau, Rebecca, Southwest Tx SU, 1983, 85, 88
Belton, Robert, Queens U, Kingston, Ont, 1987
Belzar, Mfarvin, Va Tech., 1982
Benquist, Lawrence, Keene SC, 1982, 86, 87
Benazon, Michael, Champlain C, 1987
Bence, Robert, N Adams SC,1988
Bender, Bert, Az SU, 1980, 81, 82, 83, 84, 86, 87, 88
Benedikt, Michael, U Tx, 1980
Benjamin, James, Galien, Mi, 1974
Benkov, Edith, San Diego SU, 1986, 87, 88
Bennett, Alma, Kent SU, 1988
Bennett, Arthur, Ferris SC, 1986, 87
Bennett, Gerald, A SU-Mont, 1983
Bennett, Gretchen, San Jacinto C, 1983
Bennett, H. Stith, Colo Observations, Allenspark, 1988
Bennett, Maurice, U Md, 1981, 82, 83
Bennett, Richard, U Manitoba, 1984, 87
Bennett, Spencer, CRU 1971; 72, 73, U Va
Bennett, Stephanie, Albion C, 1973, 74
Bennett-Kastor, Tina, Wichita SU, 1983
Bensch, Christopher, Winterthur Mus, 1981
Bensen, Joe, U Mn, 1984
Bensick, Carol M., U Denver,1986
Bensman, Marvin, Memphis SU, 1977, 82
Benson, Edward, U RI, 1979
Benson, John, West Mi U, 1988
Benson, Josephine, Oh SU, 1984
Benson, LeGrace, Empire SC, 1982
Benson, Thomas, Pa SU, 1984
Benstock, Bernard, U Miami, Fl, 1987, 88
Bentley, Elizabeth, Toronto, 1988
Bentley, Patricia, SUNY-Plattsburg, 1987
Benton, Vera, Morris Brown C, 1977
Beran, Paul B., Stephen F. Austin U, 1979
Bercaw, Marv, Mystic Seaport, Ct, 1988
Berchan, Richard, U Ut, 1980
Bercik, Bill, BGSU, 1984, 85, 86
Berckman, Edward M., Ind SU, 1876, 77, 78, 79
Berg, Charles, Queens C, 1976, 77; 83, 85, 87, 88, U Kansas
Berg, Philip L., U Wisc-La Crosse, 1979, 82, 86, 88
Berg, Shelley, Hunter, 1988
Berge, Carol, U NM, 1979
Berger, Allen, Syracuse, 1983

Berger, Arthur, San Francisco SU, 1973, 74, 75, 76, 77
Berger, Helen, Boston U, 1987, 88
Berger, Roger, Nor. Caro SU, 1986
Berger, Roger A., Grand Valley SC, 1988
Berger, Vicki, E Caro U-Greenville, 1986, 87, 88
Bergin, James F., Praeger Publishers, 1975
Bergman, Eugene, Gallaudet C, 1981
Bergman, Herbert, Mich SU, 1971, 72
Bergoffen, Debra, Geo. Mason U, 1984
Berk, Lynn, Fl Int U, 1972, 73, 74
Berke, Jacqueline, Drew U, 1976, 77
Berkenbile, Suzi, Ok SU, 1978, 79
Berkhoff, Rick, New Buffalo, Mi, 1980
Berkove, Lawrence I. U Mich-Dearborn, 1980
Berland, Elaine, St. Louis, Mi, 1985
Berland, Jody, Trent U, 1984
Berle, Arnie, Mercy C, 1988
Berlowitz, Marvin, U Cin, 1973, 74
Berman, David, U Pitt, 1988
Berman, Jaye, Milwaukee, Wi, 1987
Berman, Jeffrey, SUNY-Albany, 1977
Bern, Nancy, Montclair SC, 1988
Bernier, Jacques, U de Laval, 1987
Bernier, Norman, Kent SU, 1982
Bernstein, Matthew, U Wisc, 1986
Berrettoni, Lynn, Rutgers, 1986
Berrey, Carol, U Ut, 1985; 88, Salt Lake Comm C
Berringan, Dennis, Madonna C, 1988
Berry, Jay, U Ia, 1984
Berry, John, U Houston-Downtown, 1988
Berry, Kenneth, Colo SU, 1976
Berry, Lemuel, Langston U, 1982, 83; 84, 85, 86, 87, Ala SU; 88, Mercy C
Berry, Mary F., U Md, 1973
Berte, Annie, Mercy C, 1988
Bertelsen, Lance, U Tx, 1987
Berthel, Leonard, Rutgers, 1981
Berthelot, J.A., USAF Acad, 1972
Berthold, Dennis, Tx A&M, 1980, 81, 82, 84, 87
Bertolotti, David S., GMI, Flint, 1979, 80, 81, 82, 83, 84, 85, 86, 87, 88
Bertrand, Michael, U SW La, 1988
Beseda, Robert, Wright SU, 1978, 79; 80, Riverside Corr Fac, Iona, Mi
Besner,Neil, Mt. Royal C, 1984, 87
Best, James, Kent SU, 1979
Best, Steve, U Chicago, 1987, 88
Bethel, Leonard, Rutgers, 1982, 83, 84, 85, 86, 87, 88
Betts, Raymond, U Ky, 1988
Betts, Richard, Pa SU, 1985, 88
Betz, Norman, Cent Mo SU, 1988
Betz, Renee, Cent Mo SU, 1988
Beutter, Randy, SW Ok SU, 1984
Beyers, Coralie, Ut SU, 1983, 86
Beymer, James, Duquesne, 1975
Bezner, Lili, Austin, Tx, 1987
Biamonte, Gloria, Amherst, Ma, 1988
Bick, Jane, Northeastern U, 1982
Bidle, Ken, Elmhurst C, 1979, 81
Biel, Michael, Morehead SU, 1983
Bienvenue, Rita, U Manitoba, 1987
Biernacki, Conrad, Toronto, 1985

Biesinger, Joseph, Eastern Ky U, 1979
Biesty, Patrick M, Cty C of Morris, NJ 1978
Bignall, John, Az SU, 1981, 82
Bigsby, C.W.E., U E Anglia, 1972
Billeaux, David, Pa SU, 1985, 86
Billson, Marc, Ok Baptist U, 1983
Bilsky, Nat, Evanston Tsp HS, 1981
Bindas, Kenneth, U Tol, 1986
Binderman, Murray, U Al-B'ham, 1978, 79, 81
Bingham, Jane M., Oakland U, Rochester, Mi, 1980
Binion, Rudolf, Brandeis, 1980
Biocca, Frank, U Wisc., 1985
Bird, Deborah, Lafayette C., 1984
Bird, Donald A., Cent Mi U, 1973, 74, 75, 76
Bird, Elizabeth, U Ia, 1986
Bird, Laura, Ft. Benning, Ga., 1988
Bird, Roy, Washburn U, 1983, 85
Birdwell, Christine, Mich SU, 1984, 86, 88
Birdwhistell, Terry, U Ky, 1982
Birg, Laura, St. Xavier C., Chicago, 1985, 86, 87
Birkman, Marlene Ann, Webster C, 1978, 79
Birtha, Rachel, US Int'l Comm Agency, 1982
Birx, H. James, Canisiuis C, 1988
Bishop, Jay, U Alta, 1984
Bishop, Nadean, E Mi U, 1980
Bishoff, Robert, N Adams SU, 1982
Bishop, Barbara, U Louisville, 1982
Bishop, Norma, Pa SU, 1982
Bisignano, Dominic, Ind U-Indianapolis, 1985
Bitgood, Stephen, Jacksonville SU, 1984, 86
Bittner, James W., U Nor Ia, 1978, 79, 80, 82
Bizot, Richard, U Nor Fl, 1978
Bjarkman, Peter, Purdue, 1981
Bjorklund, Edith M., U Wisc-Milwa, 1974, 87, 88
Black, Jay, BGSU, 1972
Black, Ronald, McKendree C, 1988
Blackburn, Kern, Temple, 1977
Blackmon, Richard, U Sou Fl, 1987
Blackstone, Sarah, U Cent Ark, 1986
Blackwell, Charles, U Ala-B'ham, 1988
Blackwood, Roy E., Bemidji SU, 1986
Blaha, Franz G., U Neb, 1981, 82, 84
Blain, Jackie, U Tx, 1986
Blake, Cece, Long Beach, NY, 1988
Blake, Fay M., UC-Berkeley, j1980
Blake, Joseph, Ind U-Richmond, 1985
Blake, Susan, Lafayette C, 1987
Blake, William, Va Comm U, 1980
Blakely, Helen, John A. Logan C,1971
Blanch, Robert, NE U, 1987, 88
Blanchard, Dallas, U W Fl, 1986
Blanchette, Jean-Francois, Nat'l Mus of Man, Ottawa, 1984
Blankenship, Jane, U Mass, 1985
Blansfield, Karen, Greenville, SC,1981
Blasdel, Gregg, Winooski, Vt, 1984
Blaser, Kent, Wayne SU, 1983

Blatt, Gloria, Oakland U, Lansing, Mi, 1983

Blatt, Linda Anne, Ames, La, 1985

Blavney, Michael, Wayne SU, 1981

Blesch, Edwin J., Nassau Comm C, Garden City, NY, 1986, 87

Blicksilver, Edith, Ga Inst Tech, 1986

Bliss, Carolyn, Radford C, 1985

Bloch, Beverlee, U Denver, 1987, 88

Block, Joel, U Neb-Omaha, 1983, 84

Block, Kenneth, Northwestern, 1978

Blodgett, E.D., U Alta, 1984

Bloemer, William, Sangamon SU, 1978

Blomgren, Fred, Rochester, NY, 1984

Bloodworth, William, E Car U., 1978, 79

Bloom, Lynn Z., Washington U, 1973, 74; 79, W&M

Bloomquist, Jane, Chicago, Il, 1988

Blosser, Betsy, U Il, 1985

Blue, Mary, Loyola U, New Orleans, 1986, 87

Bluestein, Gene, CSU-Fresno, 1973, 84

Blum, Alan, NY St Journal of Medicine, 1985

Blumenberg, Richard, Sou Il U, 1982

Blum-West, Steve, Radford, 1981

Bluthardt, Robert F., 1982

Blythe, Hal, E Ky U, 1978, 81, 82, 85

Bobick, Bruce, W Ga C, 1980

Bockman, Guy, Tn SU, 1986

Boddinger-De Uriate, Cristina, Sommervile, Ma, 1985

Bode, Carl, U Md., 1971, 72, 73, 74, 75, 76, 77, 78, 79, 80, 81, 82, 83

Bodenhamer, David, U Sou Miss, 1988

Bodmer, George, Il SU, 1982

Bodzick, Joseph, U Minn, 1986

Boe, David, U Toronto, 1984

Bogan, James, U Mo-Rolla, 1984

Bogardus, Ralph F., U Al, 1977, 78

Bogart, Herbert, Kalamazoo C, 1976

Bogdan, Deanne, Ontario Inst for Studies in Educ, 1984

Boger, David, N Tx SU, 1983

Boggs, Carl, Los Angeles, Ca, 1986

Boggs, Joseph, W Ky U, 1983, 87

Bognar, Bela J., Wright SU, 1977, 78

Bogstad, Janice, U Wisc-River Falls, 1987, 88

Bohn, Thomas W., U Evansville, 1977, 78; 79, 80, U Tulsa

Bohne, William, Norbert C., Depere, Wisc, 1978

Bohnet, Barron, Nat'l Park Service, Phila, 1981

Bokeno, Michael, UNC-Charlotte, 1986

Boles, Jacqueline, Ga SU, 1975, 80

Bolhafner, Stephen, BGSU

Boligioni, Pierre, U Montreal, 1976

Bolland, O. Nigel, Colgate, 1984

Bolton, Richard, Morehead SU, 1984, 85

Bolton, W.F., Princeton, NJ, 1987

Boly, John R., Dartmouth, 1979

Bomert, Roger, SW Ok SU, 1983

Bond, Fred, Fisk, 1973

Bond, Hallie, Newark, De, 1983

Bond, Ronald, U Calgary, 1984

Bone, Martha, E Cumberland U, 1988

Boney, Nash, U Ga, 1975, 77, 86

Bonfiglio, Thomas, U Richmond, 1986

Bonham, Julia, NCSU, Raleigh, 1984

Boone, Garret, Earlham, 1979

Booth, Bill, Morehead SU, 1982, 83

Bordewyk, Gordon, Temple, 1980

Bordinat, Philip, W VA U., 1971

Bordue, David, U Il., 1988

Borgh, Enola, U Wisc-Milwaukee, 1975

Borgman, Paul, Northwestern Coll, Orange City, NJ, 1978, 79

Boring, Phyllis, Rutgers, 1976, 77

Boris, Eileen, Newberry Library, 1976

Boris, Harold, Tufts Med Center, 1971

Borish, Linda, U Md, 1985, 86

Born, John Dewey, Jr., Wichita SU, 1973, 83, 84

Borne, Lawrence, N Ky U, 1985

Bornstein, Daniel, U Chicago, 1977

Bortner, M.A., Az SU, 1987

Boruszkowski, Lilly, S Il U, 1984, 85, 86, 88

Borzoi, Mark, Marshall U, 1985, 87

Bosch, M. V., Dordt C, 1981

Boskin, Joseph, Boston U, 1971

Boss, Judith, U Neb-Omaha, 1981, 87

Bossert, Rex, Stanford, 1987

Boswell, Ron, U Ark-Little Rock, 1988

Botjer, George, Tampa, Fl, 1984

Botscharow, Lucy, NE Il U, 1982, 87, 88

Botterill, T. David, Tx A&M, 1985

Boudreau, Raoul, U de Moncton, Moncton, N.B, 1987

Boughter, Carol, Bloomsburg Theatre, Ensemble, Pa, 1980

Boulanger, Lisa M. SUNY Agri & Tech C, 1978

Boulding, J. Russell, Bloomington, In, 1982

Bouraoui, H. A., York U, Toronto, 1973, 75

Bourdette, Roibert, UNO, 1987

Bourque, David, U SW La, 1988

Bowden, Betsy, Pa SU, 1981

Bowen, Joanne, Col Williamsburg, 1984

Bowers, Bege Kaye, Youngstown SU, 1985, 88

Bowers, Gerald, Williamette U, 1986

Bowers, Lanny, Morristown C, 1979

Bowker, Joan, Council on Social Work Educ, NYC, 1983

Bowker, Larsen, Va Tech U, 1975

Bowles, Stephen, U Miami, Fl., 1977

Bowman, Barbara, Il Wesleyan U, 1978, 79, 80, 81

Bowman, David, Memphis SU, 1974

Bowman, Robert, Willowdale, Ont., 1988

Boyanoski, Christine, Art Gallery of Ontario, Toronto, 1987

Boyce, Debby, Defiance C., 1982

Boyd, Herb, Strasta Music Corp, Detroit, 1971

Boyd, Masry K., U Mo-Rolla, 1983, 84, 86

Boyd, Robert, St. Louis Comm C, 1983

Boyd, Veleda, Tarleton SU, 1988

Boyd, Zelda, CSU-Hayward, 1984

Boyden, Rachel, Marlboro C, 1987

Boyer, David, Marietta C, 1986

Boyer, H. Jeffrey, U Al-Huntsville, 1981

Boylan, James, MIT, Amherst, Ma, 1982

Boylan, Jay, Chapman C, 1987

Boyle, Milton, Bridgewater SC, 1988

Bozdech, James, U Dayton, 1972

Bozich, Stephen J., U Ia, 1976

Brackman, Barbara, Kansas Grassroots Art Assoc., Lawrence, 1983

Bracy, James, CSU-Northridge, 1988

Braden, Robert, Va Tech, 1984

Bradford, Bruce, Stetson U, 1978

Bradford, Mary, Lafayette C, 1975

Bradford, William, U Puerto Rico, 1987

Bradlee, M.A., Ind U, 1988

Bradley, Burton, SUNY-Stony Brook, 1984; 85, SUNY-Long Island; 88, Northwest Comm C, Powell, Wy

Bradley, Jerry, New Mex Inst of Mining & Tech, 1988

Bradshaw, David, Warren Wilson C, 1987

Brady, Kathleen, U Minn, 1983, 87

Brady, Laura, U Minn, 1987, 88

Braendlin, Bonnie Hoover, Tallahassee, Fl, 1979

Bragg, Bernard, Gallaudet C, 1981

Bragg, Linda Brown, U NC-Greensboro, 1978

Braham, Jeanne, Alleg C, 1986, 88

Brainard, Karen, Lansing, MI, 1985

Brainard, Owen, Mich SU, 1984

Braithwaite, William, Loyola U, Chicago, 1987

Brake, Robert, Il SU, 1978, 1980

Brakhage, Pamela, U Neb, 1983

Branch, Edgar M., Miami U, Oh, 1975

Brandimarte, Cynthia, Harris Cty Hist Soc, Houston, 1985

Brandt, Gail, Glendon C, Toronto, 1986

Brandt, Lawrence R., U Wisc-Steven Point, 1976

Brandt, Thompson, Jamestown C, 1987, 88

Branham, Robert, Bates C.

Branscomb, Jack, E Tn SU, 1978, 85, 87

Brant, Billy G., Friends U

Brantley, John, Trinity U, 1983

Branz, Nedra, Sou Il U-Edwardsville, 1981, 83

Brasaemle, Ruth, Munster HS, Ind, 1981, 82

Brasch, Ila, Oh U, 1973

Brasch, Walter, Oh U, 1973; 75, Temple; 84, Bloomsburg U

Brasfield, Alice, U New Mex, 1985

Brashear, Lucy, Appal SC, 1981

Brasseaux, Carl, U SW La, 1988

Braswell, Laurel, McMaster U, 1984

Braswell, Mary, U Ala-B'ham, 1986

Bratt, James, U Pitt, 1985

Bratzel, John, Mich SU, 1985, 87

Braude, Elton, Woodside, NY, 1984

Brauer, Ralph, BGSU, 1977, 78

Braun, John, Gustavus Adolphus C, 1984

Braunlein, John H., Hist. Soc of De, 1976, 82; 84, Rockwood Mus., Wilmington, De.

Braunstein, Susan, Fl Inst of Tech, 1986

Bravard, Robert, Lock Haven SU, 1987

Bravo-Elizando, Pedra, Wichita SU, 1983

Bray, Mary K., Wilmington C, 1983

Bray, Robert, E Tn SU, 1987
Bravere, Doinna, Il SU-Normal, 1984
Brazil, John, San Jose SU, 1982
Brebach, Emily, Tx Tech, 1978
Bredahl, A. Carl, Jr., U Fl, 1978, 86, 88
Brede, Richard, Kans SU, 1984, 85
Breeden, James, Sou Methodist U, 1986
Breen, Myles, Nor Il U, 1983
Bregman, Lucy, Ind U, 1973; 78, Temple
Bremseth, Anita, Tupelo, Ms, 1985;
    86, U Miss
Brenden, David, Purdue, 1981
Brengle, Richard, Ind U-Southeast, 1980
Breslin, Carol, Perkasie, Pa, 1987
Bressler, Charles, Houghton C, 1987
Breuer, Hans-Peter, U De, 1988
Brewer, Nadine, Drake U, 1984;
    85, Pueblo, Co
Brewer, Rebecca, Oh SU, 1988
Brewer, Wanda, U N Colo, 1988
Brewster, Anne, U Adelaide, South
    Australia, 1980
Bridge, Mary, U S Me, 1987
Bridges, John, BGSU, 1980; 1982, Notre
    Dame; 1986, U Central Fl
Bridges, Patricia, Grand Valley SC, 1988
Bridges, Phyllis, Tx Woman's U, 1986, 88
Briere, Eloise, SUNY-Albany, 1987
Briggs, Olin, Northlake C, 1983, 84
Brigham, William, Nat'l U, San Diego,
    Ca, 1988
Bright, Brenda, Austin, Tx, 1985;
    87, Brown U
Bright, Lewis, Humboldt SU, 1987, 88
Brigman, William E., U Houston, 1982, 83;
    84, 85, 86, 87, 88, U Houston
Briley, Ron, LSandia Prepatory School,
    Albuquerque, NM, 1986
Brinkley, Douglas, Georgetown U, 1984
Brinkley, Tony, U Me, 1988
Briscoe, Mary Louise, U Pitt, 1973
Brits, John, Ind U, 1971
Britt, John, Lee C, 1983
Brittin, Norman A., Auburn U, 1983
Brittin, Ruth, Auburn U, 1980
Broach, Glen, Winthrop C, 1988
Broadhead, Glenn J., Ia SU, 1983
Broadus, Dorothy, U Louisville, 1985
Brobston, Stanley, Brentwood, NY, 1980
Brock, D. Heyward, U De, 1979
Brockington, Celeste, Aikan Tech C, 1987
Brockington, William, U S Carolina, 1987,
    88
Brockmann, Stephen, U Wisc, 1985
Brode, Douglas, Onondaga Comm C, 1984,
    88
Broderick, Rick, Duke, 1988
Brodherson, David, Ithaca, NY, 1986
Brodsky, Allyn, West Coast U, 1988
Brodwin, Stanley, Hofstra, 1987
Broe, Mary Lynn, SUNY-Binghamton,
    1979,
    80; 87, 88, Grinnell C
Broege, Valerie, U Western Ontario, 1973,
    74; 75, 76, 77, 78, 79, 80, 81, 82, 83,
    84, 85, 86, 87, 87, Vanier C, Montreal
Broer, Lawrence R., U S Fl, 1977, 86, 87,
    88
Bromberg, Pamela, Simmons, 1988

Bromley, John, U N Colo, 1988
Bromley, Susan, U N Colo, 1988
Bronner, Stephen, Rutgers, 1987
Bronstein, Eva, U New Haven, 1985
Brook, David, Historic Pres Program & Oh
    Hist Soc, 1979
Brookes, Philip J., U Kans, 1975
Brooks, Ann, Edison C, 1988
Brooks, Barbara, McGill U, 1988
Brooks, Christopher, U Tx, 1984
Brooks, David, Jefferson Comm C,
    U of Ky, 1979, 82
Brooks, Diana, J. Sargeant Reynolds
    Comm C, Richmond, Va, 1979
Brooks, John B., U Wisc-Oshkosh, 1974
Brooks, Richard, Vt Law School, 1986
Brooks, Robert, U S Fl, 1975, 76
Brooks, Robert, Northwestern, 1974
Brophy, Robert, CSU-Long Beach, 1988
Brown, Ben, U S Fl, 1977
Brown, Burton G., U RI, 1976
Brown, Charles, Saginaw Val SC, 1987
Brown, Craig E., Manhattan, KS, 1983
Brown, Delindus, U Fl, 1977
Brown, Denise Scott, Yale, 1971, 73
Brown, Ernest Crogan, SUNY-Buffalo,
    1981
Brown, Gwen, Auburn-Montgomery, 1988
Brown, Irby, U Richmond, 1980
Brown, James L., Kansas City Comm C,
    1983
Brown, Janet, U Hartford, 1980, 84
Brown, Julie, U Ut, 1988
Brown, Kent R., U Ark, 1976, 77, 78
Brown, Lee R., U Ut, 1986
Brown, Linda G., Wright SU, 1984, 85;
    86 87, Oh SU
Brown, Lisa, Tn Tech, 1985
Brown, Lloyd, U S C, 1975
Brown, Lynda, Auburn-Montgomery, 1978
Brown, Maurice F., Oakland U, 1975
Brown, Mavis, U Richmond, 1988
Brown, May, Ga Inst. Tech, 1978
Brown, Oscar Jr., Author Destination
    Freedom, 1976
Brown, Pearl, Quinnipiac C, 1988
Brown, Peter, U Winnipeg, 1988
Brown, Robert, U De, 1982
Brown, Russell, Scarborough C, U
    Toronto,
    1978, 84
Brown, Susan S., Clemson, 1978
Brown, V.J. Shepards C., 1988
Brown, Velma, BGSU, 1979, 81
Brown, William, U Md-Catonsville, 1984
Brown, William R., Phil C Textiles, 1985,
    88
Browne, Denis, U Va, 1980
Browne, Glenn, U Minn, 1987, 88
Browne, Kevin, Green Springs, Wi, 1988
Browne, Nick, UCLA, 1982
Browne, Pat, BGSU, 1977, 82, 88
Browne, Ray B., BGSU, 1971, 72, 73, 74,
    75,
    76, 77, 78, 79, 80, 81, 82, 83, 84, 85,
    86, 87, 88
Browner, Carole, Wayne SU, 1980
Browning, Gordon, E Ky U, 1978
Brown-Manrique, Gerardo, U Ok, 1978

Broyles-Gonzalez, Yolando, UC-Santa
    Barbara, 1988
Brubaker, Lowell, Tn Wesleyan C, 1983
Bruce, Charles, Tx Women's U, 1986
Bruce, D.D., Jr., UC-Irvine, 1976
Bruce, Douglas R., Carnegie-Mellon, 1979
Bruce-Novoa, Juan, Yale, 1977, 78, 79
Bruck, Peter A., Carleton U., Ottawa
Brucker, Barbara, Mansfield News-
    Journal,
    Oh, 1980
Brucker, Carl W., Jamestown C, 1983
Bruder, C. Harry, U. SW La, 1977, 78,
    79, 83, 86
Brune, Les M, Bradley U, 1978
Brungardt, Maurice, Loyola, New Orleans,
    1988
Bryan, David, SUNY-Buffalo, 1984
Bryant, Jennings, U Mass., 1977, 78
Bryant, John, Widener C, 1979;
Bryant, Kathleen, Mich SU, 1979, 80
    86, Pa SU-Sharon
Bryant, Robert, Georgetown C,
    Georgetown,
    Ky, 1988
Bryce, Lynn, St. Cloud SU, 1980
Bryski, Bruce, Pa SU, 1982
Buchanan, Roberta, Beaver Comm C, 1973;
    1986, 87, 88, Mem U Newfoundland
Buchanan, Ron, Auburn-Montgomery,
    1988
Buchanan, Singer, Purdue, 1971
Buchheit, Robert, Morningside C, 1983
Buck, David D., U Wisc-Milwaukee, 1974
Buck, Janet, Ok SU, 1979, 80
Buckeye, Bob, Middlebury C, 1974
Buckland, Roscoe, W Wash U, 1980, 82
Buckley, Bruce, Cooperstown, NY, 1984
Buckley, James, U Mich, 1985
Buckner, Reginald, U Minn, 1984
Buckness, Barbara J., Brock U, 1978
Bucuvalas, Tina, Ind U, 1984
Budd, Louis, Duke, 1971, 72, 73, 74, 75,
    76, 77, 78, 80, 81, 82, 84, 85. 86. 87
Budge, Alice, Youngstown SU, 1980, 84,
    86, 88
Buffaloehead, Roger, U Minn, 1971
Butwack, Mary A., Colgate, 1980
Buheiry, Marwan, Amer U, Beirut, 1982,
    84
Buhle, Paul, Ed Radical America,
    Bronxville, NY, 1974
Bukoski, Anthony, U Minn-Duluth, 1982
Bulger, Petty, Fl Folklife Program,
    White Springs, 1985
Bullard, Susan, E Tx SU, 1983
Bullock-Cormier, Barbara, Los Angeles,
    Ca, 1986
Bullough, Vern, SUNY-Buffalo, 1986
Bulow, Ernest, U Ut, 1973
Bunch, Lonnie, Packer Inst, Brooklyn,
    NY, 1982
Bundgaard, Axel, St. Olaf C, 1986
Bunge, Nancy, Mich SU, 1984, 85
Bunkers, Suzanne, Mankato SU, 1986
Burcaw, Ellis, U Id Museum, 1978
Burch, Beth, Purdue, 1983
Burch, Jeanne S., George Mason U, 1981;
    82, 83, Oakton, Va

Burch, Paul, Purdue, 1983
Burch, Susan, Long Beach, CA, 1987
Burd, Gene, U Tx, 1983, 85, 86, 88
Burdick, Frank, SUNY-Cortland, 1979
Burdick, Walter, Elmhurst C, 1981
Burdison, Evonne, Ind SU, 1982
Burelbach, Frederick M, SUNY-Brockport, 1981
Burg, Judith, U Mass, 1983
Burge, Nancy, Mich SU, 1976
Burger, Douglas, U Colo, 1981
Burgess, C.F., VMI, 1983
Burggraf, David, Oh U, 1975
Burgoon, Michael, Mich SU, 1983
Burgoyne, Robert, Wayne SU, 1984
Burian, Grayce C., Schenectady Cty Comm C, 1978
Burkart, Arnold, Ball SU, 1985, 87
Burke, Catherine, Marlboro C, 1986
Burke, James Lee, Wichita SU, 1988
Burke, Martin, U Mich, 1985
Burke, Richard C., U Il, 1980
Burke, William, U Lowell, 1978, 88
Burkhardt, Jeff, U Ky, 1982
Burley, David, U Winnipeg, 1987
Burne, Glenn S., UNC-Charlotte, 1980, 84, 86
Burneko, Grace, UNC-Asheville, 1987
Burneko, Guy, Mohawk Val Comm C, 1985;
86, UNC-Asheville
Burnette, R.V., Fl SU, 1986, 87
Burnette, Rick, Old Dom U, 1988
Burnham, Christopher, N Mex U, Las Cruces, 1983
Burns, Alyson, UC-Davis, 1987
Burns, Dan, Ok SU, 1975, 77
Burns, G. Frank, Tn Tech U, 1986
Burns, Gary, U Mo, St. Louis, 1982, 83; 84, Northwestern;
85, 86, 87, 88, U Mo., St. Louis
Burns, Gerald, Wesleyan, 1988
Burns, Landon, Pa SU-Media, 1985, 86, 87
Burns, Lois, U Ark-Little Rock, 1977, 78
Burns, London, Pa SU-Delaware, 1984
Burns, Rex, U Colo-Denver, 1977
Burns, Shannon, U Ark, 1978
Burnstein, Lewis, Children's TV Workshop, PBS, 1978
Burrell, Ralph, Omaha, Ne, 1983
Burress, Lee, U Wisc-Stevens Pt, 1976
Burri, Michael, U Pa, 1988
Burrison, William, Phila, 1979
Burrows, Richard, Oh SU, 1985
Burroughs, Sylvia, Thomas Hunt Morgan Inst of Genetics, 1985
Bust, David J., Francis Marion C, 1975, 78, 88
Burton, Carmen, U S Fl, 1986
Burton, C. Emory, McMurry C, 1985
Burton, Frederick, Oh SU, 1982
Burton, Judith, U Tx, 1986
Burton, Linda, U Tn, 1980
Burton, Tom, E Tn SU, 1984, 85, 87
Burtrym, Alexander, Seton Hall U, 1982

Burzle, Toni, U Kans, 1983
Busby, Linda J., Ia SU, 1976
Busch, Briton, Colgate, 1984
Bush, Gregory, U Miami, Fl, 1984, 85, 87
Bush, Grey, Stephens Inst Tech, 1982
Bush, Terry, Il SU-Normal, 1984
Bushnell, John, Rutgers, 1987
Busia, Abena, Rutgers, 1982, 84, 85, 86, 87
Bussey, Charles, W Ky U, 1982, 83, 87
Butchart, Ronald, SUNY-Cortland, 1983
Butcher, Daniel L., LSU, 1987
Butler, Gary, Mem U Newfoundland, 1984
Butler, Jerry, U Ark, 1986
Butler, R.W., U W Ont, 1984
Butler-Wallin, Carole, LSU, 1987
Butler-Young, Sandra, Hudson Heights, PQ, Can.
Butrym, Alexander, Seton Hall U., 1983
Butsch, Richard, Rider C, 1977, 78, 79, 87
Butt, Paul L., BGSU, 1976
Butte, George, Colo C, 1987
Button, Marilyn, Lincoln U., Pa, 1986, 87
Buxton, Rodney A., U Tx, 1987
Buzzard, Karen, Northeastern U, 1986, 87
Byerman, Keith, Ind SU, 1987
Byers, Marianne, Corom, Ky, 1987
Byers, Reid, Maplewood, NJ, 1985
Byers, Thomas, Calhoun Comm C, U Ky 1979;
82, 84, 85
Byler, Bob, BGSU, 1984, 85, 86, 87
Byrd, Caroline, St. Mary's U, San Antonio, 1987
Byrd, Deborah, Lafayette C, 1985
Byrd, Forrest M., U SW La, 1976, 77, 78, 83, 86
Byrne, Ann, U RI, 1977, 78
Byrne, Edmund, IU-PUI, 1980, 81, 82, 84; 85, Ind U
Byrne, John, Il Benedictine, 1980
Byrne, Kevin, Gustavus Adolphus C, 1987
Byrum, C. Stephen, Chattanooga S Tech Comm C, 1978, 79, 80
Byrum, Henri Sue, U Sou Al, 1984
Bytwerk, Randall L., Sou Il U, 1976

Cabot, Jerri, Oh U, 1984
Cadegan, Una M., U Pa, 1986
Caesar, Terry, Clarion U, 1987, 88
Cafagna, Beth, Mich SU, 1971
Cage, Timothy, LSU, 1987, 88
Cagnon, Maurice, Montclair SC, 1975
Cahill, Dan, U Nor Ia, 1983
Cain, Michael Scott, Catonsville Comm S, Md, 1976
Caine, Robert, Columbus C, Ga, 1983
Caits, Bill, NYC, 1985
Caldwell, George, Wash SU, 1985, 87, 88
Caldwell, Harry B., Trinity U, San Antonio, Tx, 1977
Caldwell, Larry, Peru SC, NC, 1987, 88
Caldwell, Patrice, Eastern NM SU, 1983
Calhoun(-)French, Diane, U Louisville, 1981;
85, 86, 87, 88, Jefferson Comm C
Calhoun, Mary, Fl SU, 1986
Calhoun, Thomas, W Ky U, 1985
Calkins, Charles F., Carroll C, 1976
Callaghan, Michael, CINQ-FM, 1987

Callahan, Fay, U Mo-Kansas City, 1984, 85, 86
Callahan, Kathy, Kutztown U, 1987
Callahan, Patrick, 1973
Callahan, Raymond A., U De, 1977
Calloway, Catherine, U Ark, 1985, 86, 87, 88
Calvert, Kenneth, Methodist C, 1986
Calvin, William, Ill SU-Normal, 1981
Camacho, Paul, U Mass, 1987
Cameron, Charles, Sou Ore SC, 1980
Cameron, Sr. Marie Francesca, St. Catherine C, Ky, 1985
Cameron, William, U S Fl, 1984
Camfield, Marvin A., Walters St. Comm C, 1978
Camita, Tony, WXYZ, Detroit, 1980
Camp, Charles, Md Arts Council, Balti, 1977
Camp, Henry, Kans S U, Manhattan, 1984, 85, 86
Camp, Jocelyn, NYC, 1986
Campbell, Deborah, W Va U, 1986
Campbell, Donald, Carlisle, Pa, 1978
Campbell, Dowling, N Az U, 1986, 87
Campbell, Felicia, U Ne-Las Vegas, 1976, 79
Campbell, George, E Ky U, 1987
Campbell, James, U Ky, 1982
Campbell, Jane, Purdue-Hammond, 1985
Campbell, Josie, Pa SU, 1975; 76, 77, 78, 79, 80, 81, 82, 83, 84, 85, 86, 87, 88, U RI
Campbell, Kathleen, BGSU, 1980, 87, 88
Campbell, Lee, Greencastle, Pa, 1987
Campbell, Marie, Mt. St. Mary's C, 1975, 76, 77, 78, 79, 80, 81, 82, 83, 84, 85, 86, 87, 88
Campbell, Mary B., Boston U, 1982, 83, 84, 85; 86, Columbia U; 87, 88, Harvard
Campbell, Michael, Ok Baptist U, 1982
Campbell, Phillip, U Minn-Duluth
Campbell, Richard, U Wisc-Milwaukee, 1980; 81, Northwestern
Campbell, Roy, Southwest Mo SU, 1979, 80
Campbelle, Anne, U Ky, 1982
Campion, Kathleen, U NM, 1988
Canaan, Joyce, U Chicago, 1983, 84, 85
Canary, Robert H, Ed. CLIO, U Wisc -Parkside, 1975
Candido, Anne, U Ark, 1986
Caney, Arlene, Comm C Phila, 1987, 88
Canfield, John, USAF Acad, 1987, 88
Cann, Marvin, Lander C, 1987, 88
Cannistraro, Philip, Drexel U, 1985
Cannizzo, Jeanne, U Western Ontario, 1984
Cannon, Jamie, St. Louis, Mo, 1982
Canter, Louis, IU-PUI-Fort Wayne, 1978
Cantu, Roberto, CSU-LA, 1977
Capllan, Richard E., U Akron, 1983, 84, 85, 86
Caputi, Jane, BGSU, 1980, 81, 82; 83, 84, 85, U New Mexico
Carafano, James, US Mil Acad, 1987
Caraher, Brian, East Il U-Charleston, 1982

Carbone, Richard, Hayward, Ca, 1975
Card, James, Old Dom U, 1978, 79, 82, 83, 85, 87
Cardenas, Anthony, Wich SU, 1983
Candido, Anne M., Fayetteville Ark, 1987
Cardoza-Freeman, Inez, Oh SU, 1985
Cardoza, Thomas, Purdue, 1973; 74, 76, Stockton SC
Carello, Sebastian G., BGSU, 1975
Cargan, Leonard, Wright SU, 1983, 84
Carillo, Loretta, Clemson, 1981
Carlisle, Barbara, E Mich U, 1976
Carlisle, Carlos, Nor Az U, 1973
Carlisle, John C., Purdue, 1976, 84
Carlisle, Patricia, Purdue-NW Campus, 1984
Carlisle, Susan, Boston U, 1983, 84
Carlson, Alvar, BGSU, 1976, 77, 78, 79, 80, 81, 82, 84, 85, 87
Carlson, Carl, N Shore Comm C, Mass, 1978
Carlson, David, Springfield Coll, Mass, 1982
Carlson, Ingeborg L., Az SU, 1976
Carlson, John F., Kent SU, 1987
Carlson, Lewis H., W Mich U, 1972, 74, 75, 78, 80, 81, 82, 84, 85
Carlson, Norm, W Mich, 1974
Carlson, Patricia Ann, Rose-Holman Inst Tech, 1979, 80, 81, 82, 83, 84, 85, 86, 87, 88
Carlson, Paul, Tx Lutheran C, 1983
Carlson, Shirley, 1985
Carlson, Thomas, Memphis SU, 1987, 88
Carlson, Victoria, Pa SU, 1984
Carlson, W.B. Rutgers, 1983; 84, Mich Tech Inst
Carlton-Smith, Kimn, Rutgers, 1986
Carmean, Karen, Converse C, 1987, 88
Carmody, Denise, Wich SU, 1983
Carmody, John, Wich SU, 1983
Carnes, R.L. Roosevelt U, Chicago, 1975, 76
Carnes, Valerie, Roosevelt U, Chicago, 1975,76
Carney, Jo E., Pennington, NJ, 1984
Caroll, Mary, Appal SU, 1985
Carollo, Frank, BGSU, 1980
Caron, James, U Hawaii-Manoa, 1985
Carpenter, Carole, York U, Ont, 1984, 87
Carpenter, Lynette, U Cin, 1982
Carpenter, Stanley, Ga Tech, 1982
Carpenter, Theresa, W Ky U, 1986
Carper, Steve, Fairport, NY, 1984
Carr, Douglas, St.Bonaventure U, 1987, 88
Carr, Glynnis, Oh SU, 1987, 88
Carr, Jean Ferguson, Carnegie-Mellon, 1979
Carr, Laura E., Oradell, NJ, 1987
Carr, Mary, Gonzaga U, 1986, 87
Carranza, Miguel, U Neb, 1984
Carringer, Robert, U Il, 1982
Carrington, Ruth, Nat'l Gerontology Resource Center, 1984
Carroll, John, Lamar U, 1984
Carroll, Mary, Appal, SU, 1984
Carroll, Ray, U Ala, 1988
Carruthers, Guy, Chevron USA, SF, 1982

Carson, Diane, St. Louis Comm C Mo, 1986
Carson, Herb, Ferris SC, 1971
Carson, John, Kent SU, 1986, 87, 88
Carson, Sharon, Kent SU, 1985, 87, 88
Carter, Allan, C Du Page, Il., 1973, 79, 85
Carter, Dave, U S Fl, 1987
Carter, Dave, Dodge City Comm C, Ks, 1983
Carter, Douglas, Va Western Comm C, 1982, 84, 85, 86, 87, 88
Carter, Iri, U Minn-Duluth, 1983
Carter, Steven, U No Caro-Wilmington, 1976, 78, 79, 80; 82 Wilmington, N.C.
Carter, Virginia, Tandem Productions, LA, 1975
Cartland, Barbara, U Minn-Morris, 1982
Cartledge, Connie, UNC, 1986
Cartwright,Donald G., U Western Ont, 1984, 87
Caruso, Barbara, Earlham, 1981
Carvalho, Roger, Kans Newman C, 1983
Carver, Ann, UNC-Charlotte, 1984
Carveth, Rod, U Mass., 1980; 1981, Hampshire C; 82, U Ct; 83, 84, Cleveland S U; 85, John Carroll; 86, U Hartford; 87, 88
Carville, Caroline, U Ark, 1986
Cary, Emily P., 1987
Cary, John, Cleveland SU, 1987
Cary, Michael, Lock Haven U, 1987
Case, Carole, N Mex SU, 1984
Case, Charles, Riverside Church, NYC, 1983
Casebeer, Edwin, IU-PUI, 1973, 81
Casella, Donna, Mankato SU, 1987, 88
Casella, Frank, SUNY-Oswego, 1973
Casella, Kathleen J., SUNY-Oswego, 1973
Casella-Kern, Donna, Gustavus Adolphus C, 1982, 83, 84; 85, 86, Mankato SU
Casey, Daniel, SUNY-Oneonta, 1987
Casey, Edward, SUNY-Stonybrook, 1982
Casey, Ellen Miller, U Scranton, 1976
Cashdan, Sonya, E Tn SU, 1987, 88
Cashill, John R., Purdue, 1974
Casillas, Rex, Pa SU-Erie, 1986, 87, 88
Cassata, Mary, SUNY-Buffalo, 1980
Cassidy, Keith, U Guelph, 1986
Cassidy, Lawrence, St. Peter's C, 1980
Cassidy, Marsha, U Il-Chi Circle, 1982, 83
Cassorla, Albert, Phila, 1976
Castagna, Jo Ann, U Ia, 1981
Castelli, Charles D., Lehman C, CUNY
Castille, Philip, U Houston-Downtown, 1987, 88
Castleman, Craig, Kingsborough Comm C, Brooklyn, 1987
Castillo, Ana, Santa Clara U
Caswell, Lucy S., Oh SU, 1980
Cathey, Le Conte, U S Carolina, 1985
Catt, Isac, CSU-Chico, 1986
Caudill, Helen, Norwich U
Caughey, John L., U Md
Causley, Fred, Ok SU, 1983
Cavanagh, Richard, Carlton U, Ottawa
Cavanaugh, Clare, Harvard, 1986
Cawelti, John, U Chicago, 1971, 72, 73, 74, 75, 76, 77, 86
Cawelti, Mary, U Ky, 1986
Cayton, Andrew, Ball SU, 1983

Cebollero, Blanca, Emerson, 1987, 88
Cella, Charles R., Murray SU, 1979, 80, 81, 82, 83, 88
Cernek, Stephen, Colby-Sawyer C, 1981
Cerney, Ed., U S Carolina, 1985
Cerniglia, Alice, Ann Arbor, Mi, 1987, 88
Cerwek, Stephen, Ball SU, 1978
Chadwick, Robert, John Abbot C, St. Anne, Que.
Chai, Nemia, Columbus C, 1987
Chalfen, Richard, Temple, 1980, 82
Chalfont, Donald, Ga SU, 1986
Chalfont, Fran, W Ga C, 1986
Chalmers, David, U Fl, 1984
Chamberlain, Gordon, Ore SU, 1985
Chamberlain, William, Mich SU, 1986
Chambers, Bruce, Berry-Hill Galleries, Inc., NYC
Chambers, Jean, Purdue-Hammond, 1987, 88
Chambers, Raymond, Bainbridge JC, Ga, 1983
Champion, Brian, U Alberta
Champion, Dean, U Tn, 1985
Champion, E. A., BGSU, 1972, 75
Chapman, Edgar L., Bradley U, 1976, 77, 78, 79, 80
Chapman, Richard, Aurora, NY, 1987
Charba, Frank, Wichita SU, 1980
Charles, Jeffrey, Sweet Briar C, 1987, 88
Charney, Hanna, CUNY, 1981
Charney, Mark, Clemson, 1987, 88
Charney, Maurice, Rutgers, 1979, 81, 84
Charney, Wayne M., U Il, 1976
Charon, Rita, Columbia, 1982
Chase, Cida, Ok SU, 1983, 84, 85
Chase, Susan, U Tulsa, 1987
Chauncey, Helen, Georgetown, 1987
Cheatwood, Derral, U Baltimore, 1980
Cheger, Jean, Delta C, 1973
Chette, Anthony, W New Eng C, 1982
Chen, Jiafang, Miss SU, 1987, 88
Chenard, Marcelle, C St. Eliza Station, 1987
Cheney, Anne, Va Tech, 1986, 87, 88
Cheney, Michael, Rutgers, 1979; 83, 84, Drake U
Cherno, Melvin, U Va, 1986
Cherry, Dianne, St. Augustine's C, 1980
Cherry, Wilsonia E.D., Fl SU, 1979
Chesebro, James, Temple, 1977, 80
Chesebro, Patricia, Il SU-Normal, 1985
Chesser, Cheryll, Briston E HS, Ct, 1977
Chetta, Peter N., Iona C, 1987
Chiat, Marilyhn J., U Minn, 1987
Childers, Donna, Augusta C, 1986
Childress, G. Boyd, W Ky U, 1977, 79
Childs, Francine, Oh U, 1987, 88
Chin, Jennie, Kans S Hist Soc, 1983
Chittenden, Varick, SUNY, 1984
Chopyk, Dan, U Ut., 1975, 78, 79, 80, 84
Chorba, Frank J., Wich SU, 1981, 82, 83, 84; 85, 86, 87, 88, Washburn U
Chouteau, Neysa, McGraw-Hill, Manchester, Mo
Chown, Jeffrey, U Mich, 1977; 83, 84, 85, Nor Il U
Christensen, Jerome, Purdue, 1979
Christensen, John, Berkeley, Ca, 1977

Christensen, Peter, SUNY-Binghamton, 1982

Christian, Diana, Documentary Producer, 1980

Christian, Henry, Rutgers, 1983, 84

Christiansen, Cathy, U Neb, 1983

Christiansen, Hal, Murfreesboro, Tn, 1986

Christie, N. Bradley, Duke, 1987, 88

Christie, Robert M., CSU-Dominguez Hills, 1978

Christol, Gretchen, 1973

Christopher, Theresa, 1973

Churchill, Robert, Creighton, 1983

Ciaburri, Anna Mae, Pittsburg, 1979

Cicala, Alan, Wayne SU, 1976

Cicotello, Louis, U Colo, 1987, 88

Cifelli, Edward, Cty C Morris, 1987, 88

Cimbala, Paul, U S Car-Aiken, 1986

Cinquin, Chantal, Wellesley, 1987, 88

Cioffi, Frank, E NM, 1981, 83, 84

Cioffi, Kathleen, E NM, 1983

Cirksena, Kathryn, Stanford, 1985

Citron, Michelle, U Wisc, 1973

Clabaugh, Sue, Ok SU, 1978

Clampit, Maryellen H., E Mich U, 1972

Clancy, Charles J., Bradley, 1976, 78

Clardy, Gil, U Evansville, 1977

Clareson, Tom, Wooster C, 1971, 73, 75, 76, 77, 78, 83, 85

Clark, Bryan, Wich SU, 1983

Clark, Constance, Princeton Lib in NYC, 1987, 88

Clark, David L., Hope C, 1976

Clark, Edward, Winthrop C, 1987, 88

Clark, Elaine, U Mich-Dearborn, 1982

Clark, Gary, Bloomsburg SC, 1979

Clark, Glynn, Meramec Comm C, 1975

Clark, H. James, U Wisc, 1971

Clark, John R., U S Fl, 1979; 83, U Kans

Clark, Lawrence, Southwest Mo SU, 1982, 87

Clark, Meera T., North Adams SC, 1981, 82

Clark, Rebecca, Az SU, 1982

Clark, Samuel, Methodist C, 1986

Clark, Stanley, Gordon C, 1979

Clark, Stewart, U Tx-Dallas, 1983

Clark, Walter, Cedar Crest C, 1979

Clarke, Ann, St. Mary's U, South Bend, In, 1986

Clarke, Bruce, Tx Tech, 1983, 88

Clarke, Clifford, U Mich, 1987, 88

Clarke, Deborah, Yale, 1984; 88, E. Il U-Charleston

Clarke, Michael, Loyola Chicago, 1985

Clary, James, Michigan artist, 1984

Clausius, Claudia, Toronto, 1984

Clavner, Catherine, Cuyahoga Comm C, 1987, 88

Clavner, Jerry, Cuyahoga Comm C, 1979, 83

Clay, Grady, Louisville, Ky, 1987

Clayton, Lawrence, Hardin-Simmons U, 1987, 88

Cleland, Charles, Wayne SU, 1971

Cleland, Sharon, Fl Jun C, Jacksonville, 1979, 80, 81, 84, 87, 88

Clelland, Donald A., U Tn, 1981

Clements, Karen, Pennsburg, Pa, 1987, 88

Clements, William M., Arks SU, 1973, 74, 75, 76, 77, 78; 85, 86, 87, 88, St. Univ, Ark

Cleveland, Carol, 1981

Cleveland, Charles, U Hartford, 1979

Click, Patricia, U Va, 1986, 87, 88

Clift, Charles, Oh U, 1985, 86, 87, 88

Climo, Jacob J., Mich SU, 1979

Cline, Ann, Miami U, Oh, 1985

Cline, Douglas, BGSU, 1981; 83, Temple

Clines, Raymond, Lander C., 1985; 86, 87, Ore SC; 88, Jacksonville U, Fl

Clinton, Dewitt, U Wisc-Whitewater, 1983, 87, 88

Clough, Jeannette, Denver, Colo, 1983; 86, Sou Methodist

Clowers, Myles, San Diego C C, 1986, 87, 88

Clupper, Beatrice, Mt. Mercy C, 1978, 79; 81, Clarke C

Coates, Kenneth, Brandon U, Manitoba

Coates, William A., Kans SU, 1973

Cobb, James, U Md, 1976, 77

Cobb, Lawrence, Ok C U, Oklahoma City, 1984

Cobb, Roseanne L., Phila, 1978

Cobbs, John, Elizabeth City SU, NC, 1982

Coburn, George, NYC, 1985

Cochran, Robert, Ind U-South Bend, 1976

Cockcroft, Robert, U Nottingham, England, 1987, 88

Cocuzza, Ginnine, NYC, 1982, 84; 85, 86, Brooklyn, NY; 88, NYC

Codola, Gerard, Brown U, 1979

Codell, Julie F, U Mont, 1987

Coffin, Jim, Ball SU, 1985

Coffler, Gail, U Kans, 1985; 86, 87, 88, Suffolk U

Coffman, James BGSU, 1971, 71

Coffman, Sue E., U Tx-Arlington, 1983

Cogbill, Neil, U Wisc-Oshkosh, 1972, 73

Cogell, Elizabeth Cummins, U Mo-Rolla, 1978, 80, 84

Cogell, Wayne, U Mo-Rolla, 1980, 81

Coggin, Bill, BGSU, 1983

Cogswell, Robert, U Louisville, 1981, 82

Cohen, Colleen, Vassar, 1985

Cohen, Edward, Mich SU, 1987, 88

Cohen, Hubert, U Mich, 1982

Cohen, Jodi R., Pa SU, 1987

Cohen, Judith, Ottawa, Can, 1984

Cohen, Katherine W., Murray SU, 1980

Cohen, Michael, Murray SC, 1986, 87, 88

Cohen, Philip, U Ia, 1983

Cohen, Ronald D., Ind U-NW, 1976

Cohen-Stratyner, Barbara, NYC, 1985, 86

Cohn, Jack R., U Kans, 1984, 86, 87

Cohn, Jan, Carnegie-Mellon, 1971, 72, 73, 74, 75, 76, 77, 78; 81, 82, 83, 84, 85, 87, George Mason

Cohn, William, Carnegie-Mellon, 1971, 73, 75, 76, 77, 78

Colburn, George A., UC-San Diego, 1977, 81, 82; 86, Mich SU

Colburn, James, Milwaukee Brewers, 1974

Colburn, Kenneth, Sch Lib Arts, Indianapolis, 1984; 85, Ind U

Cole, Carole, Purdue, 1986

Cole, Donald, Drew, 1987

Cole, Grant, Scottsburg, Ind, 1987

Cole, John, Mercer U., 1987, 88

Cole, Richard, W New Eng C, 1987, 88

Colecchia, Francesca, Duquesne U, 1976

Coleman, Ben C., Northeastern Il U, 1975

Coleman, Dale, Tx Tech U, 1985

Coleman, Earle, Va Commonwealth U, 1982

Coleman, Floyd, Sou Il U-Edwardsville, 1978, 79; 85, Jackson SU

Coleman, Horace, Oh U, 1975

Coleman, James, Colo C, 1981, 82, 83, 84, 85, 86, 87, 88

Coleman, Janice, Houston, Tx, 1987, 88

Coleman, Larry, Howard U, 1985

Coleman, Linda, E Il U, 1988

Coleman, Ronald, U Ut, 1987, 88

Coles, Nicholas, U Pitts, 1984

Coletti, Robert, Ut SU, 1983

Colldeweih, Jack H, Teacneck, NJ, 1976

Collette, Donnie, E Tn SU, 1985

Collette, Larry, Mich SU, 1987, 88

Colley, John Scott, Vanderbilt, 1971, 78

Collier, Sylvia, 1986

Collins, Billy B., U RI, 1976, 77

Collins, Catherine, Luther C., 1980; 1983, Willamette U

Collins, Cindy, U Minn, 1986

Collins, Kenneth R., Oh U, 1987

Collins, L.M. Fisk U, 1978

Collins, Mark, SUNY-Binghamton, 1982

Collins, Marybeth, Central Piedmont Comm C, 1975

Collins, Robert A., Fl At U, 1979, 80

Collins, Stephen, Babson C, 1987, 88

Collins, William, Purdue, 1984

Colombo, John R., Toronto, 1984

Columbo, Sue, Tallahassee, Fl., 1986

Colville, Georgina, U Colo, 1988

Colvin, William E., Il SU, 1977, 78, 84

Colwell, C. Cater, Stetson, 1984

Combs, James, Valparaiso U, 1979, 81, 82, 83, 84, 85, 86, 87

Combs, William, W Mich U, 1980, 81, 86

Comiskey, Paul, U Mass, 1978

Commeret, Lorraine, U N Ia, 1988

Compesi, Ronald, San Fran SU, 1979

Conant, Roger, U Pitts, 1979, 80

Conforti, Joseph, RI C, 1984

Conger, James F., W Il U, 1982

Conliff, Steve, former Ed Purple Berries, 1976

Conliffe, Grafton, Oh U, 1976

Conlon, Paula, Carleton U, Ottawa, 1984

Connell, Kim, U Ark, 1979

Connelly, Joseph, Thomas More C, 1985

Connelly, Thomas, U S Car, 1986

Connolly, Donna, Notre Dame, 1988

Connor, John, CSU-Sacramento, 1986

Connor, Marian, Tufts, 1978, 79

Connor, Patricia Kolk, CUNY-Cortland, 1978

Conrad, James, Essex Comm C, Baltimore, 1988

Conron, John, Middlebury C, 1975

Conroy, Graham, Portland SU, 1985

Conroy, Stephen S., U Fl, 1980, 83, 84, 85,

86, 87, 88
Considine, David M., U Wis, 1981
Consigny, Scott, Ia SU, 1978
Constantina, Giovanni, Wayne SU, 1984
Conte, Robert, Greenbrier Hotel, White Springs, W Va, 1979
Conter, Alan, CBC, Canada, 1987
Contractor, Noshir, UCLA, 1986
Coogan, Peter, Kent, Oh, 1988
Cook, Fred S., Wadsworth, Oh, 1974
Cook, Frederick S., Jackson, Mi, 1971
Cook, Lyell, Burton Funeral Home, Girard, Pa, 1985
Cook, Monte, U Ok, 1979, 80
Cook, Nancy, C Lake Cy, Il, 1976
Cook, Patsy, U Ky, 1985
Cook, Philip L., W NM U, 1987
Cook, Tony, U Tol, 1986
Cook, Wister, Ga Inst Tech, 1980, 87
Cooke, John, UNO-Lake Front, 1987, 88
Cooke, T.D., U Mo, 1987
Cooley, John, W Mich U, 1981, 83, 86, 87, 88
Coonan, Mark, Ball SU, 1986
Cooncy, Scamus, W Mich U, 1984
Cooper, B. Lee., Newberry C, 1973, 80, 81, 82, 83, 84, 85, 86; 87, 88, Olivet C
Cooper, Carebanu, U S Fl, 1985
Cooper, Clara B., U S Fl, 1981
Cooper, Donna, U Ore, 1986
Cooper, India, Northwestern, 1981
Cooper, Jane, Harrisburg, Pa, 1981
Cooper, John C., Winebrenner Theo Sem, 1973
Cooper, Martha, NE Mo SU, 1984
Cooper, Wayne, Rutgers, 1977
Cooperman, Alvin, 1974
Copeland, Gary A., Pa SU, 1982
Copeland, Roger, Oberlin, 1987, 88
Cople, John, Brigham Young U, 1987, 88
Coppola, Carlo, Oakland U, 1972, 76
Corbett, Andrea, U Lowell, 1977
Corbin, David A., U Md, 1976, 77
Corbin-Sicoli, M.L., Cabrina C, 1988
Corey, Kenneth, Comm Planning, Cincinnati, 1978
Corman, Catherine Ann, Dallas, Tx, 1986
Cornelius, David, U Pitts, 1982
Cornell, Daniel, Biola U, 1988
Cornell, George, Mich SU, 1984, 85
Cornett, J. Michael, Loyola U, Chi, 1985
Cornillon, John, BGSU, 1973, 74, 75; 76, Washington U
Cornish, Sam, Emerson, 1983
Cornis-Pop, Marcel, U Nor Ia, 1986
Corozza, David, U Wisc-Milwaukee, 1981
Corrigan, Dennis, U Ia, 1984, 85
Corrigan, Robert A., U Ia, 1971, 72
Corrin, Brownlee, Goucher, 1977
Cort, Leon, Wentworth Inst Tech, 1984
Cortes, Ruth, SUNY-Binghamton, 1979
Cosgrove, Robert, SW Mo SU, 1975; 79, Tx Tech
Cosgrove, William, N Dak SU, 1981
Costa, Richard, Tx A&M, 1982
Cothran, Kay, U Md, 1974
Cotkin, George, Cal Poly, San Luis Obispo, 1981

Cotnam, Jacques, York U, Downsview, Ont, 1975
Cotner, Robert, Mont Comm C. Md, 1977
Cotter, John, U Pa, 1971
Cotter, Joseph, Pa SU,1988
Couey, Paul R., Ok SU, 1983
Couillard, Ted, Ga SW C, 1985, 86, 87
Coulter-McQuin, S., Mich SU, 1981
Covelli, Lucille, Queen's U, Kingston, Ont, 1984
Covert, Catherine, Syracuse, 1982
Covo, Jacqueline, Regis C, 1978, 79
Coward, John, U Tx, 1988
Cowser, R.L., Wharton Cty Jr C, Tx, 1983, 86
Cox, Annette, U Minn, 1981
Cox, Barbara, Elkins C, 1988
Cox, Diana, Canyon, Tx, 1987
Cox, Don Richard, U Tx, 1977
Cox, Donna J., U Il, 1987, 88
Cox, Dwayne, U Louisville, 1985
Cox, James M., Dartmouth, 1979
Cox, James S. Jr., SW La SU, 1979, 86
Cox, Joseph, Towson, 1977
Cox, J. Randolph, St. Olaf's C, 1984, 85, 86, 87, 88
Cox, Kenny, WDET-Detroit, 1971
Cox, Virginia, U Wisc-Oshkosh, 1977
Coyle, Wallace, Northeastern U, 1977
Coyle, William, Fl At U, 1981
Crabbe, Katharyn, SUNY-Brockport
Crabtree, Claire, Wayne SU, 1982
Craft, Nikki, Oshkosh, Wi, 1985
Craig, Alexander, Lennoxville, Que, 1982
Craig, Barbara, Voorhees C, 1987
Craig, Robert, Ga Inst Tech, 1984, 86
Craig, R. Stephen, U Me, 1981
Crain, Jeanie, Sou Il U-Edwardsville, 1986; 88, Mo W SC
Cramer, Carmen, TCU, 1979
Crandall, Coryl E., U Wisc-Green Bay, 1975, 76, 77
Crane, Marie, U Mich, 1982
Crane, Maurice, Mich SU, 1977, 80, 84
Crawford, Carey, Furman, 1985
Crawford, Charles W., Memphis SU, 1987, 88
Crawford, Iain, U Ala, 1985; 86, 87, 88, Berry C
Crawford, Lyall, E Mont SU, 1985, 86, 88
Crawford, Paul V., BGSU, 1977
Crawford, Ronald, Kent SU, 1981
Crawford, Scott, Geo-Mason U, 1987, 88
Crawford, Suzanne, BGSU, 1977
Crawford, T.J. Manchester, Ia, 1985
Creagh, Ronald, Montpellier, France, 1988
Creek, Mardena, Sou Il U, 1986; 87, U Neb
Creighton, Peggy, Dartmouth, 1982
Crellin, John, Duke, 1982
Crespy, Charles, Miami U Oh, 1985
Creswell, Kent, Mich SU, 1985
Cripps, Thomas, Morgan SU, 1977, 78, 79
Critelli, Joseph, N Tx SU, 1981
Croce, Lewis H., Mankato SU, 1976
Crocker, Anne, U Me, 1987
Crocker, Helen, W Ky U, 1983

Crocker, Michael, U Fl, 1987
Cronin, Cornelius, LSU, 1987, 88
Crosby, David L., Alcorn SU, 1978
Cross, John W., SUNY-Potsdam, 1979
Cross, Lawrence, Wright SU, 1986
Crouch, Laura, Ok Baptist U, 1982, 83
Crouch, Terrell, U Me, 1987
Crouch, Tom, Nat'l Air & Space Mus, 1982
Crouch, Tracy, U SW La, 1988
Crow, John, Miami U, Oh, 1977, 78, 79
Crowe-Carraco, Carol, W Ky U, 1985
Crowe, Charles, U Ga, 1974
Crowe, David W., U Minn, 1987; 88, Luther C
Crowe, Martha, E Tn SU, 1987, 88
Crowell, Doug, Tx Tech, 1983
Croy, Jeff, Mich Tech U, 1978
Cruice, Gary, Tulane, 1987, 88
Culbert, David, LSU, 1974, 75, 76, 77; 78, Nat'l Hum Inst; 79, 80, 81, 86, LSU
Culpepper, Marilyn, Mich SU, 1984, 88
Culross, Jack L., E Ky U, 1975, 77, 78
Cumbler, John, U Louisville, 1985
Cummings, Charles, Newark Pub Lib, 1984
Cummings, Daniel, Cornell, 1984
Cummings, Kay, NYU, 1985
Cummings, Michael, U Colo, 1985, 86, 87, 88
Cummings, Ronald L., Purdue, 1972; 76, Wittenberg U
Cunningham, Keith, Nor Az U, 1987
Cunningham, Merrilee, U Houston, 1986, 87, 88
Cunningham, Trish, BGSU, 1984, 85, 86, 87, 88
Curb, Roisemary K., Mo Sou SC, 1979
Curl, Donald W., Fl At U, 1978
Curran, Douglas, Banff Center, Can, 1980
Currey, Cecil, U Sou Fl, 1987, 88
Cury, Jane, U Mich, 1974
Curry, Jerome, Pa SU-Mont Alto, 1983, 85
Curry, Pamela Malcolm, Oh SU, 1979
Curtis, Bruce, Mich SU, 1981
Curtis, James M., U Mo, 1979, 81
Cusic, Don, Middle Tn SU, 1987, 88
Custred, Glynn, CSU-Hayward, 1981
Cutler, Evelyn, Ind SU, 1982
Cutler, T. J. US Naval Acad, 1987
Cutler, William W. II, Temple, 1978
Cutting, Rose Marie, St. Mary's U, 1978
Czernis, Loretta, York U, Can.
Czitron, Daniel, Mt. Holyoke, 1984

Dachalager, Earl L., U Houston, 1978
Da Costa Frontes, Manuel, Kent SU, 1986
Daher, Michael, Wayne SU, 1980
Dailey, Maceo, Smith C, 1978
Daily, Gary, Ind SU, 1972
Dakan, A. William, U Louisville, 1985
Dakich, Milan, Purdue-Hammond, 1988
Dale, J. Alexander, Alleg C, 1987, 88
Dale, James, Youngstown SU, 1979
Dale, Sharon, Pa SU-Erie, 1987, 88
D'Alessio, Dave, Mich SU, 1984
Daley, J.W., U Tol, 1985, 86, 87
Daley, Nelda K., Radford, 1980, 81
Dalke, R.W. C Ozarks, 1983
Dalstrom, E. Kay, U Neb-Omaha
Dalstrom, Hari, U Neb-Omaha

Daly, Ann, NYU, 1986

Daly, Lois, Sienna C, 88

Dambrot, Fay, U Akron, 1985, 86, 87, 88

Damewood, James, Northridge HS, Dayton,

O, 1975, 76, 77, 78; 81, Riverside Cong Church, Dayton, Oh; 84, Dayton, Oh; 86, Riverdale Cong Church

Damon, Maria, Stanford, 1987

Damsell, J.D., Central Mich U, 1980

Dancyger, Ken, York U, Can, 1984

Danet, Brenda, Hebrew U, Jerusalem, 1987, 88

Daniel, Lee, Souwestern Ok SU, 1983

Daniel, Thomas E., U Wisc-Green Bay, 1975, 76

Daniel, Walter C., U Mo, 1977, 78

Daniels, Bruce, U Winnipeg, 1987, 88

Daniels, Dan, Montreal, Can, 1987

Daniels, Roger, U Cin, 1982

Daniels, Rosalie, Jackson SU, 1984

Danker, Frederick E., Boston SC, 1973, 74, 75, 76, 77, 78, 79, 80, 82; 84, U Mass, Boston; 87, U Mass, Harbor Campus

Danker, Laura, Loyola U, NO, 1988

Danna, Sammy, Loyola U, Chi, 1980, 81, 82, 83, 84, 85, 86, 87, 88

Dansereau, Estelle, U Calgary, Can, 1984

Dansker, Emil, BGSU, 1972, 78, 80, 84, 86

Danziger, Edmund Jr., BGSU, 1979

Dargitz, Robert E., Butler, 1985, 86, 87, 88

D'Arienzo, Camille, Brooklyn C, 1986

Darmon, John, U Me-Farmington, 1978

Dart, Peter, U Kans., 1983,84; 85, 88, McNeese SU

Dasilva, Fabio, Notre Dame, 1978

Dathkorne, O.R., Oh SU, 1977, 79

Daudelin, Robert, Montreal, Can, 1987

Dauer, David, Johns Hopkins, 1983

Davenport, Brenda, U SC-Spartanburg, 1988

Davenport, Carl, Graniteville, Pa, 1988

Davern, Peggy, W Il U, 1982

David, Beverly R., W Mich U, 1973, 75, 76, 81, 82, 88

David, Charles-Philippe, Saint-Jean, Que, 1987

David, Mary Elizabeth, U Pitt, 1982

Davidson, Abraham, Temple, 1980, 81, 82, 83, 84, 87

Davidson, Arnold, Elmhurst C, 1977, 78, 79, 82, 84

Davidson, Cathy, Mich SU, 1976, 77, 78, 79, 82, 84

Davidson, David, Greenbrier, Ark, 1988

Davidson, Doug, York U, Can, 1984

Davidson, Mary, U Kans, 1985

Davidson, Penny, Des Moines, Ia, 1985

Davidson, Sol, Des Moines, Ia, 1985, 88

Davies, Christopher, U Tx, 1984

Davies, Ione, York U, Can, 1984

Davies, Laurence, Dartmouth, 1980

Davies, Lewis, Tx Tech, 1985, 86

Davila, Luis, Ind U, 1975

Davis, Allen, Temple, 1973, 74

Davis, Ann, Brescia C. Can, 1987

Davis, Barbara, U Ok, 1985, 86

Davis, Charles, U Tx, 1972

Davis, Daniel, Mich SU, 1984

Davis, David, Temple, 1987, 88

Davis, Deborah, Tx Woman's U, 1986

Davis, Delmer, Andrews U, 1986

Davis, Fred, UC-San Diego, 1978

Davis-Friedman, Deborah, Yale, 1979

Davis, Gayle, Wichita SU, 1983, 84, 85, 86, 87

Davis, Gerald L., Smithsonian Inst, 1974

Davis, J. Madison, Pa SU-Erie, 1987, 88

Davis, James, W Ky U, 1984, 86, 87, 88

Davis, Jana, U Brit Columbia, 1987

Davis, Joan, York U., Can, 1988

Davis, John, Ed, The Velvet Light Trap, 1978

Davis, John, U Sou Miss, 1987, 88

Davis, Judith, Pa SU, 1973

Davis, Kathe, Kent SU, 1987

Davis, Kenneth, Tx Tech U, 1986, 87, 88

Davis, Lloyd, W Va U, 1986

Davis, Mark, E Il U,1985

Davis, Mollie C., W Ga C, 1971, 82; 73, Queen's C

Davis, Nancy, W Ky U, 1984, 85, 86, 87, 88

Davis, Ralph, Albion C, 1980

Davis, Robert, U Ok, 1985

Davis, Ronald, Sou Methodist U, 1983

Davis, Richard, Washington U, 1975

Davis, Robert M., U Ok, 1979

Davis, Ronald, Columbia, Chicago, 1974

Davis, Stephen F., Austin Peay SU, 1973

Davis, Sue, Ind SU, 1986

Davis, Susan, Id SU,1984

Davis, Thomas, Jr., McGill U, 1973

Davis, Tim, U Tx, 1987, 88

Davis, Vivian, Warner-Amex, 1982

Davison, Kenneth, Heildelberg C, 1981

Davison, Mary H., E Ore SU, 1987

Davy, Kate, NYU, 1985

Dawley, Robert, Purdue, 1983, 84, 85

Dawson, Deborah, BGSU, 1986, 87, 87

Dawson, Harry, Austin SU, 1981

Day, Frank, BGSU, 1983; 86, Clemson

Day, Phyllis J., Purdue, 1980, 81, 83, 84, 86, 87

Daye, Douglas, BGSU, 1971

De Abruna, Laura, Ithaca C, 1987, 88

de Albuquerque, Klaus, C Charleston, 1984

Dean, Bruce, U Me-Farmington, 86

Dean, Jan, U Kans, 1983

Dean, Joan F., Purdue, 1974

Dean, John, Paris, France, 1988

Dean, Michael, U Miss, 1986

Dean, Thomas, U Kans, 1983

Dearborn, Mary, Columbia, 1983

Deardurff, Dayle, BGSU, 1975

Dearing, James, USC, 1986

Deaton, Dale, Frontier Nursing Service, 1982

Deaton, Thomas, Dalton Jr C, 1986

Deats, Sara, U SFl, 1980, 87

De Battista, Patrick, U Houston, 1987

De Battle, Geraldine P, Marlboro C, 1987

De Benedetti, C., U Tol, 1980

De Benedictis, Michel, U Neb, 1984, 85

De Berry, Clyde, U Wisc-Oshkosh, 1974

Debolt, Joseph, Cen Mich U, 1972

Debord, Larry, U Miss, 1984, 85, 86, 87, 88

Debro, Julius, Atlanta, Ga, 1986

De Burger, James, U Louisville, Ky, 1986

De Cordova, Richard, DePaul U, Chi, 1988

De Curtis, Anthony, Emory, 1980

Deegan, Mary Jo, U Neb, 1983, 84

DeEndinger, Lloyd, U Ala-Mobile, 1985

Deer, Harriet, U So Fl., 1972, 73, 78, 79, 80, 81, 86

Deer, Irving, U So Fl, 1972, 83, 76, 78, 79, 80, 81, 86

Dees, David R., Notre Dame, 1972

De Falco, Joseph, Marquette U, 1984, 85

De Finney, James, U D'Etudes Moncton, Can, 1987

De Foe, Mark, W Va Wesleyan, 1985

De Froscia, David, Bangor Comm C, Me, 1981

Degan, Jim, U Santa Clara, 1978

de Geigel, Alona Simonet, U Puerto Rico, 1984

Degenfelder, E. Pauline, Lakeland Comm C, 1974; 75, 76, Fitchburg St C

Degi, Bruce, USAF Acad, 1981

Degnan, James, Aptos, Ca., 1985, 86; 88, Santa Clara U

De Grazia, Emilio, Winona SU, 1981, 82

Dehart, Stephen, Pa SU-Erie, 1988

De Herdt, Sonja, Indianapolis, 1988

Dehnert, Edmund, Truman C, 1988

Deigh, John, Northwestern, 1988

Deihl, E. Roderick, N. Il U, 1984

De Jong, Mary, Pa SU-Sharon, 1985

de la Fuente, Patricia, Pan Amer U, 1983, 84, 85, 87

Delano, Skip, Columbia, 1988

De Larber, Nicholas S., BGSU, 1981

Del Calle, Paul, William Patterson C, 1982

de Leon, David, Howard U., 1986

de Leon, Edelma Pacita, Philippine Union C, 1978; 85, 86, Appal SU

Del Fattore, Joan, U De, 1986

Delind, Laura B., Mich SU, 1979, 80, 84, 87, 88

Dell, Jerry R., U Wisc-Green Bay

De Lorenzo, David, Gallaudet, 1985

Delorto, Theresa, BGSU, 1984

del Pino, Salvador Roidgriquez, U Colo, 1979

deLuce, Judith, Miami U, Oh, 1986

DeMarr, Mary Jean, Ind SU, 1978, 80, 81, 82, 83, 84, 85, 86, 87, 88

Demars, Stanford, RI C, 1987

Demetrakopoulos, Stephanie, W Mich U, 1975

Deming, Caren J. U Mich, 1976; 80, San Francisco SU

Deming, Robert, Fredonia SU, 1982, 86, 87

Demirdjian, Z.S., CSU-Long Beach, 1984

de Moret, A.M., U St Louis, 1975

Demos, Mary Ann, Mus of Amer Folk Art, NYC, 1985

DeMott, Robert, Oh U, 1975

Dempsey, K. Ann, St. Louis Comm C, Florissant Valley, 1985

Denisoff, R. Serge, BGSU, 1971, 72, 73, 74, 75, 76, 77, 78, 79, 89, 81, 82, 83, 84, 85, 86, 88

Dennis, Everetta E, Kans SU, 1972; 75, 76, U Minn

Dennis, Gail, York, Pa, 1984

Dennis, Larry, Mansfield SC, 1977, 78, 79; 82, 86, 88, Clarion SC

Denski, Stan, Oh U, 1984, 85; 87, C Wooster

Dent, Gene H., Lakeland Comm C, 1976, 80

De Paolo, Rosemary, Augusta C, Ga, 1981

DePree, Alice B., Greenhills School, Ann Arbor, Mi, 1980

Derden, John, Emanuel Cty Jr. C, Ga

Derounaian, K.Z., U Ark-Little Rock, 1982, 83, 84

Dervin, Daniel, Mary Washington C, 1973

Desaat, Jacob, BGSU, 1980

Descutner, David, Oh U, 1984

deSilva, Deema, Wichita SU, 1983

DesMarais, Barbara G.T., U Wisc, 1972, 73; 75, 76, U Ark

Desmarais, Ralph, Wisc SU, 1971, 72, 73

DeSchepper, Jerry, URI, 1977

Despande, Shekar, Chatham C, 1988

Dessner, Lawrence, U Tol, 1972, 73, 77

Deudon, Eric, Tx A&M, 1981

Deveny, John J. Jr., Ok SU, 1984, 85

Devereaux, E.J., U Western Ont, 1987

Devit, Bonnie, Augusta C, 1981

De Vore, Lynn, Il SU, 1982

De Vries, Peggy, Emporia SU, 1986, 87

Devries, Raymond, Westmount C, 1985

Deweese, Robert, U Tx, 1974

Dewhurst, C. Kurk, Mich SU, 1980, 84, 87

DeWill, Hoard, Ohone C, 1977

DeWing, Rolland, Chadron SC, 1984

Dewitt, Howard, Ohlone C, 1988

DeWolfe, George, DePaul U, 1988

DeYoung, Gregg, Stoneyhill C, 1984

DeYoung, Mary, Grand Rapids, Mich, 1977

Dhawan, S.K., Himachal Pradesh U, Simla, India, 1985

Diamond, Edwin, MIT News Study Group, 1981

Diamond, Sara, Vancouver, Can, 1984

Dibble, Audrey, Wash SU, 1979

Dibara, Paul, Rockland, Ma, 78

Dick, Bernard F., Fairleigh Dickinson U, 1978, 79

Dick, Lesley, BGSU, 1983, 85

Dicke, Ikenna, S Il U-Carbondale, 1983

Dickens, David, U Ky, 1982

Dickerson, Lynn, U Richmond, 1983, 84, 86

Dicks, Samuel, Emporia SU, 1983

Dickens, David, U Ky, 1981

Dickey, Susan, Ind St Mus & Historic Sites, Indianapolis, 1986, 87

Dickson, Gordon, S.F.W.A., 1971

Dickson, Marcia, SUNY-Plattsburgh, 1978

Didier, Michelle, BGSU, 1983

Diekhoff, Karen, Midwestern SU, 1978

Dienst, Richard, Duke, 1988

Dierenfield, Bruce J., Purdue, 1983

Dies, Jerry, Nathan Hale HS, 1987

Dieter, Pamela, Mich SU, 1987

Dietrich, Carol, Oh SU, 1986

Dietrich, Julia, U Louisville, 1979

Dietrich, Richard, U S Fl, 1981

Diffley, Kathleen, U Ia, 1988

Digaetani, John, Hofstra, 1987, 88

Dilley, Frank B., U De, 1979, 80, 81

Dillingham, Thomas, Stephens C, 1980

Dillon, M.C., SUNY-Binghamton, 1980, 81

DiLorenzo, Bernadette, St. Louis, Mo, 1985

DiLorenzo, Donald, St. Louis, Mo, 1984

DiLorenzo, Ronald, St. Louis, Mo, 1980, 81, 84, 85

DiMeglio, John, Mankato SU, 1983

Dinniwell, Norma, U W Ontario, 1984

Dionne, Helene, U Du Quebec, Montreal, 1984

Dilspenza, Joseph E., Am Film Inst, 1972, 73

D'Itri, Patricia, Mich SU, 1981, 84, 85, 86, 87, 88

Dixson, Barbara, U Wisc-Steven's Point, 1986, 88

Dixon, Max, W Md C, 1971

Dixon, Richard, UNC-Wilmington, 1980

Dixon, Terrell F., U Houston, 1975

Dixon-Stowell, Brenda, NYC, 1982; 85, Temple

Dizer, John, Utica, NY, 1988

Doak, Robert, Wingate C, 1982, 86

Dobkin, J.B., U SFl, 1986, 87, 88

Dobrow, Julie, U Pa, 1985

Dodd, Diane, Carleton U, Ottawa, 1988

Dodd, Gregg, MCA Distributing Co, 1986

Dodd, William, Augusta C, 1986

Dodge, Robert K., U Nev-Las Vegas, 1979

Dodson, Don, Stanford, 1975

Dodson, Edward, Governors SU, 1971

Dodson, Harriet, Fl Jun C, 1979, 80, 81, 84, 87, 88

Doeumer, Elizabeth, Ind U, 1984

Dogan, Penelope, Stockton SC, 1987

Doherty, Joseph F., U Tx, 1972

Doherty, Mary Lou, Central YMCA Comm C, Chicago, 1978

Doherty, Thomas, U Ia, 1981

Dolff, Elizabeth, U Houston, 1988

Doll, Russell, U Mo-KC, 1988

Doll, Susan, Northwestern, 1984; 1985, St. James' Press, Chi

Dolle, Raymond, Ind SU, 1988

Dombrowski, Daniel, Creighton, 1983

Dombrowski, Mark, Sienna Heights C, 1983, 84, 85, 86, 87, 88

Domzai, Teresa, Geo Mason U, 1984, 85

Donakowski, Conrad L., Mich SU, 1976

Donald, Ralph, Westfield SC, 1987, 88

Donaldson, Gary, Xavier U, NO, 1987, 88

Donaldson, Jeff, Washington, DC., 1978

Donaldson, Susan, Hampshire C, 1988

Donath, Jackie, BGSU, 1984, 85, 86; 87, 88, Wichita SU

Donegan, Rosemary, Toronto, 1984

Donelson, Ken, Az SU, 1974

Doinnelly, Dorothy, URI, 1977

Do'nnelly, Jerome, U Cent Fl, 1980, 81

Donnerstein, Edward, U Wisc, 1984

Donovan, Edward L, Sacred Heart C, 1971

Donovan, Gertrude, Nassau Comm C, 1988

Donovan, Kent, Kent SU, 1983

Donovan, Timothy P., U Ark, 1974, 75, 78, 82

Donow, Ken, Stockton SC, 1979

Doody, John, Villanova, 1988

Dooley, Linda, Kent SU, 1982, 85

Dooley, Patrick, St. Bonaventure U, 1981

Dooley, Ron, U Kans, 1988

Dooley, Tom, U West Mich, 1974

Doran, Edwina, Eurika C, 1987

Dorfman, Harlan, Vancouver, BC, 1984

Dorinson, Joseph, Long Island U, 1978, 79, 80, 84

Dorinson, Zahava K., DePaul U, 1977

Dorman, Katheryne S., TCU, 1979

Dorman, James, U SW La, 1985, 88

Dorn, Mark, BGSU, 1977

Dornor, Marjorie L., Winona SC, 1974

Dorris, Ronald, McNeese SU, 1984, 85; 86, Talladega C; 87, 88, Notre Dame

Dortmund, Erhard, W Ore SC, 1984

Dotson, Calvin, Ind U, 1974, 75, 76

Doubler, Janet, Il SU, 1986

Doughty, Howard, Seneca C, 1984, 85, 87

Douglas, Christopher, 1973

Douglas, Claudie, Central Conn SC, 1975

Douglas, Lawrence, Plymouth SC, 1983

Douglas, Otis, Longwood C, 1983, 86

Douglas, Robert, Oh U, 1985, 87; 88, U Louisville

Douglas, Sara, U Il, 1984

Douglas, Stephen A., U Il, 1975

Douglas, Susan, Hampshire C, 1984, 88

Douglass, Robert, U Louisville, 1986

Dove, George, E Tn U, 1975, 76, 77, 78, 79, 80, 81, 82, 83, 84, 85; 86, 87, 88, Johnson City, Tn

Dovring, Karin, U Il, 1973

Dow, James R., Ia SU, 1972

Dowd, Jane, Queens C, CUNY, 1982

Dowell, Linda, 1984

Downard, William L. St. Joseph's C, 1980

Downes, Margaret, UNC-Asheville, 1987

Downey, James C., William Corey C, 1978, 79; 83, William Corey C on the Coast

Downing, David, E Il U-Charleston, 1982

Downing, George J., Gloucester C C, 1978

Downing, Janay, Regis C, 1981

Dowse, Dimis, U Tn, 1979, 80

Doyle, James, Wilfrid Laurier U, 1982, 85

Doyle, Robert, Pa SU, 1976

Doyle, Terrence, Ferris SU, 1980

Drake, Carlos, BGSU, 1972, 72, 73, 74, 78

Drake, Glendon F., San Diego SU, 1978

Drake, H.L., Wayne SC, 1980, 81; 82, 84, Millersville SC

Drale, Christina, SW Mo SU, 1988

Draughdrill, Martha, Nat'l Colonial Farm, Accokeek, Md, 1981

Drayton, Arthur O, U Kans, 1983

Dreibelbis, Guy, Bradley U, 1988

Dresner, Zita Z. Washington Tech Inst, 1976, 80, 82, 83, 84, 85, 86, 87, U DC, 88

Drew-Bear, Annette, Loyola/Montreal, 1974, 75

Driscoll, Kerry, SUNY-Buffalo, 1984

Driskell, Leon, U Louisville, 1985

Drost, Dick, Naked City, 1972, 73

Druschel, Bruce, Miami Oh 1986; 1987, Oh U

Dubisch, Jill, UNC-Charlotte, 1986

DuBose, Marya M., Augusta C, 1978

Ducey, Richard, Nat'l Assoc. Broadcasters, 1985

Duchovnay, Gerald, Jacksonville U, 1981

Duckworth, Victoria, U Houston-Downtown, 1985, 87

Dudden, Arthur, Bryn Mawr, 1973, 77

Duff, Thomas, Seton Hall U, 1987, 88

Dugan, Dianne, UCLA, 1983

Dugan, Penelope, Stockton SC, 1988

Dugg, Robert W., U Portland, 1976

Dugan, James, Maumee, Oh, 1980

Duke, Charles R., Murray SU, 1979

Duke, Kathleen, Spring Hill C, 1983

Duke, Maurice, Richmond Times Dispatch. 1973; 87, Va Commonwealth U

Dukes, Thomas, U Akron, 1988

Dulai, Surjit, Mich SU, 1974, 75, 76, 79, 80, 81

Dulaney, Robin, Tx Tech, 1982

Dumm, Thomas, Amherst, 1985

Dunbar-Odom, Donna, Ind SU, 1983

Duncan, Barry, 1987

Duncan, Charles, Atlanta U, 1985

Duncan, David, Tn Wesleyan, 1986

Duncan, Joyce, E Tn SU, 1986

Duncan, Marcia, Mass C Pharmacy, 1988

Duncombe, Henry A., Ala SU, 1986

Dungey, John, Seattle, Wa, 1986

Dunham, Mellerson, 1973

Dunkle, Bob, Lafayette, IN, 1988

Dunlap, David, Kans SU, 1983

Dunlap, Robert L., Aurora Public Schools, West Side, 1972

Dunn, Daniel M., Purdue-Calumet, 1979, 80, 83, 86, 88

Dunn, Joe, Converse C., 1984, 85, 86, 87, 88

Dunn, M.G., U Sou Miss, 1988

Dunn, Margaret, Stetson, 1986

Dunn, Thomas P., Miami U-Hamilton, Oh, 1978, 80, 84, 85

Dunne, Michael, Mid Tn SU, 1985

Dunwoody, Sharon, Ind U, 1975

Duplantier, Stephen, Abita Springs, La, 1987

Dupont, Louis, U de Ottawa, Can, 1987

Dukpras, Andre, U Quebec, 1984, 87

Durand, Henry, U Cin, 1975

Durbin, Paul, U De, 1980

Durer, Christopher, U Wy, 1985

Durham, Marilyn, U Wisc-Whitewater, 1988

Durham, Philip, UCLA, 1971

Durham, Richard, 1976

Durham, T.R. Skidmore, 1988

Durkin, Mary B., Radway C, 1974

Dushane, Judy, BGSU, 1974, 75

Duvert, Elizabeth, Miami U, Oh, 1985

de Dwyer, Carlota Cardenas, U Tx, 1976

Dwight, Margaret L., U Va, 1980

Dyer, Cynthia, SUNY-Buffalo, 1984

Dyer, Thomas G., U Ga, 1977

Earle, Ed., UC-Riverside, 1979, 83

Early, Gerald, Washington U, 1984

Earnest, James, Murray SU, 1988

Eason, David, U Wisc-Milwaukee, 1980, 81

Easthope, Anthony, Manchester Poly, England,1988

Eastland, Lynette, U Ut, 1983

Eaton, Eric, U Ok, 1978

Ebanks, Milena, Temple, 1981

Eberhard, Wallace, U Ga, 1986

Eberhart, George, Amer Lib Asc, Chicago, 1988

Eby, Cecil, U Mich, 1981

Ecker, Pam, BGSU, 1975, 77; 82, U Dayton

Eckert, Edward, St. Bonaventure U, 1987

Eckert, Katherine, Mich SU, 1976

Eckert, Michael, U Fl, 1985

Eckert, Mary, U Tn, 1982

Eckert, Ralph, Pa SU-Behrend C, 1987, 88

Eckles, Gary, W Va Wesleyan, 1985

Eckley, Grace, Drake U, 1979, 80, 81, 85

Eckman, Frederick, BGSU, 1975

Eckman, Martha, BGSU, 1973, 74

Eckstein, Barbara, Tulane, 1986, 88

Ede, Lisa, Carnegie-Mellon U, 1979

Edelstein, Alan, Towson, 1987

Edelberg, Cynthia, Cleveland SU, 1986

Edgerton, Gary, BGSU, 1980, 81, 82, 83, 84, 85; 86, 87, 88, Goucher C

Edgette, J. Joseph, Widener U, 1987, 88

Edginton, Christopher, U Ore, 1986

Edginton, K., Towson, 1980, 81, 82, 84

Edgley, Charles, Ok SU, 1978, 82, 83, 84, 85, 86, 87, 88

Edmonds, Tony, Ball SU, 1986, 87

Edwards, Anthony O., Ball SU, 1973

Edwards, Bruce L., BGSU, 1983

Edwards, Dell, U Tx, 1986

Edwards, Grace, Radford U, j1986

Edwards, James J., Aurora Pub Schools, West Side, 1972

Edwards, Kathleen, U Az, 1981

Edwardson, Mickie, U Fl, 1986, 87, 88

Efron, Arthur, SUNY-Buffalo, 1980

Egan, Hugh, Loyola Chicago, 1984, 85, 86; 87, 88, Ithaca C

Egan, James, U Akron, 1980, 83, 84, 85, 86, 87, 88

Egan, Ken, Rocky Mt C, 1988

Egenriether, Ann, St. Louis, Mo, 1986, 87

Eger, Ernestina, Carthage C, 1983

Egger, Andriene, Sou Il U, 1988

Egger, C. Eugene, Va Tech, 1988

Eggleston, Noel, Radford U, 1984, 87

Ehlers, Leigh, Berry C, 1979; 80, Kenisaw C

Ehlich, Richard D., Miami Oh, 1987

Eichmann, Raymoind, U Ark, 1977, 78

Eid, Leroy V., U Dayton, 1978

Eigel, Edwin B., St. Louis U, 1975

Eiseman, James, U Louisville, 1980

Eisen, Helen, New Rochelle, NY, 1981

Eisenberg, Diane, U Md.1977

Eisenberger, Suzanne, Henrico Public

School, Richmond, Va, 1988

Eisenhour, Jerry, U Mo, 1983

Eisenman, Harry, U Mo-Rolla, 1982

Eisenman, James, U Louisville, 1988

Eisinger, Sterling, Clemson, 1980

Eisman, Gregory, Broward Comm C., Fl, 1986, 87

Eiss, Harry, Nor Mont C., 1983, 84, 85, 87; 88, E Mich U

Ekdom, Leah, Northwestern, 1982, 84, 85

Ekechi, Felix, Kent SU, 1986

Ekman, Richard, NEH, 1977, 79

Elam, Harry, U Md, 1988

Elder, Arlene A., U CU Jordan, 1983

El-Haleese, Yousef, 1983

Elhardt, Dale, Colo SU, 1977

Elias, M., Yale, 1981

Elkins, Charles, Fl Int U, 1976, 85

Eller, Jackie, Mid Tn SU, 1986, 87

Eller, Jonathan, USAF Acad, 1988

Ellery, Chris, Tx A&M, 1986

Ellinger, Jeanne, S Ok SU, 1982, 83, 87

Ellington, Jane, N Tx SU, 1981

Elliot, Gary, Harding C, 1979

Elliott, Harley, Marymount C, 1983

Elliot, Kim, Voice of Amer, 1987

Ellis, Godfrey, Ok SU, 1983

Ellis, Howard, Lorain Comm C, Oh, 1984

Ellis, Joseph, Trenton SC, 1980

Ellis, Paul, N Ky SU, 1987, 88

Ellis, Seth, UNC-Charlotte, 1987, 88

Ellis, Susan, U NM, 1988

Ellis, Tim, Duke, 1988

Ellis, William, E Ky U, 1987

Ellison, Curtis W., Miami U, Oh, 1973

Ellison, Mary, U Keele, England, 1986

Elliston, F.A., SUNY-Albany, 1980, 81; 82, Criminal Justice Res Center, Albany

Ellsworth, James, U Hawaii-Manoa, 1986, 87, 88

Elsass, David, BGSU, 1984

Elstob, Kevin, Davis, Ca, 1988

Elzey, Wayne, Miami U., Oh, 1875, 76

Embrey, Sharon, Ok SU, 1982

Emery, Donovan, Purdue, 1981

Emmett, V.J. Pitt SU, Kans, 1982

Emrys, Barbara,. Columbia C, Chicago, 1988

Emtraux, Guy, UNESCO Ed. Cultures, 1974

Endelmann, Judith, Ind U, 1985

Endres, Kathleen, BGSU, 1986

Endres, Thomas G. U Il, 1983

Engel, Beate, BGSU, 1986

Engel, Bernard, Mich SU, 1980, 86, 87, 88

Engel, Gary, Cleveland SU, 1980

Engel, Leonard, Quinnipiac C, 1985, 86, 87, 88

Engel, Mary, N Mont C, 1986

England, D. Gene, Ind SU, 1979

English, Cliff, Luther C, 1978

English, Donald W., SUC-Geneseo, 1980

English, James, Stanford, 1988

English, John, U Ga, 1975, 76, 77, 83, 85, 86, 87

English, Philip, SUNY-Plattsburgh, 1988

Enholm, Donald K. BGSU, 1976, 85, 87

Ennis, James, Harvard, 1976

Ensman, Fred, TCU, 1973

158   Index of Participants

Epple, George, RI C, 1988
Epps, Jim, Kans SU, 1985
Epstein, Alice, U Mass, 1981
Epstein, Grace, Oh SU, 1988
Epstein, Marcia, U Calgary, Can, 1985
Erde, Edmund L., U Tx Medical Branch, Galveston, 1979
Erdman, Biruta, E Car U, 1979, 89, 81, 83, 85, 87
Erenberg, Lewis, Loyola Chi, 1980, 82
Erens, Patricia, Northwestern, 1976
Erffmeyer, Thomas E., Northwestern, 1982, 83; 84, Sacred Heart U
Erickson, Gerald, U Minn, 1976
Erisman, Fred, TCU, 1974, 76, 77, 78, 80
Erlanson, David, Comm C Decatur, 1975, 76
Erlich, Richard Dee, Miami U Oh, 1978, 79, 80, 82, 83, 84, 85, 86, 88
Erni, John, U Ore, 1987
Erskine, Thomas L., Ed., Literature/Film Quarterly, 1975
Erwin, Lorna, York U, Ontario, 1987, 88
Erwin, Paul F., U Cin, 1986, 87, 88
Esbjornson, Carl, U SD, 1987, 88
Esmonde, Margaret, Villanova, 1979
Esposito, Pam, Cabrini C, 1985
Espinosa, Miriam, Tx Wesleyan C, 1986, 88
Esselman, Kathryn C., East Lansing, Mi, 1972, 73, 74, 86
Estes, Jack BGSU, 1973; 81, 82, 83, 86, 87, 88, Peninsula C, Wash
Estes, Leland, Park Forest, Il, 1983
Estrin, Barbara, Stonehill C, 1981
Etheredge, Chuck, TCU, 1988
Ettinger, Andrew, Harlequin Pub, 1983
Ettinger, Ronald F., Sangamon SU, 1979
Etulain, Richard, Ida SU, 1971, 72, 73, 77
Etzkoirn, K. Peter, U Mo-St. Louis, 1986
Eubank, William, U Nev, 1988
Eubanks, Sandra, Jefferson Comm C, 1985
Eutsler, Nellvena, E Car U, 1983
Evangelista, Anthony, Kutztown SC, 1980, 81, 84
Evans, Adria, U RI, 1984
Evans, Gary, Dawson C, Montreal, 1984
Evans, James L., Pan-Amer U, 1977, 83, 84, 85, 86, 87, 88
Evans, Jeff, U Me, 1981
Evans, Lyon, Ia SU, 1984; 85, 86, 87, 88, Viterbo C
Evans, Oliver, Dakota SC, 1974
Evans, Randy, U Il-Chicago Circle, 1978
Evans, R. Daniel, Comm C Phila, 1988
Evans, Robert, U Minn-Duluth, 1987, 88
Evans, T. Jeff, U Me, 1979, 80
Evans, Walter, Augusta C, 1973, 75
Evarts, Peter, Oakland U., Rochester, MI, 1986
Everett, James,U Il, 1983
Evers, Michael, BGSU, 1975
Everts, Dana, Bloomington, In, 1984
Eveslage, Thomas, Sou Il, 1980
Evuleocha, Stevina, Oh U, 1988
Ewell, Barbara, Loyola U, Chi, 1988
Exner, Carol, Weston, Oh, 1977
Exner, Frank, Weston, Oh., 1977
Exoo, Calvin, St. Lawrence U, 1988

Exoo, Fred, St. Lawrence U, 1988
Ezell, Masrcel, Mich SU, 1981
Ezzell, Robert M., Pitts Theo Sem, 1974,78

Faber, Cindy, Midwestern SU, 1981, 83
Faber, Ronald, U Tx, 1985
Fabin, Peter, Germantown, Md, 1985
Fabin, Steve, SIU, 1976
Fair, Alan, Manchester Poly, England, 1986
Fakeye, Brenda, Stillman C, 1978
Falk, H. Richard, CSU-Northridge, 1976
Falk, Thomas, Mich SU, 1981, 84, 85
Falke, Anne, Mich SU, 1972, 73
Falkenberg, Paul V., NYC
Falkenstein, H.R., Heildelberg, 1973
Faller, Carey, Northwestern, 1984
Fanelli, Doris, Ind U, 1980
Fanning, Elizabeth, Augusta C, 1981
Fanning, Michael, SW La U, 1982, 83
Farber, Mark, U Tx-San Antonio, 1983
Fargnoli, Joseph, URI, 1986
Farideh, Olia, U Tn, 1981
Fariss, Tina, BGSU, 1988
Farley, Pamela T., Brooklyn C, SUNY, 1987
Farley, Thomas, U Ottawa, 1984
Farnsworth, Robert, U Mo-KC, 1980
Farr, Judith, Georgetown U, 1988
Farr, Marie T., E Car U, 1983, 85, 88
Farrell, Alan, Hampden-Sydney C, 1988
Farrell, Dianne E., Ore SU, 1983
Farrell, James, St. Olaf C, 1986
Farrell, Robert, W Il U, 1972
Farrell, Walter, Jr., Cheney SC, 1977
Farrelly, James, U Akron, 1985
Farris, Sara, U Minn-Morris, 1986
Farwell, Harold, Jr., W Car U, 1979
Fass, Martin, Rochester, NY, 1982
Fauchou, Gail, York U, Toronto, 1988
Faulds, Sara, UCLA, 1982, 83; 85, 86, 87, Santa Monica, Ca
Faulkner, Claude W., U Ark, 1978, 86
Favre, Betty, Frostburg SC, 1986
Favre, Diane, UC-San Diego, 1987
Fayer, Joan, U Puerto Rico, 1984
Featherstone, Mike, Teeside Poly Middleburgh, Eng, 1988
Febles, Jorge, W Mich U, 1988
Feegel, John R., Tampa, Fl, 1979
Feehan, Michael G., U Ok, 1983
Feeney, Joseph J., St. Joseph's C, 1979, 80, 81
Fees, Paul, Brown U, 1978
Fehrenbach, Robert J, C W&M, 1985
Feibelson, David, U Wash, 1982
Feider, Lynn A., Sacred Heart C, 1972
Feinstein, Sandy, SW C Kans, 1988
Feitelberg, Richard, BGSU, 1986
Feldberg, Michael, U Mass, 1977
Feldman, David, BGSU, 1974, 75; 76, U Md; 77, 80, NBC; 88, NYC
Feldman, Seth, York U, Ont, 1984
Felheim, Marvin, U Mich, 1972, 73
Felkel, Robert, W Mich U, 1988
Felker, Bill, Cen SU, 1988
Fellman, Michael, Simon Fraser U, 1988
Fellom, Martie, SE La U, 1986
Felton, Alan, London, 1987
Feltskoig, E.N., U Wisc

Fennimore, Flora, W Wash SC, 1978, 83
Fenstermaker, John, Fl SU, 1986
Fergeson, Ric, U Ok, 1983
Ferguson, Ann, Ind U, 1985, 86
Ferguson, Beverly, Metro SU, St Paul, 1984
Ferguson, Chamblee, Kans SU, 1983
Ferguson, Dick, U Minn-St. Paul, 1982, 83
Ferguson, Mary, U Ga, 1986
Ferguson, Paul, SUNY-Brockport, 1981
Ferguson, Richard, U Minn-St. Paul, 1984
Ferguson, Robert G., Ferris SC, 1972, 73, 74, 76
Fereira, Christine, W Mich U, 1977, 78, 80, 81, 82
Fereira, James, W Mich U, 1977, 78, 79, 80, 81, 82
Ferlazzo, Paul, Mich SU, 1977
Fern, Annette, U Chicago, 1972
Fernandez, Lillian, U Colo, 1977
Fernandez-Olmos, Mfargarite, Brooklyn C-CUNY, 1988
Fernandez, Ricardo, U Wisc-Milw
Fernandez, Roberto, Fl SU, 1988
Fernandez, Rosa, Albuquerque Pub Schools, 1983
Ferrara, Patrica, Ga SU, 1986, 88
Ferrera, Dennis, Cent Mich U, 1975
Ferrero, Pat, San Francisco, Ca, 1984
Feres, John, Mich SU, 1978, 84, 85
Ferri, Joseph, U Puerto Rico, 1984, 88
Ferriano, Frank, U Wisc-Whitewater, 1986, 88
Ferris, Bill, U Miss, 1988
Ferris, John, Mich SU, 1986
Fershey, Gerald, Malcolm X C, Chi, 1977
Fertel, Randy, Le Moyne C, 1983
Fetterlyk, Judith, U Pa, 1973
Fetterman, Ken, BGSU, 1988
Feuer, Jane, U Ia, 1978
Few, Heather, BGSU, 1975
Fialkowski-McMillan, Barbara, BGSU, 1977, 78
Fick, Thomas, Albion C, 1985; 88, SE La U
Ficken, Robert, US Army Corps Engs, 1985
Ficklen, Joe, 1973
Fiddick, Tom, U Evansville, 1988
Fiedler, Leslie, SUNY-Buffalo, 1973, 74
Fiehrer, Thomas, Brown U, 1982
Fielding, Lawrence, U Louisville, 1982
Fields, Jim, U Neb, 1987
Fienberg, Lorne, Grinnell C, 1981; 88, Millsap C
Fiero, John, U SE La, 1977, 78, 79
Filar, Kenneth, McElhattan, Pa, 1982
Filewood, Alan, Toronto, Ont, 1985
Filler, Louis, Antioch C, 1973, 74, 75, 77, 80
Finch-Rayner, Sheila, Long Beach, Ca, 1983
Finder, Jan Howard, Fort Riley, Kans, 1978
Findlay, John, Pa SU, 1987
Findling, John E., Ind U-Southeast, 1978, 82, 84
Fine, Gary Alan, 1974, 75; 76, 79, 80, U Minn
Fine, John, CSU-San Bernardino, 1978
Fineberg, Lorne, Millsaps C, 1986

Finfer, Lawrence, Mich SU, 1973
Fingrutd, Meryl, SUNY-Stony Brook, 1983
Finke, Laurie, Lewis & Clark C, 1986
Finkenbein, Roy, BGSU, 1980, 81
Finn, Deborah, Emory, 1986
Finn, Geraldine, CEGEP de L'outauoais, Ont, 1984
Finucane, R., Ga Sou C, 1986
Fischer, Bernd, OH SU, 1983
Fischer, Craig, U Il, 1988
Fischer, Gabriel, Acadia U, Nova Scotia, 1984, 86
Fischer, Norman, Kent SU, 1988
Fischer, Paul, BGSU, 1981
Fischer, Roger, U Minn-Duluth, 1978, 79, 80, 81
Fischer, William, Portland SU, 1981
Fischetti, John, Chi Daily News, 1971
Fish, Kathy, Cumberland C, 1986
Fish, Marjorie, Wash SU, 1985
Fishbein, Leslie, Simmons C, 1987
Fishburn, Katherine, Mich SU, 1978, 84
Fisher, Anita, SW Mo SU, 1984
Fisher, Elaine, U Victoria, 1984
Fisher, Roy, U Mo, 1972
Fisher, Stephanie, W Mich U, 1974
Fisher, William, SW Mo SU, 1984, 85, 86, 87
Fishman, Donald, Boston C., 1975, 76, 77, 79
Fishman, Jacquelyn, Chestnut Hill, Ma, 1986
Fishwick, Marshall, Temple U, 1971, 72, 73, 74; 75, 76, Temple; 77, 78, 79, 80, 81, 82, 83, 84, Va Tech; 85, Yale; 86, 87, 88, Va Tech
Fiske, Frederick, U Pa, 1972
Fistell, Ira, WEMP, Milwaukee, 1974
Fitch, Barry, Quinnipiac C, 1988
Fitzgibbons, Dennis, Harvard, 1976
Fitzmoris, Tom, 1988
Fitzpatrick, Marjorie A., Dickinson C, 1987
Fjellman, Steven, 1985
Flack, J. Kirkpatrick, U Md, 1977
Flack, Jeffrey, Oh SU, 1983
Flammong, L.A., US Coast Guard Ac, 1988
Flammer, Philip, Brigham Young U, 1988
Flanagan, Jon, U SD, 1986, 88
Flanigan, C. Clifford, Ind U, 1986
Flanigan, Michael, U Ok, 1983
Flanigan, Rita, Mont SU, 1982
Flannery, Gerald V., SW La, 1986, 88
Flautz, John, Cedar Crest C, 1972
Fleenor, Juliann, U Tol, 1980; 83, BGSU
Fleener, Nickie, U Tulsa, 1979, 83
Fleischaker, Gail, U Louisville, 1982
Fleischer, Stefan, SUNY-Buffalo
Fleishman, Fritz, W Ky U, 1987
Fleming, Charles, Ok SU, 1985
Fleming, Larry, Wichta SU, 1983
Flesor, Devon, E Il U, 1988
Fletcher, Kathy, U Md, 1987
Flibbert, Joseph, Salem SC, 1987
Flieger, Verlyn, U Md, 1980, 82
Flint, Allen, U Me-Farmington, 1981
Flint, Debra, Westwood Ele School, Stillwater, Ok, 1983
Flint, Dianne Lynn, U NDak, 1982

Flint, Richard W., Strong Museum, 1978
Flood, James, Brigham Young, 1980
Florio, Mike, BGSU, 1973
Flosdorf, James W., Russell Sage C, 1981, 82
Flowerdsday, Fred, Detroit, 1980
Fluck, Winfried, 1988
Flynn, Charles, U Chicago, 1971; 81, Miami U, Oh
Flynn, Gerard, U Wisc-Milwaukee
Flynn, James, W Ky U, 1986
Flynn, Meredith, BGSU, 1981
Flynn, Philip, Owensboro Comm C, Ky, 1988
Flynn, Thomas, Mt. St. Mary's, 1980, 83, 84, 87
Foery, Raymond, Quinnipiac C, 1988
Fogarty, John, Ferris SC, 1973, 80, 81, 84, 87
Foley, Daniel, Wichita SU, 1983
Foley, Janis, BGSU, 1985
Foley, J.A., Nat'l U, Singapore, 1982
Folkerts, Jean, U Tx, 1983, 84; 85, Mt. Vernon C
Fontana, Ernest, Xavier U, Cin, 1985, 86
Fontane, Marilyn Stall, Ark SU, 1979
Foore, Sheila M., Hackenssin, De, 1987
Foote, Bud, Ga Tech, 1980, 82; 86, Ga Inst Tech
Foote, Walter, Grand Valley SC, 1988
Foran, Chris, BGSU, 1986
Forbes, Christopher, NE La, 1984
Forczek, Deborah, U Pa, 1979
Ford, Jesse, Tellevue, Tn, 1986, 88
Ford, John, U Mich, 1980
Ford, Thomas, U Houston, 1985, 86, 87, 88
Ford, Valerie, U NM, 1985
Forde, Victoria, Mt. St. Joseph, 1978, 84, 85
Fordyce, Rachel, Va Tech, 1981
Foreman, George, Centre C, 1986
Foreman, Joel, Geo Mason U, 1977, 83
Foreman, Ronald C., Jr., U Fl, 1975, 77, 78, 80, 83, 84, 85, 86, 87, 88
Foret, Michael, SW La, 1988
Formanek, Miriam, Rutgers, 1986
Forstenzer, Jeannie, New Brunswick, NJ, 1980
Fosberg, Thomas, BGSU, 1976
Foss, Dennis, Sangamon SU, 1978, 79
Foster-Eason, Laura, Tx Tech, 1986
Foster, Ed, Stevens Inst Tech, 1985
Foster, Frances, San Diego SU, 1980
Foster, Gary, High Point C, 198
Foster, Marie, Fl A&M, 1988
Foster, Michael, Il Central C, 1985
Foster, Michele, U Pa, 1988
Foster, Milton, E Mich U, 1983
Foster, Ray, Sharon Steel, Sharon, Pa, 1986
Foster, Thomas W., Oh SU-Mansfield, 1985
Foster, Stephen, U Ia, 1984
Foth, Vicky, Kans St. Hist Soc, Topeka, 1983
Foulke, Robert, Skidmore, 1988
Foust, Ronald, U Md, 1981
Fowke, Edith, Toronto, 1984
Fowler, Sarah, BGSU, 1985, 86
Fowles, Jib, U Houston, 1980, 83, 84, 88

Fox, John, Salem SC, 1986, 88
Fox, Matthew, Loyola U, Chi, 1972
Fox, Richard, Cleveland SU, 1980
Fox, Susan, NYC, 1988
Fox, Walter, Temple, 1981, 82
Fractenberg, David, Carnegie-Mellon, 1979
Fraden, Rena, Pomona C, 1986
Francaviglia, Richard V, Antioch, 1976, 78, 79; 80, SE Az Gov Org
Francese, Carl, Brookdale CC, 1987
Francis, David W, Chippewa Lake, Oh, 1980
Francis, Pat, U Md, 1984, 85, 86, 87, 88
Francis, William, U Akron, 1987
Frangos, S.K. Ind U, 1984
Frank, Benis, 1982
Frank, Elizabeth, Beloit C, 1984; 85, 86, Smithsonian
Frank, Luanne, U Tx-Arlington, 1988
Frank, Roslyn, U Ia, 1988
Frank, Stefania, BGSU, 1981, 83
Frank, Stuart, Kendall Whaling Mus, 1987
Frank, Virginia, U Neb-Omaha, 1986
Franke, Warren T., U Neb, 1975
Frankel, Judith, U Cin, 1975
Frankland, Ann, Oh SU-Lima, 1988
Franklin, Robert, MS SU, 1986
Frantz, John, Pa SU, 1982
Franzwa, Gregg, TCU, 1979
Fraser, Anthony, Fl Mem C, 1985
Fraser, Barbara, Austin C, 1988
Fraser, Howard, C W&M, 1980
Fraser, Kendrick, Science News, 1977
Fraser, Mary, Fed & Med Rel Div. Statistics Can, 1984
Frazee, Clara, U Cin, 1982
Frazier, J. Terry, UNC-Charlotte, 1981, 88
Frazier, Tom, Cumberland C, 1986
Frederick, Duke, Northeastern Il, 1976
Frederick, Howard, San Fran SU, 1979
Fredericks, Nancy, SUNY-Buffalo, 1987
Fredin, Erie, Ind U, 1985
Frederickson, Robert, Gettysburg C., 1988
Fredrikson, Kristine, Pro Rodeo Hall Fame, 1983, 84; 85, 86, Tx Tech; 88
Free, Van Tony, Ala SU, 1986
Freedman, Alex S., NE Ok SU, 1977
Freeman, Bee Jay, Shelby St. CC, 1979
Freeman, Bryant, U Kans, 1983
Freeman, James A., U Mass., 1982, 84, 85, 86, 88
Freeman, Thomas, Columbia C, 1971; 73, 74, 75, SUNY-Brockport
Freibert, Lucy, U Louisville, 1981
Freie, John, Lemoyne C, 1988
Freier, Mary, Ind U-Richmond, 1985, 86; 88, Dakota SC, Madison
French, Peter, U De, 1981
French, Warren, IU-PUI, 1971, 72, 73, 75, 76
French, William, W Va U, 1987
Frenier, Mimi, U Minn-Morris, 1981, 83, 88
Frentz, Suzanne, Wichita SU, 1988
Frey, R. Scott, Colo SU, 1977, 78
Freyer, Tony, U Ala, 1988
Frick, Jane, Mo WC, 1983; 84, W Mo SC

Frick, John, Pittsfield, Ma., 1984; 85,
    U Wisc-Fond du Lac
Fried, Arthur, Plymouth SC, 1986
Fried, Lewis, Kent SU, 1987
Frieden, Sandra, U Houston, 1985
Friedman, Jerome, Kent SU, 1988
Friedman, Jim, Union Grad Sch, Cin, 1982
Friedman, Lawrence, BGSU, 1976
Friedman, Lawrence, IU-PUI,
Friedman, Lenemajd, Columbus C, Ga,
    1988
Friedman, Lester D., Syracuse, 1987
Friedman, Melvin J., U Wisc-Milw, 1973,
    74
Friedman, Monroe, E Mich SU, 1988
Friedman, Norman, Queens C, Flushing,
    1988
Friedman, Norman L., CSU-LA, 1975, 77,
    79, 81
Friedman, Reva, Mobile, Al.,1976
Friedman, Stephen, Bloomfield C, 1985
Friequegnon, Marie-Louise, William
    Patterson C, 1981
Fries, Maureen, SUNY-Fredonia, 1988
Friesen, Pete, Stillwater Family YMCA,
    1982
Frisby, Elizabeth, Tallahasee Comm C,
    1980
Frisch, Adam J., U Tx, 1978, 80
Frisch, Jack, U Wisc-Green Bay, 1982, 86,
    88
Frisch, John, Morton C, 1980
Frisch, Ronald, U Windson, 1984
Fritscher, John, W Mich U, 1971, 72
Fritz, Angela, Stillwater, Ok, 1983
Fritz, Donald W., Miami U, Oh, 1979
Frizler, Paul, Chapman C, 1987
Fromman, Daniela, BGSU, 1987
Frost, Everett C., CSU-Fresno, 1982, 83
Fry, Donald, W Va U, 1983
Fry, Virginia, Kans SU, 1983
Frye, Jerry, U Minn-Duluth, 1980, 81, 82,
    83; 85, 96, Smithsonian
Frye, John F., Triton C, 1976
Frye, Lowell, 1986
Fryer, Sarah, Mich SU, 1988
Fuchs, Cindy, U Pa, 1988
Fuchsman, Kenneth, U Ct, 1983, 84, 885
Fucile, Norman, Naval Underwater Syst
    Lab, 1976
Fuerstenberg, Adam, Ryerson Poly,
    Toronto
Fukfiewicz, Jacek, Film Sch Oodz, 1984
Fulcher, James, Lincoln C., Il, 1979, 85
Fullard, Joyce, Minn., 1982, 84, 85
Fuller, Daniel, Kent SU, 1972, 74, 78, 82,
    83, 84, 85, 86, 88
Fuller, John, W Ga C., 1984, 85, 86
Fulmer, Gilbert, SW Tx SU, 1980, 88
Fulmer, Hal, Miss SU, 1988
Fulmer, Karen, Fl SU, 1988
Fulmer, Lynne, St. Mary's U, San Antonio,
    1988
Fundaburk, E. Lila, BGSU, 1983, 85
Fuoss, Kirk, LSU, 1988
Furia, Philip, U Minn, 1986
Furman, Ellen, Pa SU-Ogontz, 1988
Furniss, David, U Wisc-River Falls, 1988
Furst, R. Terry, Staten Is Comm C, 1972,

73, 74, 75
Fusch, Richard, Oh Wes C., 1979, 81
Futrell, Al, BGSU, 1983, 84; 85, 88,
    U Louisville

Gaar, Alice, Tn Tech U, 1980
Gabel, Sandra L., U Neb, 1975, 83,
Gabriel, Barbara, Ottawa, Can, 1987
Gabriel, Claire, Omaha, Neb, 1977
Gabriel, Michael, N Il U, 1988
Gadd, Dale, U Kans, 1981, 82
Gaffield, Gary, Columbia, 1980
Gagliardo, Huey S., LSU-Eunice, 1988
Gagnard, Alice, S Meth U, 1986
Gaillard, Dawson, Loyola New Orleans,
    1976, 78
Gaines, Donna, SUNY-Stony Brook, 1985,
    86
Gaither, Robin, Phila, 1988
Galasi, Frank, CUNY, 1980
Galbreath, Robert, BGSU, 1971, 72; 73, 74,
    76, U Wisc-Milwaukee
Galeinbeck, Susan C., Ia SU, 1982
Galerstein, Carolyn, U Tx, 1982
Galician, Mary, Az SU, 1988
Galin, Muge, Oh SU, 1985
Gallagher, Bernard, Cent Meth C, 1988
Gallery, Michele, BGSU 1980
Gallo, Ernest, U Mass, 1986
Gallo, Louis, Columbia C, S.C, 1979
Gamal, Adel, U Az, 1984
Gamble, David, Wich SU, 1988
Gamble, Jeffrey, Va Tech, 1984
Gamble, Michael, NY Inst Tech, 1985
Gamble, Terri, C Rochelle, 1985
Gambone, Robert, U Minn, 1984, 85, 86
Gammerdinger, Harry, Martinsville, In,
    1984
Gandolpho, Anita, W Va U, 1979, 83
Gannon, Jack, Author, 1981
Garafalo, Reebee, U Mass, 1983, 85
Garay, Ronald, LSU, 1985, 86, 88
Garbett, Ann D., Averitt C, 1984
Garcia, Linda, Pan-Amer U, 1986
Garcia, Reyes, U Colo, 1982
Gardiner, Judith Kegan, U Il, 1976
Gardner, Lenore, Pittsburgh, 198
Gardner, Saundra, U Me, 1988
Garland, Susan M., Miami Oh, 1981
Garner, R. Brooks, Ok SU, 1988
Garner, Trevalyn, Midwestern SU, 1979
Garrin, Stephen, U Tx, 1982
Garson, Helen S., Geo Mason U, 1975, 77
Garvey, Gregory, N E Comp Arts Assoc,
    1986
Garvey, Timothy, U Minn, 1976
Garvie, Peter, U Tn, 1988
Garvin, Paul, SUNY-Buffalo, 1976
Garza, R.J., Pan-Amer U, 1983
Gash, Sharon, W Ky U, 1986
Gaskill, Gayle, Clarke C, 1979, 81
Gaspar, Charles, USAF Acad, 1988
Gaston, George, Appal SU, 1978, 79, 81,
    88
Gaston, Karen, Appal SU, 1981
Gates, David, U West Ont, 1985, 86, 88
Gates, Therese, Wich SU, 1983
Gatlin, Wanda, W Ky U, 1986
Gatta, John, U Ct, 1987

Gatzke, Ken, S Ct SU, 1988
Gaude, Pamela, U SW La, 1976; 77, Rice
Gaudet, Marcia, U SW La, 1988
Gaudry-Hudson, Christine, Wich SU, 1988
Gawman, Ann, U Waterloo, 1984
Gay, Carol, Youngstown SU, 1980
Gay, Phillip T., San Diego SU, 1977, 79
Gaztambide-Geigel, Jose, U Puerto Rico,
    1988
Geherin, David J., E Mich U, 1974, 76, 80,
    84
Gehring, Wes, Ball SU, 1981, 82
Geib, Frederick A., Colby C, 1978, 84, 85,
    86, 87, 88
Geib, George, Butler U, 1981
Geist, Christopher, BGSU, 1975, 76, 77, 78,
    79, 80, 81, 82, 83, 84, 85, 86, 87, 88
Geist, Edward, Hofstra U, 1985
Geist, Jean, BGSU, 1987, 88
Geist, Joseph E., Cent Meth C, 1976
Gelb, Phillip, Sarasota, Fl, 1986
Gelber, Steven, U Santa Clara, 1981
Gelderman, Carol, UNO, 1975, 76
Gelfant, Blanch, Dartmouth, 1974
Gendron, Bernard, U Wisc-Milw, 1981,
    84, 85
Gentile, John, U Nor Ia, 1985; 86, 88,
    Kennesaw C
Gentiles, Ian, York U, Ont
Gentry, David, Gaston C, 1972,73
George, Diana, Pa SU, 1979, 80, 81
George, Paul S., Atlanta JC, 1981; 85,
    U Miama, Fl
Gerber, Mitchell, Hofstra U, 1988
Gere, Pamela, Ala SU, 1986
Gerhardstein, Mary, U Waterloo, 1986
Gernes, Sonia, Notre Dame, 1979
Geroux, Brigid, Bloomfill Hills, Mi, 1988
Gershon, Rick, Oh U, 1984
Gerson, Walter, Willamette U, 1977
Gerty, Fred, Poughkeepsie, NY, 1983, 85
Gertzman, Jay A., Mansfield SC, 1981, 85,
    87
Gerulaitis, Leonardas, Oakland U,
    Rochester, Mi, 1988
Gerulaitis, Renate, Oakland U, Rochester,
    Mi, 1988
Gery, John, UNO, 1985, 86, 87, 88
Getz, J. Greg, Tx Wesleyan C, 1984, 86
Getz, John, Xavier U., Cin, 1985
Getz, Norleen, U Cin, 1978
Ghaly, Salwa, Edmonton, Alta, 1984
Gianokos, Perry, Michi SU, 1971, 73
Gibbons, Russell, Pittsburgh, 1977
Gibbs, Kathryn, Bryan, Tx, 1979
Gibian, Jill, E Ore SU, 1988
Gibson, Bill, SMU, 87
Gibson, Kenneth, York U, Ont, 1984
Gibson, Mary, UNC-Greensboro, 1986
Giebelhaus, Gus, Ga Tech, 1986
Gifford, James M., W Car U, 1977, 80;
    81, U Wisc-Stevens Point; 82, Morehead
    SU
Giglio, Ernest, Lycoming C, 1984
Gil, Efraim, Governors SU, 1976
Gilboa, Netta, Northwestern, 81, 82, 83, 84,
    85; 86, Chicago
Gilchrist, Loretta, St. Augustine C, 1984;
    88, Marygrove C

Gildemeister, Glen A., Nor Il U, 1975
Giles, Dennis, Cleveland SU, 1980
Giles, Steven L., Mt Home VA Med Cntr, Tn, 87
Gill, June, CSU-Fresno, 1977, 84
Gill, Robert, Radford U, 1987
Gill, Walivy, U Neb, 1986
Gillen, Don, Vassar, 1982
Gillespie, Angus, Rutgers, 1985
Gillespie, David, CSU-LA. 1971
Gillespie, Judy, IU-PUI, 1974, 75
Gillies, Mary, A., Calgary, Can, 87
Gilligan, T.M., Pa SU-Allentown, 1981
Gilliland, C. Herbert, US Naval Acad, 1987
Gilliland, Joan, Marshall U, 1986
Gillin, Donald, Vassar, 1984
Gillis, Paula A., Norwich U, Vt, 1987
Gilman, Owen, St. Joseph's U, 1981, 82, 83, 84, 87
Gimble, Josephine G., Amer U, 1987
Ginsberg, Robert, Pa SU
Giovanni, Nikki, Va Tech, 1988
Girard, Jolyon P., Cabrini C, 1978, 79
Girard, Sharon, San Francisco SU, 1980
Girgus, Sam, U NM, 1983
Giry, Jacqueline, U Ut, 1979, 80
Gitenstein, R. Barbara, Cen Mo SU, 1983
Gittler, Joseph, Geo Mason U, 1984, 86, 87, 88
Givan, Richard, E Ky U, 1988
Ginant, Michael, Adelphi U, 1976, 85, 86
Gladstein, Mimi, U Tx-El Paso, 1988
Glanz, Dawn, BGSU, 1979, 81, 85
Glaser, Ehon, U Akron, 1984
Glasgow, Janis, San Diego SU, 1977
Glass, Peyton, III, Ok SU, 1976, 77
Glassie, Henry, Ind U, 1971
Glatt, Charles, Kalamazoo, Mi, 1985
Glausser, Wayne, DePauw U, 1987
Glazer, Joe, USIA, 1971
Gleason, Dan, Sou St Comm C, 1984, 85, 86, 87, 88
Gleason, James, Wright SU, 1971
Gleeson, Terence, Neumann, C, 1985, 88
Glenn, George, U N Ia, 1986, 87
Glennon, Lynda M., Rutgers, 1977
Glessing, Robert J., Canada C, 1975
Gloe, Esther, U Sou Colo, 1983, 84, 85
Glofcheskie, John, Brock U, Ont, 1984
Glorie, Jo, Strategic Writing Services, 1982
Gluck, Yoel, S. Fran Xav U, Antigonish, Can, 1987
Gluckson, Robert, BGSU, 1988
Glyer, Michael, BGSU, 1975
Goankar, Dillip, U Pitts, 1983
Goatley, Cynthia, Gustavus Adol C, 1986
Godard, Barbara, York U, Toronto, 1984
Godbout, Patricia, North Hatley, Can, 1987
Goddard, Peter, Toronto Star, Toronto, 1984
Godfrey, Lydia, N Va Comm C, 1979, 83, 84, 85, 86, 87, 88
Godin, Jean-Cleo, U Montreal, 1987
Godfried, Nathan, Northwestern, 1985
Godtredsen, Lawrence, Babson C, 1982
Godwin, Gail, Woodstock, NY, 1987
Goerman, Robert, Branckenridge, Pa, 1982
Goethals, Gregor, RI Sch Design, 1976, 77,

81
Goff, Robbie, BGSU, 1983, 86
Goggans, Barbara, Clemson, 1985
Gogol, Miriam, Fashion Inst Tech, NY, 198
Goist, Park Dixon, Case Western Res, 1971, 73
Gold, Ronald L., Taft HS, Woodville Hills, Ca, 1978
Gold, Gerald, York U, Can, 1987
Goldbeck, Jane, Id SU, 1985
Golden, Daniel, SUNY-Buffalo, 1979, 1980
Golden, James, Oh SU, 1985
Golden, Mark, U Winnipeg, 1984
Goldfarb, Alvin, Il SU, 1978
Goldfarb, Clare, W Mich U, 1984, 86, 87, 88
Goldfarb, Jeffery, New Sch Soc Research, 1988
Goldfarb, Russell, W Mich U, 1984, 86, 87, 88
Goldman, Harry, Fl SU, 1980, 81, 82, 84, 85, 86, 87, 88
Goldman, Jon, Case Western Res, 1978
Goldman, Joseph, USArmy Com & Gen Staff C, 1985
Goldman, Michael, Miami Oh, 1981
Goldman, Robert, U Ky, 1981, 82, 84; 85, 86, 87, Hobart & William Smith C
Goldsmith, Dave, Nor Mich U, 1979, 84, 86
Goldstein, Beth, U Wisc, 1984
Goldstein, Ezra, Cin, 1981, 82, 83
Goldstein, Kalman, Fairleigh Dickinson U, 1983, 86, 87
Goldstein, Laurence, U Mich, 1977
Goldstein, Richard, Mich Tech Inst, 1984, 85, 86, 87, 88
Golfman, Noreen, U Me, 1984
Goluboff, Benjamin, Lake Forest C, 1988
Gomery, Douglas, U Md, 1982
Gomez, Joseph, Wayne SU, 1984
Gontarski, S.E., Oh SU-Lima
Gonzales, Adoracion, Youngstown SU, 1979, 81, 86
Gonzales, William, U Ut, 1979
Gonzalez, Alfredo, U Minn, 1978
Gonzalez, Bobbi, U Tx-El Paso, 1988
Gonzalez, Iris, U Puerto Rico, 1988
Gonzalez, Maria, Oh SU, 1988
Gonzalez, Richard, U SD, 1971
Good, I.J., Va Tech, 1980
Goodheart, Eugene, Brandeis, 1987
Goodman, Ailene, Washington, DC, 1982, 84, 85, 86
Goodman, Lee, Purdue-Hammond, 1988
Goodman, Steven, Assumption C, 1984
Goodrich, Peter, U Mich, 1984; 85, 86, 87, 88, N Mich U
Goodwin, Barbara, London, 1988
Goodwin, Joseph, Ball SU, 1985, 86
Goodwin, Toni, Midlands Tech C, 1986
Goodwyn, Frank, U Md, 1972
Goodykontz, Bill, UC-Riverside, 1975
Gool, Reshard, U Prince Ed Is, 1987
Goostree, Laura, BGSU, 1985, 86
Gopaul, Fr Paul, St. John's U, 1971
Gorden, William, Kent SU, 1983
Gordon, Andrew, U Fl, 1986
Gordon, Avery, Boston C, 1988

Gordon, Bertram, Mills C, 1981, 82, 84
Gordon, Beverly, U Wisc, 1984, 85, 96, 87, 88
Gordon, Deborah, U Md, 1980, 81
Gordon, Jacob, U Kans, 1983
Gordon, Jean, UNC-Greensboro, 1986
Gordon, Jeffrey, BGSU, 1981, 82
Gordon, Joan, Commack, NJ, 1988
Gordon, Joan, U Ia, 1980
Gordon, Lenore, U Miami, Fl, 1986
Gordon, Martin, USMC Hist Center, Washington, 1978
Gordon, Michael, U Ct, 1971; 77, U Rochester
Gordon, Morgan, U Ark, 1983
Gore, Luther, U Va, 1971, 81, 86
Gorfain, Phyllis, Oberlin C, 1984
Gosnell, Lynn, U Tx, 1978
Gotelli, Dolph, UC-Davis, 1988
Gotera, Vincente, Ind U, 1988
Gott, Suzanne, U Tx, 1987
Gottesman, Ronald, U Wisc-Parkside, 1975
Gottesman, Steve, SUNY-Buffalo
Gottlieb, Roger, Worcester Poly Inst, 1984, 87
Gottlieb, Stephen, Quinnipiac C, 1987
Gouanvic, Jean-Marie, U Que a Trois-Riviere, 1987
Gough, Dale Edw, U Md, 1977
Gould, Christopher, SW Ok U, 1981
Goulding, James, York U, Toronto
Gourlie, John, Quinnipiac C, 1986, 87, 88
Govan, Sandra, U Ky, 1982; 86, 87, 88, UNC-Charlotte
Governer, Alan B., Columbus C Art & Design, 1977, 79
Govoni, Mark, Oh U, 1975
Gowans, Alan, U Victoria, 1972, 73, 79
Graban, Paul, Temple, 1977
Graber, Ralph S., Muhlenberg C, 1978, 79, 80
Grabill, Joseph, Ill SU, 1983
Gradford, Robert, Lafayette C., 1975
Graebner, William, SUNY-Fredonia, 1979
Graffam, Gray, Trent U, 1984
Graham, Betty, New Site HS, Al, 1986
Graham, Don, U Tx, 1986
Graham, Don B., U Pa, 1987
Graham, Elizabeth, U Fl, 1986
Graham, Richard, Minn C Arts & Design, 1978
Grahame, Peter, Ont Inst Studies of Educ, 1984
Gran, Judith A., Pub Int Law Center, Phila, 1987
Grand, Cesar, UC-San Diego, 1984
Grandgeorge, Audrey, U Wisc-Milw, 1974
Grant, Barry, Brock U, 1982, 83, 84, 88
Grant, Elizabeth, Hawthorne, NY, 1985
Grant, Philip A., Bronxville, NY, 1985
Grant, Roger, U Akron, 1985
Grant, Thomas, U Hartford, 1980
Grant, William, BGSU, 1984, 85, 87
Graper, David, U Pa, 1983
Graubert, Eric, BGSU, 1973
Graves, Allesandra, Pa SU, 1984
Graves, Barbara, Greenhill School, Dallas, 1982, 83
Graves, Lawrence L., Texas Tech, 1974

Graves, Pearletta, Loyola U, New Orleans, 1985
Graves, Shauna, U Ut, 1986
Grawe, Paul H., Winona SC, 1972, 78
Gray, Charles, Winston-Salem SU, 1986, 87, 88
Gray, David J., Hamilton C, 1987
Gray, Herman, N Car Ag & Tech, 1978; 82, 84, UC-Santa Cruz; 86, Northeastern
Gray, Jonathan, UNC, 1988
Gray, Susan, Olivet C, 1988
Gray, W. Russell, De C Comm C, 1984, 85, 86, 87, 88
Graybar, Lloyd J., E Ky U, 1979, 80
Graybar, Lloyd, E Ky U, 1982
Graziano, Cecilie, U Minn, 1975
Gredel-Mannel, Zdenka, Niagara U, 1985, 8
Greek, Cecil, Cen SU, 1988
Greeley, Andrew, U Az, 1988
Green, Beatrice, Mercy C, Dobbs Ferry, NY, 1983
Green, Donald, Kirkwood Comm C, 1988
Green, Douglas, Country Music Found, 1976, 77
Green, Edward, St. John's U, 1983
Green, Gary L., U Ok, 1981, 83, 88
Green, Gregory, Wayne SU, 1980, 81
Green, Harvey, Margaret Woodbury Strong Mus, 1984
Green, James E., Lincoln U, Pa, 1975, 76
Green, Jon D., Brigham Young U, 1981, 82, 84
Green, Mary Jean, Dartmouth, 1984
Green, Michael K., U Fl, 1987
Green, Patrick, U Ala, 1985
Green, Rayna, U Mass, 1973; 77, Amer Assoc Advancement Sci
Green, Vicki, Vernon Pub Schs, British Columbia, 1977
Green, William, Morehead SU, 1987
Greenberg, Bradley, Mich SU, 1984, 88
Greenberg, Dolores, Hunter, 1984
Greenberg, Harvey, NYC, 1988
Greenberg, Robert, Queens C-CUNY, 1984
Greenberg, Stephen, Bronx, 1984
Greene, Michael, Wentworth Inst Tech, 1984
Greene, Michele, Columbia, 1982
Greene, Roberta, Geo Mason U, 1983, 84
Greene, Suzanne Ellery, Towson SC, 1971; 72, Johns Hopkins; 73, 74, 75, 76, 77, 78, Morgan SU
Greene, Wendy T., Bennett C, 1985; 86, Methodist C
Greenfield, Beth, Lamar U, 1980
Greenfield, Concetta, Carnegie-Mellon U, 1973, 74
Greenfield, Gerald Michael, U Wisc-Parkside, 1976
Greenfield, Liah, U Chicago, 1984
Greenfield, Thomas, Bellarmine C, 1986
Greenfield, Verni, UCLA, 1983, 84
Greenhill, Pauline, Toronto, 1984
Greenwald, Fay, Mercy C, 1988
Greenwald, Marilyn, Oh U, 1988
Greenway, Cora, Dartmouth, Nova Scotia, 1984

Greenway, William, Youngstown SU, 1988
Gregg, Alvin, Wich SU, 1983
Gregory, Christopher, St. Louis U, 1988
Gregory, David, U Neb, 1986
Gregory, Donald, U Neb, 1983, 84, 85, 88
Gregory, Robert, UC-Irvine, 1981
Gregory, Timothy, Oh SU, 1982
Greg Reynold's Dance Quintet, Washington, 1982
Gregson, Terry, U Ark, 1986
Greiff, Louis K., Alfred U, 1985
Grella, George, U Rochester, 1972, 74
Gremmels, James, U Minn-Morris
Gremmels, Marion, Wartburg C, 1985
Gremore, Robert, U Minn, 1979
Greninger, Edwin T., E Tn SU, 1978, 81, 86
Greninger, Gem Kate, E Tn SU, 1978, 81
Grenoble, Penelope, Santa Monica, Ca, 1980, 81
Gresser, Saul, Baltimore, Md, 1986
Gressler, Thomas, McMinnville, Ore, 1981
Gretlund, Jan Nordby, Odense U & Vanderbil, Tn, 1985
Grider, Sylvia, Ind U, 1972
Grier, Katharine, U De, 1984
Grierson, Patricia, Jackson SU 1982
Griffin, Asheley, U Mass, 1976
Griffin, Patrick, Loyola U, L.A., 1972; 75, CAL-Long Beach
Griffin, William, Sen ed Macmillan Pub, 1977
Griggs, Scott, Mich Tech U, 1978
Grilk, Werner, U Mich, 1988
Grimes, Larry, Bethany C, 1977, 78, 79, 80, 81, 82, 84, 85, 88
Grimsted, David, U Md, 1977
Grinchuck, Robert, St. Peter's C, 1980
Grindon, Leger, NYU, 1982
Gripp, Paul, Durham, NC, 1988
Griswold, Jerry, U Ct, 1971, 73, 74; 78, Northeastern U
Grittner, Fred, U Minn, 1985
Gritzner, Charles F., Ore C Educ, 1976; 82, 85, 86, S Dak SU
Groat, Theodore, BGSU, 1988
Groce, Stephen, W Ky U, 1988
Grodal, Hanne Tang, U of Aarbus, Denmark, 1985
Grogan-Braun, Ernest, SUNY-Buffalo, 1982
Grogg, Sam Jr., BGSU, 1972, 73, 74, 75; 76, Amer Film Inst
Groiman, George, La Guardia Comm C, 1984, 86, 87, 88
Gross, Alan E, U Mo-St. Louis, 1976
Gross, Barry, Mich SU, 1975, 77, 78, 79, 80, 81, 82, 83, 84, 85
Gross, David, U Ok, 1986
Gross, Edwin J., Roosevelt U, 1976
Gross, Robert, Susquehanna U, 1988
Gross, Susan R., Va Tech, 1978
Grossberg,Michael, Case-Western,1986
Groulx, Pierre, Lachine, PQ, Can, 1987
Grover, Doris, E Tx SU, 1986
Gruber, Ellen, W Ga C., 1988
Gruenwa, Oskar, Santa Monica CC, 1976
Grumman, Joan, Santa Barbara Comm C., 1973,

74
Grundman, Adolph, Metro SC, Denver, 1981, 83
Gruner, Leroy, N Ky U, 1985
Grunes, Rodney, SW U Memphis, 1982
Grunman-Gaudet, Minette, U W Ont, London, 1985
Grusin, Richard, Ga Tech, 1988
Grytting, Wayne, 1988
Guenter, Scot, U Md, 1986
Guerin, Kathleen, Emmanuel C, Boston, 1981, 82
Guerrero, Edward, UC-Santa Cruz, 1988
Guest, Hal, U Manitoba, Winnipeg, 1984
Guffery, George, UCLA, 1982
Guillaume, Bernice, Xavier U, NO, 1984
Gula, Joanne, Ok SU, 1983
Gulledge, Jo Marie, LSU, 1982
Gullestad, Marianne, Chicago, Il, 1985
Gulliford, Andrew, BGSU, 1984, 85, 86; 88, Western NM U
Gunlicks, Arthur, U Richmond, 1986
Gunn, James, U Kans, 1982
Gunn, Scout Lee, Ok SU, 1982
Gunew, S., Deakon U, Victoria, Australia, 1980
Guo Ming, BGSU 1988
Gura, Philip, U Colo, 1984
Gurian, Jay, U Hawaii, 1974
Gust, Mary, Hennepin Ctr Performing Arts, Minn, 1984; 85, Metro SU, St. Paul
Gustafson, Thomas U Sou Cal, 1986
Gustin-Evins, W. Thomas, Nor Il, U, 1988
Gustowski, John, Ind U, 1971, 75, 76
Guzlowski, John, Il SU, 1981; 82 (E Il U)
Gwaltney, Bill, Bents Old Fort, Lajunta, Co, 1988
Gwin, Louis, Va Tech, 1985

Haas, Masrtin, Adelphi U, 1980
Haberhern, Margot, Flor Inst Tech, Melbourne, Fl, 1988
Habich, Robert David, Pa SU, 1978
Hacker, Susan, Webster U, 1988
Hackett, Amy, Washington U, 1975
Hackler, Chris, E Tn SU, 1978
Hadzipetros, Sophia, CBC, Montreal, 1987
Haerle,Rudolf. Middlebury C, 1973
Hafter, Dary, E Mich, 1980
Hagemann, E.R., U Louisville, 1978, 79, 82
Hagemann, Leita, NYU, 1982
Hagen, Lyman, Ark SU, 1988
Hagen, William, Ok SU, 1983; 85, 86, Ok Baptist U
Hagens, Elizabeth A., Governors SU, 1974, 76, 77
Hager, Kelly, UC-Irvine, 1988
Haggerty, John, U Al-B'ham, 1975
Hagler, D. Harland, N Tx SU, 1984, 85, 86, 88
Hagopian, Patrick, U Pa, 1984, 88
Hague, John, Stetson, 1973
Hahn, Bob, Hounds of Baskerville, 1976
Hahn, Sidney, U Neb, 1983
Hains, Maryellen, W Mich U, 1978, 80, 81, 82
Haines, Harry, U Ut, 1984

Haines, William, U Ut, 1984
Hair, J. David, U Pitt, 1981
Haisty, Donna, Clemson, 1986
Hakanen, Ernest, Temple, 1987
Hakola, Judy, U Me, 1988
Hala, James Paul, U Mich, 1984; 86, Elizabeth C; 88, Drew U
Halberstam, Joshua, C.W. Post C, 1982, 84
Hale, Louise, Mont SU, 1978
Hale, Steven, Berry C, 1988
Halisky, Linda, Cal Poly, San Luis Obispo, 1988
Halkovic, Stephen, Ind U, 1981
Hall, Ann C., Oh SU, 1987
Hall, Charles, Cen Az C, 1980
Hall, Colin, U Waterloo, 1984
Hall, Dennis, U Louisville, 1981, 83, 85, 86
Hall, H. Palmer, St. Mary's C, San Antonio, 1983
Hall, James, U Sou Miss, 1984, 85, 86
Hall, John, U Houston-Downtown, 1988
Hall, John U., U Mo, 1988
Hall, Patricia, Amer Assoc State/Local History, Nashville, 1977; 78, Mid Tn SU; 1985, Amer Assoc St/Local History
Hall, Perry, Wayne SU, 1983
Hall, Peter, N Adams SC, 1988
Hall, Roger, James Madison U, 1981, 88
Hall, Scott, BGSU, 1986
Hall, Stephen, Appal SU, 1988
Hall, Tony, U Sudbury, Ont, 1984
Hall, Wade, Ballarmine C, 1985
Hallahan, Kirk Edward, U Wisc, 1972
Halley, Jeffrey, SUNY-Purchase, 1981
Halli, Robert, U Ala, 1986
Hallingberg, Gunnar, U Guteborg, 1972
Halloran, William F, U W Mich, 1974
Halpern, Sheldon, BGSU, 1972, 77
Halstead, Joseph, W Chester U, 1986
Hamel, April, Harris Stowe SC, 1985
Hamill, Paul, Temple, 1974
Hamilton, Lee, Pan-Amer U, 1988
Hamilton, Mary, Pa SU, 1979; 1982, 84, 85, 86, St. Bonaventure U
Hamilton, Tamara, Loyola Marymount U, LA, 1985
Hamilton, William, Otterbein C, 1982
Hammand, Carol, U Wisc, 1982
Hammel, William, Loyola U, NO, 1977, 78, 79, 81, 82, 83, 84, 86, 87
Hammer, Adam BGSU, 1979, 80
Hammer, Angelika, Bryn Mawr, 1983
Hammer, Eugenie, U Sou Al, 1986
Hammer, Rhonda, Ont Inst Studies Educ, 1984; 86, 88, York U
Hammerdinger, Harry, Ind U, 1983
Hammer-Johnson, Deb, Knoxville, Tn, 1974
Hammill, Geoff, BGSU, 1987
Hammock, Betty, Whitesburg, Ky,1983
Hammond, Arthur, Nat's Film Board, Toronto, 1984
Hammond, Charles, SUNY-Mech & Tech C, 1978
Hammontree, Patsy G., U Tn, 1979, 80, 81, 82, 83, 84; 85, Lenoir City, In; 86, 88, U Tn
Hamod, Kay K. BGSU, 1980

Hamp, Stephen, Henry Ford Mus, 1980
Hampton, Charles Wayne, Sul Ross SU, 1979
Hampton, Wayne, U Tn, 1981
Handfield, Gerald, Ind U-Indianapolis, 1982
Handling, Pliers, Queen's U, Kingston, Ont, 1984
Hanen, Patricia, The Pentagon, 1979
Hanes, John, Duquesne, 1975
Haney, David, Newton, Ma., 1988
Haney, James, U Wisc-Stevens Point, 1984
Haney, Kathleen, U Houston-Downtown, 1988
Hank, Pamela, U No Fl, 1987
Hanke, Robert, U Pa, 1984
Hanks, Carolyn, Miami U Oh, 1980
Hanks, Craig, Duke, 1988
Hanks, Pamela, U No Fl, 1985, 86, 88
Hanks, William, Miami U Oh, 1982, 83, 86, 87
Hanlon, Lindley, NYC, 1982
Hanners, John, Alleg C, 1980, 84
Hannon, Thomas, Slippery Rock C, 1986, 87, 88
Hanrahan, John J., Morehead SU 1980, 81, 84
Hansen, Art, CSU-Fullerton, 1984
Hansen, Burrell, Ut SU, 1982, 83
Hansen, Terry, Columbia, Ky, 1988
Hansis, Richard, Valparaiso U, 1978
Hanson, Charles, Groose Pt Pub Lib, Mi, 1988
Hanson, Debbie, U Il, 1988
Hanson, Janice, Rutgers, 1983, 84
Hanson, John H., Daemen C, 1979, 80; 81, Va Commonwealth U
Hanson, Karen, Ind U, 1982
Hanson, Luelt, Youngstown SU, 1987
Hapke, Laura, Nassau Comm C, 1980; 84, 88, Pace U
Harack, Joanne E., New College, U Toronto, 1973
Harbeson, Tom, W Mich U, 1977
Hardesty, William, U Miami, Oh, 1977, 78, 79, 81, 82, 84, 86, 88
Hardick, Mark, TOTCO, 1983
Hardin, Thomas, Courier-Journal/ Louisville Times, 1985
Hardy, Andrew, U Tx, 1985
Hardy, Charles, Temple, 1981, 82
Hardy, Deborah, U Wy, 1971
Hardy, Phil, BGSU, 1981
Hardy, Priscilla, U Il, 1983
Hardy, Robert C., Ok Health SC Foundation, 1987
Harfst, Betsky, Kiswaukee C, 1983
Harkins, Patricia, U Sou Al, 1988
Harkins, Patrick, St Mary-of-the-Woods, 1985
Harkness, David, U Manitoba, 1988
Harkness, John, Kent SU, 1988
Harlan, David, U Canterbury, New Zealand, 1976
Harless, Steven, U Sou Fl, 1984, 85
Harley, Ann, U W Ontario, London, 1984
Harmon, Gary, U No Fl, 1972, 73, 74, 75, 76, 77, 78, 79, 80, 81, 82, 85, 86, 87, 88
Harmon, Mark, Xavier U, Cin, 1988,

Harmon, Maryhelen C., U Sou Fl, 1972, 73, 74, 75, 76, 77, 78, 79, 80, 81, 82, 83, 84, 85, 86, 87, 88
Harmon, Sandra, Il SU, 1983
Harp, J.M., NYC, 1981
Harper, Charles, Creighton, U, 1986
Harper, Douglas, SUNY-Potsdam, 1982
Harper, Howard, UNC, 1982, 84, 85, 88
Harper, Kenneth, U Wisc-Kenosha, 1985, 86
Harragara, Deanna Jo, U Ok, 1982
Harred, Larry, U Wisc-River Falls, 1988
Harrell, Wade, U Md, 1988
Harrington, Anne, Wentworth Inst Tech, 1987
Harrington, E. Michael, Belmont C, 1988
Harris, Charles B., Il SU, 1976
Harris, Claudia, Phila C Textiles, 1988
Harris, Diana, U Tn, 1981
Harris, Dorothy, Francis Marion C, 1988
Harris, Edward, U Cin, 1971, 73
Harris, Jack, Hobart & William Smith C, 1988
Harris, Joseph, Phila, 1987
Harris, L. David, Point Park C, 1986
Harris, Laurilyn, Wash SU, 1988
Harris, Paulette, Augusta C, 1986, 87, 88
Harris, Peter, El Cerrito, Ca, 1984; 85, Berkeley, Ca
Harris, Victoria, Il SU, 1988
Harrison, Ann, Mich SU, 1986; 88, Los Alamos, NM
Harrison, John, U No Colo, 1975, 76, 79, 80; 81, Colo SC; 82, 83, 84, 85, 86, 87, 88, U No Colo
Harrison, Sally, NYU, 1982
Harrison, Sandra, Mercer C, 1988
Harrison, Walter L., Ia SU, 1979; 81, 82, 83, 84, 85, Colo C
Harrison-Pepper, Sally, U Tx-Richardson
Harroff, William, Ok SU,1983; 86, Roxana, Il
Harron, Kenneth, Mich SU, 1981
Hart, Arthur, Ida St. Hist Mus, 1975, 76
Hart, John, U Houston, 1988
Hart, John, Lewis & Clark, 1984, 88
Hart, Sue, E Mont C, 1988
Hartje, Robert, Wittenberg U, 1976, 86
Hartley, Thomas, Ok SU, 1984, 85
Hartman, Frank, Dickinson C, 1988
Hartman, Michael, Ok SU, 1986
Hartman, Patricia, Oh U, 1983
Hartmann, Rudi, U Colo, 1986
Hartsfield, Larry K., U Tx, 983
Hartshome, Thomas, Cleveland SU, 1981
Hartung, Beth, U Neb, 1984
Harty, John, U Fl, 1988
Harvey, Bruce, Palo Alto, Ca, 1988
Harvey, Dave, Temple, 1986
Harvey, Nancy, U Cin, 1986
Harvey, Richard, Oh U, 1988
Harvey, Thomas, Pa SU, 1976, 87
Harwell, Richard, U Ga, 1977
Harwell, Thomas, Ark SU, 1978, 81, 84; 85, Austin, Tx; 86, 88, U Tx
Hasan, Zia, King Faisal U, 1983, 84
Hasayn, Abdul Rahim Abu, Amer U, Beirut, 1982
Hasbany, Dick, Mich SU, 1975; 1977,

UCLA
Haslebacher, Pauline, York U, Ont, 1986, 88
Hassan, Ihab, U Wisc-Milwaukee, 1974
Hassencahl, Fran, Old Dom U, 1980, 88
Hassler, Donald, Kent SU, 1980, 81
Hatcher, Evelyn, U Minn-St. Paul, 1984
Hatle, Harlowe, U Sou Dak, 1987
Hatlen, Burton, U Me, 1987
Hatt, Harold, Phillips U, 1983, 87
Hattemer, Leah, Oberlin, 1973
Hattemer, Therese, Oberlin, 1973
Hattenbach, Marion, WMUB radio, Oxford, Oh, 1982
Hattenhauer, Darryl, U Minn, 1979
Haubenreich, Anita, Clemson, 1988
Hauck, Richard, U Sou Fl, 1981
Hausdorff, Don, Richmond C. SUNY, 1973, 74, 76, 82, 83; 84, Staten Is Comm C; 86, C Staten Island
Haven, Annette, San Francisco, 1981
Havens, Daniel F., Sou Il U-Edwardsville, 1978, 84, 86, 87, 88
Havet, Jose, U Ottawa, 1984
Hawes, Edward, Sangamon SU, 1985
Hawes, Leonard, U Ut, 1984
Hawes, Richard, Lincoln U, Pa, 1973, 74, 75
Hawker, Ron, U Victoria, 1988
Hawkesworth, Mary, U Louisville, 1984
Hawkins, Richard, Sou Meth U, 1980, 84
Hawley, Frederick, LSU-Shreveport, 1988
Hawley, Sandra, U Houston, 1984
Haydel, Douglas, Tallahassee, Fl, 1984
Hayden, Brad, W Mich U, 1987, 88
Hayes, Elvin, Washington Bullets, 1977
Hayes, John, Temple, 1977, 78, 79
Hayes, Joseph J., CSU-Fullerton, 1976
Hayes, Michael, Wich SU, 1983
Hayne, Barrie, U Toronto, 1973, 74, 75, 76, 77; 78, 79, 80, 81, 82, 83, 85, 86, Innis C, U Toronto
Hayne, Joanne, U Toronto, 1978
Hayne, Norman, Drake U, 1977
Haynes, Robin, BGSU 1987
Harward, Camille, Seattle, Wa, 1986
Haywood, Carl, U Wisc-Eau Claire, 1984, 88
Hazard, Johnine, U Chicago, 1974
Hazzard, Plankhi Maisha, Oh U, 1985
Hazzard-Gordon, Katrina, Cornell, 1984, 85, 88
Head, Constance, W Caro U, 1980
Healey, Jim, E Mont C, 1984, 85, 86, 88
Hearell, W. Dale, Stephen F. Austin C, 1979
Hearn, Melissa, UNO, 1988
Hearron, Tom, Sanginaw Valley SC, 1988
Heath, Frederick, Winthrop C, 1988
Heath, Julia A., Bluffton C, 1978
Heath, William, Mt. St. Mary's C, 1985
Hebein, Richard, BGSU, 1981, 86
Heberle, Mark, U Hawaii-Manoa,1988
Hebert, Chantal, Quebec, Que, 1984, 87
Hecht, Stuart, Boston C, 1988
Hedeen, Paul, U Akron, 1983
Hedges, James, UNC-Charlotte, 1980, 81, 84, 85
Heenan, Edward F., Jr, BGSU, 1972; 73, Cambridge Ctr Soc Stud, Mass; 74

U Tn-Nashville
Heeter, Carrie, U Mich, 1984
Heighton, Elizabeth, San Diego SU, 1985, 88
Heil, Lillian, Brigham Young U, 1982, 83
Heilbronn, Lisa, UC-Berkeley, 1985, 86
Heilbrun, Carolyn, Columbia U, 1981, 82
Heinegg, Peter, Union C, 1981, 88
Heinze, Andrew, Richmond, Ca, 1988
Heisey, D. Ray, Kent SU, 1983
Heiss, Reid, Chapel Hill, NC, 1986
Heitzeg, Nancy, U Minn, 1988
Helbig, Alethea, E Mich U, 1980
Helbig, Louis F., Ind U, 1973
Heldreth, Leonard, N Mich U, 1980, 81, 82, 83, 84, 85, 86, 87, 88
Heldreth, Lillian, N Mich U, 1984, 86, 87, 88
Heldt, Richard, U Az, 1988
Helfand, William H., Rahway, NJ, 1982
Helitzer, Melvin, Oh SU, 1988
Heller, Joshua, Syracuse U, 1978
Heller, Terry, Coe C, 1979
Hellman, Elaine, Northeastern Il U, 1980
Hellman, John, Oh SU-Lima, 1978
Helm, Charles, W Il U, 1977
Helm, David, U Ky, 1985
Helman, Claire, Nat Film Bd, St. Laurent, P.Q. Can, 1987
Helms, Ben F., U Mo, 1977
Helphand, Kenneth I., U Ore, 1976, 77
Helphinstine, Frances, Morehead SU, 1981, 82
Helt, Richard, Rice U, 1977; 79, 80, 81, 82, Rice U
Hemenway, Robert, U Ky, 1975
Hemphill, Anita, UCLA, 1984
Hemphill, Michael, U Ark-Little Rock, 1986
Henderson, Arn, U Ok, 1983, 84
Henderson, Australia, Fl A&M U, 1977, 78, 79
Henderson, Bruce, SUNY-Farmingdale, 1988
Henderson, Lisa, U Pa, 1984
Henderson, Roxanne, U Neb-Omaha, 1983
Henderson, Terry, Ok KSU 1982
Hendley, W. Clark, U Mo-KC, 1977, 80, 84
Hendrick, Rebekah, Sou Il U, 1987
Hendricks, Jon, U Ky, 1972
Hendricks, Susan, Id SU, 1985
Hendrickson, Bob, School of Ozarks, 1986, 87
Hendrickson, Joann E., San Fran SC, 1973
Hendrickson, Jo Ann, CSU, 1974
Hengstebeck, Bill, WXYZ Detroit, 1980
Hennessey, Thomas J., Jakmaima Plain, Ma, 1975
Henninger, Francis, U Dayton, 1971, 72, 75, 85, 86, 87
Henry, Carolyn, U Tn, 1983
Henry, Harley, Macalester C, 1982, 83
Henry, J. Patrick, Eckerd C, 1982, 83
Henry, Joyce E., Ursinus C, 1985, 86, 87
Henry, Judy, IU-PUI, 1976
Henry, Lyell, Mt. U Ia, 1974; 84, 85, Mt. St. Mercy C

Henry, Patricia, Tallahasee, Fl, 1983, 86; 88, Fl SU
Hentges, D., BGSU, 1984,
Heppel, Monica, American U, 1981
Herder, Dale, Mich SU, 1972
Herdon-Schaffer, W., Dekalb Comm C, 1987
Herlan, James, U Me, 1984
Herman, Andrew, Boston C, 198
Herman, Debra, U Ga, 1982
Herman, Kali, Yale, 1988
Hermann, Gretchen, U Rochester, 1988
Hernandez, Frances, U Tx-El Paso, 1980
Hernandez, Rafael, Converse C, 1986, 87
Herron, Jane, DeKalb Comm C, 1986
Herrick, George E., Me Maritime Acad, 1987
Herrick, Robert, Westmar C, 1982, 83, 84
Herring, Connie, Dakota SC, SD, 1988
Herring, Gina, Auburn U, 1983
Herrle, Mary Alice, BGSU, 1982
Hermann, Donald, DePaul U, Chicago, 1988
Herron, Jeff, U Wisc, 1987
Herron, Jerry, Wayne SU, 1980, 84, 85, 88
Herrscher, Walter, U Wisc-Green Bay, 1985, 88
Hersh, Richard, U Fl, 1982
Hershinow, Sheldon, U Hawaii, 1975, 76, 77, 78, 79, 80; 82, Kapiolani Comm C
Hertz, Vivienne L., Sou Il U, 1987
Hertzel, Leo J., U Wisc-Superior, 1980, 83
Herwald, Michelle, Chatham C, 1979
Herzog, Melanie, U Wisc, 1987
Hess, Jean E., N NM Comm C, Albuquerque, NM, 1980
Hess, Richard, IU-PUI, 1984; 85, IU-PUI, Fort Wayne
Hessini, Marguerite, SW C, Kansas, 1988
Hester, Al, U Ga, 1980
Hester, Ernest, Gaston C, 1972
Hesterman, Vickie, BGSU, 1985
Hewett, Andrew, Cornell, 1987
Hewett, John D., Ball SU, 1985
Hewitt, William, Briar Cliff C, 1988
Hey, Kenneth R., Brooklyn C, 1986
Heyda, John SW Mo SU, 1979
Hezel, Richard, U Houston, 1982
Hgenge, Toyoba, U Tx, 1987
Hibbard, Alan, U Wash, 1984
Hibbard, Don, Ida S Hist Soc, 1977, 78
Hickcox, David H., Oh Wesleyan C, 1979
Hickerson, Jerry, Kent SU, 1971
Hickman, Larry, Tx A&M, 1983
Hickman, Lynn, 1971
Hicks, James, W Il U, 1986, 87
Hidalgo, Stephen, Notre Dame, 1988
Higashi, Sumiko, SUC-Brockport, 1979
Higgins, Charles, Ind U, 1983
Higgins, John, Oh U, 1985
Higgins, Mary A., U Akron, 19987
Higgins, William, W Car U, 1976
Higgs, Jackson, E Tn SU,1977
High, Ellesa, W Va U, 1983, 88
Hilaire, Chantal, Toronto, 1984
Hilbish, D. Melissa, U Md, 1988
Hildebrand, John, U Wisc-Eau Claire, 1988
Hildenbrandt, Daniel, Lafayette, La, 1988
Hilfer, Anthony, U Tx, 1975, 88

Hill, Carole E., W Ga C, 1971
Hill, C. William, Roanoke C, 1988
Hill, Edwin, Oh U, 1985
Hill, Elbert, SU, Durant, Ok, 1978
Hill, Elliot, Kennesaw C, 1986
Hill, Hamlin, U Chicago, 1971
Hill, Helen, E Mich SU, 1983
Hill, James Lee, Albany SC, Ga, 1979
Hill, Jane, Wayne SU, 1980
Hill, Lawrence, U N Dak, 1986
Hill, Lynda, NYU
Hill, Michael, U Neb, 1984
Hill, Randall, LSU, 1988
Hillman, Lola, U Md, 1984
Hilmes, Michele, Spring Hill C, 1988
Hilsabeck, Steven, New Trier HS,
    Winnetka, Il, 1984, 86, 87, 88
Hilton, Lloyd, Appal SU, 1977, 79
Hinds, Harold E., Jr., U Minn-Morris,
    1979, 80, 81, 82, 83, 84, 85, 86,
    87, 88
Hinkel, Robert, W Mich, 1984
Hinman, Myra, U Kans, 1984, 85, 86, 87
Hinojosa, Rolando, Tx A&I, 1976,77
Hinrichs, C.Clarke, Cornell, 1985
Hinson, Mary A.D. UNC-Charlotte, 1984,
    85
Hinton, Norman, Sangamon SU, 1978, 86
Hirsch, Adam, Fl SU 1986
Hirsch, Allan, Cent Conn SU, 1986
Hirsch, John, North Hills, NY, 1988
Hirsch, Tim, U Wisc-Eau Claire, 1983, 84
Hirsch, John E., NYU, 1983, 84
Hirschberg, Edgar, U S Fl, 1973, 74, 75,
    76, 77, 78, 79, 80, 81, 82, 83, 84,
    85, 86, 87, 88
Hirsh, Allan, Cen Ct SC, 1987
Hitchcock, Peter, Queens C, NYC, 1988
Hite, Molly, U Wash, 1980
Hlinka, Margaret, State Ohio Dept
    Development, 1972
Hlus, Carolyn, U Alberta, 1984
Hoagland, Bill, N Mont C, 1986, 87
Hoar, Jay S., U Me-Farmington, 1980, 87
Hobbs, Blair, Auburn U, 1988
Hobby, Douglas, U Louisville, 1975
Hoberg, Tom, NE Il U, 1988
Hobson, Wayne, CSU-Fresno, 1982
Hock, David, U Tol, 1973
Hockman, Ned, U Ok, 1975
Hodgdon, Dana, Northwester, 1976
Hodge, James, Bowdoin C, 1988
Hodge, Marian, High Point C, 1983, 85
Hodges, James, C Wooster, 1986
Hoekzema, Loren, Oh U, 1975
Hofer, Steve, E Ky U, 1983
Hoff, Catharine M., B'ham Sou, 1987
Hoffecker, W. Andrew, Grove City C, Pa,
    1979
Hoffman, Andrew, U Ore, 1987
Hoffman, Arnold, Adrian C, 1971
Hoffman, Donald, Northeastern U, 1987
Hoffman, Frank A., SUC-Buffalo, 1975, 76,
    77, 78, 82, 85
Hoffman, Frank W., San Houston SU,
    1984, 85, 86
Hoffman, Melvin, SUC-Buffalo, 1976
Hoffman, Nancy Yanes, St. John Fisher C,
    1979, 80, 81, 82, 83, 84, 85

Hoffman, Thomas P., Midwestern SU,
    1978, 79, 80, 84, 87
Hogan, Homer, U Guelph, 1984
Hogan, John, Colo Sch Mines, 1982, 83
Hogan, Wayne, Cookeville, Tn, 1986
Holbrooke, Wendell, Rutgers, 1984
Holcomb, Briavel, Rutgers, 1979
Holden, Dave, Il SU, 1974
Holden, Philip, U Fl, 1986
Holkeboer, Robert, Eastern Mich U, 1980
Hollahan, Eugene, Ga SU, 1979
Holland, Theodore J., Railroaders Mem
    Mus, Altoona, Pa, 1987
Hollenshead, Carol, U Mich, 1980
Holliday, Kent, Va Tech, 1981
Hollow, John, Oh U, 1980
Holloway, Karla, N Car SU, 1988
Holm, Janis, Oh U, 1983, 84
Holm, William, Hampton Inst, 1975, 76
Holman, David, UNC, 1981; 86, 88, U Miss
Holmberg, Carl, BGSU, 1983, 84
Holmes, Jack D.L., U Al-B'ham, 1978
Holmes, Robert, BGSU, 1979
Holmes, Ronald, U Louisville, 1984, 86
Holmes, Wayne, Drury C, 1983, 84
Holmgren, Philip, Kearney SC, 1983
Holsinger, M. Paul, Il SU, 1984, 85, 86,
    87, 88
Holt, Jerry, U Arts & Sciences in Ok, 1983
Holt, Wythe, U Ala, 1988
Holtan, Judith, Slippery Rock SC, 1972
Holtan, Orley, Slippery Rock SC, 1971,
    72
Holte, James Craig, E Car U, 1982, 83, 85,
    86, 88
Holton, O.D., Appal SU, 1977, 78, 79
Holton, William, U Md, 1982
Holtsmark, Erling, U Ia, 1979, 86
Holtz, Janicemarie A., CSU-LA, 1975
Holtzberg, Maggie, U Pa, 1986
Holum, Kaaren, U DC, 1984
Holwerk, Colleen, Tolson Inst, U Ky, 1973
Holwerk, David, Tolson Inst, U Ky, 1972
Homan, Delmaar, Bethany C, 1982, 83
Hones, Sheila, Weston, Bath, U.K, 1985
Honey, Maureen, Mich SU, 1979; 1980, 82,
    83, 84, 85, 86, 87, 88, U Neb
Hong, Lawrence K., CSU-LA, 1976
Honhart, Frederick, Mich SU, 1985
Hood, Connie, U Tn, 1982
Hood, Thomas C., U Tn, 1980, 81, 83, 85
Hood, Walter K., Tn Tech, 1982
Hooper, Columbus, U Miss, 1982
Hoover, Dwight, Ball SU, 1985, 88
Hoover, Judith, Vanderbilt, 1985
Hoover, Karen, Pittsburgh, Pa, 1985, 86
Hoover, Robert, Brock U, 1987
Hoover, Stewart, U Pa, 1983
Hope, Christine, Clemson, 1980
Hopkins, Anthony, Glendon C, York U,
    1972, 73, 76, 83, 84, 85, 86, 87
Hopkins, Beth, Glendon C, 1986
Hopkins, Fred, U Balti, 1985
Hopkins, Karen, SUNY-Brockport, 1975
Hoppenstand, Gary, BGSU, 1983, 84, 85,
    86, 87, 88
Hopper, Columbus, U Miss, 1983, 84, 85,
    86, 87, 88
Horn, Barbara, Nassau Comm C,1986

Horn, Pierre L., Wright SU, 1979, 80, 81,
    86, 87, 88
Horne, William, U Lancaster, England,
    1984
Horowitz, Carl, Va Tech, 1984
Horowitz, Mark, U Chicago, 1983
Horowitz, Richard F., Rutgers, 1977
Horowitz, Ronald, Belle Mead, NJ, 1982
Horowitz, Steven, U Ia, 1981; 88, Ia SU
Horsley, A. Doyne, Sou Il, 1978, 81, 82
Horton, Charles, Chatham Cty PS, Chapel
    Hill, NC, 1976
Horton, Russel M., Hope C, 1978
Horvath, David, U Louisville, 1982; 86,
    U Sou Fl
Hotalilng, Gerald, U Vt, 1979
Houck, Davis, C Wooster, 1988
Hough, David, SW Mo SU, 1988
Hough, George, Mich SU, 1975, 76
Hough, Robert, Cen Mich U, 1988
Houghton, Jay C., Doyle Dane Bernbach
    Adv, 1987
Houston, Craig, U Tol, 1987
Hovet, Grace O'Neill, U No Ia, 1979, 80
Hovet, Theodore R., U Nor Ia, 1979
Hovey, Kenneth, N Car Wesleyan C, 1983
Howard, Al, Bay De Noc Comm C, Mi,
    1986, 88
Howard, David B., Vancouver, Can,
Howard, Gene, Wellington, Al, 1986
Howard, Harry, Maryville C, Tn, 1981
Howard, Victor, Mich SU, 1973, 80, 84
Howard, Tom, Va Tech, 1977
Howe, Ken, Mich SU, 1983, 84, 85, 86, 87,
    88
Howell, Maryon, W Il U, 1984
Howell, Pamela, TCU, 1982
Howell, Sarah M., Mid Tn SU, 1987
Howell, Thomas, RI C, 1981
Howgill, Woodie, Mo West SC, 1983
Howlett, Don, Milwaukee, Wisc, 1984
Howorth, Lisa, Oxford, Ms, 1985
Howsden, Jackie L., Ok SU, 1978; 88,
    Mid Tn SU
Hoy, James, Emporia SU, 1983
Hoyle, Karen, U Minn, 1984, 87
Hrezo, William, Radford U, 1988
Hruska, Thomas, Nor Mich U, 1982, 88
Hu, Stephen, Va Tech, 1984, 85
Hubbard, Preston, Austin Peay SU, 1987
Hubbard, Rita, Christopher Newport C,
    1984, 85, 86, 88
Hubbard, Tom, U Cin, 1980
Hubbard, Marilyn Stall, Ark SU, 19974, 75,
    76, 77, 78
Huber, Carole, TCU, 1983; 1984
    Elizabethtown C
Hubert, Linda, Agnes Scott C, 1988
Hubin, Allen J, Ed The Armchair
    Detective, 1971
Hubka, Thomas C., U Ore, 1979
Huck, Karen, U Ut, 1986
Huddleston, Eugene, Mich SU, 1975, 76,
    77, 78, 81
Hudson, Harriet, Ind SU, 1986, 88
Hudson, Michael, Oh SU, 1988
Huebel, Harry Russell, Tx A&M, 1971
Huff, W.A. Kelly, Dalton C, 1988
Huffman, Carolyn S., SUNY-Buffalo, 1976

Huffman, James R., SUNY-Fredonia, 1972, 73, 74, 75, 76, 78, 79

Huffman, John, Pepperdine C, 1978

Huffman, William, Sacred Heart C, 1986, 87

Hug, W.J., Auburn U, 1985; 88, Jacksonville SU

Huggins, Martha, Union C, 1979

Hughes, James M., Wright SU, 1971, 73, 74, 76, 78, 79, 80, 81, 82, 83, 84, 85, 88

Hughes, Nina, NYC 1987

Hughes, Paul, WMUK, Western Mich U, 1980

Hughes, Shaun, Purdue, 1988

Hughes, William, Essex Comm C, 1977

Hugh, Tom, Boston U, 1988

Hagunin, Marc, BGSU, 1978, 79, 80

Hul, Bernard V., U Mich, 1987

Hull, Elizabeth A., William Raney Harper C, 1976, 78, 80, 81, 82, 83, 84, 85

Hull, Richard, Ind U-Gary, 1985

Hummel, Richard, E Il U, 1988

Hummon, David, C of Holy Cross, 1985, 88

Humphrey, George, Mass C Pharmacy, 1982

Humphreys, John, Clarion U, 1985

Hundley, Margaret, U Guelph, 1986, 87

Hundley, Pat, Ok SU, 1976; 82, 83, Phillips U

Hunt, Barbara, Columbis C, 1980, 81, 83

Hunt, Caroline, C of Charleston, 1985, 87

Hunt, Charlotte, Fl SU, 1986

Hunt, Linda, Oh U, 1983

Hunt, Lynne, U Md, 1984; 85, 86, 87, Shippensburg U

Hunt, Richarda, Trinity C, 1987

Hunter, C. Stuart, U Guelph, 1984, 85, 86

Hunter, Jean, Duquesne, 1988

Huntley, David, Appal SU, 1985; 86, 88, UNC

Huntley, Edelma, Appal SU, 1988

Huntzicker, William, U Minn, 1974

Huot, Brian, U No Ia, 1987

Hurd, Mary, E Tn SU, 1988

Hurlbert, C. Mark, Ind U Pa, 1988

Hurley, Neil P., Loyola of NO, 1977, 78, 79, 80

Hurlow, Marcia, Asbury C, 1985

Hurrell, Barbara, Mich SU, 1982, 84, 86

Hurst, Richard, Buffalo/Erie Hist Soc, 1975

Hurt, Jethro, U Il, 1975, 76

Hurt, Mandy, BGSU, 1986

Husch, Jerri, Tufts, 1988

Huse, Nancy, Augustana C, 1975

Huson, Dorothy, Wayne SU, 1985

Huss, Wayne, Villanova, 1987

Hussman, Lawrence, Wright SU, 1971

Hutch, Richard, U Queensland, Australia, 1985

Hutchinson, Allan C., York U, Can

Hutchinson, George, U Tn, 1986

Hutson, Nancy W., LSU-Shreveport, 1982

Hutson, Richard, UC-Berkeley, 1985, 86, 87, 88

Huya, Dennis, Lake City, Pa, 1986

Huyssen, Andreas, U Wisc-Milw, 1974

Hyatt, Steven, U Me, 1988

Hye, Allen, Wright SU, 1986, 88

Hyers, Conrad, Gustavus Adolphus C, 1980

Hyland, Jay, Rockport, Ma, 1986

Hyles, Vernon, U Ark-Pine Bluff, 1986; 88, Auburn U

Hyman, Colette, U Minn, 1986

Hyman, Erie, Rutgers, 1984, 85

Hyman, Linda, CUNY-Richmond C, 1974

Hynds, Ernest, U Ga, 1986

Iacovetta,Franca, York U, 1984

Iannavarone, Ronald, Pan-Amer U, 1986

Ibby, Charles, BGSU, 1985

Ibelema, M., Cen SU, Oh, 1988

Iglauer, Bruce, Alligator Records, 1976

Ilisevich, Robert D., Alliance C, 1971

Imber, Jonathan, Wellesley, 1984

Imberman, Flaurie, SUNY-Binghamton, 1979, 80

Imbert, Patrick, U Ottawa, Can, 1987

Imperia, Giovanna, Loyola U NO, 1983

Ingalls, Gerlad UNC-Charlotte, 1987

Ingalls, Meg, Lamar U, 1984

Inge, M. Thomas, Va Commonwealth U, 1973, 75, 77, 78; 81, 82, Clemson; 84, USIA; 85, 86, 87, 88, Randolph-Macon C

Ingersoll, D. W., Jr., St. Mary's C of Md, 1979

Ingle, Kathryn L., U Ia, 1987

Ingold, Charles, U Nor Colo, 1988

Inserra, Cathy, 1984

Intinoli, Michael J., Burlington Cty C, NJ, 1979

Iorio, Sharon, OK SU, 1986

Impema, Tim, E Il U, 1988

Irish, Loomis, Brooklyn C, 1985

Irvin, Helen, Transylvania U, 1979, 78, 81

Irvine, Lorna, Amer U, 1978; 79, 80, 81, 83, 84, Geo Mason U

Irwin, Edward, Austin Peay SU, 1981, 83, 87

Irwin, Zachary, Pa SU-Erie, 1985

Isaac, Frederick, 1981; 82, 83, 84, 85, 86, 87, 88, Berkeley, Ca

Isaacs, Leonard, Mich SU 1982

Isaacs, Neil D., U Md, 1977, 79

Isaacson, David, West MU, 1980

Isabella, Tony, 1974

Isen, Keith, NYU, 1986

Iskander, Sylvia, U SW La, 1984

Islam, A.K.M. Aminul, Wright SU, 1978, 84

Ismaili-Abukakr, Rashidah, Rutgers, 1985

Israel, Jerry, Il Wesleyan U, 1986

Israel, Paul, Rutgers, 1984

Isralow, Eric, SUNY-Buffalo, 1973

Itzkowitz, David, Macalester C, St. Paul, 1984

Ivers, Susan, Oh U, 1988

Iverson, Ann C., Houston, 1982

'Ivey, William, Country Music Foundation, 1974, 75, 78

Ivry, Judith, Syracuse U, 1978

Izard, Ralph, Oh U, 1985

Jackaway, Gwenyth, U Pa, 1985

Jackson, Arlene, St. Joseph's C, Phila., 1980, 81

Jackson, Bruce, 1980

Jackson, Carlton, W Ky U, 1982, 83, 86, 87, 88

Jackson, Joe, U Ark, 1979

Jackson, John, Concordia U, Montreal, 1984

Jackson, Kathy, BGSU, 1984; 85, 86, 88, Va Wesleyan C

Jackson, Martin, Encore Magazine, NYC, 1982

Jackson, Richard, Carleton U, 1976

Jackson, Richard A., Mich SU, 1986

Jackson, Sarah, Ga Tech, 1986

Jackson, Susan, Princeton, 1987

Jackson, Wendell, Morgan SU, 1981

Jackson, William, BGSU, 1980

Jackson, William, Ok SU, 1975

Jackson, William, U Nor Colo, 1988

Jackson, William K., Metro SU, Denver, 1988

Jackson-Beck, M., Cleveland SU, 1980

Jacobs, David, Temple, 1984

Jacobs, Dorothy, URI, 1987

Jacobs, Ed, U Il, 1988

Jacobsen, Cheryl, Wartburg C, 1985

Jacobsen, R. Brooke, Colo SU, 1976

Jacobsen, Sally, Nor Ky U, 1982

Jacobson, Kent, U Mont, 1975, 76

Jacobson, Richard, U Wisc, 1978

Jaffee, Harry Joe, Oh SU, 1972

Jagoe, Ann, Tx Woman's U, 1988

Jakaitis, Jake, SW Mo SU, 1980, 84

James, Barry, Rider C, 1987

Jameson, W.D, U Central Ark, 1985; 86, U Ark-Conway; 88, U Cent Ark

Jamieson, Duncan R., U Ala, 1973, 76, 77

Jamieson, Walter, U Calgary, 1987

Jamison, Susan, U Akron, 1985

Jankofsky, Klaus, U Minn-Duluth, 1976

Jansen, Raymond, Granville, Oh, 1986

Janzen, Junie, Bartlesville, Ok, 1982

Jardine, Evonne, Santa Barbar Comm C, 1974

Jarecke, George W., Auburn U, 1979

Jarrell, Michael, U Fl, 1987

Jarvie, Ian, U Pa, 1971; 84, York U

Jarvis, Dennis, Sou Il U, 1976

Jarvis, Ken, KNCT-Central Tx, 1982

Jason, Emil, S Il U-Edwardsville, 1984, 85

Jason, Philip, US Naval Acad, 1988

Jaszczun, Wasyl, U Pitt,1979

Jay, Connie, Ok SU, 1982

Jay, Elizabeth, Ball SU, 1988

Jay, Karla, Pace U, 1985

Jay, Tim, N Adams SC, 1986, 87, 88

Jayanti, Vikram, Los Angeles, Ca., 1986

Jeane, D. Gregory, Auburn U, 1977, 78, 79, 80, 81, 86

Jeanntet, Robert, U Akron, 1988

Jeansonne, Glen, Williams C, 1977

Jeay, Madeleine, McMaster U, Hamilton, Ont, 1984

Jedwab, Jack, McGill, Montreal, 1984

Jefchak, Andrew, Aquinas C, 1984, 85, 88

Jeffers, Dennis, Cent Mich U, 1982

Jeffers, Dennis W., Sou Il, 1978, 79

Jeffrey, David K., Auburn U, 1978, 81; 85, 86, NE La U

Jeffries, David, Auburn U, 1982

Jenkins, Barb, BGSU, 1975

Jenkins, Linda, Northwestern, 1981

Jenkins, Ron, Harvard, 1983

Jenkins, William, Tn Tech, 1988

Jennings, Robert, U Ind-Southeast, 1982, 85

Jennings, Wade, Ball SU, 1980, 81

Jensen, Joli, U Il, 1982

Jensen, Margaret, Hamline U, 1981, 86

Jensen, Media, 1976

Jensen, Rayhmond. Ok SU, 1987

Jervey, Edward D, Radford C, 1975, 76, 77, 78, 79, 80, 82, 83, 84, 85, 86, 87, 88

Jervey, Thora, Dublin Elem Sch, Dublin, Va, 1984

Jeske, Jeff, Guilford C, 1988

Jeter, James, Fl A&M, 1986

Jewell, Richard B., USC-LA, 1982

Jewett, Robert, Morningside, C, 1976

Jezierski, John V., Saginaw Valley SC, 1980

Jiang, Xin-Zhu, BGSU, 1986

Jillson, Teresa, U Rochester, 1988

Jiminez, Francisco, U Santa Clara, 1979

Jiobu, Robert, Oh SU, 1979, 80

John, Lisa, Ok SU, 1984, 85, 86, 87

Johns, John, Dallas, Tx, 1988

Johnson, Annette, BGSU, 1971

Johnson, Barbara, U Sou Car, 1986

Johnson, Byron, U Colo, 1986

Johnson, Charles, U Richmond, 1985, 86

Johnson, Connie, U Mich, 1986

Johnson, Dan, U Minn-Duluth, 1976, 78

Johnson, David M., N Caro A&T, 1979; 81, Columbus C, Ga

Johnson, Deidre, U Minn, 1984, 86

Johnson, Diane, U Minn, 1988

Johnson, Donald, Bridgewater SU, 1981; 82, Wake Forest U; 85, E Tn SU

Johnson, Eithne, Albuquerque, NM, 1985; 88, Emerson C

Johnson, Gary, Ferris SC, 1988

Johnson, Glen, U Louisville, 1980, 81

Johnson, James H., U Wisc, 1977

Johnson, James L., E NM U, 1984

Johnson, Jeff, E Ore SC, 1988

Johnson, Judith, Oh SU-Newark, 1981

Johnson, Laura Kaye, Lamar U, 1979

Johnson, Marla, Ok SU, 1984

Johnson, Mary, U Kans, 1983

Johnson, Mary, E Tn SU, 1982

Johnson, Michael L., U Kans, 1972, 75, 76

Johnson, Paul, CSU-San Bernardino, 1982

Johnson, Robert, SPEBSQSA, 1975

Johnson, Robert, Miami U, Oh, 1983, 85, 88

Johnson, Stephen, NYC, 1982

Johnson, Stuart, Atlanta, Ga, 1986

Johnson, Tanya, Duke Medical Center, 1983

Johnson, Virginia, C Charleston, 1988

Johnson, W. Lee, UNC-Wilmington, 1987

Johnson, William, Mich SU, 1980

Johnson, William, Sou Il U, 1988

Johnson, William J., Augusta C, 1988

Johnson-Grau, Brenda, Los Angeles, 1986

Johnson, James J., Griswold-Eshleman Co, Cleveland, 1972

Johnson, Jessica, U Md, 1988

Johnston, Robin, Temple, 1981

Johnston, Ruth D., John Jay C Criminal Justice, 1976, 82

Johnstone, Anne, U N Ia, 1988

Joiner, Dorothy, W Ga C, 1987

Jones, Anne H, U Tx Medical Branch, 1979

Jones, Archie, Fort Lewis, Ore, 1971, 72

Jones, Charles E., Houghton-Mifflin, 1972

Jones, Charles E., Stephen F. Austin SU, 1984, 85

Jones, Dan, U Houston-Downtown, 1988

Jones, Daryl E., Mich SU, 1983

Jones, Donald, U Cen Fl, 1980

Jones, Edward T., York C, Pa, 1988

Jones, E.R., U S Caro, 1985

Jones, Elizabeth, U Wisc-Green Bay, 1984

Jones, E. Michael, St. Mary's C, Notre Dame, 1981

Jones, Gary L., U Nev-Las Vegas, 1985

Jones, Gerald, Tiffin, Oh, 1988

Jones, James, Tn Hist Comm, 1986

Jones, Joel, U NM, 1977

Jones, Joyce Meeks, Ark SU, 1977

Jones, Kathryn, OK SU, 1973

Jones, Kellie Corlew, U Tn-Martin, 1978

Jones, Laura, Araphoe, CC, Colo, 1987

Jones, Leander, W Mich U, 1978, 79, 89, 82, 83, 84, 85, 86

Jones, Lethonee, W Mich Sch Soc Work, 1979; 80, 81, W Mich U, 83, 84, 85, 86, 87, 88

Jones, Lonnie, Chicago, Il, 1978

Jones, Loyal, Berea C, 1982

Jones, Madison, Auburn U, 1986

Jones, Michael Owen, 1971, 88

Jones, Miriam, York U, Can, 1988

Jones, Myrl Guy, Radford U, 1986

Jones, O.P., Ohio Wesleyan U, 1974

Jones, Robert A., C Wooster, 1973; 80, Bradley U

Jones, S. Jeffrey, Cleveland SU, 1986

Jones, Shirley, Ok Baptist U, 1982, 83

Jones, Soyna, Alleg C, 1986, 88

Jones, Steve, U Wisc-Eau Claire, 1988

Jones, Steven, Cleveland SU, 1988

Jones, Thomas, Coastal Car C, 1987

Jones, Victor, Ind SU, 1988

Jordan, Amy, U Pa, 1988

Jordan, Brigitte, Mich SU, 1979

Jordan, Elizabeth, Purdue, 1981

Jordan, Peter, Tn SU, 1984, 85, 86, 87, 88

Jordan-Squire, Jeannine, BGSU

Jorgenson, Jane, U Pa, 1982

Joseph, Cheryl, Munster HS, In, 1981, 82

Joseph, Paul, Tufts, 1987

Joseph, John, Ok SU, 1983, 84

Joslyn, Richard, Temple, 1982

Jowett, Garth, 1971; 80, 81, 82, 84, 85, U Houston

Joyaux, Georges, Mich SU 1972, 73, 75, 77

Joyce, Constance, Radford, Va., 1987

Joyner, Charles, St, Andrews Presby C, 1974

Joyner, Nancy, West Car U, 1976, 77, 78, 79, 81, 82

Joys, Joanne, U Tol, 1981

Judd, Larry, U Houston, 1982

Judkins, Bennett, Belmont Abbey C, 1983

Judkins, David C., U Houston, 1983, 84

Juffras, Angelo, William Patterson C, 1981

Juhasz, Joseph, 1976

Juhasz, Suzanne, U Colo, 1977

Jules-Rosette, Bennetta, UC-San Diego, 1977, 80

Juleus, Nels, Alleg C, 1986

Juliano, Herb, Notre Dame, 1981

Julius, Patricia, Mich SU, 1984

Jun, Zhao, BGSU, 1987

Juneja, Renu, Valparaiso U, 1988

Juravich, Tom, Pa SU-Reading, 1987

Jurkiewicz, Kenneth, Cent Mich U, 1980, 81, 82

Kader, Chery, U Wisc-Milwaukee, 1986

Kafalenos, Emma, Wash U, St Louis,

Kagan, Richard C., Hamline U,

Kahlbacher, Catherine, Gallaudet C, 1981

Kahlbeck, Mel, U Minn-Morris, 1982

Kahn, Diana Grossman, Oberlin, 1985

Kahng, Grace, 1985

Kakonis, Tom, U Wisc-Superior, 1971; 76, Ferris SU

Kaleialoha, Carol, U Hawaii, 1978

Kaler, Anne, Gwynedd-Mercy C, 1986

Kalikoff, Beth, U Puget Sound, 1988

Kalin, Berkeley, Memphis SU, 1985

Kallan, Richard A, U Nev, 1975, 76, 77

Kallen, David J., Ferris SC, 1988

Kalson, Albert, Purdue, 1973, 80, 82

Kamalipour, Yahya, Purdue-Hammond, 1988

Kamau, Lucy Jane, Northeastern Il U, 1979

Kamholtz, Jonathan, U Cin, 1986

Kamholtz, Sara E., U Cin, 1988

Kaminsky, Edmund P., Kent SU, 1983, 85, 86, 87

Kaminsky, Stuart, Northwestern U, 1973, 74, 76, 80, 81, 82

Kamphoefner, K.R., Northwestern U, 1988

Kanarek, Rita, York U, Can, 1987

Kane, Ilene, Union C, 1987

Kane, Jeremy, BGSU, 1987

Kane, Kate, Northwestern U, 1985, 86, 87, 88

Kaner, Norm, Temple, 1973

Kang, Hyeong-Dew, Sou Il U, 1981

Kang, Jong, U Mass, 1985, 86

Kang, Shin, U Mass, 1986

Kanter, Sanford, San Jacinto C, 1984

Kantra, Robert A, Villanova, 1972

Kaplan, Abraham, U Mich, 1972

Kaplan, Ann, Monmouth C, 1973

Kaplan, Bruce, Flying Fish Records, 1976

Kaplan, Frederick I, Mich SU, 1971, 75, 76, 79, 80, 81

Kaplan, Karen, Georgetown U, 1988

Kaplan, Shirley, U Tol, 1981

Kaplan, Sidney J, U Tol, 1981

Karageorge, Uri, E Car U, 1984

Karagueuzian, Maureen M., Kensington, Ca, 1988

Karam, A., U Kuwait, 1982

Karp, Mort, U Ark, 1980, 84

Karpen, Jim, BGSU, 1983

Karpen, Stephen, People's Housing, Topanga, Ca, 1985

Karpinski, Joanne B., Regis C, 1988

Karrenbrock, Marilyn, U Tn, 1986
Karrer, Kathryn, Catholic U, 1986
Karriker, A. Heidi, U Ok, 1988
Karsten, Peter, U Pitt, 1987
Kasmer, Lisa, U Hartford, 1988
Kaspar, Elizabeth, W Il U, 1985, 86
Kasson, John F., UNC, 1975
Kasson, Joy S., UNC, 1975
Kastner, Kent, U S Fl, 1988
Kates, Don B., San Francisco, Ca, 1988
Katriel, Tamar, U Haifa, Israel, 1988
Katsh, Ethan, U Mass, 1986
Katsiaficas, George, Wentworth Inst Tech,
   1988
Katz, Milton S., Kansas City Art Inst, 1978,
   80
Katz, Neil, Syracuse U, 1980
Katz, Steven B., NC SU, 1988
Katzman, Natan I., Mich SU, 1971
Kauffmann, Barry L., Lewisberry, Pa, 1988
Kaufman, Barbara, Seton Hall U, 1984, 85
Kaufman, Gershen, Mich SU, 1984
Kaufman, Janet E., Amer U, 1977; 78,
   Lafayette C, 79, Worcester,
   Ma,; 86, Kutztown U
Kaufman, Leslie, Burlington Cty C, 1982
Kaul, Arthur J., Sou Il U, 1980; 83,
   W Ky U
Kaups, Matti, U Minn, 1976, 84; 85,
   U Minn-Duluth
Kaur, Serjit, BGSU, 1986
Kavanaugh, Thomas, SUNY-Buffalo, 1984
Kaveny, Philip A., Madison, Wi, 1988
Kay, Arthur, U Az, 1979
Kay, Helen, Mich S U, 1984
Kayser, Christopher, SUNY-Brockport,
   1974
Kazuo, Yoshida, BGSU, 1983
Kealy, Edward, Bayonne, NJ, 1980, 82
Kearney, Shery S., U Ky, 1988
Keating, Clark, U Ky, 1973
Keddie, Shirley, Keene C, 1985, 86
Keefe, Tim, Lansing, Mi, 1984
Keefer, Fred, Miami U, Oh, 1980, 81; 82,
   Franklin, Oh
Keel, William, U Kans, 1983
Keenan, Hugh, Ga SU, 1982
Keesing, Hugo, U Md, 1978, 79, 80, 81, 82,
   83, 84, 85, 86, 87
Keeter, Larry, Appal SU, 1986, 88
Keiser, Dennis, Bloomsburg SC, 1980
Kelcey, Barbara, Victoria, BC, 1988
Kell, Carl, W Ky U, 1983, 84, 85, 86,
   87, 8
Kellerman, Robert, Mich SU, 1988
Keller, J.R., Indiana U-Indianapolis, 1985
Keller, Richard, Kans STC, 1974
Kelley, Andrew L., Shelby S Comm C,
   Memphis, Tn, 1979
Kelley, Colleen, Pa SU-Erie, 1988
Kelley, David, Vassar, 1984
Kelley, Karol, BGSU, 1980; 86 Tx Tech
Kelley, William, writer of Gunsmoke
   episodes, 1984
Kellman, Steven, U Tx-San Antonio, 1981,
   82, 83, 84
Kellner, Douglas, U Tx, 1980, 81, 82, 84,
   85, 86, 88
Kelly, Becky, Sou Tech Inst, 1982, 85

Kelly, David, Nixdorf Computer, Boston,
   1983
Kelly, Edward, SUNY-Oneonta, 1981
Kelly, Frank, Wich SU, 1982, 83, 84
Kelly, Gordon, U Pa, 1971, 72
Kelly, John, Boston U, 1984, 85
Kelly, Keith, NYU, 1982
Kelly, Philip H., Gannon U, 1988
Kelly, Priscilla, Slippery Rock SC, 1973
Kelly, Richard, Setawket, NY, 1982; 85,
   U Tn
Kelly, William P., CUNY, 1979
Kelso, Susan U Kans, 1984; 85,McNeese SU
Kemp, Homer, Tn Tech U, 1986
Kendig, Doug, Comic Research Lib,
   Cassidy, BC, 1978
Kendle, Burton, Roosevelt U, 1976
Kenen, Regina, Trenton SC, 1985
Kennard, David, NYC, 1985
Kennedy, Ann, BGSU, 1987
Kennedy, Cornelia, U Ia, 1988
Kennedy, Devereaux, SUNY-Corland, 1986
Kennedy, G.W., U Il-Chicago, 1978
Kennedy, Michael J., Tx Tech, 1988
Kennedy, Pamela, Coker KC, 1981
Kennedy, Veronica, St John's U, 1983, 84;
   85 NYC, 86, St. John's U
Kenner, Janette, Pa SU-McKeesport, 1987
Kent, George, Murray SU, 1988
Kent, Thomas, Ia SU, 1980; 81
   Miami U. Oh
Kepley, David R., Hyattsville, Md., 1976
Kerman, Judy, Kent SU, 1985, 86, 87, 88
Kern, Louis J., Hofstra U, 1988
Kern, Ronald C., Ashland C, 1971
Kerr, Dennis, U Pa, 1982
Kerrane, Kevin, U De, 1974, 75, 86, 88
Kershner, Irwin, Motion Picture Director,
   1974
Kersten, Lawrence, E Mich U, 1973, 74, 76
Kessler, Carol F., U Pa, 1976, 77; 78, West
   Chester SC; 81, Pa SU-Mount Algo; 1984
Kestenbaum, Justin, Mich SU, 1984
Ketner, Joseph, Wash U, 1987
Ketterer, David, Concordia U, 1984
Kettler, Mary, Ga Sou C, 1986
Keune, Manfred, Pa SU, 1973, 74, 77
Keyishian, Harry, Fairleigh Dickinson U,
   1976
Khan, Razia Amin, Dhaka U, Bangladesh,
   1983, 84
Khanna, Lee, Montclair SC, 1984
Khliefat, Awad, U Jordan, 1983
Khokle, Vasdant, Mich SU, 1974
Kidney, Jennifer, Ok SU 1977
Kiehl, Kathy, Mankato SU, 1983
Kielich, Lawrence, Aquinas C, 1985
Kiesby, Suzanne, Nor Mich U, 1983
Kiewe, Amos, C Wooster, 1988
Kilbourne, Jean, Boston, Ma, 1985
Kileff, Clive, U Tn-Chattanooga, 1983, 85
Kilgo, Reese, U Ala-Huntsville, 1982
Kilgore, John, E Il U, 1982
Kilgour, Kathleen, Oh SU, 1980
Killeen, Barbara, E Il U, 1982
Killen, Linda, Radford U, 1984
Killingsworth, M. Jimmie, Tx Tech U,
   1988
Kilmer, Elizabeth, Montclair SU, 1985

Kilmer, Hugh, Hoboken, NJ, 1982, 84, 85,
   86, 87, 88
Kimball, Jeffrey, Miami U, Oh, 1986
Kimball, Sue L., Methodist C, 1985, 86, 87,
   88
Kimberling, C. Ronald, SCU-Northridge,
   1976
Kincaid, John, N Tx SU 1980
Kind, Joshua, Nor Il U, 1980
King, Christopher R., U Windsor, 1977
King, Holly Beth, Rutgers, 1979, 80
King, G. Wayne, Francis Marion C, 1981
King, Janis, U Ia, 1986
King, John, Los Angeles, 1985
King, Kathleen, Ia SU, 1987
King, Margaret, BGSU, 1971, 72; 75,
   U Hawaii; 76, Honolulu; 77, East-West
   Center; 78, U of Hawaii-Manoa; 79,
   Yellow Springs, Oh; 80, Antioch C,
King, Michael J., Nat'l Humanities Inst,
   1977
King, Michele, Westwood Ele Sch, Ok, 1983
King, Sarah S., National Humanities Inst,
   1977
Kingsbury, Stewart, N Mich U, 1986
Kingsland, Helen K., Drew U, 19898
Kingsley, Karen, Va Tech, 1980
Kingston, Raye, URI, 1977
Kingston, Roger, Belmont, Ma, 1982
Kinnamon, Kenneth, U Il, 1977; 84, U Ark
Kinnard, Cynthia, Johns Hopkins U, 1975,
   76
Kinner, Jack, Gallaudet C, 1984
Kinney, Katherine, U Pa, 1988
Kinney, Thomas L., BGSU, 1978
Kinsella, Marjorie, BGSU. 1981; 82, Il SU
Kinsella, Toby, CINQ-FM, Montreal, Can,
   1987
Kinstenberg, Cindy J., UNC, 1988
Kinzer, Nora Scott, Purdue, 1973
Kirkham, E. Bruce, Ball SU, 1981
Kirkhorn, Michael, U Ky, 1982
Kirkland, Barney, Carbondale, Il, 1987
Kirkland, Catherine, U Pa, 1983
Kirkpatrick, R. George, San Diego SU, 1983
Kirlin, Thomas, U Wisc, 1977
Kirsch, George, Manhattan C, 1984
Kirschenbaum, Baruch, RI Sch Design,
   1978, 79, 81
Kirshner, Alan M., Ohone C, 1977
Kirson, Arthur, NYC, 1981
Kiser, Kenneth J., Ok SU, 1978
Kiske, Rebeccah, Anniston, Ala, 1986
Kissane, Sharon, Barrington, Il, 1983
Kitch, Sally, Wichita SU, 1983, 85
Kitching, Gavin, SUC-Cortland, 1988
Kithcart, Phillip E., Prairie View A&M,
   1977
Kittrell, Jean, Sou Il-Edwardsville, Il, 1984
Kitzenbeck, Alan, Miami U, Oh, 1982
Kivlin, Joseph, BGSU, 1975
Kivlin, Laura, BGSU, 1980
Kizer, Elizabeth, U Mo-St. Louis, 1982, 83,
   84, 85; 86, Austin, Tx, 88
Klak, Alice, E Ore SC, 1984
Klaphake, Clement, Bellevue C, 1983
Klass, Dennis, Webster U, 1985
Klatch, Rebecca, UC-Santa Cruz, 1988
Kleck, Gary, Fl SU, 1988

Klee, John, Maysville Comm C, 1981
Klein, Kathleen G., IU-PUI, 1974, 75, 76, 77, 78, 79, 80, 81, 82, 84, 84; 85, Indiana U, Indianapolis, 86, 87, 88
Klein, Lloyd, Brooklyn C, 1985
Klein, Yvonne, Dawson C, Can, 1987
Kleinberg, Susan J., U Tn, 1978
Kleinhans, Chuck, Co-ed Jump Cut, 1974, 75, 76
Kline, Galen, Va Tech, 1981, 88
Kline, Paule G., Hampden Sydney Ci, 1988
Kline, Rufus, U Ct, 1985
Klingenberg, Vaughn, U Fl, 1986
Klipper, Lishe A., Ind U, 1979
Klipstein, Steven, Suffolk Cty Comm C, 1978
Kloenne, Gregg, Portland Mus, Louisville, Ky, 1985
Klopenstein, Bruce, BGSU, 1986
Klotman, Phyllis R., Ind U, 1972, 73
Klotter, James, Ky Hist Soc, 1982
Klug, Dorothy, Sears Roebuck Co, Dayton, Oh, 1979
Klymasz, Robert, St. Andrews C, Winnipeg, 1984
Knafo, Danielle, CUNY, 1987
Knapp, Peggy A., Carnegie-Mellon U, 1979
Knatt, Kathaerine, Williamsburg, Va, 1982
Knecht, Antoinette, Lourdes C, 1981, 82, 84
Knecht, Richard, U Tol, 1980, 82, 83, 84, 86
Knee, S., Syracuse, NY, 1984
Kneebone, John, U Ala, 1986
Knepper, George W, U Akron, 1981
Knepper, Marty, Morningside C, 1985, 86, 87, 88
Kneupepper, Charles, Carnegie-Mellon, 1979
Knight, Bill, Prairie Sun Comm, Peoria, Il, 1982, 83
Knight, David, Carleton U, Ottawa, 1984
Knight, Edward, UNC—Ashville, 1980
Knight, John H., Il Valley Comm C, 1983
Knight, Patricia, Amarillo C, 1988
Knighton, Billie, Wichita SU, 1983
Knobel, Dale, Tx A&M, 1979
Knobloch, Frank, Brookville, Tn, 1982
Knoper, Randall, Lafayette C, 1988
Knopp, Josephine, Harcum Jun C, 1982, 83
Knowlton, Roberta, Rutgers, 1983, 85, 86
Koch, Bill, Kans SU, 1983
Koch, David V., Morris Lib, Sou Il, 1977
Koch, Lewis, Photographer, Madison, Wisc, 1983
Koch, Susan, Mich SU, 1972
Kochanski, Matthew, U Md, 1988
Koe, Barbara, Heritage Hall Schools, Ok City, 1983
Koegler,Karen, U Ky, 1984, 85
Koelsch, James R, Cleveland, Oh, 1987
Koenig, Frederick, Tulane, 1978, 79, 81
Koenigsberg, Lisa, Smithsonian Inst, 1985
Koester, Robert, Delmark Records, 1976
Koff, Stephen P., Syracuse U, 1988
Koffler, Judith S., Pace U, 1987
Koger, Alicia, Kent SU, 1986
Kohl, Linda, Mich SU, 1988

Kohl, Rhonda, Il SU, 1987
Kohl, Seenal, Webster C, 1975
Kohler, Turner, Tx Woman's U, 1984
Kohler, Vincent, U Pitt-Johnstown, 1974; 82, 86, U Pitt-Bradford
Kois, Craig, Northwestern, 1987
Koivumaki, Judith, Harvard, 1974
Kokrff, Sybil, Perrysburg, Oh, 1979
Kolb, Turner, Tx Woman's U, 1985
Kollar, Marvin, Kent SU 1982
Kollmann, Judith, U Mich-Flint, 1980, 84, 88
Kolmerton, Carol, Hood C, 1984
Kolodzcy, Jody, Temple, 1984; 86, U Pa
Koloski, Bernard J., Mansfield SU, 1977
Kolmerton, Carol, Hood C, 1979
Kolton, Ronald, Washington, D.C., 1984
Komichak, Michael, WPIT, Pittsburgh, 1979
Komprides, Nicholas, York U, Toronto, 1983
Konetschni, Walter, Shippensburg U, 1988
Konshak, Dennis, U Neb, 1982
Kontos, Paulette, Ind SU 1973
Koon, William, Clemson, 1981
Koons, Kenneth F., VMI, 1987
Kopel, David, NYC
Koppelman, Susan, BGSU, 1972, 73; 75, Wash U; 78 St. Louis U; 79, 80, 81, 82, 85, 86
Koppenhaver, Allen J., Wittenberg U, 1983, 84
Korn, George, Oh U, 1985
Kornbluth, Joyce, U Mich, 1980
Kornfeld, Eve, Princeton, 1985,86, 87
Korsok, Albert, U Akron, 1978,79
Kosberg, Roberta, Northeastern U, 1987
Kosek, Steven, Elgin Comm C II, 1985
Kosinski, Mark, U Fl, 1981
Kotker, Joan, Bellevue Comm C, 1985, 86, 88
Kotter, Jacqueline, Salt Lake City, 1985
Kottler, Hugh, Amer Embassy, Mexico, Laredo, 1985
Kottsey, Steven, U Cin, 1984
Kotywek, Roy A., Oakland U, Rochester, Mi, 1980
Kountz, Peter, Roosevelt U, 1975
Kovas, Susan, Drake U, 1985
Kovich, Charles, U N Ia, 1979
Kovisars, Judith F., Ok SU, 1973
Kowalski, Rosemary, U Mich, 1985, 86
Kraetschmer, Kurt, U Neb-Omaha, 1983
Kraft, Ruth B., NUY, 1983
Krajewski, Bruce, U Ia, 1987
Krajewski, Walter, Dawson C, Cal, 1987
Krakow, Amy, US News & World Report, 1980, 81; 82, WINS Radio, NYC; 84, Promotion Dir World Tennis
Krakow, Gary, NBC-TV, NYC, 1984
Kramer, Gary, Ball SU, 1985
Kramer, Gerald H., Pittsburg SU, Kans, 1983
Kramer, John, SUNY-Brockport, 1984
Kramer, Temma, CSU-Northridge, 1986
Kramer, Victor A., Ga SU, 1988
Kramme, Mike, Culver-Stockton C, 1985
Krasney, Marty, Princeton, 1971
Krasniewicz, Louise, SUNY-Albany, 1982
Kratsas, James R, Kans Hist Soc, 1982, 83

Kraus, Jeffrey, Kingsborough Comm C, NY
Kraus, Linda, Ind U, 1985
Kreamer, Jean, U SW La, 1988
Krebs, Fred, Johnson Co Comm C, Kans, 1982, 83, 84, 85
Kreig, Martha Fessler, U Mich, 1978
Kreiling, Albert, S Meth U, 1982
Kreizenbeck, Alan, St. Mary's C, Md, 1981; 82, 83 Miami U, Oh; 84, 85, U Denver; 86, U Houston-Clear Lake, 87, 88
Krell, Roberta, UCLA, 1983
Kremer, Lillian, Kans SU, 1983
Kremer, Pem, U Ky, 1985
Kremer, S. Lilliah, Manhattan, Kans, 1984
Kremers, Marshall, NY Inst of Tech, 1985
Kresel, Peggy, U Il, 1986
Kretchmer, Susan, Johns Hopkins, 1987
Kretchmer, Susan, U Hartford, 1986
Kreyche, Gerald, DePaul U, Chicago, 1985, 87
Krieg, Joan, Hofstra U, 1983
Krier, William, Notre Dame, 1984, 85, 86, 87
Kroker, Arthur, Concordia U, Montreal, 1988
Kroller, Eva-Marie, UBC, Vancouver, Can, 1987
Kronegger, Marlies, Mich SU, 1987
Krouse, Agate Nesuale, U Wisc-Whitewater, 1975, 76, 77, 78
Krouse, Harry, U Wisc-Whitewater, 1976, 77, 78
Krueger, John, Ind U, 1973
Krueger, John R., Ind U, 1981
Kruegler, Chris, Syracuse U, 1980
Kruegler, Dvora, BGSU, 1980
Krummer, Michael, Mus Tent Repertoire, Mt. Pleasant, Ia, 1984
Kubiak, Lavinia, E Ky U, 1985
Kucyj, Vivi, Detroit, MI, 1980
Kuebbeler, Michelle, BGSU 1980
Kuebrich, David, Geo Mason U, 1981
Kuechmann, Christopher, Edinburg Pub Lib, Tx, 1986
Kuemmerlin-McLean, Joanne, Mont SU, 1988
Kuhel, Pat, Pittsburg SU, Kans, 1983
Kuhlberg, Raoul, U DC, 1978, 79, 80, 81, 82, 83, 84, 85, 86, 87, 88
Kuhlman, Deborah, Galveston C, 1987
Kuhlman, Thomas, Creighton U, 1983, 84
Kujawa, Sheryl, Boston C, 1983
Kukla, Edward R., Washington SU, 1987
Kula, Sam, Amer Film Inst, 1972, 83
Kulenkamplemmers, Felicitas, Belmont, Ma, 1984
Kullman, Colby, U Kans, 1983, 84
Kumagai, Akiko, Tokyo U Agri, 1988
Kummer, George, Case-Western, 1971
Kuney, Julius, Brooklyn C, 1985, 87
Kunin, Carolyn, UCLA, 1977
Kunz, Donald, URI, 1984, 85
Kunzle, David, UCLA, 1979
Kuo, Michael, E Il U, 1986, 88
Kurth, Suzanne, U Tn, 1983
Kus, Bonnie, CSU-Fresno, 1980
Kuwahara, Yassue, BGSU, 1986, 87, 88
Kyle, Richard C., Tabor C, 1983

Laack, Susan, U W Mich, 1974

Laatsch, William G., U Wisc-Green Bay, 1976

Lab, Susan, BGSU, 1988

Laba, Martin, Simon Fraser U, 1987

Laban, Lawrence F., Va Commonwealth, 1987

LaBarbara, Jim, WLW, Cin, 1978

LaBelle, Maurice, Drake U, 1988

Labossiere, Camille, U Ottawa, 1987

LaBrecque, Richard, U Ky, 1985

LaCasse, Don, Ball SU, 1988

LaCava, Elizabeth, IU-PUI, 1982

Lacey, Theresa, Tusca, Ala, 1988'

Lacombe, Michele, York U, Toronto, 1984

Ladd, Anthony E., U Tn, 1980

Ladue, Buffi, Tacoma, Wa, 1988

Ladwig, Ronald V., Oh Nor U, 1979

Lafleur, Ingrun, SUNY-Plattsburg, 1988

LaFollette, M., Harvard/MIT, 1980

LaFontaine, Cecile, Edmonton, Alta, 1984

LaFontant, Julien, U Neb-Omaha, 1983

Laforse, Martin, Ithaca C, 1981

Laforte, Robert S., Nor Tx SU, 1988

Lagana, Gretchen, U Il-Chicago, 1985, 87

Lahti, Glenn, Macomb Cty Comm C, 1980

Lahurd, Carol, Greenville, Pa, 1984

Lahurd, Ryan, Thiel C, 1981, 84

Lain, Laurence B., U Dayton, 1987

Laird, David, CSU-LA, 1977

Lakin, Michael, Alfred U, 1986

Lally, Tim D.P., BGSU, 1978

Lalonde, Christopher, SUNY-Buffalo, 1985; 86, N Car Wesleyan

Lama, Donald, Grayslake HS. 1976

Lamb, Margaret, Fordham, 1979

Lamb, Marvin, Tn Tech, 1984

Lambert, Patricia, Ok SU, 1978; 79, U Ok

Lambriola, Alberrt C., Duquesne U, 1979

Lamont, Austin, Ed Film Comment, 1974

L'Amour, Louis, Novelist, 1977

Lampe, David, SUNY-Buffalo, 1985

Lance, Larry M, UNC-Charlotte, 1979, 80

Land, Gary, Andrews U, 1981

Landerson, Joyce, Mich SU, 1981

Landon, Brooks, U Ia, 1982, 83, 84

Landon, Philip J., U Md-BC, 1988

Landrum, Larry, BGSU, 1973, 79; 77, 78, 80, 83, 84, 85, 86, 87, Mich SU

Landry, Albert M, U Montreal, 1976

Landry, Donna, U Mich, 1984, 85

Landry, Drew, Ut SU, 1983

Landsman, Miriam, U Ia, 1981

Lane, Sylvia, SUNY-Buffalo, 1982

Lane, Thomas D., E Tn SU, 1979, 80, 85, 88

Lang, Elsie, SW Ok SU, 1983

Lange, Ann, Bentley C, 1981, 82, 84

Langer, Sandra, USC-Columbia, 1986

Langford, Frances S., Ia SU, 1983, 84

Langford, Michele, Pepperdine C, 1988

Langham, Thomas C., U Sou Dak, 1988

Langley, Harold D., Smithsonian, 1988

Langner, Lorinda L., U Neb-Omaha, 1977

Langum, David J, Truett-McConnell C, 1981

Lanier, Doris, Ga Sou C, 1986

Lansing, Carol, U Tn, 1986

LaPaglia, Nancy, SW C, Chicago, 1976

Lapping, Mark, SUNY-Oswego, 1971; 73, Va Tech

Lanquist, Norman, E Az C, 1988

Larabee, Ann, SUNY-Binghamton, 1987

Lareau, Gerald R., Ia SU, 1980

Larkey, Edward, U Md-BC, 1986

Larner, Daniel, W Wash U, 1981, 82, 83, 84, 85

Laroche, Jacques, N Mex SU, 1986

Larossa, Paul, Brandeis, 1987

Larrier, Wanda, Mich SU, 1985, 87

Larsen, David M., Cleveland SU, 1980

Larsen, Lotte, W Ore SC, 1985, 86, 87, 88

Larsen, Michael J., St Mary's, Halifax, NS, 1988

Larson, Arthur, Westmark C, 1984

Larson, Charles, N Il U, 1984, 85

Larson, Cheri, UC-Irvine, 1988

Larson, David, SUNY-Fredonia, 1974, 75

Larson, Mary S., N Il U, 1985

Larsson, Donald F., U Wisc, 1979

Laskowsky, Henry, U Wy, 1981, 85, 88

Lasner, Phyllis, U Mich, 1987

Lasseter, Rollin, N Car SU, 1972

Lassiter, Laurie, Tisch Sch of Arts, 1984

Latkovski, Leonard, Louisville, Ky, 1985

Latosi-Swain, Elizabeth, Mo WSC, 1982, 83

Latta, Brenda, Ind SU, 1988

Lau, C. Kay, Mungkuk Lutheran Sch for Deaf, Hongkong, 1982, 83

Laughlin, Charlotte, Howard Payne U, 1982

Laughlin, Elaine, Cornell, 1986

Laughlin, Jody, Owensboro Comm C, Ky, 1988

Laukes, Jim, Governors SU, 1976

Laurence, Frank M., Miss SU for Women, 1978, 80, 81

Laurence, Richard, Mich SU, 1975, 76, 77, 78, 80

Laurette, Patrick C., Art Gallery NS, Halifax, NS

Lauritson, Robert, Toronto, Can, 1988

Lavazzi, Thomas, SW Mo SU, 1984

Lavery, David L., U Fl, 1979

Law, Richard, Kutztown SC, 1982, 84, 85; 86, Kutztown U

Lawler, John J., Ind SU, 1972, 73

Lawrence, Barbara, Sou Il-Edwardsville, 1980, 81, 83, 86

Lawrence, Floyd B., Edinboro SC, 1977, 79

Lawrence, Frank, Miss U for Women, 1979

Lawrence, John, Morningside C, 1976, 80, 81

Lawrence, Robert, Jefferson Comm C, Louisville, Ky, 1980, 81, 84, 85

Lawson, Anita, Murray SU, 1984

Lawson, Benjamin, Albany SC, Ga., 1985

Lawson, Elaine, Don Mills Can, 1987

Lawson, Elaine, York U, Toronto, 1983

Lawson, Jackie, U Mich-Dearborn, 1988

Layman, Richard, Bruccoli, Clark Publishers, 1982

Layne, Gweldolyn, Vanderbile, 1983; 85, Chicago, Il

Lazar, Barry, CBC, Montreal, 1987

Lazier-Smith, Linda, Oh SU, 1987

Le, Pham, BGSU 1978

Leach, Don, Tx SU, 1983

Leach, Gene, Trinity C, 1982, 84, 85, 87, 88

Leach, Jim, Brock U, St. Catharine's, Ont, 1984

Leady, Linda, BGSU, 1975

Leahy, Edward,P., E Car U, 1987

Lealand, Geof, BGSU, 1981, 82, 83

Lears, Jackson, U Mo, 1982

Leary, John, U Md, 1977, 79

Leatherwood, Kristi, Oh U, 1988

Leblanc, Edward, Ed Dime Novel Roundup, 1984, 85, 86, 87, 88

LeBlanc, Robert, U New Hamp, 1986, 87

Lebling, Dave, Infocom, Inc, Cambridge, Ma, 1986

Leckie, Ross, U Toronto, 1987

LeCroy, Anne E., Tn SU, 1979; 80, 81, 82, 83, 84, 85, 86, 87, 88, East Tn SU

Leddy, Edward, Tarleton SU, 1988

Leder, Priscilla, U Ok, 1983

Lederer, Katherine, Mo SU, 1986

Lederman, Marie Jean, CUNY, 1978, 79

Ledford-Miller, Linda, U Tx, 1983

Ledingham, John, U Houston, 1983

Ledwin, Lenora, Notre Dame, 1988

Lee, Bartholomew, San Fran, Ca, 1982

Lee, Patrick E, C. of Great Falls, Id, 1978, 79, 80, 81

Lee, Stan, NYC, 1974, 77

Leeds, Barry, Cent Ct SC, 1987

Leeson, Richard, Fort Hays SU, 1983

Leff, Leonard J., Ok SU, 1983

Leftwich, Linda Rowan, Geo Mason Elem Sch, Richmond, Va, 1979

LeGacy, Arthur, Syracuse U, 1975, 76, 77

Leggett,Susanne, New Trier HS, Il, 1988

Lehan, Richard, UCLA, 1986, 88

Lehman, Neil B., Ind SU Pa., 1979, 80, 81, 85, 88

Lehman, Rhea, U Wisc, 1986

Lehnerer, Melodye, York U, Toronto, 1985, 86, 87, 88

Lehr, John C., U Winnipeg, Manitoba, 1984

Lehrhaupt, Linda, NYU, 1983; 84, W. Germany

Lehrman, Frederick, Shr Jung Cntr for Culture/Arts, NYC, 1974

Lehrman, Walter, U Akron, 1983, 84, 85, 87, 88

Leib, Elliot, Yale, 1985

Leibacher-Ouvard, Lise, U Az, 1987

Leibowitz, Flo, Ore SU, 1982,84, 86, 87

Leiby, David, Orange, Ca., 1984

Leichtle, Kurt R., U Wisc-River Falls, 1988

Leigh, Frederic, Az SU, 1982

Leith, Linda, John Abbott C, Ste. Anne of Bellevue, 1987

Lekas, Michelle, U Fl, 1987

LeLond, Christopher, SUNY-Buffalo, 1984

Lemaster, Angela, Sou Il U, 1981

Lemaster, Joyce, Morehead SU, 1985

LeMoine, Frannie, U Wisc, 1973

Lemon, James, U Toronto, 1984

Lemon, Randall, Highland Sch, Ind., 1982

Lemontt, Bobbie Burch, U Tn, 1979

Lenard, G.T., Stockton SC, Pomona, NJ, 1986, 87, 88

Lenhart, Paul, Ok SU, 1982

Lenihan, John H., U Md, 1976, 77; 84, Texas A&M
Lepovitz, Helena, SUNY-Geneseo, 1987
Lennon, J. Alan, Toronto, Ont, 1982, 84
Lennon, John, Sangamon SU, 1975
Lennon, Peter, Local Govt Affairs Dept., Springfield, Il, 1979, 80, 81, 82, 83. 84
Lenox, Gary J., U Wisc-Rock County, 1979
Lent, Tina, Rochester Inst Tech, 1986
Lentz, Richard, U Ia, 1980
Lentz, William, U Va, 1980; 84, Chatham C
Leo, John R., URI, 1977, 79, 80, 83, 84, 85, 86, 88
Leo, Peter, Towson SU, 1987
Leonard, G.T., Stockton SC, Pomona, NJ, 1985
Leonard, Stephen, Metro SC, Denver, 1986
Lerner, Elinor, Stockton SC, Pomana, NJ, 1984, 85, 87
Lerner, Saul, Purdue-Calumet Campus, 1979; 80, 84, Purdue-Hammond
Lesch, William, Baylor, 1983
Leslie, Larry Z., U Sou Fl, 1988
L'Esperance, Jeanne L., Nat Archives Canada, Ottawa, 1988
Lessne, Greg, URI, 1984
LeSure, Valentino, Langston U, 1983
Letson, Russell, St Cloud, Mn, 1978, 79, 80
Levang, Lewis D., U Minn-Duluth, 1980
Levenduski, Cristine, U Minn, 1984, 85
Leventhal, Naomi, Dunkirk Pub Sch System, NY, 1979
Leventman, Seymour, Boston C, 1988
Leverence, William John, BGSU 1972, 73
Levernier, James A., U Ark, 1978
Levesque, George, Ind SU, 1981
Levin, Carole, U Ia, 1983, 84
Levin, Jack, Northeastern U, 1984
Levin, Judith, U Pa, 1986
Levin, Richard, UC-Davis, 1988
Levin, William, Bridgewater SU, 1984
Levine, Herbert, Harvard, 1971
Levine, Howard, Lansing, Mi, 1984
Levine, Judy, NYU, 1985
Levine, Nancy, U N Fl, 1986
Levine, Peter, Mich SU, 1974
Levine-Keating, Helaine, Pace U, 1985
Levitov, Betty, Doane C, 1985
Levy, Donald, Brooklyn C, 1982, 83
Levy, Emanuel, Yeshiva U, College for Women, 1984, 85
Levy, Helen, U Mich, 1984, 85, 86
Levy, Joseph, U Que,1984
Levy, Richard, Rensselaer, Poly Inst, 1982
Levy, Suzanne, Hunter, 1988
Lewin, Harlan, San Diego SU, 1986
Lewis, Anthony, SUNY-Buffalo, 1979; 80, 84, 87, SUC-Buffalo
Lewis, Arthur O., State College, Pa, 1988
Lewis, Douglas, St. Mary's C Md, 1979
Lewis, George, C Pacific, 1987, 88
Lewis, Hanna, Sam Houston SU, 1983,84
Lewis, Howard, Nat'l Acad Sciences, 1977
Lewis, Jerry, Kent SU, 1971, 72, 73, 75, 82
Lewis, John, L'Oreal Lancome, NY, 1984
Lewis, Jon, Ore SU, 1984, 87, 88
Lewis, Leon, Appal SU, 1978

Lewis, Lisa, W Il U, 1982
Lewis, L.M., Tx Southmost C, 1985
Lewis, Lloyd B., Grinnell C,
Lewis, Marty, Brownsville, Tx, 1984
Lewis, Raymond J., E Ky U, 1979, 84, 87, 88
Lewis, Robert, U B'ham, United Kingdom, 1983
Lewis, Sonja P., Temple, 1988
Lewis, Vashti, U Il-Chicago, 1983
Lewison, Edwin R., Seton Hall U, 1988
Lhamon, William T., Fl SU, 1973, 74, 75, 76, 84, 85
Liba, Richard, Mich Tech U, 1979, 81, 84, 85, 86, 87, 88
Liberman, Terri R., Norwich U, 1988
Libman, Brenda, Roosevelt U, 1975
Lich, Glenn E., Baylor, 1988
Lichenstein, Allen, SUNY-Buffalo, 1980; 84, 86, 87, 88, Brooklyn C,
Lichenstein, Diane, Minneapolis, Mn, 1986
Lichty, Larry, U Wisc, 1977; 88, Northwestern
Lieberman, Leonard, Cent Mich U, 1984
Lieberman, Leslie, Cent Mich U, 1984
Liebow, Ely M., Northeastern Il U 1976, 78, 82
Lieberman, Terri, Norwich U, 1987
Liebowito, Flo, Ore SU, 1981
Lidston, Robert C., Loyola C of Md, 1981
Liedel, Donald, SUNY-Albany, 1971
Light, Allie, Film Maker, San Fran, 1984
Lightfood, William, Oh SU, 1976
Ligibel, Ted, BGSU, 1979, 80
Lijeron, Hugo, U Akron, 1988
Lilly, Paul R., Jr, SUNY-Oneonta, 1981
Lim, Soon-Heng, Duke, 1986
Lima, Robert, Pa SU, 1973
Limbacher, James L., Libraries, Dearborn, MI, 1980, 84
Lin, Nien-Sheng, Lamar U, 1983, 84
Linck, Charles, E Tx SU 1983
Lincoln, Kenneth, UCLA, 1971
Lindauer, Martin S., SUNY-Brockport, 1988
Lindberg, David C., U Wisc, 1974
Lindberg, Laurie, Ball SU, 1984
Lindberg, Stanley W., Oh U, 1975, 76
Lindell, Richard, Wayne SU, 1980
Lindeman, Yehudi, McGill U, Montreal, 1987
Linden, Blanche, Brandeis, 1981
Linden-Ward, Blanche, Emerson, 1988
Lindfors, Bernth, U Tx, 1972, 85
Lindgren, James M., SUNY-Plattsburgh, 1987
Lindley, Lester G., Union C, 1975
Lindlof, Thomas, Pa SU, 1982
Lindmark, Joyce, Northwestern, 1976
Lindner, Barbara J., BGSU, 1980
Lindquist, Vernon, Trinity C, 1988
Lindsay, Bryan, Converse C, 1974
Lindsey, Sarah, Wichita SU, 1983
Lindsey, Suzanne E., U Al-B'ham, 1988
Lindstrom-Best, Varpu, York U, Toronto, 1984
Linenthal, Ed, U Wisc-La Crosse, 1982
Ling, Amy, Rutgers, 1984
Ling, Jan, U Goteberg, Sweden, 1975

Linick, Anthony, Mich SU, 1971, 78, 79, 81
Linick, Dorothy, East Lansing, Mi, 1971
Linkfield, Thomas P. Mich SU, 1980
Linnemann, Russell, U Tn-Chattanooga, 1988
Lipke, William, U Vt, 1975
Lippy, Charles H., Clemson, 1978, 80
Lipsitz, George, U Houston-Clear Lake, 1982, 83, 84, 85, 86, 87
Lipski, John M., Mich SU, 1981
Lipsky, Richard, Queens C., Flushing, NY, 1982
Lis, Marie, Cabrini C, 1987
Lisenby, Foy, U Cen Ark, 1981, 82, 88
Lisk, Thomas, U Sou Car, 1984
List, David C., Syracuse U, 1980
Listerman, R.W., U Miami, Oh, 1986
Litchfield, Lawrence, Castleton, Vt, 1981
Litman, Barry, Mich SU, 1980
Litoff, Judy, Bryant C, 1986, 87, 88
Little, Greta, U Sou Car, 1986
Littlefield, Daniel, LSU, 1981; 85, U Ark
Litton, Joyce Ann, Athens, Oh, 1982, 86, 87, 88
Liv, Scott, U Tx, 1985
Livesay, Harold C., Tx A&M, 1988
Livesay, Harold, U Mich, 1974
Livesay, Jeff, Colo C, 1984
Livingston, Kriemhilde I.R., U Akron, 1987
Livingston-Weber, Joan, Ind U, 1984
Lizotte, Alan, SUNY-Albany, 1988
Lloyd, Craig, Columbus C, Ga, 1986
Lloyd, Franklin, U Ia, 1974
LoBalbo, Anthony, St. Johns U, 1983
Lobdell, Jared, Garland Pub, NYC 1987, 88
Lobe, Thomas, USD, 1987, 88
Lockard, Hal, Bensalem HS, Pa, 1980
Locke, Virgil, Purdue, 1973
Locker, Jack, Gettysburg C, 1984
Lockwood, Yvonne, U Mich, 1980
Lodge, Peter, Belmont Abbey C, 1983
Loeb, Helen, Northeastern U, 1983
Lofaro, Michael, U Tn, 1985
Logan, Joshua, 1974
Logan, Thad, Rice U, 1979
Logsdon, Guy, Tulsa U, 1983
Lohof, Bruce A., Heildelberg C, 1972, 73; 75, 76, U Miami, Fl
Lomonaco, Martha, NYU, 1983, 84; 85, Wantagh, NY; 86, NYU
Lomonaco, Martin, Wantagh, NYU, 1985, 87
Long, Elizabeth, Rice U, 1980, 82, 85, 87
Long, Gary, U Miss, 1984, 85, 86
Long, Terry, Oh SU-Newark, 1986, 88
Long, Thomas, U Cin, 1981
Longhurst, Derek, Sunderland Poly, England, 1986
Longstaff, Steven, Atkinson C, North York, Ont, 1988
Looks, Bernard, Great Neck, NY, 1985
Lopez-Aranguren, Eduardo, Univ Del Pais Vasco, Bilbao, Spain, 1988
Lopez, Michael, Mich SU, 1985, 86
Lopez, Santos, W Ky U, 1986
Lopez, Toni A., U Fl, 1979

Lora, Ronald, U Tol, 1974
Lorch, Sue, US Caro, 1986
Lasano, Waykne A., Rens Poly Inst, 1973, 75
Loss, Archie K., Pa SU-Erie, 1988
Lossau, Carl, SIU-Edwardsville, 1988
Lothstein, Arthur, C.W. Post C, 1984
Lott, Brett, C Charleston, 1987
Lott, Sandra, U Montevallo, 1988
Lott, Tommy, U Mass-Boston, 1982, 84
Louden-Hanes, Marie, BGSU, 1987, 88
Loudon, Michael, U Ok, 1983; 85, E Il U
Louder, Dean, U Laval, Quebec, 1987
Louie, Suzanne, St. Louis U, 1987
Loukides, Paul, Albion C, 1974, 75, 76, 77, 78, 79, 80, 81, 82, 83, 84, 58, 86, 87
Lounsbury, Barbara, U Nor Ia, 1980
Lounsbury, Myron, U Md, 1984, 87
Loux, Karen, Albright C, 1983
Love, James, Brock U, 1985
Loveland-Iglauer, Jan, Alligator Records, 1976
Loveland, Marion P., Mattatuck Comm C, 1978, 79
Loveless, Warren H., Ind SU, 1983
Lovely, Bernie, U Ky, 1978, 79
Lovin-Boyd, Stacy, Purdue-Hammond, 1986, 87
Loving, Cathleen, Tx A&M, 1988
Lovis, William A., Mich SU, 1979
Lowe, Benjamin, Governors SU, 1975
Lowe, Clayton, Oh SU, 1985, 87
Lowe, John, St. Mary's C, Notre Dame U, 1985
Lowe, Virginia, Ball SU, 1988
Lowenstein, Michael, Harris-Stowe SC, 1981
Lowery, Michael, Stillwater, Ok, 1984
Lowry, Mary, Kent SU, 1983, 85, 88
Loy, Pamela, U Hartford, 1979, 80
Loy, Philip, Taylor U, 1986
Lucas, Jerry, CSU-LA, 1980
Lucas, Robert, San Diego SU, 1987
Lucas, W.F., Carpketbag Theater, Inc. 1973
Luck, Susan, Lorain Cty Comm C, 1981
Luckett, Gary Don, BGSU, 1973
Ludington, Townsend, UNC, 1978, 79, 80; 81, Intl Comm Agency
Ludwig, Edward G., Mich SU, 1975; 76, SUNY-Fredonia
Ludwig, Jay, Mich SU, 1974
Lueck, Terry, BGSU, 1985, 87
Luegenfiehl, Heinz, Rose-Hulman Inst Tech, 1982
Luehrs, Robert, Fort Hays SU, 1982
Luere, Jeane U N Colo, 1986
Lugenbiehl, Heinz, Rose-Hulman Inst Tech, 1984
Luke, Allen, James Cook N Queensland, Australia, 1988
Luke, Carmen, James Cook N Queensland, Australia, 1988
Lukehart, Jeff, Willamette U, 1983
Lukenbill, W. Bernard, U Tx, 1978, 79
Lukens, Rebecca, Miami U, Oh, 1978, 81
Lukic, George, U Pitt, 1979
Lukinsky, Joseph, Jewish Theo Sem, 1984
Lule, Jack, U Ga, 1986
Lund, Jens, BGSU, 1971, 72, 73; 76,

Ind U; 77, IU-PUI-Columbus
Lundin, Anne H. U Sou Miss, 1988
Lundy, Jo, Sou Tech Inst, Marietta, Ga, 1986
Lundy, John, BGSU, 1974, 75
Lupack, Alan, Wayne SU, 1985, 86, 87, 88
Lupack, Barbara, Wayne C, Neb, 1983, 84, 85, 86, 87, 88
Lupack, Barbara T., Empire SC-SUNY, 1988
Lupton, Mary Jane, Morgan SU, 1978, 79, 80; 72, Baltimore
Lupton, William, Morgan SU, 1975
Lussier, Mark, New Orleans, La, 1983
Lutton, Jeannette, Atlanta, Ga, 1986
Lutz, Gretchen, San Jacinto C, 1988
Lyle, John D., Stratford C, 1973
Lyman, Barbara, U SW Louisiana, 1982
Lynch, Dennis, U Akron, 1982, 85
Lynch, Kathleen D., Rutgers U, 1987
Lyons, Anne W., Bemidji, Mn, 1976
Lyons, Anne W., Marlton, NJ, 1978
Lyons, H. David, Memphis, Tn, 1988
Lyons, John, U Wisc, 1975, 76
Lyons, Paul, Stockton SC, 1987
Lyons, Robert, Bemidji SC, 1972, 73, 74, 75, 76
Lysonaki, Steven, URI, 1984

MacAndrew, Elizabeth, Cleveland SU, 1973
MacCurdy, Carol A., Cal Poly Tech, 1988
MacDaniel, Elizabeth, Oh SU, 1987, 88
MacDaniel, Stan, Sonoma SU, 1982
MacDonald, Alice, U Akron, 1985
MacDonald, Andrew, Loyola U, NO, 1988
MacDonald, Andrew, U Tx, 1975
MacDonald, Deborah, OSU, 1984
MacDonald, Gina, Loyola U, NO, 1988
MacDonald, J.A., Campion C, Regina, Can
MacDonald, J. Fred, Northeastern IU, 1971, 72, 73, 74, 75, 76, 78, 79, 80, 81, 82, 83, 84, 85, 86, 88
MacDonald, Susan, St. Louis Comm C, 1980
MacDonald, Virginia, U Tx, 1975
MacDougall, Jim, Ball SU, 1982, 83, 84, 86
MacDougall, Jill, NYC, 1988
MacDowell, Marsha, Mich SU, 1987
MacFadden, Fred, Coppin S C, 1972, 73,74
MacFee, Wilber C., Sou Il
MacGillivary, Don, UC Cape Breton, 1987
MacGillivary, Royce, U Waterloo, Ont1984
MacGregor, Robert, Bishops U, Lennoxville, PQ, 1987, 88
MacGregor, Robert, Bishop's U, Que, 1986
Machanic, Mindy, E Car U, 1986
Machann, Clinton J., Tx A&M, 1979
MacInnes, John, New C, 1986
MacIntyre, Wendell, U Prince Ed Is, 1984, 86
Mackay, Jock, Memorial U NF, 1988
Mackie, Jan, Metro SC, Denver, 1981
MacKenzie, Gordon O., U NM, 1985
MacKillop, Ian, U Sou Cal, 1984
MacLean, Gerald, Wayne SU, 1984, 85
MacPhee, Laurence, Seton Hall U, 1982
MacPherson, G.R., U Victoria, BC, 1984

MacPike, Loralee, CSU-San Bernardino, 1980, 81
MacKinnon, Richard, UC Cape Breton, Nova Scotia, 1988
MacKintyre, Wendell, U Prince Edward Is, 1987
Macklin, F. Anthony, Wright SU, 1975; 82, U Dayton
MacRae, Suzanne, U Ark, 1979, 82, 84
MacRae, Suzanne H., U Ark, 1987, 88
Macris, Peter, SUC-Oneonta, 1988
Madden, David, LSU, 1971, 72, 73, 76, 77, 78
Madden, Fred, Ithaca C, 1987, 88
Maddox, Lynda, Sou Il, 1977; 84, Geo Wash U, Va.
Maddux, Thomas R., CSU-Northridge, 1988
Madigan, Mark, U Vt, 1988
Madison, Robert, Northwestern U, 1982, 83; 84, US Naval Acad, 85, 86, 87, 88
Madrid, Arturo, Ida SU, 1975; 77, U Minn
Madsen, Nadive, Drake U, 1983
Magiocco, Sabina, Ind U, 1984
Magistrale, Anthony, U Vt, 1984, 85, 87
Magnuson, Landis, Urbana, Il, 1984, 85; 86, U Il
Maguire, William J., Ga Sou C, 1988
Mahamdi, Cynthia, BGSU, 1984
Mahamdi, Yahia, BGSU, 1984
Mahan, Beth, BGSU, 1973
Mahkan, Jeffrey, Northwestern, 1980, 81, 87
Mahom, William, Milwaukee, 1986
Mahoney, Betsy, Cabrini C, 1987
Mahoney, Mary Kay, U Kans, 1982, 83; 85, 86, 87, 88, Brighton, Ma
Maik, Thomas A., U Wisc-Lacrosse, 1988
Maine, Barry, Wake Forest U
Maines, Rachel, Ithaca, NY, 1988
Maio, Eugene A., U Akron, 1987, 88
Majerszyk, Elliot, CBC, Montreal, 1987
Mak, Collette, U Il, 1988
Malamuth, Neil, Comm Studies, Calif, LA, 1984
Maland, Charles, U Tn, 1983
Malcolm, Andrew, Rochester Inst Tech, 1982, 83
Malcolm, Clark, Facility Mnge Inst, Ann Arbor, Mi, 1987
Malcom, Shirley, Nat'l Sc Found, 1977
Malik, Madhku, U Va, 1979
Malk, Linda L., U Wisc-LaCrosse, 1988
Malley, Terence, Long Island U, 1973
Mallison, Elise, Ithaca, NY, 1985
Malm, Linda, Pitzer C, 1982; 86, Pitzer C, Mt. Baldy; 88 Pasadena Comm C
Malmsheimer, Lonna M., Dickinson C, 1976, 77
Malnig, Julie, NYU, 1984, 87
Malone, Bill C., Wisc SU, 1971; 75, 76, Tulane
Maloney, Joseph, U Louisville, 1982
Maloney, Martin, Northwestern, 1974
Malplezzi, Frances M., Ark SU, 1977, 78; 85, 86, SU Ark
Maluk, Anna, Pittsburgh, Pa, 1979
Man, Glenn, U Mass, 1986
Manbeck, John, Kingsboro Comm C, 1984,

86, 87

Manca, Luigi, Medaille C, Buffalo, NY, 1984; 88, Antioch C

Mancell, Robert B, Eastern Mich U, 1978, 79, 80, 81, 88

Manchise, Don, Tn SU, 1978

Mancini, Elaine, NYU, 1982; 84, NYC

Mandell, Richard, U So Caro, 1976

Mandzuik, Roseann, U Ia, 1986

Manear, John, South Hills Cath HS, Pittsburgh, 1979

Manion, Eileen, Dawson C, Lafontaine Camp, Montreal, 1987

Mann, Dennis Alan, U Cin, 1977, 78, 79, 80, 81, 82, 84, 85, 86, 87

Mann, Harold W., Radford C, 1978, 83, 84, 87, 88

Mann, Robert, Il St Representative, Chicago, 1976

Manna, Anthony, Kent SU, 1985

Mannheimer, Monica, U Goteberg, Sweden, 1975

Manning, Frank, U W Ontario,

Manning, Gerald F., U Guelph, 1987 London, 1984

Mansfield, Steven, Augusta C, Ga, 1986

Mantley, John, Exec Dir, Gunsmoke, 1984

Mantooth, Sara, Baylor, 1986

Manzo, Joseph, Concord C, 1985

Marable, Manning, Tuskegee Inst, 1978

Marc, David, Brandeis, 1887

March, Kathleen, U Me, 1988

Marchalonis, Shirley, Pa SU, 1979

Marchand, C. Roland, UC-Davis, 1976

Marchesani, Joseph, Pa SU-Hazleton, 1981

Marchetti, Gina, Northwestern, 1982

Marchkese, Ronald T., U Minn-Duluth, 1979, 80

Marcos, Juan Manuel, Ok SU, 1984

Marcou, Howard, Mercer Cty Comm C, 1988

Marcus, Irwin, Ind U Pa, 1981

Marcus, Jane, U Il-Chicago Circle, 1976

Margolies, Edward, Staten Island Comm C, 1972; 74, NYC; 84, C Staten Island

Marin, Pilar, Universidad de Sevilla, Spain, 1985

Marino, James G., U Pitt, 1979

Marion, Sheila, Az SU, 1988

Mark, Norman, Chicago Daily News, 1976

Mark, Paul, U New Haven, 1978

Markle, Joyce B., Loyola U Chicago, 1973; 76, Evanston, Il

Markley, Robert, Ga Inst Tech, 1986

Markowitz, Judy, Towson SU, 1977

Marks, Henry S., Northeast Al S Jr C, 1972; 73, Huntsville, Al; 75, 76, 78, Northeast Al S Jr C

Marks, Marsha Kass, Al A&M U, 1972, 73; 75, 76, 78, Al Agr & Mech U

Marks, Melissa, Princeton, 1987

Markson, Stephen, U Hartford, Ct, 1986, 87

Marler, Robert, Temple, 1981

Marling, Karal, U Minn, 1984

Marling, William, Case-Western U, 1981

Marlowe, Dan J., 1971

Marmarelli, Ron, Temple U, 1977; 79, Cent Mich U,

Marohl, Joseph, US Caro, 1986

Marois, Claude, U Montreal, 1987

Maroney, H.J., McMaster U, 1977

Marovitz, Sanford, Kent SU, 1981

Marquis, Alice, La Jolla, Ca., 1983, 84, 85, 88

Marra, James, Tx Tech, 1981, 82, 83, 84

Marre, Katy, U Dayton, 1981

Marschall, Richard, World Ency of Comics, 1977

Marsden, James R., U Ky, 1973

Marsden, Madonna, BGSU, 1972, 76, 77, 78

Marsden, Michael, BGSU, 1971, 72, 73, 74, 75, 76, 77, Nat'l Hum Inst, Chicago; 78, 789, 80, 81, 82, 83, 84, 85, 86, 87, 88, BGSU

Marsh, Ben, Pa SU. 1978

Marsh, John L., Edinboro SU, 1972, 77, 79, 81

Marshall, Betty, Morehead SU, 1982

Marshall, Cynthia, Rhodes C, 1986

Marshall, Denise, BGSU, 1976, 84; 86, 87, Heidelberg C

Marshall, James, URI, 1980, 82

Marshall, Thomas, Kent KU, 1972

Marsicano, Edward, Bainbridge Jr C, Ga, 1980, 81, 84

Martens, Hedda, SUNY-Brockport, 1974, 75

Martens, James, U Winnipeg, 1988

Marthan, Joseph, Pa SU-Media, 1987

Marti-Olivella, Jaume, Tx A&M, 1988

Martin, Bill, U Kans, 1986, 87

Martin, Elaine, U Ala, 1985, 87

Martin, Eleanor Jean, Rutgers, 1975, 76, 77, 78, 79

Martin, Floyd, U Ark, 1986

Martin, James, BGSU, 1971

Martin, Jerry, Muskingum C, 1982, 83, 84, 85, 86, 87

Martin, Laura, Cleveland SU, 1983

Martin, Lawrence, U Akron, 1987, 8

Martin, Reginald, Memphis KSU 1986

Martin, Richard, Fashion Inst Tech, 1975, 77, 78

Martin, Robert, Dekalb Comm C, Ga, 1987

Martin, Robert, Concordia U, 1982, 87

Martin, Sadie, Cortland C, 1974

Martin, Thomas, Colo SU, 1976

Martin, Walter, UNC-Charlotte, 1985, 86, 87, 88

Martin, Wendy, Queens C CUNY, 1984

Martin, William, Leander C, 1987

Martin, William C., Rice U, 1974, 75, 76, 77; 86, Ga SU

Martin, William T., Lander C, 1980

Martin, W.R., Mich SU, 1978, 80

Martinez, Daniel, U Neb-Omaha, 1982

Martinez, Tomas, U Colo, 1977

Martinsdale, Kathleen, York U, Ont.

Martinson, Karen, U West Mich, 1974

Martz, David, BGSU 1985

Marvin, Ann, Carl Menninger Found, 1983

Maryati, A., U Kuwait, 1982

Marynow, Maurice, Maxwell AFB, 1988

Marzolf, Kingsbury, U Mich, 1971

Marzulli, Larry, U Tol, 1987

Maschio, Geraldine, U Ky, 1985, 86, 88

Masco, Vincent, Temple, 1982

Masel-Walters, Lynne, Cen Mich U, 1976, 78; 79, U Al

Mashata, Majid, U Busra, Iraq, 1983, 84

Mashburn, Everett, WMPB-TV, Owings Mills, Md, 1977

Masinton, Charles, U Kans, 1983, 84, 85

Masinton, Charles G., U Kans, 1987

Mason, Julian, UNC-Charlotte, 1986, 87

Mason, Patricia, BGSU, 1984

Mason, Paul, Duquesne, 1988

Mason, Phillip L., Raleigh, NC, 1987

Mass, Roz, Baruch C, SUNY, 1974, 75

Massengale, John, E Wash U, 1985

Massetti-Miller, Karen, U Ia, 1983, 87

Mast, Anna, Augusta C, 1986

Mast, Gerald, Richmond C, CUNY, 1975

Mast, Robert, Augusta C, 1986

Masteller, Jean C., Whitman C, 1988

Masteller, Richard, Whitman C, 1988

Masters, Kathy, Ark SU, 1980; 81, U Ark; 82, 83, 84, 85, 86, 87, 88, Ark SU

Masters, Lee, Henson Broadcasting, Louisville, 1982

Masters, Mitchell, Ark SU, 1982, 83, 84, 85, 86, 87, 88

Masterson, John T., U Miami, Fl, 1986

Masterson, Pat, Vanier C, Snowdon Campus, Montreal, 1987

Matchie, Thomas, N Dak SU, 1985, 86, 88

Mates, Julian, Long Island U-CW Post Ctr, 1988

Mathis, Kary, Tx Tech, 1988

Mather, Cotton, U Minn, 1976

Matherne, Beverly, Kans SU 1977

Mathers, Gray, Trenton SU, 1980

Mathisen, James, Wheaton C, 1988

Matilla, Alfredo, SUNY-Buffalo, 1975

Matonti, Charles, St. John's U, 1983

Mattern, Claire, U Neb, 1985

Matthews, Glenice, Wichita SU, 1983

Matthews, Herman, U Evansville, 1976

Matthews, Roy T., Mich SU, 1976, 79

Matthews, Wayne, Ok SU, 1983

Matthewson, Tim, McFaddin-Ward Hist Mus, 1988

Mattson, Jeremy, Mich SU, 1976, 77, 80

Matturi, John, NYC, 1988

Matturro, Richard, Albany Bus C, 1984

Matuzak, Lorraine, Delta C, 1973

Matviko, John W., West Liberty SC, 1988

Matzq, Diane, Syracuse U, 1982

Maulsby, Portia, Ind U, 1976, 80

Maurer, Peter, 1971

Maurr, J., BGSU 1984

Mawer, Noel D., Moore C of Art, Phila, 1986

Mawson, Marlene, U Kans, 1986

Maxfield, Malinda, Converce C, 1988

Maxwell, Bill, Duke, 1988

Maxwell, Rhoda, U Wisc-Eau Claire, 1988

May, Anita Rasi, Health Sciences Cent Okla, 1975

May, Charles E., CSU-Long Beach, 1975, 76, 85

May, Jill P., Purdue, 1978, 85

May, Jude Thomas, Health Sciences Cent Okla, 1975

May, Martha, St. Lawrence U, 1988

May, Robert E., Purdue, 1978

Mayberry, Susan N., Alfred U, 1987

Mayer, Elsie F., Henry Ford Comm C, 1977

Mayer, Hans, U Wisc-Milwaukee, 1974

Mayer, Henry, U Louisville, 1985

Mayker, Suzanne, Western Il U, 1985

Mayo, Deborah, Va Tech, 1980

Mayo, Edith, Smithsonian Inst, 1978, 80, 82, 83, 85, 86

Mays, David, Va Tech, 1983

Mazel, Henry, NY Inst Tech, 1984

Mazis, Glen, N Ky U, 1981, 82, 84

Mazow, Julia Wolf, U Houston, 1976

Mazuek, Ray, Reading, Pa, 1988

Mazurana, Steve J., U Nor Colo, 1988

Mazzola, L. Charles, Corning Conn C, 1987 U-Edwardsville, 1977, 80

McAndrew, Robert L., Pikes Peak Comm C, 1979

McArthur, Jan, UNC-Greensboro, 1986

McBride, Gordon, Westminster c, 1978

McBride, Robin, Mercury Records, 1976

McBride, Ruth, Hanover C, In, 1981

McBride, William, SUNY-Buffalo, 1987

McCabe, Casey, Young & Rubicam, San Fran, 1988

McCaffrey, Donald, U ND, 1980, 84

McCaffrey, Joann, Grand Forks, ND, 1984

McCaffrey, John, Lowell U, 1975, 76

McCaffrey, Larry, San Diego SU, 1979

McCaghy, Charles, BGSU, 1971

McCall, William W., Mich SU, 1988

McCallum, Brenda, BGSU. 1988

McCann, William, 1973, 74

McCardell, Wallin, U Tx-Tyler, 1986,88

McCardell, William, LSU-Shreveport, 1983

McCarron, Gary, York U, Ont., 1988

McCarter, William, Channel 11, Chicago, 1976

McCarthy, Patrick, BGSU, 1983; 85, 86, 88, Ind SU

McClain, Meredith, Tx Tech, 1983

McClaren, Peter, Miami U, Oh, 1988

McClary, Andrew, Mich SU, 1979, 80

McClary, Ben Harris, Mid Ga C, 1978

McClellan, E. Fletcher, Elizabethtown C, 1987

McClelland, Averil, Kent SU, 1982

McClintock, James, Mich SU, 1982, 83, 87, 88

McClintock, Michael, U Mont, 1980, 82, 84

McClure, Arthur, Cent Mo SU, 1974

McClure, Paul, N Ga C, 1986

McComb, Judith, BGSU 1982

McCombs, Judith, Wayne SU, 1984

McConachie, Bruce, W&M C, 1984, 85, 86, 87, 88

McConnell, Frank, Northwestern,1980

McConnell, Robert, Winston-Salem SU, 1981

McCord, Nancy N., Albion C, 1980

McCormakc, P.A., U St Thomas, Houston, 1981; 82, Loyola NO

McCormick, James, CSU-Sacramento, 1988

McCoy, Joan, U Fl, 1982

McCracken, Ellen, U Mass, 1980

McCracken, Grant, U Guelph, 1987

McCraw, David, Marist C, 1984

McCullough, Jack, Trenton SC, 1980, 81, 83, 84, 85, 86, 88

McCullough, Marilyn, U West Ont, 1973

McCray, Curt, Saginaw Valley C, 1971

McCroskey, Bert, U Ida, 1975

McCutcheon, W.J., Beloit C, 1971

McDaniel, Drew, Oh U, 1988

McDaniel, Elizabeth, Oh SU 1988

McDaniel, Stanley, Sonoma SU, 1981

McDannell, Colleen, U Denver, 1978; 85, U Colo

McDermott, Douglas, CSU-Stanislaus, 1979, 86

McDermott, Mark, BGSU, 1986, 87

McDiarmid, John F., Pa SU-Behrend C, 1981

McDonald, Archie, Stephen F. Austin SU, 1986

McDonald, Bob, Mich SU 1974

McDonald, James, Milliken U, 1985

McDonald, Michael, U Tn, 1977

McDonald, Robert A., U Ct, 1978

McDowell, Betty, Mich SU, 1980

McDowell, Dixon, Sou Il U, 1986

McDowell, Margaret, U Ia, 1976

McDowell, Marsha, Mich SU, 1980, 84

McDowell, Peggy, UNO, 1987, 88

McElrath, Joseph R., Fl SU, 1987

McElroy, F.L., Ind U, 1981

McEvoy, Alan, Wittenberg U, 1978

McEwen, Barbara, Brock U, Ont, 1984

McFadden, Mara, Ind U, 1986

McFarland, Keith, E Tx SU, j1983

McFerrin, Ted R., Encino, Cal, 1980

McGaw, Doug, Emporia SU, 1983

McGee, Marsha, TCU, 1987

McGillis, Roderick F., U Calgary, 1976

McGinty, Sue, Tarleton SU, 1988

McGlade, Jacqueline, U Neb-Omaha, 1983

McGlinn, Jeanne, UNC-Asheville, 1985, 86, 87

McGlocklin, Jon, Milwaukee Bucks, 1974

McGlone, Becky, Franklin U, 1984

McGlone, Gregory, W Il U, 1983; 84, Franklin U

McGoff, Kathy, Portage, Mi, 1987

McGowan, Barbara, Notre Dame U, 1978, 80

McGowan, Martha, U Lowell, 1987

McGowan, Richard, Milwaukee Sch Engineering, 1987, 88

McGrath, Kathy, BGSU, 1972

McGregor, Gaile, Toronto, 1987

McGuire, Michael, U Ga, 1976, 87

McGuire, Patrick, SUNY-Stony Brook, 1983

McGuire, Phillip, UNC-Wilmington, 1985

McGuirk, Carol, Fl Atl U, 1986

McGukin, Drew, Auburn U, 1988

McHale, Ellen, U Pa, 1987

McInerny, Kathleen, Augusta C, 1985

McInerney, Thomas, Marshall U, 1980

McInnis, John, Monroe, La, 1984; 85, 86, Northeast U, Monroe, La

McIntyre, Bryce, Stanford, 1984

McKale, Donald M., Clemson, 1980, 81

McKay, Linda, U Windsor, Can, 1980, 86

McKee, Macey, W Il U, 1985

McKee, Melanie B., E Il U, 1988

McKennon, Joseph, Sarasota, Fl, 1972, 82

McKeown, Bruce, Seattle Pac U, 1983

McKernie, Grant, U Ore, 1988

McKerns, Joseph, Sou Il U, 1982

McKinley, Archibald, U Chicago, 1976

McKinley, Robert H., Mich SU, 1979

McKinnon, Isiah, City of Detroit Police Dept, 1982, 83

McKinnon, Peter, Mich SU 1979

McKintry, Susan, Carleton C, Northfield

McKnight, Kenneth, Purdue, 1984

McLachlan, James, Princeton, 1973

McLaren, Joseph, Mercy C-Dobbs Ferry, 1986, 87, 88

McLaren, Peter, Miami U, Oh, 1986

McLaughlin, John, U Kans, 1983

McLaughlin, Thomas, BGSU, k1980

McLaurin, A. Porter, U SCar, 1984, 85, 86, 87

McLay, Catherine, U Calgary, Can, 1984

McLean, Gerald, Wayne SU, 1988

McLean, Polly, U Tx, 1984; 85, 86, U Colo

McLean, Stuart, U Chicago, 1983

McLemore, Jay, Tulane U, 1987

McLemore, Joy E., Pikeville C, 1988

McLennan, Kathleen, Augustana C, 1986

McLeod, Patrick G., Jackson U, Fl, 1978, 86

McLeon, Jim, Denison C, 1985

McMahon, Helen, SUNY-Fredonia, 1975

McManus, Joseph, Brighton, Ma, 1986

McMath, Robert, Ga Tech, 1986

McMeniman, Linda, Glassboro C, 1988

McMillan, Bill, Chicago, Il, 1988

McMillen, David Byron, Kent SU, 1974, 75

McMillen, Marilyn, U Il, 1975

McMillen, William, BGSU, 1978; 84, Medical Col Oh

McMullan, Ruth, College Station, Tx, 1983

McMurray, Mary, U Ia, 1971, 72, 73

McNair, John, UNC-Charlotte, 1986

McNair, Martha, U Ark, 1985

McNair, Wesley, Colby-Sawyer C, 1980

McNall, Sally, U Kans, 1983, 86

McNara, Eugene, U Windsor, 1982, 84, 85, 86

McNara, Richard D., U Ia, 1972

McNearney, Clayton L., Marshall U, 1978, 80

McNeil, W.K., Ind U, 1971, 73

McNelly, Cleo, Rutgers, 1985

McNulty, Teresa, Cabrina C, 1987

McQuarie, Donald, BGSU, 1978

McQueen, Charles, U Il, 1974

McReynolds, William, U Colo, 1972, 83

McVay, Christy, Columbia, Mo, 1979

McWhinney, Norman, U Pitt-Greenburg Campus, 1988

McWhorter, George, U Louisville, 1985

McWilliams, Dean, Oh SU, 1978

McWilliams, Warren, Ok Baptist U, 1983

McWhorter, Gerald, U Il, 1980

Mead, Joan, Marshall U, 1983, 84, 85, 86, 88

Mead, Joan L., Marshall U, 1987

Meaghan, Diane, Seneca C, Willowdale, Ont, 1985

Meagher, Eileen, Marycrest C, 1975
Mechikoff, Roberta, San Diego SU, 1987
Mechling, Elizabeth, CSU-Hayward, 1980
Mechling, Jay, UC-Davis, 1980
Mechta, Andrzej, Mich SU, 1982
Meckier, Jerome, U Ky, 1985
Medford, Joy, U Tn, 1980
Medoff, Jes, U Mass-Boston, 1979
Medvedev-Khazanov, Marina B,
  Brookline, Ma, 1977
Meeker, Josephine P., Brock U, Ont., 1978
Meese, Elizabeth A., U Al, 1976
Meffert, John, Nat'l Trust Hist
  Preservation, 1986
Meglio, John Di, Mankato SU, 1972
Mehlman, Michael H., Cleveland SU, 1972
Mehta, Xerxes, U Md-Ba, 1988
Meihls, J. Lee, Nat U
Meikle, Jeffrey, Colby-Sawyer C, 1978
Meile, Richard, U Neb, 1984
Meiss, Guy T., Central Mich U, 1982
Meissinger, Eileen M., Ok SU, 1978
Melanson, Wayne, U Tn, 1985
Melhem, D.H, CUNY, 1977, 82
Melko, Matthew, Wright SU, 1981
Mellendez-Hayer, Theresa, U Tx, 1984
Mellenkamp, Patricia, U Wisc-Milwa,
  1982
Mellerski, Nancy, Dickinson C, 1985
Meller, Kirsten Busck, U Aaarhus,
  Denmark, 1985
Melloy, Jerry D., WHAS-Am-WAMZ-
  Louisville, 1982
Melton, Gary W., Ark SU, 1988
Melton, J. Gordon, Spritual Frontices
  Fellowship, 1974, 75, 76, 80
Mclton, Judith, Clemson U, 1986
Meltzer, Judy, Baltimore Hebrew C,
  Baltimore, 1988
Mendelsohn, Harold, U Denver, 1979
Mendelson, Edward, Yale, 1973; 76,
  Washington
Mendelson, Michael, Ia SU, 1982, 84
Mendez-Egle, Beatrice, Pan-Amer U, 1985
Mendez-Faith, Teresa, St. Ansclm C, 1987
Menig, Harry, Ok SU, 1973, 74, 75, 76; 77,
  Langston U
Menkote, S., BGSU, 1985
Menke, Finn, U Minn, 1987
Mennen, Richard, UNC-Greensboro, 1981
Menter, Brett, U Tol, 1981
Mercer, George, SUNY-Oneonta, 1982
Mercer, John, Sou Il U, 1975
Mercier, Denis, Glassboro SU, 1987, 88
Meredith, James H., USAF Acad, 1987, 88
Merlihan, James, Comm C Baltimore, 1977
Merlock, Kathy, BGSU, 1979, 82, 83
Merlock, Ray, Highland Park, Il, 1975, 76;
  77, 79, Oh U; 80, 81, 82, 83, U Ok;
  86, 87, 88. Clemson
Merril, Judith, Science Fiction Writer, 1984
Merrill, Gordon, Carleton U, Ottawa, Can,
  1984
Merrill, Robert, Washington, D.C.
Merriman, John, Wayne SU, 1983, 84; 85,
  86, Valdosta SC,
Merrit, Bishetta, Howard U, 1988
Merritt, James D., CUNY-Brooklyn, 1977,
  80

Merritt, Russe!l L., U Wisc, 1971
Merrix, Paul, U Akron, 1987, 88
Merrix, Ribert, U Akron, 1984, 85, 86
Mersmann, James, U Ala-B'ham, 1975
Mertz, Robert J., BGSU, 1974, 75, 76
Meserve, Ruth, Ind U, 1981
Meserve, Walter, Ind U, 1981
Messaris, Paul, U Pa, 1982
Messenger, Christian, Wittenburg U, 1975,
  76, 77; 81, 84, U Il-Chicago Circle
Messent, Peter, U Nottingham, England,
  1986
Messer, Richard, BGSU, 1983
Messerole, Harrison, Pa SU, 1983
Mester, Richard, Pa SU-Behrend, 1986
Meszaros, Paul F., Mt. Sarnario C, 1981
Metaband, Paula, Howard U, 1985, 86
Metcalf, Greg, U Md, 1986
Metcalf, Steve, U Tn, 1985
Metcalfe, Alan, U Wisc, 1973
Metchikoff, Robert, Tx Tech, 1980
Metereau, Jeane-Pierre, Austin, Tx, 1985
Metwalli, Achmed, CS Poly, Kellogg-
  Voorhis, 1973
Metzgar, Jack, Roosevelt U, Chicago, 1981
Meyer, Jane, U De, 1987
Meyer, Michael, CSU-Northridge, 1976, 86
Meyer, Richard, W Ore SC, 1985, 86, 87,
  88
Meyer, Wayne, Ball SU, 1986
Meyer, W. Paul, BGSU, 1983
Meyers, Mary, U Ct, 1986
Meyers, Robert, BGSU, 1972
Meyrowitz, Joshua, UNH, 1982
Michael, Donald L., Jr., Durham, NC, 1987
Michaels, Doyd, Alleg C, 1987
Michaels, Lloyd, Alleg C, 1987
Michalczyk, John A., Boston C, 1988
Michalowski, Raymond, UNC-Charlotte,
  1986
Michel, Sonya, Brandeis, 1982
Michel, Thomas, St. John's U, 1987
Michel, Tom, BGSU, 1982; 84, 85, Clarion
  U; 86, St. John's U
Michelson, Bruce, U Il, 1987, 88
Michelson, Paul, U Neb, 1987, 88
Michta, Natalie C., USNaval Acad, 1988
Mickel, Howard, Wichita SU, 1983
Miclenhausen, Eileen, Montclair SC, 1988
Middleton-Keirn, Susan, CSU-Stanislaus,
  1984, 85, 86; 88 Mid Tn
Miersky, Norman, Hebrew Union C, 1975
Mielke, Robert. NE Mo SU, 1988
Mikesell, Tim, Eastman Sc of Music, 1985
Mikotowicz, Tom, NYU, 1982
Milano, Fred, Appal SU, 1986
Milburn, Jud, Ok SU, 1974
Miles, Geoffrey, York U, Ont., 1984
Miles, Grady G., Barber-Scotia C, 1980
Miles, Vernon, U Ark, 1983, 85, 86
Miles, William, Clarke Hist Library, Mt.
  Pleasant, Mi, 1975
Millard, Bradley, U Puget Sound, 1982
Miller, Adrienne, UC-Berkeley, 1986
Miller, Anthony, U Tn, 1983
Miller, Arthur, 1974
Miller, Bill, KAKZ Radio, Wichita, Kans,
  1983
Miller, Carol, Meramac Comm C, 1977

Miller, Chris, Loyola, NO, 1984, 85
Miller, Chris, Ind U, 1986
Miller, Christanne, Pomona C, 1984; 85
  U Wisc; 86, 87, 88, Pomona C
Miller, Christine, BGSU, 1987
Miller, David, Purdue, 1973; 81, Clark U;
  82, 87, Oh SU
Miller, David, Cameron U, 1983
Miller, David N., Oh SU, 1988
Miller, Douglas T., Mich SU, 1974
Miller, E. Joan, Il SU, 1977
Miller, Eugene, Appal SU, 1986
Miller, Fred, BGSU, 1981
Miller, Gene, Appal SU, 1988
Miller, George, Wayne SU, 1971
Miller, Heather, U Ark, 1986
Miller, John W., Ind Hist Soc, 1987
Miller, John C., Gettysburg, C, 1979
Miller, Jordan Y, URI, 1975, 76
Miller, Joseph, St. Mary's C, 1978
Miller, Joseph H. SE La U, 1984, 85
Miller, Kathryn, U Kans, 1982
Miller, Rush, BGSU, 1987, 88
Miller, Martin, Psychoanalyst, Waban, Ma,
  1986
Miller, Mary J, Brock U, Ont, 1984
Miller, Miriam Y. BGSU, 1978; 79, Tx
  Tech; 81, UNO
Miller, Patricia M., U Ct, 1985
Miller, Paul, Contributing ed Adam
  Magazine, 1984
Miller, Robert A., Purdue, 1976
Miller, Robert V., DePauw U, 1984
Miller, Sam, U Va, 1973
Miller, Tice, U Neb, 1986
Miller, Wayne, 1982
Miller, William Oh U, 1985
Millichap, Joe, W Ky U, 1988
Millichap, Joseph R., U Tulsa, 1974, 76,
  77, 79; 85, 86, W Ky
Millin, Judith, Toronto, Ont, 1986
Milling, Jill, U Tx-Richardson, 1986
Mills, Dennis L., Studebaker Drivers Club,
  St. Louis, 1981
Mills, Gary B., U Ala, 1988
Mills, Margaret A., Harvard, 1979
Mills, Marrianne, U Mich, 1982
Milner, Jay G., E Tn SU, 1979
Mincks, Sue, BGSU, 1972
Minda, Gary, Brooklyn Law School, 1987
Miner, Madonne, SUNY-Buffalo, 1982
Mink, Joanna, U SW La, 1986
Minor, Dennis, LSU, 1982
Minor, Lucien, SUNY-Fredonia, 1977
Minor, Michael, U Ky, 1975
Minoves-Myers, Irma, Ind U-Northwest,
  1987
Mintz, Lawrence E., U Md, 1971, 73, 74,
  75, 77, 78, 79, 81, 83, 84, 85, 86, 88
Mira, Edward, BGSU, 1971
Mirabito, Michael, BGSU, 1980, 82; 83,
  U Tulsa
Mirel, Barbara, E Mich U, 1981; 84 U Mich
Mirella, Louis, Duke, 1988
Mirotznik, Jerrold, CUNY, 1985
Mirza, H.A., Newing C,
  SUNY-Binghampton, 1977
Mishkin, Daniel, BGSU, 1978
Missman, Susan, Broadway Fashions, Ltd,

1976
Mistichelli, Judith, Lib of Congress, 1980
Mitcham, Carl, St. Catherine's C, Ky, 1982
Mitchell, Bruce M., E Wash U, 1988
Mitchell, Chuck, Downbeat Mag, 1976
Mitchell, Edward, Oh U, 1975, 76, 77
Mitchell, Judith, RI C, 1980, 83, 86
Mitchell, Laura, SW Mo SU 1984
Mitchell, Lee C., Princeton, 1988
Mitchell, Lisle, USC-Columbia, 1986
Mitchell, Michelle, Charleston, Il, 1985
Mitchell, William, Ok Baptist U, 1983
Mitleman, Amy, Hampshire C, 1988
Mitsch, William, Oh SU, 1988
Mitterling, Phillip, U Colo, 1980
Miville, Patricia, Big Cheese Pizza Co, Wichita, 1983
Mizejewski, Linda, Wheeling C, 1981
Mobley, G. Milton, Ga SU, 1980
Mobley, Jane, SUNY-Binghamton, 1975
Mobley, William, Wilbraham, Mass, 1985
Moe, John, Ind U., 1973, 74; 75, Heidelberg C; 76, Ind U; 78, 79 Central Mich U; 81, Case Western U; 84, Oh SU; 85, Ball SU
Moeller, Madelyn, U Louisville, 1981
Moffat, Frederick, U Tn, 1979
Moffeit, Tony, Ok SU 1973
Moffet, Rosemary, Elizabeth Comm C, 1978
Moffett, E. Albert, Ga SU, 1987
Mohl, Raymond, Fl Atl U, 1976
Mohler, Gary, 1974
Mohr, Clarence, Yale, 1977
Mohr, Wayne, Baylor, 1983
Mohray, Judy, Sou Meth U, 1983
Mojica, Perla, Ok SU, 1983
Molak-Dinkel, Sharon, Lourdes C, 1982
Molinar, Jose, U Ok, 1979
Molnar, Thomas, Brooklyn C, 1981
Molson, Francis J., Central Mich U, 1978, 80, 81, 84, 85
Moltner, Rachel, Rhoses Sch, NY, 1978
Molyneaux, Gerry, U Wisc, 1971
Monaco, Martha Lo, Wantagh, NY, 1987
Mong, Melissa, Kent SU, 1988
Mongeon, Joanne, Bryant C, 1976
Monroe, Ruth, Westmar C, 1982, 83, 84, 85; 86, 87, Drury C
Monson, Richard, Cent Mo SU, 1978, 81
Montesi, A.J., St. Louis U, 1988
Montgomery, Catherine J., U Pitt, 1988
Montgomery, Kathryn, CSU-LA, 1979, 80, 82
Montgomery, Lyna Lee, U Ark, 1975, 76, 77, 78, 85
Montgomery, Martha, Drexel U, 1982
Montgomery, Robin, SW Ok SU, 1984
Moody, Carolina, BGSU, 1985
Moody, Michael, U Ida, 1988
Moody, Suzanna, U Minn, 1985, 86
Mookerjea, Sourayan, U Toronto, 1988
Mookiah, M.S., U Colombo, Sri Lanka, 1982
Mooney, Hughson F., Cent Ct SU, 1979, 85
Mooney, Robert, U Il, 1986
Moore, Arlene, Wichita SU, 1987, 88
Moore, Barbaraa, U Tn, 1988
Moore, Charles, Contemporary Jazz

Quartet, Detroit, 1971
Moore, Charles W., LSU-Shreveport, 1985
Moore, David, Loyola, NO, 1981, 82, 83, 84, 85, 87
Moore, Dennis, Greenville Tech C, 1982
Moore, Jack, U Sou Fl, 1972, 73, 82, 83, 84, 85, 86
Moore, James, National Archives, 1977
Moore, John D., E Il U, 1988
Moore, Johnny S., Hollins C, 1987
Moore, Lewis D., UDC, 1987, 88
Moore, Malvin, Sou Il U, 1984, 85
Moore, Marian, BGSU, 1983; 87, Yellow Springs, Oh
Moore, Mary, Ind Cent U, 1984
Moore, Oscar, Al A&M, 1972
Moore, Rick, U Ore, 1986, 87
Moore, Rosa, U Tn-Chattanooga, 1980
Moore, Tom, Sou Meth U, 1979
Mootry, Maria, Northwestern, 1977, 78, 79; 82, 83, 84, 86, Sou Il
Mootz, William, Louisville Courier-Journal, 1982
Mor, Iris, York U, 1983
Morace, Robert, Daemon C, 1978, 79, 80, 84
Morales, Alejandro, UC-Irvine, 1979
Moran, Barbara B., SUNY-Buffalo, 1980; 84, 85, 86, 87, 88, UNC
Moran, Joseph, SUC-Buffalo, 1980, 87, 88
Moran, Michael, Clemson, 1982, 86
Moran, Peggy, Purdue-Calumet, 1979, 81, 82, 83, 85, 86, 87
Moran, Stephanie, BGSU, 1985, 86, 87
Morefield, John, Erwin, Tx, 1987
Moreland, Laurence W., Citadel, 1987
Morgan, Ann Lee, The New Art Examiner, Chicago, 1981
Morgan, Bill, St. Cloud U, 1979, 81
Morgan, Diane, Ok Baptist U, 1986
Morgan, Edward P., Lehigh U, 1988
Morgan, Ellen, Bucks Cty Comm C, 1976
Morgan, Gwendolyn, U Sou Fl, 1988
Morgan, Hugh, Miami U, Oh, 1981, 82
Morgan, Jeanne, Santa Barbara, Ca, 1984
Morgan, John, Emory & Henry, 1987, 88
Morgan, John P., U Rochester, 1977; 80, U Tn; 85, 86, McNeese SU
Morgan, Margaret E., Temple Terrace, Fl, 1976
Morgan, Michelle, CSU-Fresno, 1986
Morgan, Peter, U Toronto, 1984, 85
Morgan, Wayne, Ottawa, Can, 1987
Morgan, William T., U So Fl, 1975, 76, 78
Morganstern, Barry F., Wm Pattercon C, 1987
Morganstern, Donna, Environmental Design Bldg, Boulder, 1981
Morgenstern, Barbara, BGSU, 1982, 83
Moriarty, Sandra, Mich SU, 1981
Morioka, Heinz, Shibuya-Ku, Tokyo, 1988
Morisett, Jean-Maurice, U du Quebec, Montreal, 1988
Morrill, Calvin, Harvard, 1984
Morris, Ann, Stetson, 1986
Morris, Barbara, U Mich, 1985
Morris, Dan, U Mo, 1983
Morris, Jon, U Louisville, 1982

Morris, Ray, York U, 1987
Morris, Susan, E Il U, 1985, 86
Morrison, K.C., Syracuse U, 1984
Morrison, Rhoda, Public Art Workshop, Chicago, 1976
Morrison, William, Brandon, Manitoba, Can, 1986
Morrow, Lynn, SW Mo SU, 1983
Morrow, Patrick, USC, 1972, 74, 75; 85, 86, Auburn
Morsberger, Robert E., Cal St Polytechnic U-Kellogg-Voorhis, 1973, 77
Morse, Richard E., Maxwell AFB, 1988
Morsy, Soheir, Mich SU, 1979
Morton, Gerald, U Tn, 1989; 1981 Winthrop C; 1986, Auburn U
Morton, Richard K. Jacksonville, Fl, 1972
Morvitz, Sanford, Kent SU, 1982
Mosellie, B.M., Yale, 1985
Mosely, Carolyn, U Pa, 1978; 79, 81, 86, Princeton, NJ
Moses, Wilson J., U Ia, 1973
Mosier, John, Loyola U. NO, 1979, 80, 81, 82, 83, 85; 85, 86, Film Buffs Inst, NO
Moss, Anita, UNC-Charlotte, 1980, 84
Moss, Jane, Colby C, 1980, 81, 84
Moss, George, City C, San Francisco, 1976
Moss, Richard, Colby C, 1981
Moss, William, Wake Forest U, 1981
Mossman, Beal, E Mont C, 1985
Mostocci, John J., Willowbrook HS, 1976
Mostow, Joshua, U Pa, 1983
Mott, Don, Xavier U, NO, 1988
Motte, Warren, U Pa, 1981
Motto, Anna Lydia, U S Fl, 1979
Motz, Marilyn, BGSU, 1982, 83, 84, 85, 86, 87
Moubarak, Walid, Kuwait U, 1982
Moudry, Joe, U Al, 1975
Mould, David H., Oh U, 1984, 85, 86
Mount, Grame, Laurentian U, 1984
Mount, Maxine, Cin, Oh, 1981
Mourraq, Manuela, U Il, 1988
Mousette, Marcel, Laval U, Quebec City,1984
Mowder, Bill, State Planning, Boulder, 1988
Mowder, William, Govern's Office, Colo, 1985
Mowitt, John, U Minn, 1984
Moylan, Thomas A., U Wisc-Waukesa, 1988
Moyle, Natalie K., U Va, 1979, 80
Mrozek, Donald J., Kans SU, 1976, 78, 79
Mudge, Bradford, U Tx, 1986
Mueller, Donald J., U Wisc-Milw, 1973
Mueller, Frederick, Morehead SU, 1982
Mueller, Milton, Cato Inst, Washington, D.C., 1984
Mukerji, Chandra, UC-San Diego, 1977, 84
Mukherjee, Arun, U Regina, 1984
Mullen, Patrick, Oh SU, 1972, 73
Mullen, Richard, Ind SU, 1973
Mullet, Olive G. Ferris SC, 1977
Mulligan, Mary C., Bloomfield C, 1974
Mulligan, Paul, Mich SU, 1988
Mullis, Tom, Radford U, 1988
Mulready, P.M., NYU, 1985

Munib-ur-Rahman, Oakland U, 1974
Munley, John, Pine Manor C, 1982
Munro, Ian, William Jewell C, 1983
Munson, Linda G., Mercer U, 1988
Murdock, Libby, Oh SU, 1984
Murdock, Marianne, Sou Il U, 1977
Murphy, Allen F., Bloomsburg SC, 1979
Murphy, Avon J., Ferris S C, 1980
Murphy, Bonnie, Ok SU, 1975
Murphy, Earl, Harris-Stowe SC, 1983
Murphy, Frank W., U Tol, 1984
Murphy, J. Thomas, U Il, 1985
Murphy, James, Sou Il, 1980, 81, 82
Murphy, John, U Wash, 1984
Murphy, Julie, DePaul U, Chicago, 1982
Murphy, Lawrence R., Wayne SU, 1988
Murphy, Lori, BGSU, 1984
Murphy, Michael B., Chicago, 1988
Murphy, Patrick, W Va U, 1971
Murphy, Sharon, Sou Il U, 1982
Murphy, William T., National Archives, 1975
Murray, Davis Robert, U Ok, 1985
Murray, Brian, Youngstown U, 1988
Murray, Ellen, Ok SU, 1975
Murray, Francis J., Belmont Abbey C, 1973
Murray, James A., Oh U, 1978
Murray, James Briggs, Schornburg Library, 1981
Murray, Lawrence L., SUNY-Fredonia, 75, 76; 77 (St. John's U
Murray, Michael, U Louisville, 1982
Murray, Patricia, SE Mo SU, 1986
Murray, Paul T., Siena C, 1988
Murray, Randal, Sou Il U, 1985
Musgrave, Marian, Miami U Oh, 1986
Mussell, Kay, U Ia., 1971; 72, U Va; 73, Geo Mason U; 75, 76, 77, 82, American U
Musselwhite, Lynn, Cameron U, 1986
Musser, Donald, Stetson, 1988
Musser, Joseph, Oh Wesleyan U, 1987
Mussulman, Joseph A., U Mont, 1974, 75, 76
Mustazza, Leonard, Pa SU-Abington, 1986
Mutersbaugh, Bert M., E Ky U, 1985
Myer, Roy, Mankato SU, 1973
Myers, Constance Ashton, U Sou Car, 1974
Myers, David, Loyola U, NO 1988
Myers, Elizabeth, Sacred Heart of Mary HS, Rolling Meadows, Il, 1976
Myers, Mashall, Ky Wesleyan C, 1985
Myers, Norman J., BGSU, 1988
Myers, Robert E., Bethany C., 1979, 81
Myers, Robert R., West Ga C, 1988
Myers, Russ, Creator of "Boom-Hilda," 1971
Myers, William G. Oh Hist Soc, 1973, 75
Naby, Eden, Harvard, 1979
Nachbar, Jack, BGSU, 1972, 73, 74, 75, 76, 77, 78, 79, 80, 81, 82, 83, 84, 85, 86, 87, 88
Nachbar, Lynn, Bowling Green, Oh, 1984
Nachman, Jay, Temple, 1980
Nadel, Ira B., U British Columbia, 1984
Nader, Benjamin, U Neb, 1982
Nagel, Eric R., U Pitt, 1981
Nagel, James, Northeastern U, 1972, 76
Nagle, Stephen, U SC-Coastal Car C, Inst.,

1982
Nagourney, Peter, Wayne SU, 1978, 79, 80
Nagy, Michael, Concord C, 1985
Nakajavani, Erik, U Pitt, 1982
Nakayama, Thomas, U Ia, 1986
Nance, Guin A., Auburn U-Montgomery, 1978
Nandyal, R.K., Ok SU 1983
Napierkowski, Thomas J, U Colo-Colo Springs, 1979
Napp, Ralph von Tresckow, Winston-Salem U, 1978, 79
Narvaez, Peter, Mem U Newfoundland, 1977, 86, 87, 88
Nash, Anedith, U Minn, 1982
Nash, Lynne, Shippensburg SU, 1988
Nasser, Munir, U Pacific, 1982
Natanson, Nicholas, U Ia, 1985
Nath, Vishwanadhja Hari Hara, Tx Tech, 1979, 80
Nathans, Elizabth Studly, Duke, 1973
Nathanson, Paul, Montreal, Can, 1987
Natoli, Charles, St. John Fisher C, 1982
Nault, Lylvie, U Quebec, Montreal, 1987
Nazzarini, Judy, U Cin, 1973
Neal, Arthur, BGSU, 1984, 85, 86, 87, 88
Neal, Larry, U Ore, 1986
Nealon, Jeffrey, Loyola U, Chicago, 1988
Neapolitan, Jerry, Tn Tech U, 1988
Neckerman, Kathy, 1988
Nedelkovice, A., Yugoslavia, 1980
Nederman, Cary, York U, Toronto, 1980, 81, 82, 83, 84
Needleman, Bert, SUNY-Oswego, 1977
Neel, Jasper, Francis Marion C, 1985
Neff, David, U Al-Huntsville, 1983
Nehring, Michael, Long Beach, Ca, 1988
Nehring, Neil, U Tx, 1988
Neil, J. Meredith, Boise, Ida, 1975, 78
Neils, Patricia, CSU-Sacramento, 1985
Nellis, Marilyn K., Clarkson U, 1987, 88
Nelsen, Harry, Ball SU, 1985
Nelson, Bill, Wichita SU, 1983
Nelson, Byron, W Va U, 1979
Nelson, C.E., U Neb, 1975; 83, CSU-Sacramento
Nelson, Charles, Mich Tech U, 1977, 78, 79, 80, 81, 82, 84, 85, 86, 87, 88
Nelson, Doris, CSU-Long Beach, 1983
Nelson, Emmanuel, U Tn, 1982; 84, Univ Center, Knoxville, Tn
Nelson, F. William, Wichita SU, 1984
Nelson, John Wiley, Pitt Theological Seminary, 1975, 76, 77, 79
Nelson, Mac, Pa SU, 1979
Nelson, Malcolm, SUC-Fredonia, 1980
Nelson, Margaret, Ok SU, 1974, 82
Nelson, Richard, U Wisc-Oshkosh, 1979
Nelson, Richard, U Houston, 1982, 83, 84, 85
Nelson, Stephen, Shorewood, Wis, 1986
Nelson, Stephen S., NYU, 1983, 84, 87
Nelson, Stephen, Hunter, 1988
Nelson, Thomas F., Oh U, 1975
Nelson, William F., Carnegie-Mellon U, 1979
Nemecek, Maureen, Ok SU, 1985
Nesin, Jeff, SUNY-Buffalo, 1972
Nesteby, James, BGSU, 1978; 86, Paducah

Comm C
Nestor, Loretta, Granada Hills, Ca, 1979
Netzhammer, Emile, U Ut, 1986, 87, 88
Neuendorf, Kimberly, Cleveland SU, 1983
Neuleib, Janice, Il SU, 1977
Neuman, David, BGSU, 1971, 72, 73, 75
Neumann, Mark, U Ut, 1984
Neumann, Richard, SW Mo SU, 1988
Neuringer, Charles, U Kans, 1983
Neustadter, Roger, Mt. St. Mary C, Newburg, NY, 1984
Neuswanger, R.R., U Wisc-Superior, 1980
Neville, Anthony, Fl SU, 1982
Nevins, Francis, 1971; 72, 74, 75, 76, 77, St. Louis U
Newcomb, Horace, Saginaw Valley C, 1971; 76 U Md; 80, U Tx
Newcomb, James W., Memphis SU, 1986
Newhouse, Tom, SUNY-Buffalo, 1984
Newlin, Keith, Colo SU, 1982
Newman, Edgar Leon, NM SU, 1976
Newman, John, Colo SU, 1983
Newman, P.B., Queens C, 1977
Newman, Ronald, U Miami, Fl, 1977
Newman, Shelley, Columbia U, 1983
Newman, Stanley, Phila, 1985
Newton, Francis, NYC, 1983
Newton, Sandra S., Mattatuck Comm C, Ct., 1988
Nice, Pamela, Gustavus Adolphus C, 1985
Nichol, Charles, Ind SU, 1983, 86, 88
Nicholl, James R., W Car U, 1979
Nichols, Kathleen L., Tx Tech, 1978; 83 Pitt SU
Nichols, Marilyn, Towson SU, 1980, 81
Nickels, Cameron, James Madison U, 1984
Nickell, Frank, SE Mo, 1984, 85
Nickell, James M., St. Mary's C Md., 1979
Nicks, Joan, Brock U. St. Catherine's Can., 1979, 84
Nicol, Charles, Ind SU, 1981, 82
Nicolosi, Robert, U Ala, 1978
Nicoloso, Elaine, Tallahassee, Fl, 1986
Nichols, Kathleen L., U Neb, 1975
Nieburg, H.L., SUNY-Binghamton, 1977
Niederman, Sharon, Metro C, Denver, 1979
Nielson, Angela, U Il, 1974
Nielson, Ted, Hope C, 1978
Nielson, Richard P., U Il, 1974
Niemann, Thomas, N Ky SC, 1974
Nieminski, John, co-ed Baker St. Miscellanea, 1976
Nigro, August, Kutztown SC, 1979, 87
Nilon, Charles H., U Colo, 1979, 80, 81, 82, 83, 84, 85, 86, 87, 88
Nimmo, Don, U Tn, 1981
Nist, Joan S., Auburn U, 1976
Nixon, Charles, U Colo, 1978
Nixon, Helen M., U Neb-Omaha, 1988
Nixon, Laurence, Concordia U, Montreal, 1987
Noble, Allen, U Akron, 1978
Noble, David, U Minn, 1977
Noble, Donald R., U Ala, 1981, 82, 85, 86, 87, 88
Nochimson, Martha, Mercy C, 1987
Nochimson, Richard L., Yeshiva U, NYC, 1987
Nokony, Denis, Saskatchewan Culture &

Recreation, Regina, 1984
Noland, Richard, U Mass, 1986
Noodhoorn, Max, Albion C, 1988
Norberg, Arthur, Nat'l Science Foundation, 1980
Norbu, Thubten, Ind U, 1981
Nord, Doublas, U Minn-Duluth, 1986
Norden, Martin, U Mass, 1982, 84, 87
Nordley, Dave, Bemidji SU, 1984, 85
Norman, Mary Anne, Norman's Int'l Exchange, Dallas, 1981, 82
Norris, Darrell A., SUNY-Geneseo, 1987
Norris, Darrell, SUNY-Geneseo, 1984
Norris, Jo A., Wayne SU, 1982
Norse, Clifford, Radford U, 1985, 86, 87, 88
North, Uboesha Cloud, U Neb, 1982
Norton, Suzanne, Purdue, 1985, 86
Norvell, Margaret, BGSU, 1981, 82, 88
Norwood, Glenda, Carrollton C, 1986
Norwood, Vera, U NM, 1982
Noun, Louis R., Grinnel C, 1987
Novak, Linda, NYU, 1986
Novelli, Martin, Phila C, 1984, 86, 87; 88 Rutgers
Noverr, Douglas, Mich SU, 1974, 75, 76, 77, 79, 81, 82, 85, 86, 87, 88
Nowicki, Joseph, U Mass, 1981, 82, 83
Nowland, Robert, S Ct SU, 1986
Noyes, Sylvia, Hussan C, 1987
Nuessel, Frank, U Louisville, 1986, 87
Nugent, Donald G., U Ky, 1972
Nunn, Robert, Brock U, Can, 1984, 88
Nunnally, Patrick, U Ia, 1986
Nutting, P. Bradley, Framington SC, 1979
Nye, David, Union C, 1980; 82, MIT
Nye, Peter, E Mich U, 1971
Nye, Russel B., Mich SU, 1971, 72, 73, 74, 75, 76, 77. 78, 79, 80, 81, 82; 83, 84, 85; 86 U So Fl
Nye, William, Hollins C, 1984, 85, 87, 88
Nystrom, Elsa, Cary, Il, 1983, 84; 85, Loyola U, Chicago
Oakes, Ray, U Louisville, 1982
Oaster, Thomas, U Mo.-KC, 1987, 88
Obertubdesing, Carol, Malden, Ma, 1978
O'Brien, Ellen, Guilford C, 1981
O'Brien, George, U Minn-Duluth, 1976, 86
O'Brien, James, C New Rochelle, 1985
O'Brien, Kenneth, SUC-Brockport, 1983, 84
O'Brien, Marie, Lowell U., 1975, 76, 77, 79; 87, Auburn U
O'Brien, Matthew C., Ga Inst Tech, 1978, 86
O'Brien, Patrick, Emporia SU, 1983
O'Brien, Sharon, Dickinson C, 1977; 79, Phila., 82
O'Brien, Sheila, Ind U, 1986
Ocasio, Rafael, U So Ala, 1988
O'Connor, Alan, York U, Can
O'Connor, Gerard, Lowell U, 1971, 72, 73, 74, 75, 76, 77, 78,79, 80, 81, 82, 83, 84, 85, 86, 87, 88
O'Connor, John, Geo Mason U, 1987
O'Connor, John, NJ Inst Tech, 1977, 82, 83; 84, Bloomfield, NJ; 85 NJ Inst Tech

O'Connor, Karen, Cabrini C, 1987
O'Dell, Doris, Queen's Univ, Kingston, Ont, 1986
O'Dell, Leslie, Wilfrid Laurier U, Waterloo, Ont
Odine, Maurice, Northeastern La U, 1985
Odom, Keith, TCU, 1983, 84, 85
O'Donnell, Mabry, Marietta C, Oh,1981
O'Donnell, Patrick, U Az, 1981
Oebling, Richard, Assumption C, Mass, 1977, 82, 84
Oestereicher, Emile, New Sch Soc Research, 1975
Ogden, Karen, 1984
Ogden-Malouf, Susan, Bethel C, 1982
Ogilvia, Charles F., U Tn, 1978
Ogles, Robert M., Purdue, 1988
Oglesbee, F.W., Sou Il U, 1982, 83, 84, 85, 86, 87, 88
Ohlgren, Thomas, Purdue U, 1972, 73
Ohmer, Susan, Wayne SU, 1988
Ognibene, Elaine, Sienna C, 1975
Ohr, Michael, C Charleston, 1979
Ohrn, Steven, Ia Arts Council, 1984
Oiwa, Keibo, Montreal, 1987
Ojior, Omoh, U Benin, Benin, Nigeria, 1988
Okamura, Lawrence, U Mo, 198
O'Kane, Karen, Carnegie-Mellon, 1988
O'Keefe, Heather C., UND, 1988
Okhamafe, E. Imafedia, U Neb-Omaha, 1988
Okouneff, Dov, Marianpolis C, Montreal, 1987
Okotie, Atutumama, N Il U, 1984
Oldani, John, Sou Il U-Edwardsville, 1979, 82
Olderman, Raymon, U Wisc, 1974
Oldham, Perry, Casady School, Ok City, 1982
O'Leary, James, Daemen C, 1983, 84, 85
Oliva, Leo, Fort Hays SC, 1972
Olivella, Manuel Zapata, Howard U, 1976
Oliver, William R., N Ky U, 1988
Olivia, Judy L., Buffalo Grove, Il, 1987
Ollenquist, Jody L., N Il U, 1988
Olmos, Margarita, Brooklyn C, 1988
Olmstead, A.D., U Calgary, 1987
Olmstead, Donald W., Mich SU, 1984
Olsen, W. Scott, Lander C, 1987
Olson, Scott R., Cent Ct SU, 1987
Olson, Thomas O., Kent SU, 1987
Olt, Blair, Wright SU, 1978
O'Malley, Lurana, U Tx, 1988
O'Mara, Joan, U Bridgeport, 1988
O'Meara, Anne, U Minn, 1988
O'Meara, Don, U Cin, 1987, 88
O'Meara, Jean, U Mich-Dearborn, 1978
O'Neal, Amy, Living Blues Magazine, 1976
O'Neal, Frederick, Actor's Equity, 1971
O'Neal, Jim, Living Blues Magazine, 1976
O'Neal, John, Free Sou Theater, NO, 1976
Opie, John, Duquesne U, 1982
Opt, Susan K., Oh SU, 1988
Opubor, Alfred E., Mich SU, 1973; 77, U Lagos, Nigeria
Ord, Priscilla A., Longwood C, 1988
O'Reilly, Mary R., C St. Thomas, St Paul, 1984

Oriard, Michael, Ore SU, 1977, 87
Orlik, Peter B., Cent Mich U, 1984
Orloff, Kossia, 1982
Orlov, Paul A., Pa SU-Media, 1987
Orlov, Paul, Pa SU, 1984, 85, 86, 87, 88
Orman, Patricia, U S Colo, 1985
Ormiston, Gayle, U Colo, 1988
Ornelas, Kriemhilde, BGSU, 1984
Orozco, Luz Marie, Marycrest C, 1979
Orr, David, U Pa, 1977; 78, 79, 80, 81, Nat'l Park Service, Phila
Orr, Jay, Country Music Hall Fame, 1985
Orr, John C., U Ok, 1983; Duke, 1988
Orso, Ethlyn, UNO, 1988
Ort, Daniel, S Ct SU 1986
Ortiz, Norma, U Ark, 1986
Ortro, Richard, Ore SU, 1973
Orwan, Patricia M., U S Colo, 1987
Ory, William K., U Pitt, 1977
Osadnik, Waclaw M., Katowice, Poland, 1985
Osborne, Martha, U Tn, 1986
Osburn, Michael, Memphis SU, 1982
Oseguera, A. Anthony, Valdosta SC, 1979
Osgood, Richard, WXYZ, Detroit, 1980
Oshana, Mary Ann, Northwestern, 1983, 84, 85, 86, 87, 88
O'Shaugnessey, Margael, St. Mary's C, 1988
Osing, Gordon, Memphis SU, 198
Ostman, Ronald E., Sou Il U, 1978, 79; 84, 85, Cornell U
Ostrach, Herbert, Boston C, 1977, 78
Ostroff, David, BGSU, 1982, 83, 84, 85
Otitibge, Samuel, W Il U, 1982, 82; 84 Emerson C
O'Toole, Thomas, Science Ed Washington Post, 1977
Otting, John D., WQMF-Jefferson, In, 1982
Otus-Baskett, Belma, Mich SU, 1986
Overstreet, Charles, OK SU, 1985
Owen, Guy, NC SU-Raleigh, 1980
Owen, Patricia, NYC, 1988
Owen, Thomas, U Louisville, 1982
Owen, Virginia, Il SU-Normal, 1982
Owens, Irene, Chester Heights, Pa, 1988
Owens, James, Lynchburg C, 1973
Owens, Jo, Vanderbilt, 1985
Owings, Kathleen, U Guam, 1980, 84
Ozier, Mervin, Champaign, Il, 1985
Paananen, V., Mich SU, 1980
Pace, Barney, CUNY, 1985
Packard, Cynthia, BGSU, 1976, 77
Packard, William, Ed. New York Quarterly, 1982
Pacton, Diane, U Ottawa, 1987, 8
Padilla, Fernando, U Colo, 1977
Pady, Donald S., Ia SU, 1987
Paehlke, R.C., Trent U, Peterborough, Can. 1977
Page, Barry, Mich Tech U, 1978
Page, Rebecca, Purdue, 1981
Page, Vicki, Briar Cliff C., 1988
Pahlka, William H., U Tx, 1978
Paikowsky, Sandra, Concordia U, Montreal, 1987
Paine, Katharine, LSU, 1988
Paletz, David L., Duke, 1976
Pallister, Jan, BGSU, 1981, 83
Palmer, Bruce, U Houston, 1986

Palmer, Carole, BGSU, 1987

Palmer, Jerry, City London, Poly, England, 1980

Palmer, J. Jesse, USMiss, 1988

Palmer, Leota, William Rainey Harper C, 1982, 83

Palmer, Michael, Louisburg C, N Caro, 1983, 85, 86

Palmer, R. Barton, Ga SU, 1976, 86

Palmer, William J., Purdue, 1973, 79

Paludan, Phillip, U Kans, 1987

Palumbo, Donald, N Mich SU, 1979, 89, 81, 82, 83; 84, 85, 86, 87, 88, Loraine Comm C

Pandian, Jacob, CSU-Fullerton, 1988

Panek, LeRoy, W Md C, 1981

Panico, Ambrose, W Suburban Assoc for Special Educ, Cicero, Il, 1979

Pankin, Robert M., SUNY-Oswego, 1973, 74

Pannbacker, Alfred R., Edinboro U, Pa., 1987

Pannill, Linda, U Ky, 1981, 82, 85

Panowski, James, N Mich U, 1983

Paoletti, Jo B., U Md, 1985, 86, 87

Papay, Joseph, St. Peter's C, NJ, 1985

Papay, Twila Y., Caldwell C, 1980; 85, Hofstra U

Papish, Barbara, BGSU, 1983

Papke, David R., New Haven, Ct., 1982; 86, Ind U., Indianapolis

Papke, David, Ind U-Indianapolis, 1987

Papoulis, Irene, UC-Santa Barbara, 1987, 88

Papson, Stephen, St. Lawrence U, 1984, 85, 86, 87

Paradis, Roger, U Me-Fort Kent, 1984

Paravisini, Lizabeth, Lehman C-CUNY, 1986

Parent, George, U Laval, Quebec, 1980

Parins, James, U Ark-Little Rock, 1985

Paris, Bernard J., Mich SU, 1976

Park-Curry, Pamela, Oh SU, 1980

Park, Shelly M., Duke, 1988

Parker, Alice, U Ala, 1988

Parker, David, Library of Congress, 1977

Parker, Jill, Cornell U, 1985

Parker, Kay, Adult Film Actress, 1986

Parker, Patricia, Oh U, 1985

Parker, Richard, Middle East Inst, Washington, D.C., 1982

Parker, Robert, Author "Spenser" crime novels, 1977, 78

Parks, Alfreita, U Ia 1980, 82

Parks, Henry, U Md, 1981

Parks, John G., Miami U, Oh, 1977, 87

Parks, Ward, LSU, 1985, 88

Parnell, Paul, BGSU, 1980, 81

Parnes, Howard, Frostburg SC, Md, 1987

Parowski, Ann, Va Tech, 1986

Parris, Nina, Columbia Mus Art, SC, 1986

Parrish, James, U So Fl, 1985

Parsinnen, T.M., Temple, 1971

Parsons, Arthur S., Smith C, 1987

Parsons, David, U Saskatchewan, Can, 1985, 86

Pasadeos, Yorgo, U Al; 82, 83, U Tx; 84, U Al

Paskoff, Louis, Kent SU, 1984, 85, 86, 87

Paterson, Douglas L., U Neb-Omaha, 1983

Paterson, James D., U Calgary, 1987, 88

Patino, Rosa, General Motors, 1980

Patnaik, Eira, Frostburg SC, 1986, 88

Patrick, Marietta, E Ky U, 1985, 87

Patrick, Michael D., U Mo-Rolla, 1978

Patrik, Linda, Union C, 1985

Patrouch, Joseph F., Jr., U Dayton, 1972

Patterson, David, Ok SU, 1983

Patterson, Eric, Hobart & William Smith C, 1981

Patterson, Oscar, Tx Tech U, 1983; 86 Pembroke SU

Patterson, Richard, Miss SU, 1977, 81, 87

Patterson, Sylvia W., U Southeastern La, 1977, 78; 79, 80, 81, 82, U Southwestern La

Patti, Anthony V., Lehman C, CUNY, 1976

Paul, Terri, Ia SU, 1980

Paulin, Ed., Ok SU, 1986, 87, 88

Paulin, Philip, Ok SU, 1985

Paulson, Kristoffer, Simon Fraser U, 1983

Pauly, John, Fordham, 1980

Pauly, Susan, BGSU, 1986

Pauly, Thomas H., U De, 1974, 75, 76, 77

Pavelich, Joan, Concordia U, Montreal, 1984

Pavlides, Merope, 1987, 88

Pavlik, Katherine, Nor Mich U, 1981, 82, 83, 84, 85, 87, 88

Payne-Carter, David, NYU, 1984, 87

Payne, Judy, Sibley House Assoc, Mendota, Mn, 1988

Payne, Linda, U De, 1987

Payson, David, Northwestern, 1987

Peacock, John, Md Inst Art, 1988

Pearl, Schlamie, McMaster U, 1987

Pearman, William, Millersvile U., 1985

Pearse, James A., Baylor, 1983; 85, W Il U

Pearson, Barry Lee, Ind U, 1971; 77 U Md

Pearson, Carol, U Md, 1977

Pearson, Masie K., W Mich U, 1982

Pearson, Michael, Lagrange C, 1985, 86

Pearson, Pat, Ia SU, 1983

Pease, Donald, U Chicago, 1971, 73

Peavler, Bill, Ok SU, 1983

Peavy, Charles, U Houston, 1972, 73, 74, 75

Pecile, Jordon, US Coast Guard Acad, 1985

Peck, Robert, Washington, D.C., 1988

Pecor, Charles, Macon Jr C., Ga, 1986

Pecora, Norma, 1984

Peddle, Walter W., Newfoundland Mus, St. Johns, 1988

Pedersen, Diana, Carleton U, 1988

Pederson, Ann, UND, 1988

Peek, George S., Ark SU, 1974, 76, 77

Peet, Richard, Clark U, 1985

Pegg, Barry, Mi Tech U, 1987

Peirce, Carol, BGSU, 1984, 85

Peirce, Maggi, Fairhaven, Wa, 1987

Pelensky, O.A., Boston U, 1986

Pell, Johnetta, U Il, 1984

Pellow, Kenneth, U Colo-Colo Springs, 1979

Pelz, William, Roosevelt U, 1975, 76, 77

Pelzer, John D., Ball SU, 1988

Pelzer, Linda C., Ball SU, 1987, 88

Pembroke, Randall, U Mo-KC, 1987, 88

Pendleton, Gayle T., Emory U, 1979

Pendleton, Thomas A., Iona C, 1978

Penee, Terry, N Ky U, 1984

Penelope, Julia, U Neb, 1983

Penezic, Relja, BGSU, 1986

Penezic, Vida, BGSU, 1987, 88

Penn, Ray, Radford U, 1988

Pennell, Jane C., Sou Il U-Edwardsville, 1980, 81, 82, 83, 84, 85, 86, 87

Pennell, Melissa M., U Lowell, 1987

Perebinosoff, Phillipe, U Il, 1972

Peregoy, Marjorie, Tx A&M, 1985

Peregrino, Santiago, Delta C, 1974

Peretti, Burton, UC-Berkeley, 1988

Perkins, Agnes, E Mich U, 1980

Perl, Robert D., Tx Tech, 1981

Perling, Toni, Northwestern, 1986

Perlmutter, Ruth, Phila Inst Cinema, 1975

Perlstadt, Harry, Mich SU, 1984

Peroutka, Shirley, Goucher, 1988

Peroutka, Shirley, Oh U, 1985

Perpich, Mary, SD SU, 1988

Perpich, Mary, U Wisc-Oshkosh, 1985, 86

Perrell, Jeff, Regis C, 1988

Perricone, Christopher, Jr., CUNY-Baruch, 1981

Perricone, Philip, Wake Forest C., 1988

Perry, Charles, Wright SU, 1982

Perry, Nancy, Jamestown-Yorktown Foundation, Williamsburg, 1986

Perry, Richard, St. Lawrence U, 1988

Perry, Robert, BGSU 1971, 72, 73, 74, 75, 84, 86

Pershey, Edward, Thomas Edison Nat'l Hist Site, 1983, 84

Persico, V.R., Ga Sou C, 1988

Persky, Joel, TCU, 1984, 85

Persky, Joel, SW Mo SC, 1988

Persoon, James, Grand Valley SC, 1988

Pest, Robert SW Mo SU, 1979

Peter, D.M., U SW La, 1983

Peterfreund, Stuart, U Ark-Little Rock, 1978

Peterman, John, William Paterson C New Jersey, 1981

Peters, Adelia, BGSU, 1986, 87, 88

Peters, Bruce, U Ky, 1988

Peters, Marian, Beaverbrook, Oh, 1986

Peterson, Claire, USC, 1988

Peterson, Betsy, Ind U, 1979

Peterson, Deborah, Il SU, 1984

Peterson, Gene, Dept Nat' Resources, 1971

Peterson, Jon, U Ala, 1983; 86, Pa SU

Peterson, M. Dianne, N Mich U, 1986

Peterson, David R., Greenbrier, Ark, 1988

Peterson, Pamela, Rolling Meadows HS, Il, 1976

Peterson, Richard A., Vanderbilt, 1971, 72, 73, 74, 75, 78, 79, 82, 84

Peterson, Richard, Mich SU, 1984, 85, 87

Peterson-Lewis, Sonja, U Ut, 1984, 85

Peterson, Yen, St Xavier C, 1986

Petite, Joseph, Columbus C., Ga., 1983

Pettewski, Paul, Columbus C., Ga., 1987

Petreman, David A., Wright SU, 1988

Petress, Kenneth, N Il U, 1984

Petrey, Jack, WAKY-Louisville, Ky, 1982

Petrik, Joseph, N Ky U, 1982

Pett, William. URI, 1977, 79
Pettengell, Michael, BGSU 1988
Pettengill, Ann H., JFK Mem Lib, CSU-Los Angeles, 1976
Pettis, Joyce, E Car U., 1977, 78; 79, Carrboro, NC; 80, 82, 83, 84, 85; E Car U; 86, 87, 88, N Car SU
Pettit, Robert B., Lafayette, Ind, 1981; 86, Ft. Wayne, In
Pevey, Jo Lundy, Sou Tech Inst, 1985
Peyrouse, Jack, Methodist C, 1988
Pfaelzer, Jean, U De, 1987
Pfeifer, Leona, Fort Hays SU, 1983
Pfeiffer, John R., Cen Mich U, 1971
Pfeiffer, Richard, Louisville, Ky, 1982
Pfliger, Pat, U Minn, 1986
Pfohl, Stephen J., Boston C, 1987
Phifer, Susan Cen Piedmont Comm C, 1975
Philips, David, E Ct SU, 1987, 88
Philips, Gene, Loyola U Chicago, 1982
Philips, R. Craig, Mich SU, 1980
Phillips, Billie, San Antonio C, 1974
Phillips, Don E., Washburn U, 1987
Phillips, Gary, Ball SU, 1987
Phillips, Gene, Loyola U Chicato, 1983
Phillips, Inez, Ok SU, 1976
Phillips, Robert, Lander C, 1985, 87
Phromsuthirak, Maneeplin, Silpokorn U, Thailand, 1982
Piacentino, Edward, 1986
Picard, John, Cen SU, Ok, 1983, 85
Pichaske, David, SW SU, Mn, 1983, 86
Pickett, Joseph, U Mich, 1987
Picklesimer, Dorman, Boston C, 1977, 79
Pictor, James, St Frances C, Ft Wayne, In, 1982
Piehl, Charles, Mankato SU, 1983, 84
Piehl, Kathy, Mich Tech U, 1981; 83, 84, 86, Mankato SU
Pielke, Robert, Geo Mason U, 1978, 79, 80, 81, 82
Pierce, Allan, St. Ann's Sch, Brooklyn, 1980
Pierce, Carl, U Tn, 1986
Pierce, Carol, Biola U, 1986
Pierce-Daniel, M.E., Lamar U, 1988
Piernot, Craig A., Colo SU, 1977
Pierson, William, Fisk U, 1985
Piety, James, Wilbur Wright C, Chicago, 1984, 85; 86, 87, Roosevelt U
Pike, Gerald, UC-Davis, 1988
Pike, Larry, Macomb Comm C, 1985
Pildrich, Charles, Rutgers, 1977
Pilgrim, Donald, York U, Toronto, 1984
Pilipp, Frank, UNC, 1988
Pilling, Arnold, Wayne SU, 1971
Pitch, Charles, John Jay C Criminal Justice, NY, 1985
Pinckney, Warren R., UCLA, 1987
Pingry, David E., Va Tech
Pino, Frank Jr., Mich SU, 1972, 73, 74; 75, 76, 77, U Tx-San Antonio
Piorkowski, Joan L., C St. Thomas, St. Paul, 1988
Piper, Dan, Sou Il U, 1972
Piper, Judith, 1986
Pisano, Dominic, Nat'l Air & Space Mus, 1986
Pitt, Bruce, U Ia, 1983
Pitt, Joseph C., Va Tech, 1979, 80, 82

Pitts, Bill, Baylor, 1987, 88
Pitzer, Donald, U Sou Ind, 1986, 87
Plank, Robert, Case Western U, 1982
Plank, William, E Mont C, 1986
Plasketes, George, BGSU, 1984, 85; 86, Auburn U
Plasse, Marie, Boston U, 1985, 88
Plato, Don, McNeese SU, 1988
Platt, Jane, U Kans, 1983
Platte, Mary K., BGSU, 1980, 81; 83, Az SU
Plattner, Steve, Macalester C, 1973
Playmountain, Stephen, Hollywood In'tl, 1986
Pleskin, Gloria, Cote St. Luc, Can,. 1983
Plesur, Milton, SUNY-Buffalo, 1971, 72, 73, 74, 75, 76, 77, 79, 81
Pletcher, Galen, Sou Il U-Edwardsville, 1980
Plichta, Annette, Mid Tn SU, 1988
Plotnicki, Rita, Hunter, 1978; 80, Sou Il
Plummer, Bonnie C., E Ky U, 1979, 81, 82, 86
Plymell, Charles, Silver Springs, Md, 1983
Pochran, Tom J., 1973
Pocius, Gerald, Mem U Newfoundland, 1984, 85
Pockrass, Robert, Mankato SU, 1988
Poe, Donald B., Jr., Cornell, 1979
Poe, Jon W., Wichita SU, 1983
Poesch, Jessie, Tulane, 1986
Poffenbarger, Gary C., Ok SU, 1975, 76; 82, Tx Tech
Pogel, Nancy, Mich SU, 1975, 76, 77, 78, 79, 80, 81, 82, 83, 84, 85, 86, 87, 88
Pohl, Frederick, Sci Fi Writer, 1977, 82, 85
Poissant, Marie-Sylvie, U du Quebec, Montreal, 1987
Pokrywczynski, Jim, U Ga, 1985, 86
Pole, Nelson, Cleveland SU, 1981, 84
Polino, Eric, Northwestern, 1985
Polivka, Dennis, Geo. Mason, 1987
Polivka, Jirina, Geo Mason U 1983, 84, 86, 87
Polk, Barbara, Wayne SU, 1973
Poll, Susan, Northwestern U, 1982
Pollack, Mark, Nor Il U., 1983
Pollay, Richard, U British Columbia, 1984
Pomerantz, Donald, Cen Conn SC, 1981
Pomeroy, Charles CSU-Long Beach, 1977
Poole, Jerry, U Cen Ark, 1988
Poole, Richard L., U Nor Ia, 1988
Poole, Robert, Reason Fndt, Santa Barbara, Ca, 1984
Poor, Sue, Ok SU, 1983; 85, 86, 87, 88, Wharton Cty C, Tx
Pop-Cornis, Marcel, U N Ia, 1984
Pope, Daniel, U Ore, 1984
Popelnik, Rodolfo, Interamer U, Hato Rey, PR, 1988
Popham, Elizabeth, Mem'l U Newfoundland, 1986
Popov, Boris Jakob, U Mass, 1974
Poretz, D.H., Flow General, Inc., Va., 1983
Portales, Marco, UC-Berkeley, 1979
Porter, Catherine, Marquette U, 1984
Porter, Christopher, Surrey Consulting, Denver, 1987
Plorter, Claire, 1986

Porter, Curtiss E., Black Comm Educ, Pittsburg, 1978
Porter, Dale H., W Mich U, 1981
Porter, David, Wm Penn C, Iaa, 1984
Porter, Gregory S., Marquette U, 1984, 85, 86, 87
Porter, Lasle, Muskingum C, 1987
Porter, Lynette, Findlay C, 1985
Porter, Marc, U Sou Al, 1987
Porter, Robert, Va Tech, 1981
Porter, Thomas E., U Detroit, 1977; 80, Oh U
Porterfield, Nolan, SE Mo SU, 1979
Portillo, Estela, El Paso PS, 1976
Posey, Marcia, Clemson, 1988
Posselt, Nancy, Mid Tech C, SC., 1988
Post, Constance J., Ia SU, 1987
Postal, Todd, Chicago, Il, 1985
Poteet, Maurice, U du Quebec a Montreal, 1984
Potter, Dorothy Bundy, Lynchburg, Va, 1974
Potts, Steve, Mankato SU 1988
Poulds, Ed, Ottawa, Can, 1987
Pounds, Wayne, Austin Comm C, 1986, 87
Powell, Christus N., Fort Valley SC, 1988
Powell, Ethel, 1982
Powell, Helen, E Ky U, 1984, 85
Powell, Paul R., UNC-Ashville, 1988
Powell, Walter, York C, Pa, 1984
Powers, Richard, U Mass, 1971; 73, 74, 75, 76, Richmond C CUNY; 78, 79, 80, 81, 82, 83, 84, 85, 86, 87, 88, C Staten Island
Powers, Ron, Chicago Sun Times, 1976
Prasad, Yuvaraij, U Md, 1982
Prasch, Thomas, Ind SU, 1988
Pratt, Judith, U Neb., 1983
Pratt, L.H., Fl A&M, 1987
Pratt, Ray, Mont SU, 1985, 86, 87
Preddy, Jane A., Brooklyn, NY, 1988
Predelli, Marie, U Montreal, Que., 1978
Prehn, John W., Gustavus Adolphus C, 1978, 79, 80, 81, 83
Preiss, Richard, Suffolk U, 1986, 87, 88
Prescott, Lawrence, Ind U, 1972, 76
Prescott, Renate W., BGSU, 1988
Presley, John, Augusta C, 1985, 86
Preston, Charles, UNM, 1985
Preston, David, San Diego SU, 1979
Preston, Dennis R., SUC-Fredonia, 1972, 78, 79
Preston, Frederick W., U Nev, 1988
Preston, Robert M. Mt St Mary's C, Md, 1980, 81
Preu, Dana, Fl A&M, 1982, 8
Prevos, Andre, U Ia, 1980, 81, 82, 83; 84, 85, 86, 87, 88, Pa SU-Dunmore
Prevos, Yves, Pa SU-Worthington, 1985
Prevost, Verbie L., U Tn-Chattanooga, 1988
Price, Grady, Stillwater, Ok, 1984
Price, Joseph, Whittier C, 1986, 87, 88
Price, Mark, Spinnker Software Corp, 1985, 86
Price, Steve, U Ia, 1987
Price, Tyrone F., Kearney SC, 1987
Pridgen, Allen, Chowan C, 1987
Pries, Nancy, Seattle Pac U, 1986

Prigozy, Ruth, Hofstra U, 1975, 76
Prill, Penelope K., Columbus, Oh 1978
Primeggia, Pamela, Adelphi U, 1988
Primeggia, Salvatore, Adlephi U, 1988
Prince, Daniel, Venice, Ca., 1984
Princic, Walter, U Colo, 1985, 87, 88
Pring, Robert K., Herkimer Comm C., NY, 1988
Pringle, Mary Beth, Wright SU, 1978, 79, 84, 85, 86, 87, 88
Prinsky, Norman, Augusta C, 1984, 85, 86, 88
Prioli, Carmine, N Car SU, 1985
Prisco, Salvatore III, Stevens Inst Tech, 1977, 78
Pritchard, David Ind U, 1987
Pritscher, Conrad, BGSU, 1978
Prochaska, David, U Il, 1986
Procopliow, Norma, U Md, 1978
Procter, Jack, Kosair Temple, Louisville, 1985
Prokop, Leota P., William Rainey Harper   C, 1977
Proper, Stan, Wentworth Inst Tech, 1987
Proshan, Chester, U Minn, 1987
Prosser, Daniel, Montclair SC, 1976
Prostak, Elaine, U Kans, 1983
Pruett, Robert, Wright SU, 1979
Pruitt, Elaine, N Car Sch of Arts, Winston-Salem, 1985

Pruitt, John, WXIA TV, Atlanta, 1979
Pry, Elmer R., De Paul U, 1974, 75, 76, 78, 89
Pryor, John, U Windsor, 1987
Puckette, John, Sou Ore SC 1980
Pudaloff, Ross, Wayne SU 1980, 84, 85
Pugh, David G., Ore SU, 1979
Puglia, Gerardo, Cameraperson, 1980
Puhr, Kathleen M., St Louis U, 1981; 84, 86, Clayton HS, Mo
Pundsack, Vichy, U Cin, 1978
Purdon, Liam, Doane C, 1988
Putterman, Theodore, CSU-Sacramento, 1988
Pyle, Ransford, U Cen Fl, 1986
Pyron, Daren A., Fl Int'l U, 1978, 81

Quam, Michael, Sangamon SU, 1979
Quandt, Eldor, W Mich U, 1986
Quantic, Diane, Wichita SU, 1983
Quarantelli, E.L., Oh SU, 1976
Querary, Louis B., Cent Ore CC, 1987
Qeuvreaux, Teri, St. Louis, 1985
Quick, James R., Duquesne U, 1988
Quinn, Joseph A., U Windsor, 1987
Quinn, Mary L., U Sou Me, 1988
Quinn, Sandra, San Jacinto C, 1984
Quivey, James, E Il, 1986
Quillen, Dennis, E Ky U, 1984
Quinby, Lee, Hobart & William Smith C, 1987, 88
Quinlan, Kieran, Vanderbilt U, 1981
Quinn, James, Loop C, Chicago, 1978
Raack, Richard, CSU-Hayward, 1975
Rabillard, Sheila, Oh SU, 1984
Rabin, Cathy, CSU-LA, 1983
Rabinow, Paul, CUNY-Richmond C, 1974

Rabinowitz, Nancy, Kirkland C, 1976
Rabinowitz, Peter, Kirkland C, 1976l; 82, 83, Hamilton C
Rabinowitz, Sima, SUNY-Binghamton, 1979
Race, Timothy, BGSU, 1980
Rachleff, Peter, U Pitt, 1977
Radaker, Kevin, Pa SU, 1987
Radcliff-Umstead, Douglas, Kent SU, 1987
Raddle, Bruce, San Jose SU, 1980
Radespiel, U Ia, 1981
Radford-Hill, Sheila, Central YMCA Comm C, Chicago, 1979
Radhakkrishan, Rajagopalan, U Mass, 1986
Radner, Hilary, U Tx, 1987
Radoway, Jan, Mich SU, 1975, 76, 77, 78; 79, 80, 81, 82, 83, U Pa
Rafalko, Robert J., UNC-Wilmington, 1987
Raffel, Buroton, U Denver, 1984
Ragsdale, Charles, Columbus C, Ga., 1986
Railsback, Jo Helen, Tn SU, 1986
Raines, M. Diane, U Alaska, 1986
Rainey, Carol, N Ky U, 1985
Rainey, Daniel, Geo Mason U, 1982
Rainey, Kenneth T., Memphis SU, 1987
Ralston, Michael, U Tx-Arlington, 1986
Ralston, Richard, U Wisc, 1980, 84
Ramaswamy, Mel, Easterline Angus Instr Co, Indianapolis, 1982
Rambeau, James, Pa SU, 1978
Rambo, Sharon, Mich SU, 1985, 88
Ramet, Carlos, U Il Chicago, 1988
Ramirez, Arthur, Ida SU, 1975
Ramirez, Salvador, 1986
Rampolda, Mary L, Colgate, 1987
Ramsey, Cynthia, Fl SU, 1980
Ramsey, Jeffrey, Kans SU, 1983
Ramsey, Lee C., Nat'l C Educ, Evanston, Il, 1976
Ramsey, Neil Phillip, Va Wesleyan C, 1981
Ramsey, Paul, Ed Testing Service, Princeton, 1980
Ramsey, Priscilla, Howard U, 1985
Ramsey, Ronald Lanier, ND SU, 1979
Ramsing, Kenneth, U Ore,1987
Randall, Aaron J., Appal SU, 1987, 88
Randall, Joan, Va Tech, 1987, 88
Randall, Keith, Radio Can. Int'l, Montreal, 1987
Randall, Neil, U Waterloo, Can, 1987
Randall, Stephen, McGill U, Montreal, 1984
Randall-Tsuruta, Dorothy, Sou Il U, 1980
Randle, Bill, Cleveland, Oh, 1978
Rangan, Jayanthi, Emerson C, 1987
Ranieri, Paul W., Ball SU, 1987
Rank, Hugh, Governors SU, 1982
Ransom, Holly, San Francisco, 1987, 88
Ranson, Nicholas, U Akron, 1983, 84, 86, 87, 88
Ranta, Taimi R., Il SU, 1980
Ranucci, Karen, Brooklyn, NY, 1987
Rapf, Joanna, U Ok, 1977, 78, 79, 80, 83, 86, 87, 88
Raphael, Lev, Mich SU, 1984, 87
Rapp, Dean, Wheaton C, 1988
Rapp, Margaret, Geo Washington U, 1987

Rapping, Elayne, Robert Morris C, 1987, 88
Raskin, Miriam, Geo Mason U, 1984, 87
Raskin, Victor, Purdue, 1981
Raspa, Richard, Wayne SU, 1983
Rasporich, B., U Calgary, 1984
Ratcliff, Gerald L., Montclair SC, 1979
Ratcliff, Kathryn, U Minn, 1985
Ratclffe, Krista, Oh SU, 1987
Rath, Sura P., LSU-Shreveport, 1987
Ratzan, Scott, Harvard, 1986
Raub, Patricia, BGSU, 1983. 85, 86, 87
Raubicheck, Walter, Pace U, 1984, 85, 86
Rauche, Anthony, U Hartford, 1983
Ravage, Jack, U Wy, 1982, 83, 84
Rawlings, Donn, U Denver, 1980
Rawson, Ian, U Pitt, 1979
Ray, Harold, W Mich U, 1987
Ray, Leroi, W Mich U, 1981
Ray, R. Alan, St Louis Comm C, 1985
Ray, Robert, U Fl, 1980
Ray, T.J., U Miss, 1988
Raymer, Anne, NYC, 1976
Raymond, Diane, Bently C, 1980, 81, 82, 84, 85, 86, 87, 88
Raymond, Michael W, Stetson, 1978
Rayson, Ann, U Hawaii, 1983, 84
Read, Allen W., Columbia, 1984
Read, Colin, Huron C, London, Ont., 1984
Reagan, Betty, U Tx-Arlington, 1984
Reagan, Charles E., Kans SU, 1983
Real, Michael R., UC-San Diego, 1975, 76, 77,78, 79, 80, 88
Reamer, Owen J., U SW La, 1977
Reaves, R.B. URI, 1976, 77
Recchia, Edward, Mich SU, 1975, 84, 86
Rechtman, Janet, Atlanta, Ga., 1982
Recoulley, Alfred L., Sou Tech Inst, 1988
Redd, Larry, Mich SU, 1983, 84, 86, 87
Reddick, David, Butler U 1984, 85
Reddy, Albert, Fairfield U, Can, 1981
Redenius, Charles, Pa SU-Erie, 1984, 85, 86, 87
Redhead, Steve, Manchester Poly, England, 1988
Reed, A.K., U Ky, 1980, 82
Reed, Glenn, Nor Az U, 1986
Reed, Harry, Mich SU, 1977, 78, 81
Reed, James, U Tx-Arlington, 1983, 84
Reed, Lawrence, Mich SU, 1985
Reed, Michael, Pan-Amer U, 1984, 85, 86, 87, 88
Reed, Patricia, Boston C, 1987
Reed, P. Larus, Va SU, 1986
Reed, T.V., Kresge C, 1988
Reeder, L., W Ga C, 1985
Reedy, Jeremiah, Macalester C, 1976
Reedy, Michael, U Ut, 1985
Reel, Jerome, Clemson, 1983, 84, 85, 87
Reep, Diana, U Akron, 1982, 85, 86, 87, 88
Reese, Robert, Foundation Cultural Arts & Media, 1984
Reeve, Clayton C., Tn SU, 1979, 80, 81, 82
Reeves, Jimmie, U Tx, 1983
Regan, Betty, Kutztown U, 1985
Regan, Nancy, U Va, 1976
Rehder, John, U Tn, 1979

Reiber, Karen, U Wash, 1982
Reicher, William, BGSU, 1971
Reid, Jayne, U Cin, 1973
Reid-Nash, Kathleen, U Denver, 1983
Reilly, Edward, Ark SU, 1983
Reilly, John M., SUNY-Albany, 1975, 76, 77, 79, 82
Reilly, Joseph, BGSU 1974
Reilly, Robert, Rider C, 1983
Reimer, James, Marshall U, 1984, 85
Reimer, Robert, UNC-Charlotte, 1983
Reimer, Rollin, Ok St Leg., Cheyenne, Ok, 1984
Rein, Irving J., Northwestern, 1979
Reinartz, Kay F., SUNY-Albany, 1975; 76, Ida Falls, Id
Reinburg, Virginia, Boston C, 1986
Reinig, Ronald B., Edinboro SU, 1973, 76
Reinstein, P. Gila, SE Mass U, 1977; 79, 80, 81, RI C
Reisler, Marc, Syracuse U, 1986
Reisner, Junius, Aristo's Boutique, 1976
Reitzel, Armeda, Humboldt SU, 1987,88
Remington, Patricia, BGSU, 1984
Remington, Thomas, U N Ia, 1977, 78, 79, 80, 82, 83, 84
Remley, David, UNM, 1983
Remmington, Patricia Weiser, BGSU, 1979
Rendell, Ruth, Mystery Writer, 1982
Renner, Craig, York C, Pa., 1986
Renner, G.K., Gannon C, 1980; 83, Mo Sou SC; 84, Gannon U; 85, Mo Sou SC
Renner, Stanley, Il SU, 1984
Reno, Victor, KLR Engineering, Keene, NH, 1984
Rensi, Ray, N Ga C, 1981
Renz, Mary Ann, N Ky U, 1982
Restaino, Katherine M., St. Peter's C, 1978, 79
Reufli, Terri, Daemon C, 1984
Reuss, Carol, UNC, 1978
Reuss, Richard A., Wayne SU, 1971, 73
Rewa, Michael, U De, 1974
Reynolds, Cecilia, Brook U, St. Catherine's, 1988
Reynolds, Clay, Lamar U, 1983
Reynolds, D.A., Vincinnes U, 1988
Reynolds, Dawn, Pullman, Wa., 1987, 88
Reynolds, R.C., Lamar U, 1984, 85, 86, 88
Reynolds, William, Hope C, 1981, 82, 84, 85, 86, 87, 88
Rezmerski, J.C., Gustavus Adolphus SU, 1983, 86
Rhees, David, U Pa, 1984
Rhoda, Mark, Col C, 1988
Rhodes, Carolyn, Old Dom U, 1982, 85
Rhodes, Jewell, U Md, 1980, 81; 82, SUNY-Buffalo; 84, U Md
Rhody, Donald, Kaiser Aluminum, Oakland, Ca, 1982
Ribaufo, Leo, Geo Washington U, 1982
Ribble, Marcia, U Ut, 1988
Ribbler, Eileen, Kettering, Oh, 1983, 84, 85
Ricci, Glenn, Lake-Sumter Comm C, Fl, 1978, 79
Rice, Anthony H., Wesleyan C, 1978
Rice, Nancy, Il SU, 1984
Rice, Paul, UNC-Ashville, 1980, 81

Richard-Allerdyce, Diane, U Fl, 1988
Richards, Al, Cent Ct SC, 1978
Richards, Cora, Transylvania U 1987
Richards, David A., Lake City Comm C, Fl, 1979
Richards, Edward, Norwich U, 1982, 83, 85, 87
Richards, Milton, Mohawk Valley Comm C, NY, 1985

Richards, Peter, Cambridge, Ma, 1980
Richardson, Gaylord, U Kans, 1984
Richardson, H. Edward, U Louisville, 1982
Richardson, Rose, Tx Tech, 1988
Richman, Jan, Montreal, Can
Richmond, Ellen, Flossmoor, Il, 1986
Richter, Sara, Ok SU, 1982, 83
Rickert, William E., Wright SU, 1976, 81
Rics, John S., U Al, 1978
Rideout, Chris, U Puget Sound, 1988
Ridgley, Ronald, Brunswick Jr, C, Ga, 1986
Ridgeway, Sally O., Adelphia U, 1984
Ridless, Robin, NYC, 1982; 84 NYU
Ridley, Chauncey A., Grand Valley SC, 1988
Ridlon, Harold, Bridgewater, Ma, 1986, 87, 88
Riedel, Johannes, U Minn, 1977, 80
Riedy, James L., Truman CC, Chicago, 1988
Rieff, John D., U Mich, 1980
Riegel, Dieter, Bishops U, Lennoxville, Can, 1984, 85, 86, 87, 88
Riegelman, Milton, Centre C, Ky, 1983
Rieger, Branimir, Lander c, 1986, 87, 88
Rieger, Jon, U Louisville, 1984
Riemer, James D., BGSU, 1982; 84, Marshall U,
Riess, Nils,Oh Nor U, 1982, 84, 85
Rigal, Laura, Stanford U, 1987
Riggin, Judith, Nor Va Comm C, 1981
Riggins, Stephen, Laurentian U, 1984
Riggio, Thomas, U Ct, 1982
Rigney, Ernest, C Charleston, 1986
Rigsby, Roberta, Moores Hill, In, 1980; 81, U Cin
Riker, Richard, Brandywine C, Widener U, 1988
Riley, Barbara, Nat'l Mus Man, Ottawa, 1978
Riley, Craig, Tri-County Tech C, 1985
Riley, Judas, Ok SU, 1983
Riley, Kathryn, LSU, 1983
Riley, Linda, Temple U, 1977
Riley, Philip, Kent SU, 1986
Riley, Sam, Va Tech, 1982, 83, 84, 85, 87, 88
Riley, Thomas J., U Il, 1988
Rinder, Irwin D., Macalester C, 1981
Ringer, Gerald, Sun City, Ca., 1987
Rinehart, Stephen, Purdue, 1980
Rink, Stefan, Washington SU, 1988
Ripley, Jonathan G., Wentworth Inst Tech, 1987
Ripmaster, Terence, William Peterson C, 1986
Risatti, Howard, U Al-B'ham, 1980; 81, Va Commonwealth

Rister, Gene, E Cent U., Ada, Oh, 1983
Ritchie, Harry, U Denver, 1987, 88
Ritter, Jeff, BGSU 1983
Ritter, Judith, CBC, Montreal, Can
Ribage-Seul, Michael, Berea C, 1981
Rivera, Rosendo, BGSU, 1975
Robards, Brooks, Westfield SC, 1982, 83, 84, 85, 87, 88
Robbins, Douglas, Pratt Inst, 1988
Robbins, Edward, MIT, 1984
Robbins, Fred, Sou Il U-Edwardsville, 1985, 87, 88
Robbins, Gregory, A., Wichita SU, 1987
Robbins, Jan C., U Nor Ia, 1979, 80, 86
Robert, Sister Mary, Mercy C, 1988
Roberts, Audrey, U Wisc, 1975, 76
Robert, Churchill, U W Fl, 1988
Roberts, Dan, Clemson U, 1988
Roberts, Dorothy, Sacred Heart C, 1985, 86
Roberts, Fredric, Mich SU, 1986, 87, 88
Roberts, Garyn, BGSU, 1983, 84, 85, 86; 87, 88, Mich SU
Roberts, Gerald, U Mo., 1973
Roberts, Gerald, Berea C, 1985
Roberts, John W., U Mo, 1977, 81
Roberts, Robin, U Pa, 1984, 85; 86, 87, LaFayette C
Roberts, Scott, U Miss., 198
Roberts, Sheila, Mich SU, 1980
Roberts, Sidney I., Youngstown SU, 1987, 88
Roberts, Toni, U Fl, 1988
Roberts, Warren, Ind U, 1973
Robertson, Joan A., USAF Academy, 1988
Robertson, Richard, Al Humanities Center, 1982
Robillard, Douglas, U New Haven, 1988
Robinson, Anna T., U Wisc, 1971
Robinson, David E., Winona SC, Mn, 1976, 82, 83, 88
Robinson, David, U Houston, 1986
Robinson, Geogeann, Barttesville, Oh, 1982
Robinson, James, U Md, 1979; 80, U Nor Ia, 1987
Robinson, James, Purdue, 1981
Robinson, James D., U Dayton, 1986
Robinson, J. Gregg, UC-San Diego, 1981; 82, U Md
Robinson, Jo Ann, Morgan SC, 1975
Robinson, Kay, Bemidji SU, 1984, 85, 86, 87, 88
Robinson, Lillian, SUNY-Buffalo, 1973
Robitaille, Marilyn, Tarleton SU, 1988
Robles, Robert M., U Il, 1979
Robson, David, U Wy, 1982
Rocha, Rina, Chicago, Il., 1976
Rochberg-Halton, Gene, U Chicago, 1976, 77
Rochelle, Larry, Johnson Cty Comm C, 1980, 81, 82, 83, 87, 88
Rockaway, Robert, Tel Aviv U., Israel, 1982
Rockett, W.H., Seton Hall U, 1982
Rockland, Michael A., Rutgers, 1978, 87, 88
Rockler, Michael J., Rutgers, 1986, 87, 88
Rodabaugh, Karl, E Car U, 1988
Rodabaugh, Rita, Beaufort Cty Comm C, 1988

Roderick, John, U Hartford, 1984
Rodgers, Raymond S., N Car SU, 1981
Roderick, Rick, Duke, 1988
Rodner, William, W Mich U, 1981
Rodnitzky, Jerome L., U Tx-Arlington, 1971, 72, 73, 75, 76, 83, 84, 85, 88
Rodrique, Christina M., Clark U, 1978
Rodriquez, Maria C., U Puerto Rico, 1988
Rodriquez-Seda, Gladys, CUNY-Brooklyn, 1977, 78
Roemer, Eleanor, BGSU, 1982
Roeming, Robert F., Center 20th Centy Studies, U Wisc-Milw, 1974
Roepken, Henry, Harper Comm C, 1976
Rogers, Anne M., Washington, D.C.
Rogers, Deborah, Des Moines, Ia, 1983, 86, 87
Rogers, Deborah, U Me, 1988
Rogers, Denis, Bromley, Kent, England, 1985
Rogers, Forrest A., Fort Wayne, In, 1987, 88
Rogers, Jimmie, U Ark, 1981, 83, 84; 85 Ind U-Richmond
Rogers, Judy, Morehead SU, 1982
Rogers, Lyndon, 1984
Rogers, Suzyk, U Wisc-River Falls, 1988
Roggenbuck, Mary J., Catholic U, 1977, 78, 79
Rogiers, Charles L., USD, 1987
Rogosin, Donn, KLRN-TV & KLRU-TV, Austin, Tx, 1983
Rogovin, Mark, Pub Art Workshop, Chicago, 1976
Rohler, Lloyd E., UNC-Wilmington, 1988
Rohrberger, Mary, Ok SU, 1977
Rohrkemper, John, Elizabeth C,1987
Rohrkemper, John, Central Mich U, 1981; 83, 84, 85, 86, 88, Elizabeth C
Rohrman, Nicholas, Colby C, 1986, 87, 88
Roland, Catherine, U Cin, 1973
Roland, Paris, U Cin, 1973
Rollin, Lucy, Clemson U, 1984, 85, 87
Rollin, Roger, Franklin & Marshall C, 1973, 74; 76, 77, 78, 79, 80, 81, 82, 83, 84, 85, 86, 87, 88, Clemson U
Rollins, Janet, Ok SU, 1982, 84
Rollins, Peter C., Harvard, 1971, 72, 73; 74, 75, 76, 77, 78, 79, 80, 81, 82, 83, 84, 85, 86, 87, 88, Ok SU
Rollyson, Carl E., Detroit, Mi, 1982; 84, 86, 87, Wayne SU
Rolph, Debra, Kans SU, 1983
Romanowski, William D., BGSU, 1987, 88
Romberg, William, Milwaukee, Wi, 1981
Romotsky, Jerry, Rio Hondo C, 1978, 79, 81, 82, 84, 88
Romotsky, Sally, CSU-Fullerton, 1978, 79, 81, 82, 84, 87, 88
Rompkey, R.G., U Me, 1984
Roney, R. Craig, Wayne SU, 1982
Roney-Hughes, Ellen, Smithsonian, 1986
Rooney, John F., Jr., Ok SU, 1976, 79
Roos, Michael E., U Cin, 1982, 87, 88
Root, Robert L., Cent Mich U, 1980, 81, 82, 84
Rosandich, Thomas, W Mich U, 1974
Rose, Brian, BGSU, 1977, 78; 80

Brookyn C
Rose, Dan A., Amer Film Inst, 1975
Rose, Charles, Auburn U, 1986
Rose, Jonathan, Drew U, 1988
Rose, Ken, Case-Western U, 1983
Rose, Patricia, Brown U, 1988
Rose, Peter, Miami U, Oh, 1981
Rose, Vattel T., Howard U, 1977; 84, 85, 87, Oh U
Roseen, Clarice, U Wisc, 1971
Roselot, Gerald, UNC-Wilmington, 1982
Rosen, David, York U, 1973
Rosen, Harry W., USAF Acad, 1979
Rosen, Philip, Gannon U 1984
Rosen, Philip, 1988
Rosenauer, Kenneth, Mo W SC, 1983
Rosenbaum, Howard, Syracuse U, 1978
Rosenberg, Bernard, City C NY, 1975
Rosenberg, Bruce A., Pa SU, 1974; 79, 86, Brown U
Rosenberg, Jan, Empire SC, 1977
Rosenberg, Marc, U Pa, 1971, 73
Rosenberg, Neil V., Mem Univ Newfoundland, 1974, 76, 88
Rosenberg, Norman, Macalester C, 1983, 84
Rosenberg-Mapar, Ruth, Rochester, NY, 1984
Rosenblum, Martin J., Shorewood, Wi, 1981
Rosencranz, Mary Lou, U Ct, 1986
Rosenfeld, Richard, Rensselear Poly Inst, 1978
Rosenthal, Bianca, Calif Poly SU, 1987, 88
Rosenthal, Bob, U Hartford, 1986
Rosenthal, Judy, CSU-Fresno, 1984
Rosentrater, Douglas, Harrisberg Comm C, Pa, 1988
Rosinky, Natalie M., U Wisc, 1979
Rosenova, Michael, Il Inst Tech, 1982
Ross, Dale, Ia SU, 1971, 73
Ross, Debbie, BGSU, 1975
Ross, Don, U Wisc-Whitewater, 1982
Ross, Harris, Spring Hill C, 1983
Ross, Helaine, Boston U, 1980, 81, 82, 83, 84
Ross, Helaine, NWSU, La, 1987, 88
Ross, Janice, Tuskagee Inst, 1982
Ross, Ronald, BGSU, 1980, 81; 83, U Mo
Ross, Theopil, NW Mo SU, 1983
Ross, William, U SFl, 1973
Rosselot, Gerald S., UNC-Wilmington, 1981, 82
Rossen, Howard, Mich SU, 1983
Rossi, Eileen, Los Angeles, Ca.,1974
Rossi, Lee, Los Angeles, Ca., 1974
Rossiter, Frank, U Tx-Dallas, 1983
Roth, Audrey, Miami Dade Jr. C. North, 1973
Roth, Lane, U Fl, 1978; 79, 80, 83, 85, 86, Lamar U
Roth, Maury, Chicago Bureau Chief, Variety, 1976
Rothaus, Leslie, U Wisc, 1984
Rothberg, Abraham, St. John Fisher C, 1981
Rothfork, John, NM Tech, 1980
Rothkrug, Lionel, Concordia U, Montreal, 1984

Rothman, Mark D., Paul D. Schreiber HS, 1976
Rothmyer, Sue, Luther C, 1980
Rotto, Irvin, Bemidji SU, 1988
Rotundo, Barbara, SUNY-Albany, 1987
Roufberg, Ruth, Toy Consultant, Kendall Pk, NJ, 1983
Rouse, Moe, U Cin, 1977
Rout, Kathleen, Mich SU, 1982, 83, 84, 85, 87
Routt, William, W Mich SU, 1971
Rowe, Carel, SUNY-Purchase, 1987, 88
Rowe, D. Veston, Phillips U, 1982
Rowland, Diane, U Ark-Little Rock, 1980
Roy, Roberta Teague, E Tn SU, 1979
Royot, Daniel, Dijon, France, 1974
Roysden, Christine, Lehigh U, 1980
Royster, Philip M., SUNY-Albany, 1977, 78; 79, 81, 82, Syracuse U; 83, 84, 85, 86, 87, 88, Kansas SU
Rozema, Hazel, U Ark-Little Rock, 1986
Rubanowice, Robert, Fl SU, 1986
Rubanowicz, Robert J., Fl SU, 1976
Rubens, Philip M., Mich Tech U, 1978
Rubenstein, Bruce A., U Mich-Flint, 1978, 84, 85, 86, 88
Rubenstein, David, Adelphi U, 1984
Rubenstein, Diane, U Cin, 1985
Rubenstein, Elliot, CUNY-Staten Island, 1982
Rubenstein, Joseph, Stockton SC, 1978, 79
Rubenstein, Murray A., Baruch C-CUNY, 1977, 78, 86, 87
Rubenstein, Richard, Roosevelt U, 1975
Rubin, Benny, Hollywood, 1972
Rubin, Jason, NYU, 1984
Rubin, Sharon, U Md, 1975, 76
Rubinstein, David, Adelphi U, 1980
Rubinstein, M.A., CUNY-Baruch, 1979
Ruble, Raymond, Appal SU, 1982, 84
Rubrecht, August, U Wisc-Eau Claire, 1988
Rucker, Robert E., U Nev, 1988
Rudd, Robert, Wash SU, 1985
Ruddy, Mike, St. Louis U, 1978; 83, Kent SU-Tuscarawas Campus; 84, St. Louis U
Rude, Carolyn, Tx Tech U., 1985
Rudin, Seymour, U Mass, 1983
Rudinger, Joel, BGSU-Firelands, 1975, 76, 78, 81, 83, 85
Rudner, Larry S., N Car SU, 1979, 80, 82, 84, 85, 86
Reuve, Mary, U Cin, 1973
Rugg, William J., Ok SU, 1983, 84, 85, 86
Ruffin, Winfrey, Shippensburg SU, 1988
Rugg, Kathy, U SW La, 1986
Rugg, W.J., Ok SU, 1987
Rugoff, Kathy, U SW La, 1988
Rumble, John W., Vanderbilt, 1979
Runfola, Ross, Medailie C, 1975
Runte, Hans R., Dalhousie U, 1987
Runzo, Sandra, Ind U, 1984
Ruppersburg, Hugh, U Ga, 1986
Rush, Florence, NYC, 1983
Rush, Forest, Auburn U, 1988
Rushing, Allen, E Tn SU, 1987
Russ, Joanna, Harpur C, SUNY-Binghamton, 1973
Russell, Evalu, Yukon, Ok, 1982

Russell, Bruce, Montreal, Can, 1987
Russel, Patricia, Stephen F. Austin SU, 1986
Russell, Rosalind, 1974
Russell, Sharon, Ind SU, 1985, 86, 87, 88
Russell, Virginia, U Md, 1987
Russum, Barbara, Pub Art Workshop, Chicago, 1976
Rust, Kenneth, Madonno C, 1988
Rusted, Brian, Northwestern, 1984, 85
Rutherford, John, Radford U, 1986
Rutledge, Amelia, Geo Mason U, 1984
Rutherford, Paul, U Toronto, Ont., 1984
Rutterman, Theodore L., CSU-Sacramento, 1987
Rux, Paul, Community Unit Schools, Warren, Il, 1986
Ryan, Frank L., Stonehille C, 1979
Ryan, Helen, U Akron, 1986, 87, 88
Ryan, Maureen, U Sou Miss, 1988
Ryan, Michael, Northwestern, 1987
Ryan, Pat M., Greensboro, N.C., 1981
Ryant, Carl, U Louisville, 1980, 82, 83, 84, 85, 86, 87, 88
Ryburn-Lamonte, Terri, Il SU, 1983
Ruchtyuckji, Doria, Assoc Ukrainian Women, Detroit, 1980
Ryrie, Elizabeth, CSU-Fullerton, 1988

Saalbach, Louis, E Mich U, 1983, 87
Saalmann, Dieter, Wichita SU, 1987
Saar, Doreen, Phila, 1986
Saba, Cheri, Bradner, Oh, Elementary Sch, 1973
Sabar, A., UCLA, 1976
Sabbath, David J., BGSU, 1982
Sabrie, Elaine, Oh U, 1987
Sachar, Marcia, Lehigh U, 1973
Sachs, Pamela, Dawson C, Viger, Can, 1987
Sacks, Sheldon, U Chicago, 1974
Sacapulos, Eugenia, Froebel JHS, 1976
Sadler, David, W Mich U, 1981, 82
Sadler, Glenn E., Bloomsburg U, 1987
Sadler, Lynn, Bennett C, 1984; 85, 86, 87, 88, Methodist C
Sadoff, Dianne, Antioch C, 1974
Sadomskaya, U Ct, 1978
Sadowsky, Alice L., 1980
Saeger, Wain, Knoxville C, 1980
Saffle, Michael, Va Tech, 1980, 81, 82
Safir, Margery, Yale, 1977
Safran-Naveh, Gila, U Cin, 1987
Sage, George, U N Colo, 1985
Sahin, Haluk, Cleveland SU, 1980
Saito, Kikuji, Mich SU, 1984
Saito, Kikyji, Adachi-Ku, Tokyo, 1988
Saleh, Mohammed, Woodstock Collegiate Inst, Ont, 1984
Salem, James, U Ala, 1975, 76
Salerno, Douglas, Ann Arbor, Mi, 1984
Salerno, Henry, SUNY-Fredonia, 1976, 79
Salevouris, Michael J., Webster U, 1987
Salien, Jean-Marie, Fort Hays SU, 1983
Salinas, Judy, U Tulsa, 1975, 76; 76, SUNY-Binghamton, 78, 79
Salinas, Oscar, Pan-Amer U, 1986, 87, 88
Salisbury, Joyce, 1984
Salisbury, Robert, Ill Art Council, 1979
Salmon, Mark, NUC, 1985

Saloman, Roger, Case Western Reserve, 1971
Salter, John UND, 1988
Saltman, Judith, UBC, 1987
Salvidio, Frank, Westfield SC, 1980
Salvino, Dana N., E Lansing, Mi, 1987
Salvino, John F., E Lansing, Mi, 1987
Salwen, Michael B., U Miami, Fl., 1987, 88
Salzman, Jack, Long Island U, 1975, 76
Sammons, Jeffrey T., U Houston, 1983
Sammons, Martha, Wright SU 1985
Sample, Irene, 1983
Samson, John, Tx Tech U, 1983, 84, 85, 86, 87, 88
Samuels, Lennox, Marquette U, 1978
Samuels, Stuart, U Pa, 1971, 77
Samuels, Wilfred, U Colo, 1980
Sanbuenaventura, Steffi, U Hawai-Manoa, 1985
Sanchez, Aurelio, 1986
Sanchuk, Kim, York U, Can, 1987
Sandarg, Robert, UNC-Charlotte, 1985, 86
Sandell, Karin, BGSU, 1982, 83; 84, 85, 87, U Oh
Sanderlin, Reed, U Tn-Chattanooga, 1985, 86
Sandels, Robert, Quinnipiac C, 1987
Sanders, Bill, Milwaukee Journal, 1971
Sanders, Clinton, Alternatives, Inc, 1973; 75, 76, Temple U; 77, 80, 81, 82, 87, 88, U Ct
Sanders, David, Clarkson C,1973; 79, 80, Harvey Mudd C
Sanders, Joe, Lakeland Comm C, Oh, 1980, 85
Sanders, Joseph E., Ind SU, 1980
Sanders, Wayne, U Pitt, 1981
Sanderson, James, Odessa C, Tx, 1983, 85
Sandford, Mariellen, The Drama Review, NYC, 1986
Sandler, Richard, U Pa, 1980
Sandler, Richard L., Southfield, Mi, 1981
Santino, Jack, BGSU, 1985, 86, 87, 88
Santraud, Jeanne-Marie, U Paris, France, 1986
Sapieha, Lew, London, 1972
Sapolsky, Barry, Fl SU, 1978
Saponaro, Rick, UC-Irvine, 1986
Saraf, Irving, San Francisco, 1984
Sargent, Lyman T., U Mo-St. Louis, 1987, 88
Sarracino, Carmine, Elizabethtown C, 1984, 85
Sasaki, Miyoko, Shibuya-Ku, Tokyo, 1988
Sassaman, Stephen, Westfield SC, 1985
Sassower, Raphael, U Colo, 1987, 88
Sather, Lawrence, Midland C, 1983
Sather, Suzanne, Midland C, 1983
Satlof, Marilyn, Columbus C, 1980, 81, 82, 85, 87, 88
Saton, Barbara, BGSU, 1982
Sattelmeyer, Riobert, U Mo, 1984
Satterfield, Leon, Neb Wesleyan U, 1982
Sauciuk, Olena L., Inter-Amer U, Puerto Rico, 1978
Saunders, Gordon, Trinity C, 1980
Saunders, John, Comic Strip Author, Toledo, Oh. 1972

Saunders, Thomas J., U Victoria, Can, 1988
Saur, Pamela, Auburn U-Montgomery, 1986
Sauret, Tom, Lander C, 1987
Savage, Lon K., Va Tech, 1977
Savells, Jerry, Wright SU, 1988
Savin, Janet, William Rainey Harper C, 1976
Savoie, Norman R., U Ut, 1975, 76; 84, 85, 86, Ut SU
Sawchuk, Kim, York U, Can, 1988
Sawyer, Corinne, Clemson, 1983, 84, 85, 86, 87, 88
Sawyer, Faye, Appal SU, 1985, 86
Sawyer, Martha, Bensalem HS, Pa,1980
Sayer, James, Wright SU, 1979, 80
Saylor, V. Louise, Spokane, Wa, 1985
Scafella, Frank, W Va U, 1979
Scaglion, Richard, U Pitt, 1979
Scalet, Elizabeth Butler, Lawrence, Ks, 1974
Scanlan, Tom, U Minn-St. Paul, 1984
Scanlan, Lee, Humbolt SU, 1987
Scanlan, Lee, Washburn U, 1985
Scarborough, Alex, BSSU, 1973
Scarborough, Danny, Ok SU, 1982, 83, 84, San Diego SU,
Scatena, Paul, U Rochester, 1987,88
Scavetti, Scott, U N Ia, 1980
Scavone, Daniel, Ind SU, 1985
Schade, Rosemarie, York U, Toronto, 1982, 87, 88
Schaefermeyr, Mark, Va Tech, 1985
Schaeffer, John D., Columbus C, Ga., 1988
Schaeffer, Lynne, Marygrove C, 1984
Schaeffer, Mary, BGSU, j1973
Schaffer, Deborah, E Mont C, 1988
Schaffer, Lisa, UNC, 1986
Schaffer, Rachel, E Mont C, 1988
Schafer, William J., Berea C, 1977
Schaffer, Mark, U Md, 1979, 80; 85, Germantown, Md,
Schaik, Karolyn, Pa SU, 1983
Schall, Keith L., Hampton Inst, 1977
Schall, Larryetta, Hampton Inst, 1976
Scharchburg, Richard, GMI Inst, Flint, Mi, 1985, 86, 88
Scharine, Richard, U Ut, 1981
Scharnhorst, Gary, U Tx-Dallas, 1980, 81
Schatz, Thomas, U Tx, 1980, 85, 87
Schechter, Harold, Queens C-CUNY, 1979
Schechter, Russell, Cornell, 1986
Scheef, Charles W., Mich SU, 1972
Scheele, Carl, Smithsonian Inst, 1980, 86
Scheese, Don, U Ia, 1985
Scheffler, Judith, Drexel U, 1980, 81
Scheibe, Cynthia, Cornell, 1984
Scheide, Frank, U Ark, 1978, 82
Scheer, Ronald, Mansfield SC, Paa., 1978, 79
Schelde, Per, NYC, 1988
Schenker, Daniel, U Al-Huntsville, 1986
Scher, Saul, N York Inst Tech, 1982
Scherer, Don, BGSU, 1977
Scherer, Tim, Mich SU, 1981
Scherer, V. James, Boot Hill Mus, Dodge City, 1984
Scheuer, Timothy, BGSU, 1976, 77; 82, 84, 86, 87, Franklin U
Scheurle, William, U S Fl, 1985

Schib, John L., Carthage C, 1978
Schichtman, Martin, U Ok, 1983
Schiff, Ellen, N Adams SC, 1983
Schille, Candy, Il SU, 1986
Schiller, Scott, Miami U, Oh, 1983
Schilz, J.L.D., TCU, 1983
Schilz, Thomas, TCU, 1984
Schinke, Oscar, Ky Wesleyan C, 1985
Schitoskey, Elizabeth, Ok SU, 1983
Schleh, Eugene P.A., U Me-Portland-
Gorham, 1978; 85, 86, 87, 88,
U Sou Me
Schleifer, Robert, Ok SU, 1983
Schlich, Pam, Ind U, 1985
Schlinger, Peter J., IU-PUI, 1971
Schmid, William R., U Wisc, 1974
Schmidt, Dorey, BGSU, 1979; 80, 81, 82,
83, 84, 85, 86, 87, Pan-Amer U
Schmidt, Henry, Tx A&M, 1980
Schmidt, Lorna, 1986
Schmidt, Mathias R., Fed Rep Germany,
1979, 80
Schmier, Louis, Valdosta SC, 1978
Schmitt, Peter, W Mich u, 1974
Schmitt, Ted, Universal/16, 1974
Schmitz, Carolyn, BGSU, 1985
Schmul, Robert, Ind U, 1971
Schneider, Carl, Essex, Ma, 1986
Schneider, Dorothy, Essex, Ma, 1986
Schneider, Gilbert D., Oh U, 1973, 83
Schneider, Mary Jo, U Ark, 1984
Schneider, Michael J., N Il U, 1984
Schneider, Robert, N Il U, 1984, 85
Schneider, William, Phila, 1977
Schneiderman, H.G., Lafayette C, 1988
Schnell, Jim, Miami U, Oh, 1984; 85, 86,
87, 88, U Cin
Schoenecke, Michael K., Ok SU, 1975, 76,
77, 78, 79; 80, Bellevue C; 81, 82,
83, 84, 86, 86, 87, 88, Tx Tech
Schofield, Anne, U Kans, 1985
Schofield, Lemuel B., U Miami, Fl, 1984,
86
Schofield, Mary, St Bonaventure U, 1986,
87, 88
Scholey, Christine, Purdue, 1981
Schollaert, Paul, Old Dom U, 1986
Schoonmaker, Ann, Sunrise House, Eliot,
Me, 1984, 86, 87
Schorin, Gerald, Mich SU, 1984, 85
Schraamer, James J., St. Paul, Mn, 1984;
85, U Minn
Schrank, Louise Welsh, Palatine, Il, 1974
Schraq, Robert, UNM, 1980
Schrath, Evelyn, W Il U, 1980
Schreffler, Peter, BGSU, 1987
Schreiber, Earl G., Arts Council, Tampa,
Fl, 1980
Schreiber, Lee L., Temple, 1980, 81, 82, 83,
84, 85, 86, 87, 88
Schreinder, Paul, Munster HS, 1982
Schreir, Barbara, U Mass, 1985
Schroeder, Eric J., UC-Davis, 1988
Schroeder, Fred E.H., U Minn-Duluth,
1972, 73, 74, 75, 76, 77, 78,
79, 80, 81, 82, 83, 84, 85,
86, 87, 88

Schroeder, Jan, Duluth Pub Lib., Mn, 1976
Schroeder, Natalie, U Miss, 1987
Schroeder, Ronald, U Miss, 1987, 88
Schroth, Evelyn, W Il U, 1982, 83, 84, 85
Schubert, Joseph, Mars Hill C, 1986
Schuchat, Molly, Washington, D.C.
Schuchman, John, Gallaudet C, 1986
Schuchmay, Hedvah, NJ Inst Tech, 1982
Schudson, Michael, U Chicago, 1979
Schueller, Malini, U Fl, 1988
Schuller, Janice, U Ore, 1985, 86, 87, 88
Schuller, Susan, UC-Riverside, 1975
Schultz, Elizabeth, U Kans, 1984, 85
Schultz, H.J., Vanderbilt, 1984
Schultz, Lucile, U Cin, 1984
Schumaker, Hazen, U Mich, 1988
Schuman, David, Deep Springs, Col, 1976
Schuman, Jeff, U Ark, 1983
Schunk, Susan, U Akron, 1987, 88
Schurk, Bill, BGSU, 1971, 72,73,74,75, 76,
77, 78, 79, 80, 81, 82, 83, 84, 85,
86, 87, 88
Schurman, Lydia, N Va Comm C, 1988
Schuster, Barbara E., U Mich, 1987
Schuster, Marilyn, Smith C, 1975
Schuth, H. Wayne, Oh SU, 1971; 74, LSU
Schuyler, William M., Jr., U Louisville,
1979, 80, 81, 82, 85, 86
Schvey, Henry M., Webster U, 1987
Schwab, Allen, Colgate U, 1981, 82
Schwan, Katherine, BGSU, 1977
Schwartz, C. Michael, Purdue, 1981
Schwartz, John, Plymouth, Mi, 1982
Schwartz, Kathryn Mettelka, U Mich, 1976
Schwartz, Martin, E Car U, 1986
Schwartz, Robert, Ore SU, 1979
Schwartz, Sarah J., Oh U, 1975, 76
Schwartz, Thomas, Oh SU, 1984, 85, 86
Schwartz, Henry, Duke, 1988
Schwed, Warren W., Loyola, NO, 1981
Schweitzer, John, Ok SU, 1983
Schweizer, Paul, Munson-Williams-
Procter Inst, 1984
Schwind, Jean, U Minn, 1985
Schwitt, Ted, Universal Pictures, 1973
Scodari, Christine A., Towson C, 1988
Scofield, Richard, Hillsborough Comm
C, Fl, 1978, 81
Scott, Barbara, Cameron U, 1982
Scott, Carolyn, Univ. City, Mo, 1974
Scott, Clifford H., Ind U-Fort Wayne, 1972,
85, 88
Scott, Gina, San Francisco, Ca,1986
Scott, Gini, Oakland, Ca, 1984, 85
Scott, John S., BGSU, 1973, 74, 75, 84, 85,
86, 88
Scott, Joseph L., Pa SU, 1973
Scott, Joseph, Columbia C, 1971
Scott, Ronald B., U Ut, 1987, 88
Scott, Shirley, W Mich U, 1974
Scott, Wayne, Pa SU-Erie, 1975
Scott-Chandler, Patricia, Oh U-
Chillicothe, 1981
Screven, Tom, W Va Dept. Commerce, 1976
Scriba, Robert, Bemidji SU, 1981
Scriven, Karen, U Tol, 1979
Scrocco, Phyllis A., BGSU, 1988
Scruggs, T.M., U Tx, 1986
Seager, Dennis, SUNY-Binghamton, 1980

Seaman, David, Davis & Elkins C, 1986
Searle, William, E Il U, 1979, 80, 81, 82,
84, 85, 86, 87, 88
Sears, Diane, Cent MU, 1975
Sears, Donald, CSU-Fullerton, 1988
Sears, Jeff, Ia SU, 1980
Sears, Priscilla, Dartmouth, 1980
Seaton, Beverly, Oh SU, 1977; 81, 84, 86,
87, 88, Oh SU-Newark
Seaton, James, Mich SU, 1978, 79, 80, 81,
83, 84, 85, 86, 87, 88
Seaton, John A., Alexandria, Oh, 1979
Seaton, William, U Ia, 1983
Seddig, Robert, Alleg C, 1986
Seege, Ken, Ashland C, 1978
Seeley, Clinton, U Chicago, 1983
Seeleye, John, U Ct, 1972, 83
Sefler, George F., Mansfield SC, 1979, 81
Segal, Eli, W Mich U, 1973, 80
Segal, Howard, U Mich, 1980
Segel, Elizabeth, U Pitt, 1981
Segerlind, Fern A., Duke, 1976
Sehlinger, Peter J., IUPUI, 1971
Seidel, Kathryn, U Md, 1986
Seidner, Eva, Toronto, Can, 1983
Seigworth, Gregory S., U Cin, 1988
Seikaly, Samir, Amer U, Beirut, Lebanon,
1982
Seiter, Ellen, U Ore, 1982
Seiter, Richard, Cent MU, 1981, 82, 83, 84,
87
Seitz, Barbara, Bloomington, Ind, 1986
Selavan, Ida Cohen, Non-Formal Acad
Jewish Studies, 1979
Self, Peter, U Fl, 1981
Self, Robert, Nor Il U, 1984
Selig, Michael, Northwestern, 1983
Seligmann, Claus, U Wash, 1980
Sellers, Pamela, Grand Valey SC, 1988
Selley, April, C Saint Rose, 1986
Selnow, Gary, Blacksburg, Va., 1984, 87
Selsor, Marcia, E Mont, C, 1985
Seltzer, Robert A., Phila, 1987
Semark, Douglas, Case Western
Reserve,1980
Semmel, Keith D., Ball SU, 1987, 88
Semmes, Cloves, U Il-Chicago Circle, 1983,
85
Senatore, Margaret, USC, 1983
Senese, Phyllis, U Victoria, Can, 1986
Senf, Carol, Ga Inst Tech, 1986
Sequeria, Isaac, Osmania U, India, 1980
Serlen, Ellen, Mich SU, 1976
Serr, Robbie, UCLA, 1986
Sessions, Kyle, Il SU, 1986
Sevastakis, Michael, Manhattan C, NY,
1982
Severance, Sibyl, Pa SU-Media, 1985
Severson, Marilyn S., Seattle Pac U, 1988
Sevier, John, Ind U-South Bend, 1980
Sewell, Dorita, U Wisc-Parkside, 1977
Sewell, Edd, Va Tech, 1977, 82, 84
Sewell, Ernestine, U Tx-Arlington, 1983
Sewell, John, Former mayor of Toronto,
Can, 1984
Sewell, Michael, Radford U, 1982, 83
Sexson, Lynda, Mont SU, 1979
Sexson, Michael W., Mont SU, 1979
Shackelford, George, Va Tech, 1984

Shade, William, LeHigh U, 1982, 83, 85
Shadish, Elizabeth, Miami U, Oh, 1982
Shafer, Ingrid, U Science & Arts, Ok, 1983, 84, 85, 86, 87, 88
Shafer, Michael, Rutgers, 1988
Shafer, Yvonne, Fl SU, 1986
Shaffert, Charles, Castleton SC, 1981, 82, 83, 84, 86, 87
Shaheen, Jack, Sou Il, 1974, 84, 85, 86, 87, 88
Shain, Russell, U Colo, 1975
Shale, Richard, Youngstown SU, 1977, 78, 79, 80, 82, 84, 87, 88
Shamp, Scott, U Ga, 1988
Shank, Gary, Meinrad C, 1985, 87
Shannon, Anna, W Va U, 1982, 83, 86
Shannon, Steve, U Md., 1977
Shapiro, Diane, R.J. Kelroy & Assoc, 1985
Shapiro, Gerry, U Mass, 1987
Shapiro, Mitchell, U Miami, Fl, 1982; 83, Il SU; 84, U Miami, Fl
Shapiro, Paul, New School, NYC, 1987
Shapiro, Stephanie, U Md, 1985
Shapiro, Stewart, Bentley C, 1984
Sharma, R.S., 1983
Sharnhorst, Gary, U Tx-Richardson, 1983
Sharpe, Patricia, Ann Arbor, Mi, 1983
Sharples, Win, U Film Assoc, 1976
Sharpe, William F., Temple U, 1987, 88
Sharpless, John B., U Wisc, 1987
Sharrett, Christopher, Valley Forge Mil Jr, 1982, 83; 84, Jersey City SC; 85, 86, 88, Sacred Heart U
Shaughnessy, Mary Rose, 1973
Shaver, Anne, Denison U, 1979
Shaw, Eugene F., U Tn, 1978
Shaw, Harry, U Fl, 1975, 77, 81, 84, 86, 87, 88
Shaw, Ian, Brock U, Ont., 1986
Shaw, Jennifer Z., Nanaimo, BC, Can, 1987
Shaw, Judith, Pitt SU, 1983
Shawhan, Ralph, Ind U, 1974
Shea, Michael, Sou Ct. U, 1987
Shea, William, U Mich, 1985, 86, 87, 88
Shearer, Cindy, Mankato SU, 1986
Sheef, Charles, Mich SU, 1971
Sheehan, Stephen, Wayne SU, 1988
Sheehy, Colleen, U Minn, 1984, 85, 86
Sheide, Frank, U Ark, 1979
Shekwo, Joseph, Ahmadu Bello U, Kongo-Campus, Zaria, Nigeria, 1986, 87

Shelton, Frank, Limestone C, 1985, 86
Shelton, Michael, Seton Hall U, 1985; 86, Lexington, Ky
Shelton, Robert, Oberlin C, 1988
Shen, Jane, Vanier C, Snowdown Campus, Can, 1975
Shenhar-Alroy, Alja, Haifu U, 1987
Shenkman, Harriet, Chapel Hill, NC, 1984
Sheorey, Ravi, Ok SU, 1983
Shepard, Marcus, Oberlin C, 1986
Shepard, Philip, Mich SU, 1980
Shepard, Sanford, Oberlin C, 1986
Shepard, Juanita, Chicago Heights, Il, 1980
Shepard, William H., Wash SU, 1988
Sheppard, Alice, E Ore SC, 1983, 87
Sheppard, Sally, U Ut, 1984

Sheppard, William, Hampton Inst, 1981
Shereikis, Richard, Sangamon SU, 1975, 76, 77, 78, 79, 83, 85
Sherer, Emily, W Va Wesleyan C, 1985
Sheridan, Daniel, UND, 1977, 79
Sherk, Nancy, Albion C, 1985
Sherman, Barry L., U Ga, 1987
Sherman, Marilyn, U Sou Fl, 1978, 79, 80
Sherman, Sherri, Ind U, 1973
Sherman, W.D., Open Univ. London, England, 1978
Sherrill, Susie, Emory U, 1986
Shevey, Sandra, Hollywood, Ca., 1974
Shicker, Stephen, W Mich U, 1972
Shields, Donald, U Mo-St. Louis, 1984; 86, Ind SU
Shields, Tom, U Tn, 1987
Shields, Steven U Wisc-Whitewater, 1988
Shienbaum, Kim Ezra, Rutgers, 1979
Shifreen, Lawrence J., U Md, 1977, 78, 79; 83 U Ala
Shilts-Panksepp, Sara, BGSU, 1975
Shine, Carol E., Springfield C, 1988
Shine, Jean, U Fl, 1980
Shine, Walter, U Fl, 1980
Shinn, Thelma, Az SU, 1981
Shive, Kenneth, US Mil Acad, 1988
Shivers, Gary, U Kans, 1974, 75
Shoemaker, Rebecca Ind SU, 1986
Shoesmith, Brian, W Australia C Advanced Educ, 1983
Shohan, Herschel, North Adams SC, 1981
Shokoff, James, SUC-Fredonia, 1980; 81, 84, 87, SUNY-Fredonia
Sholle, David, Oh U, 1985
Shor, Francis, Wayne SU, 1981, 84, 86, 88
Shorb, Terry L., Northwest Comm C, Wyoming, 1976
Shorer, Ed, BGSU, 1987, 88
Shorin, Rebecca, U Tx, 1986
Shorr, Jonathan, U Baltimore, 1985
Shosid, Norman, UC-Berkeley, 1980
Shovery, Imad, Ind SU, 1973
Shrader-Frechette, Kristin, U Louisville, 1982
Shrestha, Mohan, BGSU, 1977, 78, 80, 81, 84
Shreve, Gregory, Kent SU-Geauga Campus, 1982; 85, Kent SU
Shuffelton, Frank, U Rochester, 1984
Shuldiner, David, Los Angeles, Ca., 1984
Shumate, Nancy, Austin Peay SU, 1983
Shumlinson, Jack, US Marine Corps, 1976
Shumway, David, Miami U, Oh, 1980, 81, 82, 84, 85; 86, 87, 88, Carnegie-Mellon
Shupe, Anson, U Tx-Arlington, 1981
Shurbutt, Sylvia, Ga Sou C, 1986, 87; 88, Shepherd C
Shuster, Rona, Montclair SC, 1987, 88
Shy, Bob, Paducah Comm C, Ky, 1986
Sichi, Edward Jr., Pa SU, 1979
Siciliano, Sam, U Wisc-Whitewater; 77, 78, Mich SU
Sicoli, M.L. Corbin, Cabrini C, 1986
Siddiqui, Ashraf, Bangla Academy, Bangladesh, 1982
Sidel, M. Kent, NY Inst Tech, 1984
Siegel, Ben, Cal St Poly, Kellogg-Voorhis

Campus, 1973, 74; 75, 76, Cal Poly-Pomona
Siegel, Mark, U Wy, 1979
Siegelman, Stuart, Hostos Comm C, CUNY, 1987, 88
Siegman, Jack, U Neb, 1988
Sieper, Jean, Carnegie-Mellon, 1988
Sies, Mary, Waltham, Ma., 1984; 85, Gainesville, Fl
Sikorski, Henry, Hofstra U, 1984, 85, 86, 87, 88
Silberman, Joan, Rockland Comm C, NY, 1977
Silberman, Rob, U Minn, 1984, 85
Silverman, Sheldon, U Calgary, Can, 1987
Sill, John, Meth C, 1986
Silver, Sheila, U Md, 1976
Silver, Susan, U Neb-Omaha, 1982, 83
Silverblatt, Arthur, Webster U, 1985, 88
Silverman, Lawrence, Wayne SU, 1974; 75, Roosevelt U
Silverman, Sheldon A., U Calgary, Can, 1976
Silvian, David Alllen, Loyola, NO, 1978
Simeral, Fred, Hackensack, NY, 1982
Siminoski, Dan, Tx Tech, 1983
Simmons, Carla, W Il U, 1983, 84
Simmons, Charles, U Evansville, 1977; 78, Lake Erie C
Simmons, Jane, Youngstown SU, 1985
Simmons, John, Colo C, 1984
Simmons, Mary L., NM SU, 1988
Simmons, Mike, Pa SU-Behrend C,, 1987
Simms, L. Moody, Il SU, 1976
Simon, Stephen, Appal SU, 1981
Simon, William, U Houston, 1980
Simonds, Peggy, Washington, D.C., 1984
Simoneau, Joseph R., Graham Jr C, Boston, 1979
Simons, John, Colo C,1982, 88
Simons, Thomas, SUNY-Oneonta, 1987
Simpson, Ethel C., U Ark, 1987
Simpson, Hassell A., Hampden-Sydney C, 1988
Simpson, Jeanne, E Il U, 1981, 82, 85, 86, 87
Simpson, John E., Savannah SC, 1977
Simpson, John Mack, E Il U, 1981
Simpson, Marie, New School for Soc Research, NYC, 1982
Simpson, Thomas, CUNY-John Jay C, 1974, 75
Sims, Anastasia, Ga SC, 1987, 88
Sims, Barbara, LSU, 1976
Sims, Martha, Oh SU, 1987
Sims, Norman, U Mass, 1980, 81
Simson, Eve, Ind U, 1976
Sinclair, Michael, U Tol, 1986
Singer, Linda, Miami U, Oh, 1982, 85, 86, 87, 88
Singer, Linda, Miami U, Oh, 1981, 84
Singer, Merrill, Amer U, 1981
Singh, Yahoda N., BGSU, 1980
Singhal, Arvind, BGSU, 1984, 85, 86
Singleton, Carl, Ft. Hays SU, 1987
Singleton, Gregory, NE Il U, 1986
Sink, David, U Ala-B'ham, 1985
Sinning, Nancy, Kent SU, 1987
Sinor, Denis, Ind U, 1981

Sipes, Sherrie, Mich SU, 1984
Sipple, JoAnne, Robert Morris C, 1974
Siry, Joseph V., Rollins C, 1988
Siska, William, U Ut, 1983
Sitton, Thad, Dominican C, New Orleans, 1979
Sjovall, Jeanne, BGSU, 1977
Skaggs, Merrill Maguire, Drew U, 1978
Skalski, Anne, Toledo, O, 1981, 83
Skelly, Richard, Kent SU, 1982
Skerry, Philip, Lakeland Comm C, 1985, 86, 87, 88
Skill, Thomas, U Dayton, 1986
Skillman, Amy, UCLA, 1982; 84, Santa Monica, Ca; 85, Topango, Ca; 86, 87
Skillman, Timothy, U Mich, 1982
Skinner, C.J., U Lethbridge, Can, 1984, 86, 87, 88
Skinner, Izora, Pan-Amer U, 1985
Skinner, James, Brandon U, Can, 1984
Skipper, James K., W Ontario U, 1971
Skotnes, Andor, Rutgers, 1977
Skrzypiec, Jacquie, U Akron, 1987
Skyzypiec, Sam, Akron, O, 1987
Skyrms, James, Westmar C,1983
Slabey, R.M., Notre Dame U, 1984, 85, 86, 87, 88
Slaght, Lafayette C, 1988
Slate, Joseph, U Tx, 1977, 78, 79, 80, 81, 82, 83, 84
Slater, Don, London, England, 1986
Slater, Jerome, SUNY-Buffalo, 1988
Slater, Judy, U Mass, 1987
Slater, Thomas, Ok SU, 1982, 83
Slattery, Dennis, Sou Meth U, 1984
Slaughter, William, U NFl, 1986
Slavensky, Sonia, Chicago Pub Schools, 1973
Slavick, William, U SMe, 1985, 87, 8
Slaymaker, William, Midway C, 1985
Slethaug, Gordon E., U Waterloo, Can
Sloan, De Villo, Auburn U, 1987
Sloan, Kay, Miami U, Oh, 1985, 8887
Slocum, Sally, U Akron, 1983, 84, 86, 87, 88
Slott, Jonathan, Urbana C, 1972
Slout, Bill, San Fran SU, 1973
Sluder, Claude, Ind U, 1988
Small, Melvin, Wayne SU, 1984
Smalling, Michael, S Ark U, 1977
Smallman, Kirk T., Springfield Tech Comm C, 1988
Smedman, Sarah, UNC-Charlotte, 1981
Smelstor, Marjorie, U Tx-San Antonio, 1976, 81, 83
Smetak, Jacqueline, U Ia, 1984, 85, 86, 87, 88
Smith, Ben A., U Sou Miss, 1988
Smith, Bruce, Notre Dame, 1988
Smith, Carol Ann, U Mo-Rolla, 1981, 82
Smith, Chris, Az SU, 1976
Smith, Christine, Troy, Mi, 1982
Smith, Christopher, SUNY-Albany, 1984
Smith, Claude, Fl Jr C, Sou Campus, 1988
Smith, Corless, San Francisco SU, 1985, 87
Smith, Craig, Freedom Expression Foundation, 1984
Smith, C. Zoe, Marquette U, 1984, 85, 86
Smith, David, U Me, 1987, 88

Smith, David, Williams C, 1985, 86, 87, 88
Smith, Deborah, Winterthur Mus., 1981; 82, Ky Mus, W Ky U
Smith, Don, U Ia, 1982
Smith, Donald H., Old Dom U, 1986
Smith, Doris, U Sou Ala-Mobile, 1984
Smith, Dorothy, Ont Inst for Studies in Educ, Toronto, 1984
Smith, Dwight, Miami U, Oh, 1981
Smith, Ernest, NYC, 1984
Smith, Ernest J., Boston U, 1988
Smith, Geoffrey, Queen's U, Ont., 1984
Smith, Herbert, U Victoria, Can, 1986, 87
Smith, Hollister, St. Louis Med Medical Museum, 1982
Smith, Howard W., Spring Hill C, 1978, 84
Smith, Ingrid, U Ia, 1988
Smith, Ivan, Utica, NY, 1987, 88
Smith, James F., Pa SU-Ogontz, 1975, 76, 79, 80, 81, 83, 84, 85
Smith, J. Allen, Miss C Law, 1986, 87, 88
Smith, James H., Augusta C, 1984, 85, 86
Smith, Jeff, BGSU, 1987
Smith, Jim, Pa SU-Ogontz, 1976, 77, 78, 79, 80, 81, 82, 83, 84, 88
Smith, Jennifer, Wright SU, 1986, 87, 88
Smith, J. Stephen, U Pa, 1979
Smith, Julian, Ithaca C, 1973, 77; 79, U Fl
Smith, Larry David, U Ark-Little Rock, 1986
Smith, Larry, Oh SU, 1985
Smith, Leonora, Mich SU, 1987
Smith, Leverett, Edinburgh SC, 1972; 74, N Car Wesleyan C
Smith, Linda C., Allentown, Pa, 1986
Smith, Linda, Maumee U, Oh, 1980
Smith, Lorrie, St. Michaels C, 1987
Smith, Louis C., U Il, 1971
Smith, Mark, U Tx-San Antonio, 1983
Smith, Michael, Ball SU, 1988
Smith, Norman, Ok SU, 1973, 74, 75; 77, Walsenburg, Colo; 82
Smith, Nicholas D., Va Tech, 1979, 80, 81, 82
Smith, Paul, Miami U, Oh, 1985
Smith, Pauline, Cleveland Indian Educ Services, 1981
Smith, Philip, U Pitt, 1979
Smith, R.I., Auburn U, 1879, 86, 88
Smith, R. Sue, BGSU, 1982
Smith, Ray T., San Diego SU, 1988
Smith, R.T., Auburn U, 1979, 86
Smith, Sharon, U Houston, 1984, 85
Smith, Stephen A., Fayetteville, Ark, 1976; 83, 84, 85, U Ark
Smith, Susan, U Pitt, 1979
Smith, Susan A., Springfield, Mo, 1986
Smith, Susan M., U Minn, 1985
Smith, Suzanne, Carnegie-Mellon, 1988
Smith, William Andrew, Alleg Cty Comm C, 1978
Smithermar, Geneva, Wayne SU, 1980
Smolenski, Ira, Monmouth C, 1987
Smolenski, Reiner, Ga SU, 1988
Smolla, Rodney, U Ark, 1987
Smoodin, Eric, Amer U, 1988
Smoot, Calder, APPALSHOP,

Whitesburg, Ky, 1977
Smythe, Willie, UCLA, 1986; 88 Ok Arts Council
Snall, Peg, WMUK, W Mich U, 1980
Snell, Joel C., Kirkwood Comm C, 1988
Snipes, Katherine, E Wash U, 1974, 87, 88
Snodgrass, David, URI, 1986
Snow, Robert, Mich SU, 1975, 76, 77, 80; 82, 83, SUNY-Potsdam
Snow, Sara, Augusta C, 1985
Snowden, Fraser, NW La SU, 1978, 79
Snyder, Eldon, BGSU, 1973, 74, 75, 83
Snyder, Ellen M., Brooklyn Hist Soc, 1987
Snyder, Jacqueline, Wichita SU, 1982, 83, 84, 85, 87
Snyder, John R., U Houston-Clear Lake, 1976
Snyder, Robert, U SFl, 1983, 84
Snyder, Robert J., Athens, Oh, 1988
Snyder, Tom, Evanston, Il, 1985
Snyder, Wayne, Sangamon SU, 1978
Sobchak, Tom, U Ut, 1973, 74,, 80, 83
Sobchak, Vivian, U Vt, 1978
Sobieska, Lynn, Hunter, 1987, 88
Sochen, June, NE Il U, 1980
Sodhi, Penny, Neb Hist Soc, 1983
Sodowsky, Alice, U N Ia, 1981, 83
Soens, Al, Notre Dame, 1987
Sohl, Patricia, York U, Can
Soifer, Aviam, Boston U, 1987, 88
Soiffer, Stephen M., U Rochester, 1988
Soitos, Stephen, U Mass, 1987, 88
Sojka, Gregory, Wichita SU, 1981, 82, 83, 84, 85, 86
Sokol, David, U Il-Chicago, 19896, 87, 88
Solensten, John M., Mankato SC, 1971
Solez, Elaine, Towson SU, 1980
Sollars, Verner, Columbia U, 1983
Solomon, Albert J., U Scranton, 1987
Solomon, Howard, Tufts U, 1984
Solomon, Jon, U Az, 1987, 88
Soloman, Marvi, Sou Il U-Edwardsville, 1981
Soloski, John, U Ia, 1982
Solt, Marilyn, BGSU, 1980, 81, 82, 83, 84
Somer, Richard, Hamilton C, 1984
Somera, Rene D., U Philippines, 1982
Somers, Paul M., Mich SU, 1975, 76, 77, 80, 81, 82
Somkin, Fred, Cornell, 1988
Somoza, Oscar U., CSU-Bakersfield, 1979
Sondergard, Sidney, USC, 1983
Songer, Marcia J., E Tn SU, 1987, 88
Sorkin, Adam, Pa SU, 1983, 84, 85, 86, 87, 88
Sorlen, Ellen, Mich SU, 1977
Soroka, Michael P., U San Diego, 1988
Sorrell, Richard, Brookdale Comm C, NJ, 1987
Sorrell, Victor, Chicago SU, Chicago, 1987
Sossaman, Stephen, Westfield SC, 1986, 87, 88
Sottile, Victoria, N Il U, 1983
Southard, Sherry, Ok SU, 1982, 83
Sovine, Melanie, MacNeal Hospital, Il, 1985
Sowd, David, BGSU, 1973
Spade, George, Columbia U, 1980

Spalding, Phinizy, U Ga, 1986
Spangehl, Stephen D., U Louisville, 1987, 88
Spangler, Bud, WDET-FM, Detroit, 1971
Spangler, Jack, 1979
Spangler, Sharon, Clemson, 1986
Spangler, Stells, Daemen C, 1984
Sparks, Elisa, Clemson, SC, 1986
Sparks, Isabel, W Mo SC, 1980, 83, 84, 87
Spartano, Philip J., U Puerto Rico, 1988
Speaks, Michael, Duke, 1988
Spear, Karen I., U Ut, 1988
Spears, H. Keith, Marshall U, 1982
Speck, Bobbie J., Cumberland U, 1988
Speck, Paul, Frostburg SC, 1982
Specter, Bert, Longview Comm C, Mo., 1980
Spector, Judith, IUPUI-Columbus, 1982, 84
Speer, Jean, Va Tech, 1977
Speers, Susan, Va Tech, 1979
Spellman, A.B., Nat'l Endowment Arts, 1980
Spence, Susan, Lindenwald, NJ, 1986, 87
Spencer, Kathleen, Wright SU, 1977, 78, 79, 80, 81, 82, 84,87, UCLA, U Neb, 1988
Spengemann, William C., Claremont Grad School, 1973
Sperling, Lynda J., U Ia, 1988
Spetnagel, Harry T., U Denver, 1973, 74, 78, 79
Spetz, Dennis, U Louisville, 1985
Spiegel, Carole Damien, BGSU 1973
Spiegle, Rick, Woodmore Jr. HS, Oh, 1973
Spielberg, Joseph, Mich SU, 1979
Spielvogel, Jackson, Pa SU, 1987
Spiesman, Barbara, Fl A&M, 1988
Spinden, Frank, Ok SU, 1976
Spiney, Donald, U Ct, 1980
Spinks, C.W., Trinity U, San Antonio, 1976, 83
Spinks, C.W. Lewisburg, Pa, 1984
Spinks, Mark, W Mich U, 1980
Spliney, Donald, U Ct, 1980
Spongehl, Stephen, U Louisville, 1980
Sponsler, Claire, Ind U, 1986
Sporn, Paul, Wayne SU, 1978, 79, 81
Spornnick, Nick, U DC, 1984
Sprague, Stuart, Morehead SU, 1984 81, 82
Spraker, Jean, U Minn, 1984
Spreitser, Elmer, BGSU, 1974, 75, 76
Spreser, James, Columbia, Tn, 1984
Sprich, Robert, Bentley C, 1982, 84, 85, 86, 87
Springer, Claudia, Northwestern, 1983
Springer, Haskell, U Kans, 1981, 82, 83, 84, 85; 86, 87, 88, U Paris, Sorbonne
Springer, Lisa, Ok SU, 1979
Springman, Joanne, Woodstock, Il, 1979; 80, U Wisc-Whitewater, 1979, 80
Sprouse, Rex, E Ore, 1988
Spurlock, Jacqueline B., E Ky U, 1988
Squires, Linda, BGSU, 1975
Squires, Stanley W., Oakville Pub Lib, Ont., 1978
Srebnik, Henry, U Mich, 1984; 87 Washington Jewish Weekly

Srebnik, Patricia, Gettysburg C, 1987
Sronce, Nancy J., S Il U, 1987
St. Andrews, B.A., Upstate Medical Center, Syracuse, NY, 1986
St. Clair, Robert, U Louisville, 1980
St. Germain, Amos, Sou Tech Inst., 1975, 78, 79, 85, 86; 87 Wentworth Inst, 87, 88
St. James, Margo, Coyote, San Francisco, 1984
St. John, Jacqueline, U Neb, 1983, 86
St. Louis, Ralph, U Evansville, 1979
St. Romain, Rose Anne, LSU, 1988
Stacey, Pamela, Long Beach, Ca., 1985
Stade, George, Columbia U, 1979
Stadelman, Bonnie, Tx A&M, 1974, 75
Stadlley, Scott, Sou Il, 1987
Staehle, Williams, Rutgers, 1979
Stafford, Randy, Macalester C, 1983
Stafford, William, Purdue, 1972, 73, 74, 76
Stage, Sarah, UC-Riverside, 1982
Stahlberg, Lawrence, Va Tech, 1982
Staley, Janellyn, Ia SU 1974
Stambolian, George, 1973
Stamper, Virginia, Marquette U, 1986, 88
Standerfer, Christina, U Ark-Little Rock, 1986
Standley, Scott, Sou Il U, 1986
Stanford, Rainey, Castro Valley, Ca, 1978
Stanger, Gretta, Tn Tech, 1987, 88
Stanley, Isabel B., E Tn SU, 1988
Stanley, Owen R., Lewiston, Ida, 1976
Stansfield, Charles, Glassboro SC, 1979
Stanton, Max, Brigham Young U, 1986
Star, Michael, Hiram C, 1982
Stark, Bruce R., U Wisc-Milwaukee, 1974
Stark, Harry, Rutgers, 1987
Stark, John, UC-Santa Barbara, 1982
Stark, Meritt W., Suffolk, Va, 1987
Staroshchak, Ivanna, Pittsburg, 1979
Starks, Charlotte, U Ut, 1987
Starr, Claudia, Churchill Downs, Ky, 1982
Starr, Jerold, W Va U, 1981
Startup, Kenneth M., Sou Baptist C, 1988
Startzman, L. Eugene, Berea C, 1985
Staton, Carolyn E., U Miss, 1988
Stav, Ilana, Hebrew U, Jerusalem, 198
Stave, Shirley, U Minn, 1984; 86, W Va U; 87, 88, Oxford U, Oh
Stebbins, Gene, Kent SU, 1987
Steck, Henry, SUNY-Cortland, 1988
Stedman, Jane W., Roosevelt U, 1976
Steed, Robert, Citadel, 1986, 87
Steele, Elizabeth, U Tol, 1973
Steele, Michael R., Mich SU, 1974; 77, Pacific U
Steen, Ivan, SUNY-Albanyu, 1980
Steere, Geoffrey H., U Kans, 1987
Stefaniak, Gregory, Ok SU, 1983, 84, 85
Steffen-Fluhr, Nancy, NJ Inst Tech, 1985, 86
Steger, Charles, Va Tech, 1986
Steiger, Richard, Murray SU, 1979
Stein, Elisabeth, Tallahassee Comm C, 1984, 87
Stein, Karen, URI, 1978
Stein, Roger, SUNY-Binghamton, 1984
Stein, Rose, Columbia U, 1985
Steinberg, Levi, Mich SU, 1981, 82

Steinberg, Mark, Lansing, Mi, 1985
Steinberg, Michael, Mich SU, 1976, 77
Steinberg, Saline Harju, NE U, 1976
Steinen, Karl T., W Ga C, 1982
Steiner, Rodney, CSU-Long Beach, 1986
Steinfirst, Susan, UNC, 1984, 86, 87
Steininger, Judith, Milwaukee Sch Engineering, 1983, 85
Steinke, Gary, U Tn-Martin, 1982
Steinle, Pamela, CSU-Fullerton, 1986
Steinmetz, Lee, E Il Un, 1976, 78
Stell, Lance, Davidson C, 1988
Stelpflug, Peggy, Auburn, Ala, 1986
Stenberg, Henry, Salem SC, Ma., 1988
Stengel, Wayne, U Cent Ark, 1985
Stenross, Barbara UNC, 1987, 88
Stenson, Linnea, Minneapolis, Mn, 1985
Stephan, Sandra, Youngstown SU 1987, 88
Stephens, Anne, BGSU, 1988
Stephens, Bruce, Pa SU, 1986
Stephens, Jane, SE Mo SU, 1986
Stephens, Michael, BGSU, 1988
Stephenson, Peter, Pa SU, 1976
Stepp, Nancy, BGSU, 1973
Steppenfield, Dan, Tallahassee, Fl, 1986
Sterk, Helen, Marquette U, 1987
Stern, Carrie, NYU, 1988
Stern, Elaine, WXYZ-Detroit, 1980
Stern, Jerome, Fl SU, 1974, 75, 76, 78, 80, 81, 82, 83, 84, 85, 86, 87, 88
Stern, Michael, Harvey Mudd C, 1979
Stern, Milton, U Ct, 1979
Stern, Robert, Wayne SU, 1974
Sternsher, Bernard, BGSU, 1979
Steuding, Bob, Ulster Cty Comm C, NY, 1979, 82
Steuernagel, Trudy, Kent SU, 1986
Stevens, Carol Daddazio, Oakland U, Mi, 1978, 79, 80; 82, E Il U; 83, 84, 85, 86, 87, 87, 88, Eastern Il U
Stevens, Charles S., Depaul U, 1988
Stevens, David, Oakland U, Mi, 1978, 79, 80, 81, 82, 84; 85, 86, 87, 88, Sou Il U
Stevens, Felicia, Madison, Wi, 1988
Stevens, Freeland R., West Coast U, 198
Stevens, George, Jr., Amer Film Inst, 1975
Stevens, John D., U Mich, 1972, 73, 74, 75, 81, 84, 86, 88
Stevens, Norman, U Ct, 1987
Stevens, Peter, U Windsor, 1985, 87
Stevenson, Catherine, U Hartford, 1984
Stevenson, Mary, Prince George's Comm C, 1973
Stewart, Alfred D., Midwestern SU 1975, 76, 78, 79, 80, 81
Stewart, Charles, Purdue, 1985
Stewart, Don J., USC-Aiken, 1988
Stewart, Donald, Temple U, 1985, 87
Stewart, Grace, Henry Ford Comm C, 1980, 87
Stewart, James R., USD, 1987, 88
Stewart, Jefferson, Cent Mich U, 1983
Stewart, John, U Santa Clara, 1985
Stewart, Lucy A., E Mich SU, 1985, 86
Stewart, Margaret, U Wisc, 1981; 82, 85, Hanover C
Stewart, Mary, Cent Mich U, 1983
Stewart, Matthew C., Emory U, 1988

Stewart, Ralph, Acadia U, NS, Can, 1985
Stewig, John, U Wisc-Milw, 1978, 86
Stiebel, Arlene, CSU-Northridge, 1988
Stiffler, Beth, W Il U, 1983, 85
Still, Sandra, Crown Publishing, 1988
Stilling, Roger, Appal SU, 1986
Stock, Wendy, Human Sexuality Center, 1984; 85, Tx A&M
Stockton, Edwin L., Radford U, 1987
Stoddard, Frank, WTMJ Radio/TV, 1974
Stoddard, Karen, U Md, 1977
Stokes, Frank, E Il U, 1978
Stokes, Thomas, Cumberland C, 1987
Stone, Edward, Oh U, 1978, 82
Stone, Gaynell, SUNY-Stony Brook, 1987
Stone, Lisa, Milwaukee, 1984; 85, Chicago
Stone, Lyle, Dept Natural Resources, 1971
Stone, Michael, World Coll West,1975
Stoner, Ronald E., BGSU, 1980
Stott, Jon C., W Mich U, 1975; 80, Seminole, Fl.; 84, U Alberta, Can
Stout, Janis, Rice U, 1986
Stout, Joe, Ok SU, 1973, 74, 75
Stout, Neil R., U Vt, 1988
Stover, Sharon, U Tx, 1985
Stowell, Marion B., Ga Mil C, 1987
Stoyak, Sharon, Mich Tech U, 1979
Strada, Michael, W Liberty SC, WVA, 1984, 85
Strandness, Marilyn, ND SU, 1987, 88
Strandtman, Sara, U Tx, 1986
Stratfield, David C., U Wash, 1978
Stratyner, Barbara, NYU, 1982, 83, 84, 87
Strauss, David, Kalamazoo C, 1976
Strazulla, Ron, Dev. Research Sch, Tallahassee, 1986
Straw, Richard, Radford U, 1988
Streb, Edward, St Univ Coll Arts & Sciences, Geneseo, 1976, 78, 79
Street, Douglas, Tx A&M 1980
Streeter, Sandra, 1983
Streissguth, Michael, Ind U Pa., 1988
Strickland, Carol, SUNY-Stony Brook, 1988
Strickland, Johnnye, U Ark-Little Rock, 1985, 87
Strickland, Michael, Clemson, 1986
Strickland, William Bradley, Truett-McConnell C, 1978, 79
Stricklin, David, Baylor, 1988
Striker, Fran, Runnemede, NJ, 1986
Stringer, A.E., Va Tech, 1983
Strohmeyer, Virgil B., West Coast U, 1988
Strom, Yale, San Diego, Ca., 1986, 87
Strombach, Werner, U Dortmund, 1987
Strong, Paul, Alfred U, 1986
Strothers, Evette, Oh SU, 1982
Stroud, Kenneth M., Ind U-Indianapolis, 1987, 88
Strozier, Robert, Wayne SU, 1978, 80
Struebig, Patricia, U Houston-Downtown, 1988
Strumwasser, Gina, CSU-Fresno, 1988
Stubbs, Andrew, U Guelph, 1987
Stugrin, Michael, U Pitt, 1979
Stulman, Andrea, Great Neck, NY, 1987, 88
Stults, Taylor, Muskingum C, 1973, 78
Stump, Jeanne, U Kans, 1985

Stump, Roger, SUNY-Albany, 1985
Stumpf, Stuart, Tn Tech, 1978
Stupple, David, E Mich U, 1972, 73, 74, 75, 76, 81, 82
Sturm, Rebecca, Nor Ky U 1988
Sturino, Frank, York U, Toronto, 1984
Suarez-Muriae, Marguerite C., U Wisc-Milwaukee, 1974
Subercaseaux, Bernard, U Wash, 1980
Suderman, Elmer, Gustavus Adolphus, 1972, 73, 74, 75, 76, 77, 78, 79, 80, 82, 83, 84, 86, 87
Suderman, Norma, Gustavus Adolphus, 1983, 87
Suggs, J.C., John Jay C Crim Justice, 1987, 88
Suggs, H.L., Clemson, 1986
Suhor, Charles, Nat'l Council Teachers English, 1985, 86
Suhr, Heldrun, U Mich, 1987
Suid, Lawrence, Case Western U, 1976, 77; 78. Washington, D.C.; 79, U Vt; 80, Virginia; 81, Alexandria, Va
Sullenberger, Tom E., SW Mo, U, 1973
Sullivan, Barbara M., Sacred Heart C, 1971; 72, 73, 74, Gaston C; 75, 76, 77, 78, Cent Piedmont C
Sullivan, Bill, Keene, SC, 1987
Sullivan, Charles W., III, E Caro SU, 1978
Sullivan, Mary R., U Colo, 1984
Sullivan, Patricia, Ok SU, 1973
Sullivan, Robert J., RI C, 1987
Sullivan, Sherry, U Ala-B'ham, 1982, 84
Sullivan, Tom, U Puerto Rico, 1973, 85, 88
Sullivan, Zohreh, U Il, 1988
Summerhayes, Don, York U, Toronto, 1971, 84
Summerlin, Mitchell, Truett-McConwell C, 1981
Summersell, Charles G., U Ala, 1975
Sundel, Michael, Schulte, Roth & Zobel, NYC, 1986
Surber, Jere, U Den, 1981
Surratt, Sam, CBS, NYC, 1975, 77
Susman, Warren, Rutgers, 1984
Susser, David, Ok SU, 1977
Sussman, Lyle, U Louisville, 1982
Sustakoski, Henry, SUC-Buffalo, 1976
Suter, John M., E Cent U, Ok, 1978, 79, 80
Sutherland, Anne, Macalester C, 1988
Sutherland, Connie, NE Mo SU, 1988
Sutton, Donald S., Carnegie-Mellon, 1979
Svoboda, Frederick, U Mich-Flint, 1986
Swackhammar, Mac, Little Current, Ont, 1984
Swafford, Dale, Wichita SU, 1985
Swain, Bruce, U Ga, 1986
Swan, Michael, U Ut, 1986
Swan, M. Beverly, URI, 1977
Swann, Paul, Temple, 1985, 86
Swartz, James, Sou Meth U, 1986
Swaffer, Janet, U Tx, 1988
Swanger, Eugene, Wittenberg U, 1987
Swann, Paul, Temple U, 1987, 8
Swedberg, Deborah, Boston U, 1983, 84
Sweeney, Barbara, Auburn U, 1983
Sweeney, James, Old Dom U, 1985

Sweet, Charlie, E Ky U, 1978, 81, 82, 85
Sweet, Timothy, U Minn, 1987, 88
Swenger, Eugene, Wittenberg U, 1983
Swensen, Alice, U N Ia, 1984, 85
Swenson, Connie, U Akron, 1987, 88
Swenson, Gretta, North
Swetnam, Susan H., Ida SU, 1987
Swiderski, Richard M., CUNY-Richmond, 1974; 83, Bridgewater SC, Ma
Swigger, Keith, U Ia, 1971
Swindell, Warren, Ind SU, 1987, 88
Swiss, Cheri, Mary Washington C, 1986
Switzer, Charles, E Il U, 1983
Switzer, Les, U Houston, 1985
Smypira, F., U Alberta, Can, 1988
Sydie, R.A., U Alberta, Can, 1984
Synnot, Anthony, Concord U, Montreal, Can, 1984
Syrett, Mary L., U SW La, 1988
Szcezpanik, Michael, U Kans, 1975
Szklardzyk, Illian, Montclair SC, 1975
Szostek, John, Governors SU, 1976
Szporer, Michael, Oh SU-Mansfield, 1985

Tabakow, Lou, Cincinnati, Oh, 1978
Taborsky, Edwina, Toronto, 1984
Tafelski, Robert L., U Ga, 1977
Taft, Edmund, Pa SU 1982
Tagge, A.W., Lasell Jr C, Ma, 1985, 87
Tait, Alice, U Detroit, 1985, 86
Takenouchi, Nobuyuiki, Sophia Jr. C., Tokyo, 1982
Talamini, John, U Bridgeport, 1973
Talbot, David A., E Tx SU, 1984
Talburt, Nancy Ellen, U Ark, 1986, 77, 78, 79, 80, 81, 82, 83, 84, 85, 86, 87, 88
Talention, Arnold, SUNY-Cortland, 1980
Tallmadge, John, U Ut, 1980
Tammer, David, Stafford, Az, 1987
Tankel, Jonathan, Ithaca C, 1987
Tannenbaum, Joy, Hampshire C, 1981
Tannenbaum, Leslie, Oh SU, 1987
Tanner, James L., Wichita SU, 1983
Tapping, Craig, U British Columbia, 1984
Tashjian, Ann, UC-Irvine, 1976, 87
Tashjian, Dickran, UC-Irvine, 1976, 87
Taskin, Richard, North Adams SC, 1987, 88
Tate, David, Mo Sou SC, 2986, 87, 88
Tate, Douglass, SC SU, 1972
Tate, Joel C, Germanna Comm C, Va, 1988
Tatum, Charles, NM SU, 1977, 79, 80
Tatum, Steve, U Ut, 1983, 86
Tavares, Frank, Nat'l Public Radio, 1980
Tavormina, M. Teresa, Mich SU, 1986
Tawa, Nicholas E., U Mass, 1976
Taylor, Andrew, Toronto, Can, 1987
Taylor, Beverly, UNC, 1988
Taylor, Bruce, U Wisc-Eau Claire, 1987, 88
Taylor, Carole Anne, Bates C, 1985
Taylor, Ella, Northeastern U, 1982
Taylor, Harris, Guelph U, Can, 1984
Taylor, Jack, Fl SU, 1988
Taylor, Jon, Fl Jr C, Jacksonville, 1977
Taylor, Koko, Blues Recording Artist, 1976
Taylor, Lawrence, W Mich U, 1984
Taylor, Matthew, Rice U, 1987, 88
Taylor, Michael, Marietta C, 1981

Taylor, Patricia, W Ky U, 1987
Taylor, Ramona, St Louis U, 1988
Taylor, Verta, Oh SU, 1976, 77
Taylor-Roepke, Sharon, Kalamazoo, Mi, 1978
Tebbe, Jennifer L., Mass C Pharmacy, Boston, 1979, 81, 82, 83, 84
Techter, David, 1971, 72, 84
Tedesco, Albert S., U Pa, 1973
Teilhet, Jehanne, UC-San Diego, 1977
Teitelbaum, Benjamin, U Que, Can, 1984
Teiteleman, Edward, Architect.ural Hist, Camden, NJ, 1982
Telotte, Jay P., Berry C, 1978, 79; 86, 88, Ga Inst Tech
Templeton, Alice, W Ky U, 1988
Tener, Robert, Kent SU, 1986
Terborg-Penn, Sosalyn, Morgan SU, 1976
Tergesen, Anne, Princeton, 1987
Terrar, Toby, Encino, Ca., 1988
Terrebonne, Nancy, Forest Park Comm C, St. Louis, 1976
Terrie, Philip, BGSU, 1982
Terry, Lucille, BGSU, 1985
Teske, Robert, Wayne SU, 1976
Teski, Kris, Stockton SC, 1988
Teski, Marea, Stockton Sc, 1988
Tesler, Rita W., Jersey City, NJ, 1976; 77, Flushing, NY
Test, George A., SUNY-Oneonta, 1979
Testa, Michael, Northwestern, 1985
Tetley, Rosslyn, Montreal, Can, 1984
Tetreault, Mary A., Old Dom U, 1987
Teunissen, John J., U Manitoba, Winnipeg, 1988
Tevis, Ray, Ball SU, 1983, 84, 85, 86, 87
Thacker, Robert, St. Laurence U, 1987
Thalberg, Irving, U Il, 1980
Thayer, Fred, Radford U, 1986
Theisen, Arnold, E NM U, 1987
Theisen, Lee, Cent Az Mus, Phoenix, 1982; 86, Ind S Museum, Indianapolis
Theoharis, Zoe G., Emporia SU, 1979, 80, 83, 84, 85, 88
Thiebaux, Marcelle, St. John's U, 1979, 82
Thigpen, Ann, Pa SU, 1984
Thigpen, Kenneth A., Pa SU, 1974, 75, 76
Thilsted, Uranda, Ok SU, 1982
Thomas, Carolyn, SUNY-Buffalo, 1980
Thomas, Frank, Albion C, 1976
Thomas, Gwendolyn A., U Denver, 1977
Thomas, James, Wichita SU, 1982, 83, 84, 86, 88
Thomas, Jimmie, Wharton Cty Jr C, Tx, 1983
Thomas, Mattie, Purdue, 1977
Thomas, Peter, Lake Superior SC, 1971
Thomas, Philip Drennon, Wichita SU, 1972, 73
Thomas, Samuel, Mich SU, 1983, 87
Thomas, Sari, Temple, 1982
Thomas, Shirley, Atlanta U, 1983
Thomashow, Mitchell, Antioch-New England Grad Sch, 1987
Thomason, Michael, U Sou Ala, 1983, 84
Thomlinson, Vivian, Denton, Tx, 1986
Thomlison, T. Dean, U Evansville
Thompson, Christine, Mich SU, 1981

Thompson, Dorothy, U Wisc-Richland Center, 1988
Thompson, Elizabeth, Shippensburg U, 1988
Thompson, George, Emporia kSU, 1978
Thompson, Guadalupe, U Ok, 1976
Thompson, Irene, U Fl, 1973
Thompson, Joyce, Tx Woman's U, 1985, 86, 88
Thompson, Julius, SUNY-Albany, 1984
Thompson, Lawrence, U Denver, 1982, 83
Thompson, Lee, UVt, 1978, 79, 81, 83, 84
Thompson, Leslie M., Stephen F. Austin SU, 1978, 79
Thompson, Lou, NM Inst Mining & Tech, 1988
Thompson, Lupita, U Ok, 1979, 82
Thompson, Michale, U Sou Ala, 1982
Thompson, Richard, UCLA, 1972
Thompson, Robert, Luther C., 1982, 83; 84, 85, 86, Northwestern
Thompson, Robert, SUNY-Cortland, 1987, 88
Thompson, Tom, KCET-TV, 1980
Thompson, Tommy, U Neb-Omaha, 1983
Thorman, Monique, Santa Clara U, 1987
Thornburn, David, Yale, 1976
Thorndike, Jonathan L., Mich SU, 1987
Thorndyke, Jonathan, Mich SU, 1984, 85
Thorndyke, Nick, Alma, Mi
Thornton, Jerome, SUNY-Albany, 1984
Thornton, William, St. Mary's C, 1986
Thorpe, Claiborne B., Winston-Salem SU, 1978, 79, 91, 83, 84, 85, 87, 88
Thorpe, Vivian C., Winston-Salem SU, 1987, 88
Thorson, Gerald, St. Olaf C, 1982
Thralls, Charlotte, Ia SU, 1988
Thronson, Ron, Chapman C, 1988
Thuma, Linnie, U Mich, 1984; 85 Mich Tech U
Thuma, Serna, Jane, Oh U, 1984
Thundy, Zacharias, N Mich U, 1984
Thurman, William, Ga SW C, 1981, 82, 86
Thurston, Carol, Austin, Tx., 82, 83, U Houston
Tichy, Charles, La Vista, Ne, 1984
Tick, Stanley, San Francisco SU, 1987
Tiessen, Hilda, Wilfred Laurier U, Can, 1987
Tilford, Earl H, Jr., Maxwell AFB, 1988
Till, David, Austin Pea SU, 1986
Tilley, E. Allen, U NFl, 1974, 77
Tilley, Lewis, U S Colo, 1982
Tillman, Gregory, BGSU, 1987
Timberg, Bernard, U Neb, 1980, 81, 83
Timmerman, John H., Calvin C, 1979
Timson, Beth, UNC-Charlotte, 1980, 81
Ting, Lee-Hsia, W Il U, 1985, 88
Tingley, Stephanie A., Youngstown SU, 1988
Tinkler, John, U Tn, 1987
Tipper, Jack, Mus Cartoon Art, 1977
Tipton, Catharine A., Duluth, Mn, 1988
Tischler, Barbara, Barnard C, 1987
Titen, Jennifer, Lake Sumpter Comm C, 1979

Titterton, Mike, Va Tech, 1977, 78
Titus, Kim, Tx Util Service, Dallas, 1983
Tobin, Gary, Brandeis U, 1988
Tobin, Mary F., U Md, 1977
Todd, Bonnie, Stephen F. Austin SU, 1984
Todd, Ellen, Geo Mason U, 1986
Todd, James, U Mont, 1979, 80
Todras, Arthur, U Richmond, 1984, 85, 86
Tokaarczyk, Michelle, Hofstra U, 1986, 87
Tolchin, Neal, Rutgers, 1985
Toll, Larry, Ball SU, 1985
Toll, Robert, UC-Berkeley, 1973
Tolstedt, Mark, U Mo-KC, 1985; 86, Geo Washington U
Tomasch, Otto, York C, Pa, 1979, 80, 81, 82
Tomasson, Jill, U Toronto, Can, 1985
Tomasulo, Frank, Ithaca C, 1984, 85
Tome, Sandra, Toronto, Can, 1984
Tomeh, Aida, BGSU, 1971
Tomlinson, Timothy, Northwestern C, St. Paul, Mn, 1984, 87
Toner, James, Norwich U, 1985
Tong, John, U Ut, 1979, 80
Tonsfeldt, H. Ward, 1987
Tonso, William, U Evansville, 1987, 88
Toogood, Alex, Temple, 1983, 85, 86, 87
Toolin, Cynthia, Amherst, Ma., 1982; 86, Warick, RI
Toplovich, Ann, Tn Dept Conservation, 1986
Topping, Gary, Salt Lake City, 1974
Torczon, Vernon J., UNO, 1984
Torke, James, Ind U Sch of Law, Indianapolis, 1987, 88
Torres, Kay, CSU-LA, 1980
Torres, Lucy, Ind U, 1976
Torry, Bob, U Wy, 1986
Toth, Emily, Johns Hopkins U, 1973; 75, UNO; 76, 77, 78, UND; 79, 80, 81, 82, 83, 84, 85, 86, 87, 88, PA SU
Toubia, Nabil, BGSU, 1984
Tournier, Robert E., C Charleston, 1978, 79, 81; 86, 88, Charleston, SC
Tovar, Inez Hernandez, U Houston, 1974, 75; 76 U Tx
Towers, Frank, UCLA, 1988
Towers, Tom, Wisc SU, 1971; 73, 74, 75, 76, 77, 78, 79, 80, 81, 82, 83, 84, 85, 86, 87, 88, URI
Town, Caren J., Stetson, 1988
Towns, Stuart, U WFl, 1985
Townsend, Charles, W Tx SU, 1983, 88
Townsend, Guy, Madison, In., 1982
Trachtenberg, Alan, Yale, 1972
Trachy, James, BGSU, 1975
Tracy, Eleanor, Washington, D.C., 1987
Tracy, Steven, Managing Editor MELUS, 1982; 85, 86, 87, U Cin
Tranquilla, Ronald, St. Vincent C, 1987
Traub, Patricia, Flora Park, NY, 1988
Traub, Stuart H., SUNY-Cortland, 1988
Trauth, Denise, BGSU, 1978, 83
Travis, Marie, Geo Washington U, 1986
Travis, Molly, Oh SU, 1987
Travis, Russell, CSU-Bakersfield, 1988
Travis, Vivian K., Winthrop C, 1977
Treacy, Mary J., Simmons C, 1988
Treadwell, Thomas, W Chester U, 1986

Treckel, Paul, Alleg C, 1984, 86

Treece, Peggy Belle, Findlay, Oh, 1976

Treves, Nicole, UCLA, 1975; 77, 78, San Diego SU

Tribble, Joan, Jefferson Comm C, Ky, 1980, 81

Tribe, Ivan, Rio Grande C, 1985

Trickey, R. Patricia, U Pa, 1974

Trimble, Steve, Minn Comm C, 1985

Trimmer, Joseph F., Ball SU, 1972, 77

Trimpey, John E., Ark SU, 1978, 79

Trinity, Mary, St Bonaventure U, 1984

Tripp, Joseph, Citadel', 1983

Trobian, Helen, Bennett C, 1984, 85

Tropman, John, U Mich, 1980

Trouard, Dawn, U Akron, 1982, 84, 86

Trout, Bill, Wooden Records, 1976

Trout, Tom, Coastal Car C, 1982

Trowbridge, Sara, U Tn, 1985

Troyan, Marilyn V., U Wisc, 1988

Troyan, Scott, U Akron, 1984

Trudell, Dennis, U Wisc-Whitewater, 1988

True, Marshall, UVT, 1985

Trumtbour, Jack, Stanford, 1984

Truzzi, Marcello, New C, Sarasota, 1972, 74; 75, 76, E Mich U

Tsukashima, Ronald, CSU-LA, 1982

Tucci, Candice, St. Bonaventure U, 1984

Tucker, Carolyn, UFI, 1984

Tucker, Elizabeth, SUNY-Binghamton, 1979

Tucker, Memye, Marietta, Ga., 1984

Tucker, Sylvia, U Cin, 1973

Tuckey, John S., Purdue-Calument, 1974

Tuerk, Richard, E Tx S, 1983

Tueth, Rev. Michael S.J., American Civ, Dept, NYU, 1975

Tuiloss, Thomas, U Md, 1976; 77, W Md C

Tumas-Serna, Jane, Oh U, 1985

Tunbridge, John, Carleton U, Ottawa, 1984

Tunis, Betsy, Colby-Sawyer C, 1980

Turk, Edward B., MIT, 1987, 88

Turner, A., El Reno Jr C, 1982; 83, Ok Hist Soc

Turner, Colin, Queens C, 1976

Turner, Darwin, U Ia, 1972, 78

Turner, Dennis, Wayne SU, 1984

Turner, Eldon, UFI, 1984, 85, 86, 87

Turner, Frederick H., Rider C, 1976

Turner, John P., Humboldt SU, 1983

Turner, John S., Oh U, 1988

Turner, Lynn H., Marquette U, 1987

Tuska, Jon, Ed Views & Reviews, 1972

Tutt, Ralph, URI, 1976, 77, 78

Tutt, Roberta, URI, 1977, 78

Tweedie, Stephen, Ok SU, 1979

Tweet, Jonathan, Rock Island, Il, 1986

Tweton, Jerome, UND, 1972, 73, 80, 81

Twomey, Alfred E., Cent Mo SU, 1975

Twomey, John, Ryerson Poly, Toronto, Can, 1984

Tyler, Bruce, U Louisville, 1986

Tymn, Marshall, E Mich U, 1983

Tynan, Daniel, Colo C, 1982, 83, 84

Tyrrell, William Blake, Mich SU, 1975, 76

Tyssen, Muriel, Lee C, 1983

Udoff, Alan, Baltimore Hebrew C., 1987

Uecker, Bob, Sports Announcer, 1974

Uffen, Ellen, East Lansing, Mi, 1981; 82 Mich SU

Ullman, Pierre, U Wisc-Milwaukee, 1974

Ullsperger, Christian, U Wisc, 1987

Ulvis, Betty, Television Writer, 1974

Umland, Sam, U Neb., 1987

Umphlett, W. Lee, U WFl, 1981

Underwood, Alva, Moberly Jr. C, Mo., 1982

Underwood, Virginia, Ia SU, 1982

Unger, Lynette, Miami U, Oh, 1985

Unsworth, Michael, Colo SU, 1983

Uphaus, Susan, Mich SU, 1977, 79, 81

Upton, Lee, Grand Valley SC, 1987, 88

Urbanowicz, Victor, Ia SU, 1977

Uren, Marjorie, Portland SU, 1974, 75

Urqurait, Don, Fl SU, 1982

Urithiam, Douglas, Ok SU, 1982

Uruburu, Paula, Radford U, 1984; 85, 86, 87, 88, Hofstra U

Uslan, Michael, 1975

Utley, Francis Lee, Oh SU, 1973

Utter, Glenn H., Lamar U, 1980, 81, 83

Utterback, Raymond V., Ga SU, 1976

Uzendoski, Emily, Platte Cent Comm C, 1983; 84, Cent Comm C, Neb

Vaca, David, CSU-Fullerton, 1986

Vacha, J.E., Cleveland, 1973

Vachon, Lorraine, BGSU, 1984

Vail, Mark, BGSU, 1988

Vaile, Barbara, Minn, Mn, 1985

Valencia, L.B., U Philippines, 1982, 83

Valentine, Les, Omaha, Neb, 1983

Vales, Robert L., Gannon C, 1988

Valis, Noel Maureen, U Ga., 1978

Valley-Fischer, Lois, Acadia U, Nova Scotia, 1984, 86

Valliere, D.W., Gambling Quarterly, 1976

Valline, Tracy, Carnegie-Mellon, 1988

Van Campen, Rebecca, Evansville, In, 1985

Van DeBurg, William, U Wisc, 1986

Van Dellen, Robert, Rocky Mt. C, 1974, 75, 76

Vanden Bergh, Bruce, Mich SU, 1984, 85

Van der Bogert, Frans, Appaal SU, 1982

Vandergriff, Jim, Cent Mo SU, 1983

Vander Waude, Matthew, York U, Ont, 1986

Van Deusen, John, U Mass, 1971

Van Dover, J. Kenneth, Newark, De., 1983, 84, 85, 86

Van Gorder, Helen, Youngstown SU, 1981, 86

Van Der Osten, Ferris SC, 1988

Valentino, Leo, Cabrini C, 1987

Vander Closter, Susan, RI Sch Design, 1988

Vander Woude, Vanier, York U, Can, 1988

Vanderwood, Paul J., San Diego SU, 1988

Vandoren, John W., Fl SU, 1988

Van Dover, J. Ken, Newark, De, 1988

Van Dover, Sarala A., Lincoln U, Pa, 1988

Van Herk, Aritha, U Calgary, Can., 1984

Van Name, Mark, Pa SU, 1977

Van Sickle, Larry, Rollins C, 1987

Vann, Helen, Albuquerque, 1988

Vanouse, Donald, SUNY-Oswego, 1976

Vansword, Robert C., U Ala-B'ham, 1978

Van Wert, William F., Bloomington, In, 74; 76, Temple U

Varacalli, Joseph A., Adelphi U, 1988

Varan, Duane, U Houston, 1985

Vargas, George, U Mich, 1985

Vargas, Margarita, Yale, 1979

Vartorella, William F., Alliance C, 1979

Varzas, Nicole, Berenson & Kates, San Francisco, 1987

Vasbinder, Samuel, U Akron, 1982

Vasquez, Richard, La Times, 1971

Vattel, Rose, Oh U, 1982

Vaughn, David, Park C, 1982; 84, 86, 87, U Me

Vaughan, David K., Wright-Patterson AFB, 1988

Vaughan, Lori M., Clemson, 1978

Vaughn, Mina, U Ut, 1985, 86

Vaughn, Stephen, U Wisc, 1986

Vauthier, Simone, Strasbourg, France, 1979

Veeder, Gerry, N Tx SU, 1983

Veeder, William, U Chicago, 1976

Veeser, Harold A., Wichita SU, 1988

Veler, Richard P., Wittenberg U, 1979

Velez, Lili, Carnegie-Mellon U, 1988

Velluci, Daniel, U Md, 1976

Venek, Elizabeth-Ann, Roosevelt U, 1976

Vera, Hernan, Notre Dame U, 1972

Verden, Paul, U Santa Clara, 1981, 84, 85, 87

Vesper, Ethel, Phillips U, 1983

Vester, Heinz-Gunter, Der Unwig Maximilians U, West Germany, 1988

Vestrich, Roy M., U Hartford, 1988

Vestrich, Roy, Northampton, Ma., 1986 87

Via, Jon, Mercer U, 1978, 79

Vicinus, Martha, Ind U, 1976

Vidutis, Ricardas, Ind U, 1984

Vierville, Jonathan, San Antonio, Tx., 1983

Villarino, Jose, San Diego SU, 1982

Villarreal, Jose A., Pan-Amer U, 1983

Vincent, Debra, Ok SU, 1983

Vincent, Richard, Slippery Rock SC, 1981; 83, W Il U; 84 Sou Il U

Vincent, Sylbil, Perrysberg, Oh, 1980, 81

Vincent, William A., Mich SU, 1975, 78, 80, 81, 83, 84

Vinson, Audrey L., Ala A&M, 1977, 78, 84, 85, 86, 87

Vipond, Mary, Concordia U, Montreal, 1984

Vissing, Yvonne, Ferris SC, 1987, 88

Vitanza, Dianna Mullen, E Il U, 1978, 79

Vitanza, Victor J., E Il U, 1976, 78, 79

Vivion, Michael, U Mo-KC, 1983

Vlach, John, U Md, 1976

Voelker, Paul, U Wisc-Richland, 1984

Voelkl, Cynthia J., Chicago, Il, 1988

Vogel, Harold, Sedalia, Mo., 1983

Vogt, Anne, William Paterson C, 1976

Voigt, David Q., Albright C, 1973, 76, 81, 82

Voiku, Daniel, Albany SC, Ga., 1986

Volz, Jim, Wright SU, 1980

Von Gunden, Heidi, U Il, 1984, 87

Von Hoffman, Ann B., URI, 1975, 76

Von Sauer, Franz, Ok SU, 1975

Von Schilling, James, BGSU, 1978, 79, 80; 86 Somerville, NJ

Vorhees, Duane, BGSU, 1985

Vosevich, Kathi, U Denver, 1987, 88

Vowell, Faye Nell, Emporia St. C, 1978, 82

Waage, Frederick O., Northwestern, 1972; 76, Rutgers; 80, 82, 86, 87, E Tn SU

Wachhorst, Wyn, Stanford, 1976; 83, San Jose SU; 1984, Atherton, Ca

Wachsberger, Ken, Lansing, Mi., 1984, 85, 86

Wacker, Fred, Ann Arbor, 1972

Wacker, Peter, Rutgers, 1982

Waddell, Eric, U Laval, 1987

Waddey, Lucy, U Tn-Chattanooga, 1982

Wade, Gary, Ia SU, 1987

Wade, Philip, W Car SU, 1986

Waffin, Les, National Archives, 1977

Wagers, Robert, San Jose SU, 1985

Wagner, Ann, St Olaf C, 1986

Wagner, Jon G., Knox C, 1974

Wagner, Linda, Mich SU, 1975

Wagner, Melinda, Radford U, 1981

Wagner, Nancy, Northwestern, 1987

Wagner, Ms., U Md, 1986

Wahl, Lynda E., U Ark-Little Rock, 1988

Wahlstrom, Billie J., USC, 1976, 80, 81

Wainscott, Ronald, Towson SU, 1986, 87, 88

Waite, Robert E., Vanderbilt, 1975

Waite, Rogene Smerage, Vanderbilt, 1975

Walden, Daniel, Pa SU, 1971, 77, 78, 79, 80, 81, 82, 83, 84, 85, 87, 88

Waldie, Donald J., Jr., CSU-Long Beach, 1976

Waldman, Gloria, CUNY, 1977, 78

Waldmeir, John, U Chicago, 1984, 88

Waldmeir, Joseph, Mich SU, 1972, 73, 74, 80, 84, 86, 87, 88

Walker, Cynthia, Geo Washington U, 1977; 80, U Alaska, Fairbanks

Walker, Craig S., Richmond Hill, Ont, Can, 1987

Walker, David, Mid Tn SU, 1985

Walker, Gail, Kennesaw C, 1985

Walker, James, Memphis SU, 1988

Walker, Jeanne, U De, 1988

Walker, Jeffrey, Ok SU, 1983

Walker, Jim M., E Ky U, 1988

Walker, John, Neb Wesleyan, 1981, 85

Walker, K.B., U Colo, 1986

Walker, Lewis, UNC-Wilmington, 1982

Walker, Nancy, Stephen's C, Mo., 1982, 83

Walker, Roslyn A., Bloomington, Il, 1976

Wall, Carey, San Diego SU, 1980, 88

Wall, Donald C., E Wash SC, 1975, 77, 78, 80, 81, 82, 84, 85, 86

Wall, Robert, Towson SU, 1980, 81, 82

Wallace, David, Morristown C, 1979

Wallace, Douglas, Daly City, Ca., 1983

Wallace, Jack, Miami U, Oh, 1979, 81

Wallace, Jacqueline, Miami U, Oh, 1981

Wallace, Robert, Glendon C, Toronto, 1984

Wallace, Roger, U Scranton, 1982

Walle, Alf, Ashland C, 1978, 79; 80, Alice Lloyd C; 84, John Carroll U; 85, U Akron

Wallendorf, Melanie, U Az, 1988

Wallenstein, Peter R., U Toronto, 1977

Waller, Gregory, U Louisville, 1981

Waller, Robert, Clemson U, 1986

Walling, James I., Cent MU, 1978, 79

Wallisck, William, USAF Acad, 1982

Walls, Peggy, Auburn U, 1985; 86, Benjamin Russell HS, Al

Walsh, Frank, U Lowell, 1976, 77, 78, 79

Walsh, James, Oberlin C, 1983, 84, 85

Walsh, John, Miami U, Oh, 1983

Walsh, Mary R., U Lowell, 1977, 78

Walsh, Richard, Methodist C, 1986

Walter, Charles L., Mt Home Va Med Center, Tn, 1987

Walter, James, NH C, 1984

Walters, Charles T., York C Pennsylvania, 1977; 78, 79, 80, 83, 84, 86, Bloomsburg SC

Walters, David, UNH, 1980

Walters, Dorothy, Wichita SU, 1983

Walters, Edward, Ok SU, 1973

Walters, Eric, Long Island U, 1980

Walters, Gordon, DePaul U, Ind, 1984

Walters, Pia, W Ky U, 1987

Walters, Suzanne, CUNY, 1987

Walton, Thomas, Catholic U, 1988

Waltzer, Kenneth, Mich SU, 1984

Wander, Philip, San Jose SU, 1979

Wands, John, Carnegie-Mellon U, 1979

Wang, C.K., Nat'l Taiwan U, 1986

Wang, Joseph C., Va Tech, 1980

Wang, Quignan, BGSU, 1988

Warbold, Carolyn, U Tx-San Antonio, 1984

Warburton, Terence, Pa SU-Erie, 1985, 86

Warch, Rick, Yale, 1971

Ward, Amy, Ed., Radical History Review, NYC, 1986

Ward, Carol M., U Tn, 1979, 82; 86, Clemson

Ward, Catherine, W Ky U, 1985, 86, 87

Ward, Cynthia, NYC, 1983

Ward, Dan, BGSU, 1981, 82, 83, 84, 86, 87, 88

Ward, Denis M., U Mo-KC, 1979, 80

Ward, George, BGSU, 1981, 82, 83

Ward, Robert, U Nor Ia, 1984

Ward, Robert, W Ky U 1985

Ward, Susan, St. Lawrence U, 1977

Warde, William, N Tx SU, 1981, 83, 84, 85, 86, 87

Ware, Paul W., NM SU, 1980

Warner, Charles, BGSU, 1987

Warner, Edward A., Ind SU, 1979

Warner, Priscilla K., Northwestern, 1987

Warner, Keith, Howard, 1985

Warren, Clay, UC Cape Breton, NS, 1988

Warren, John C., Milton Acad, 1988

Warren, John W., Tn Tech, 1988

Warren, Lisa, Roanoke C, 2986

Warren, Patricia, UC-Irvine, 1975

Warren, Thomas, Ok SU, 1983, 85

Warren, Traci, Appal SU, 1988

Warsh, Cheryl, U New Brunswick, 1987

Washburn, Carol, Ok SU, 1982

Washer, Robert E., 1971

Washington, Jerry, Sul Ross SU, 1979

Washington, Michael, U Cin, 1975

Washington, Robert, Bryn Mawr, 1988

Wasserman, Julian, Loyola U, NO, 1987

Wassmuth, Birgit L., U Mo, 1988

Waters, John, U Ga, 1986

Watson, Douglas, Ok Baptist U, 1983, 85

Watson, Sam, Carnegit-Mellon U 1979

Watt, Donald, SUNY-Geneseo, 1977

Watters, David, UNH, 1984

Watts, Larry, U Ala-B'ham, 1988

Watts, Thomas, U Tx-Arlington, 1983

Watts, Penny K., U Ok, 1983

Waugh, Robert H., SUC-New Paltz, 1980

Waugh, Susan, St. Louis Comm C, Mo, 1986

Wawanash, Sheila, Toronto, Can., 1984

Wawrzaszek, Patricia, SUNY-Syracuse, 1987

Waxman, Wright, Chicago, 1974

Way, R. Bruce, Tiffin U, 1986

Weadow, Mark P., USAF Acad, 1988

Wear, Delese, Northeastern Oh U, 1987 88

Weatherly, Joan, Memphis SU, 1984

Weaver, Jack, Winthrop C, 1982

Weaver, Jeanne C, Oh SU, 1987

Weaver, Laura, U Evansville, 1982, 85, 87

Weaver, Rockkmarie, Boston Pub Lib, 1986

Webb, Bernice Larson, U SW La., 1978, 79; 80, 81, 82, 83, 84, 85, 86, 87, 88

Webb, Charles, Il SLU, 1980

Webb, David, BGSU, 1984

Webb, Don, NM SU, 1979

Webb, Lynn, Tx Tech U, 1985

Webb, Robert M., U SW La, 1980, 81

Weber, Brom, UC-Davis, 1982

Weber, Charles, Wheaton C, 1988

Weber,Ronald, Notre Dame, 19791, 76

Weber, William, CSU-Long Beach, 1972

Webner, Thomas, Prince George's Comm C, 1975

Webster, Sheila, U Md, 1987

Weedman, Jane, Tx Tech, 1984, 85, 86

Weeks, Willis E., Kans SU, 1975

Wei, Dong, Ga SU, 1986

Weibel, Irene, Sou Il U, 1981

Weibel, Kay, Mich SU, 1972, 76

Weigl, Bruce, Pa SU, 1987

Weiher, Carol, U Tx-San Antonio, 1976

Weil, Vivian, Il Inst Tech, 1981

Weiland, Stephen, U Cin, 1976

Weiler, Mary T., St. Louis, Mo., 1988

Weinberg, Bob, 1974

Weinberg, David, BGSU, 1972, 76

Weinberg, Helen, Cleveland Inst Arts, 1974

Weiner, Joel, CUNY, 1986

Weinstein, Ann, Dowson C, 1987

Weinstein, Deena, DePaul U, 1984

Weinstein, Idit, U Toronto, 1984

Weinstein, Stephen, NYC, 1984

Weirather, Larry, Rocky Mt. C, 1975, 76

Weis, Lyle, U Alberta, 1986

Weisbaker, Dimis T., U Tn-Chattanooga, 1978

Weisblat, Tinky, U Tx, 1986

Weiseman, Jack, C DuPage, Il, 1973

Weisenborn, Ray, Mont SU 1982

Weiss, Gene, U Md., 1977

Weiss, Irving J., SUNY-New Paltz, 1972, 78

Weiss, Liz, WXYZ-Detroit, 1980

Weiss, Marion, U Md, 1977

Weiss, Naomi, U Pa, 1972

Weiss, Rube, WXYZ-Detroit, 1980

Weisz, Carole, Pa SU, 1982

Weixlmann, Joe, Ind SU, 1984

Welch, Kathleen, U Ok, 1983

Welch, Richard, U Denver, 1983; 84, 85, 86, Villanova

Weller, Donald, U Hawaii, 1973

Wells, Alan, Cent MU, 1988

Wells, James, Ok SU, 1984

Wells, Jane F., Marshall U, 1988

Wells, Joan, Phila., 1978

Wells, John D., Mary Baldwin C, 1985, 86

Wells, Rosemary, Northwestern, 1982

Wells, Samuel, U Sou Miss, 1982

Wells, Tanya, U Tx-Arlington, 1985, 86

Welsch, Andrew, Rutgers, 1985

Welsch, Jack, Abilne Christian U, 1985

Welsch, Janice R., W Il Un 1976

Welsh, James M., Literature/Film Quarterly, 1975

Welsh, John F., Pittsburg SU, Kans, 1987

Welsh, Susan E., 1985

Welsh, William, BGSU, Firelands, 1987

Welty, Gordon, Wright SU, 1981, 84

Wendell, Carolyn, Monroe Comm C, NY, 1980, 84

Wendell, Peter, Duke, 1988

Wendland, Albert, U Pitt, 1979

Wenke, John, Marquette U, 1985

Werchan, James, E Tx SU, 1985, 86

Werness, Hope, CSU-Stanislaus, 1986

Wert, Hal, Kansas City Art Inst, 1980

Werth, Lee F., Cleveland SU, 1980, 81, 84, 85, 86, 87

Wertheim, Arthur Frank, USC, 1976

Wertheimer, Barbara, Cornell U, 1980

Wesley, George, Appal SU, 1984

Wesolowski, James, W Ky U, 1986

Wesson, David, Marquette U, 1985, 87

West, Kenneth, U Mich-Flint, 1986

West, Marc, Green Bay, Wi, 1980

West, Mark, BGSU, 1981, 82; 86, Campbell U

West, Mark, Elon C., 1988

West, Robert, Kent SU, 1986, 87

Westbrook, Brett, U Ok, 1983

Wester, Donald, Ok Baptist U, 1983

Wester, Janey, Ok Baptist U, 1983

Westfall, Susan, Lafayette C, 1984

Westrum, Ronald, E Mich U, 1975, 76

Wexman, Virginia W., U Il-Chicago, 1978

Whalen, Matthew D., U Md, 1977; 79, Temple U

Whalen, Terence, Duke, 1988

Whaley, A.B., Kent SU, 1983, 84, 86

Whaley, Charles, UNC, 1979; 81, UNC-Charlotte

Whaley, Marie W., Kent SU, 1983, 86, 87

Whannel, Paddy, Northwestern U, 1973, 76

Wharton, Donald, Castleton SC, 1984

Whatley, George C., U Ala-B'ham, 1976, 77

Whatley, Virginia, U Ala-B'ham, 1975

Wheeler, Anne, BGSU, 1988

Wheeler, Macel, N Ky Highland U, 1985

Wheeler, William Bruce, U Tn, 1977

Whelan, Robert, U Me, 1988

Whetmore, Edward Jay, Lewis & Clark C, 1975, 76; 77, 78, U Hawaii; 79, 80, 81, 82, 83, U San Francisco

Whillock, David, Stephen F. Austin SU, 1984; 86, 87, U Mo

Whillock, Rita, U Mo, 1986, 88

Whipp, Les, U Neb, 1984

Whitaker, Elaine, U Ala-B'ham, 1986

Whitaker, Walter, III, Girard, Pa, 1985, 86, 88

White, C. Clarkson, Armstrong SC, 1984

White, David, St. John Fisher C, 1980, 82, 84

White, David M., UC-San Diego, 1977

White, David Manning, Boston U, 1973

White, Doug, Tulsa, Ok., 1983

White, Elizabeth, U Ia, 1982; 84, Loyola U, Chicago

White, Hayden, Wesleyan U, 1974

White, Isabelle, E Ky U, 1984, 86

White, John Franklin, William Rainey Harper C, 1976; 85, N Ky U, 1985

White, Les, U Tn, 1982; 86, UNO

White, Leslie A., UNO, 1987

White, Margaret Ripley, E Tn SU-Kingsport Center, 1982

White, Marilyn, W Ky U, 1985, 87

White, Marybeth, SE Mo SU, 1985

White, Maxine, San Jose SU, 1984, 85

White, Patrick, Westmar C., 1979, 81, 82, 83, 84; 86, 87, 88, Pfeiffer C

White, Peter, UNM, 1983

White, Ray, Ball SU, 1980, 81, 83, 84, 85, 86

White, Robert, York U, Toronto, 1971, 72, 80, 84, 86, 87

White, Robert A., Citadel, 1988

White, Sharon, Yale, 1978

White, Vernon, WXYZ-Detroit, 1980

Whiteaker, Bruce, James Madison U, 1979

Whitehead, Ralph Jr., U Mass, 1978

Whitehill, Sharon, Grand Valley SC, 1988

Whitlock, William B., Dekalb Comm C, Ga, 1987

Whitlow, Roger, E Il U, 1976, 77, 78, 79, 83

Whitman, Joan, N Ky U, 1985

Whitney, Charles, Alfred, NY, 1987

Whitney, Sharon, NYC, 1982

Whitson, Mont, Morehead SU, 1982, 85

Whittenberger-Keith, Kari, U Tx, 1984, 85

Whordley, Derek, Mercer U, 1978, 79

Wickham, Christopher, U Il-Chicago, 1987, 88

Wicoxson, Kirby, Sioux Falls C, 1988

Widdison, Harold A., N Az U, 1987

Widdowson, William, U Cin, 1977, 78

Wiedeman, Barbara, U Ala-Huntsville, 1987

Wiedemann, Barbara, U Sou Fl, 1984, 85, 87

Wieder, Rosemary, Everson, Wa, 1983

Wiegand, Bruce, Vanderbilt, 1985

Wiegand, Wayne A., U Ky, 1978

Wiegman, Robyn, U Wash, 1986

Wiener, Joel H., CUNY, 1979, 80

Wiener, Paul, SUNY-Long Island, 1982

Wier, Alison, York U, Toronto, 1988

Wiethoff, William, Ind U, 1986, 87, 88

Wiggins, Alfred, Ok SU, 1986

Wiggins, Lee, York U, Toronto, 1988

Wiggins, William, Ind U, 1971, 73, 74, 75, 81, 82

Wilcox, Fred A., SUNY-Albany, 1987, 88

Wilcox, Gary, U Tx, 1985

Wilcox, Leonard, U Canterbury, Christchurch, NZ, 1986, 88

Wilcox, Sarah, U Ct, 1986

Wilden, Anthony, Burnaby, BC, 1984

Wilder, Hugh T., Miami U, Oh, 1980; 82 U Charleston

Wilentz, Gay, E Caro U, 1986, 87, 88

Wiley, George, Ind U Pa., 1979, 82, 88

Wilhelm, Albert, Tn Tech U, 1986

Wilhelm, Hubert G.H., Oh U, 1987

Wilhide, Chris, BGSU, 1988

Wilke, Carol, U Scranton, 1982

Wilke, Janet, Doane C, 1983

Wilkins, Lawrence, Ind U-Indianapolis, 1986

Wilke, Ray, Villanova U,1988

Wilkin, Karen, U Pa, 1987, 88

Wilkinson-Bus, T. Patrick, NYC, 1987

Willardson, Ann, Denison U, 1979; 80, U Wash

Willauer, G.J., Ct C, 1988

Wille, Steve, Augusta C, 1985

Willems, David M., U Wisc-Green Bay, 1979

Willett, Ralph, U Hull, England, 1975, 76

Williams, Albert, Tn Tech, 1987

Williams, Brett, Amer U, 1978, 80, 81

Williams, Carol T., Roosevelt U, Chicago, 1974, 75, 76, 79, 80, 81; 82, U Chicago; 84, 85, 86, 88, Roosevelt U

Williams, Clyde V., Miss SU, 1974, 75

Williams, Daniel, Orange Park, Fl., 1983; 86, U Miss

Williams, Edith, E Ky U, 1985, 86, 87, 88

Williams, Edwin W., E Tn SU, 1978

Williams, Ernie, S. Leo C, 1986

Williams, Gilbert, Mich SU, 1984, 85

Williams, Gloria, U Minn-St. Paul, 1984, 85

Williams, Harry, U Mo, 1983

Williams, J.P., Wayne SU, 1987, 88

Williams, J. Carol, Va Commonwealth U, 1978

Williams, Jeanne, Kent SU, 1982; 84, 85, Oh SU

Williams, Jerome, U Colo, 1985

Williams, J. Peter, Cty C, Morris, NJ, 1987

Williams, Kenny, NE Il U, 1976

Williams, Lance A., Los Angeles, Ca., 1978

Williams, L.C., U Md, 1977

Williams, Mara, NYU, 1984

Williams, Marvin, UNO, 1979

Williams, Michael, Aquinas C, 1985

Williams, Nudie, U Ark, 1983

Williams, Peter, Cty C, Morris, Randolph, NJ, 1988

Williams, Tony, S Il U, 1986, 87, 88

Williams, Wenmouth, Ithaca C, 1987
Williams, William, E Wash U, 1984, 88
Williamson, Juanita, LeMoyne-Owens C, 1977
Williamson, Katya, UCLA, 1983
Williamson, Mary, U Neb-Omaha, 1979
Williford, Julian, BGSU, 1980, 84
Willinsky, John M., Laurentian U, Ont, 1983
Willis, Alan, Richmond Heights, Mo., 1975
Willis, Susan, E Ky U, 1984, 85
Willmer, John E., SUNY-Cortland, 1977
Willson, David, Green River Comm C, 1986
Wilson, Ann, York U, Toronto, 1984
Wilson, Ben, W Mich U, 1982
Wilson, Carolyn A., Mn Hist Soc, St. Paul, 1987
Wilson, Charles, U Miss, 1985, 86
Wilson, Christina, Sou Il U, 1986
Wilson, Christopher, Middlebury C, 1988
Wilson, David S., UC-Davis, 1974
Wilson, Debbie, U Louisville, 1984
Wilson, Donald, Clarion U, 1986
Wilson, James D., Ga SU, 1974
Wilson, James H., U SW La, 1977, 78
Wilson, John Scott, U S Caro, 1977, 78, 81, 82, 83, 84, 85, 86, 88
Wilson, Kevin, St. Leonard, P.Q., Can, 1984; 85 U Montreal
Wilson,. Paul, Methodist C, 1986
Wilson,. Paule A. U Tn, 1978
Wilson, Sharon, U N Colo, 1984, 85, 86, 87
Wilt, Judith, Boston C, 1986
Winans, Robert B., Wayne SU, 1980
Winchell, Mark Royden, U Sou Miss, 1982; 86, Clemson
Winder, Terry, B. Columbia Inst Tech, Burnaby, 1985
Winderl, Carl A. Eastern Nazarine, 1988
Winders, James, Appal SU, 1980
Wingate, Nancy, WVUE-TV, New Orleans, 1976; 77, Newark, De., 78, 88
Winn, Ruth, Suffolk U, 1984
Winning, Robert, Chicago, Il, 1986
Winsell, Keith A., IUPUI, 1971, 73, 74, 75, 76; 78, Wittenburg U; 84, Northfield, Mn
Winston, Robert, Dickinson C, 1982, 85
Winters, Donald, U Minn, 1979; 81, 82, 85, Minn Comm C
Winton, Calhoun, U Md, 1976
Wires, Richard, Ball SU, 1985, 86, 88
Wise, George, General Electric Corp, 1981
Wise, James N., U Mo-Rolla, 1987
Wise, Paul, U Akron, 1984
Wiseman, John, Frostburg SC, 1986, 87
Wishart, David, U Neb, 1988
Witkoski, Michael, U S Caro, 1978
Witkowski, Paul, Radford U, 1981
Witkowski, Terrence, CSU-Long Beach, 1982; 83, 84, U Tx; 85, CSU-Long Beach
Wittmer, George, Stillwater, Ok, 1983
Wixon, Richard L., Sou Il, 1981, 85, 87
Woehling, Mary, St. John's U, 1983
Wohl, David, W Va SU, 1987
Wohlpart, James, Colo SU, 1988
Wolck, Wolkgang, SUNY-Buffalo,1976
Wolf, Howard, SUNY-Buffalo, 1979, 80
Wolf, Jack, SUC-Brockport, 1984

Wolf, Leonard, San Francisco SC,1973
Wolfe, Arnold S., Triton C, 1979
Wolfe, Billy, TCU, 1985
Wolfe, Charles, Mid Tn SU, 1973, 74, 75, 76, 77, 78, 88
Wolfe, Gary K., Roosevelt U, 1975, 76, 77, 79, 80, 81
Wolfe, Irving, U Montreal, 1987
Wolfe, Gary, Roosevelt U, 1974
Wolfe, Kary, U Chicago, 1974
Wolfe, Peter, U Mo-St. Louis, 1976, 77, 78, 86, 87
Wolfe, Ralph, BGSU, 1972, 86
Wolfe, Steve, Mankato, Mn, 1981
Wolford, Chester, Pa SU-Behrend, 1986, 87
Wolfram, Manfred, Trinity U, San Antonio, j1984
Wolins, Julie M., Ind U, 1987
Wolitz, Seth L., U Tx-San Antonio, 1976
Wolk, Claudia, U Hartford, 1979
Woll, Allen, Camden C Arts & Sciences, 1980
Wollam, Jean, U Ut, 1973
Wollan, Laurin Λ., Fl SU, 1988]
Wollen, Peter, Northwestern, 1973
Wolniewicz, Richard, USAF Acad, 1977, 79
Wolter, Lou, Drake U, 1984
Wonders, Karen, U Victoria, B.C.
Wood, George, UNO, 1988
Wood, Harvard C., Lansdown, Pa, 1987
Wood, John E., James Madison U, 1988
Wood, Martin, U Wisc-Eau Claire, 1988
Wood, Robert, Ga Inst Tech, 1986, 87, 88
Woodall, Elaine, Pa SU, 1980
Woodard, Philip. Loyola Marymount, 1974
Woodhouse, Mark, Ga SU, 1980
Woodlief, Ann, Marymount C Kans, 1980
Woodman, Betsy, Historic Resources Newburyport, Ma, 1984
Woodruff, Charles, W Mich U, 1980
Woodruff, Fred, Ok SU, 1976
Woodruff, Juliette B., Fl Jn C, Jacksonville, 1980, 82, 84, 88
Woods, Alan, Oh SU, 1988
Woods, Louis, U N Fl, 1982, 86, 88
Woods, Paula M., Ind SU, 1980; 82, 83, 84, 85, 86, 87, 88, Baylor
Woods, Ronald E, Mich U, 1986
Woods, W.C., Longwood C, Va., 1984
Woodward, William, Seattle Pacific U, 1985, 86, 86, 87, 88
Woolcott, Donna, U Guelph, Can., 1987
Woolfolk, Alan, Sou Methodist U, 1984
Wooster, Martin M., Silver Spring, Md, 1981
Workman, Mark, Oakland U, 1980, 81, 87
Worley, Bill, Clovis, NM, 1984; 85, N Ky U
Worley, Joan, Oh U, 1975, 78; 79, 80, 81, 82, 83, 86; UC-Santa Barbara
Worth, Lee, Cleveland SU, 1982
Worthen, Tom, E Il U, 1988
Worthington, Mariane, Ball SU, 1987
Wortman, Roy R., Oh SU, 1971; 72, 73, 88, Kenyon C
Wosk, Julie, SUNY-Maritime C, 1983
Wren, James, Trussville, Ala, 1983
Wright, Catherine, BGSU 1985
Wright, David C., U Wisc

Wright, David E. Mich SU, 1974, 75, 76, 77, 80, 81; 82, 83, Washington, D.C.
Wright, R. Glenn, Mich SU, 1972, 73, 77
Wright, Gwendolyn, Sou Ct SU, 1986
Wright, James D., U Mass, 1988
Wright, Jon D., SW Mo SU, 1986
Wright, John, BGSU, 1974, 75, 76; 80, Henry Ford Mus
Wright, Larry, Beer Can Collectors of America, 1973
Wright, Robert, Kingston, Ont., 1985, 87, 88
Wright, Robert, Mich SU, 1972, 73
Wright, Talmadge, UC-Irvine, 1984, 85
Wright, William C., U Houston, 1975
Wrobel, Arthur, U Ky, 1975, 76, 79, 80, 81
Wuerth, Hans, Moravian C, 1987
Wyatt, Robert, U Tn, 1974
Wydeven, Joseph, Bellevue C, 1983
Wylder, Delbert, SW Minn SC, 1972, 75; 88, Murray SC
Wylie, Kenneth, Mich SU, 1986, 87
Wymer, Thomas, BGSU, 1973, 75, 76, 79, 80, 81, 82, 85
Wyass, Hal, Albion C, 1974

Yacovelle, Lynn, U Md, 1987
Yacowar, Maurice, Brock U, 1972, 73, 74, 75, 77, 78, 79, 80
Yahnke, Robert E., U Minn, 1981
Yamaguchi, Joanne, UBC, Vancouver, 1984
Yamamoto, Akira, U Kans, 1984, 85
Yamamoto, Fumiko, U Kans, 1984, 85
Yancey, Melville, Ind U, 1974, 75
Yancey, Thomas, Cent Methodist C, 1976
Yanelli, Andrew, Temple, 1980
Yang, Kyuchul, Temple, 1986
Yanarella, Ernest, U Ky, 1988
Yanwen, Xia, BGSU, 1988
Yap, Gloria, BGSU, 1986
Yaple, Henry, U Wy, 1985, 86
Yarowsky, Morris, Va Commonwealth U, 1973
Yates, Donald, Mich SU, 1971, 72, 73, 74, 75, 80, 81
Yates, Moris, Ia SU, 1971
Yau, Esther, BGSU, 1983
Yawella, Philip, Temple, 1973, 74, 81, 82
Yawney, Carole, York U, Toronto, 1984
Yearwood, Gladstone, Oh U, 1982
Yeats, Gary, Ok SU, 1983
Yeh, Michelle, CSU-Long Beach, 1984
Yeh, Nora, UC-Santa Barbara, 1987
Yoder, Linda, W Va U, 1985
Yoggy, Gary, Corning Comm C, 1984, 86, 87, 88
Yoke, Carl, Kent SU, 1982, 85
Yokopenic, Patricia, UC-Berkeley, 1975
Yon, Paul, BGSU, 1979, 84
Yorio, Carlos, CUNY-Lehman C, 1986
York, Randy, Miami U, Oh, 1983
Yorke, Jean M., Lawrence, Ks, 1983
Yoshimori, Dorothy, Mich SU, 1984
Young, Dolly, Austin, Tx, 1983
Young, Edward, Shr Jung Center Culture/Arts, 1974
Young, Frederic, U Dayton, 1987
Young, Iris, Miami Oh, 1980

Young, James Bradford, U Il, 1982
Young, Jennifer Smith, Lansing, Mi, 1982
Young, John, Lincoln U, Mo., 1986
Young, Juana R., U Ark, 1988
Young, Mallory, Tartleton SU, 1988
Young, William, BGSU, 1985, 86
Young, William H., Lynchburg C, 1975, 76, 77, 80, 88
Youngelson, Helen L., Portland SU, 1987, 88
Youngs, William T., Kenyon C, 1972
Youra, Steven, U Me, 1986, 87
Yu, Li-Hua, BGSU, 1985, 86, 87
Yunker, Douglas, Quad-Cities Socialwork Center, 1976

Zacharias, Lee, U Ark, 1975
Zaharias, Jane, Cleveland SU, 1985
Zak, Rose, Boston C, 1984, 87
Zaki, Hoda, Hampton Inst, 1982, 83, 88
Zalampas, Michael, Jefferson Comm C, 1981, 82, 83, 86, 87, 88
Zalampas, Sherree, Jefferson Comm C, Ky, 1981, 83, 86, 88
Zamora, Carlos, Pa SU, 1977, 78
Zamora, Lois, U Houston, 1979
Zanot, Eric, U Md, 1988
Zanes, John, Clemson, 1986

Zanger, Juks, S Il U, 1973, 79, 86, 87
Zaniello, Thomas A., N Ky SC, 1973, 75, 76, 77, 78
Zanot, Eric J., Pa SU, 1977, 78; 78, 87, U Md
Zapatka, Francis, Amer U, 1984, 87
Zapatka, Frank, Amer U, 1988
Zapinski, Jim, U Wisc, 1974
Zatalava, J.D., U Pitt, 1977
Zatliln, Linda, Morehouse C, 1975
Zavala, Diana A., U Puerto Rico, 1988
Zbar, Flora, U S Fl, 1980
Zehlow, Paula M., Mo Western SC, 1983
Zeiger, William, CSU-San Diego, 1987
Zelman, Tom, Ia SU, 1984
Zelman, Thomas, Stevens Point, Wi, 1987, 88
Zemka, Sue, Stanford, 1988
Zerbinos, Eugenia, Marquette U, 1986
Zerby, Diane, Kent SU, 1987
Zero, T., Il SU, 1982
Zharen, W. Van, Skaarup C & Odense U, Denmark, 1982
Zhao, Li, BGSU, 1986
Zia, Yah Wen, BGSU, 1987
Zibelman, Steve, 1973
Zieff, Robert L., Carlisle, Pa, j1982
Ziegler, Robert, Mont C Mineral Science

& Tech, 1979, 80, 81, 82, 83, 84; 86, New Phila, Oh
Ziewacz, Lawremce. Mich SU, 1981, 85, 86, 87, 88
Ziff, Melody, Fairfax, Va., 1984, 85
Zimmerly, Belle M., Columbus C, Ga, 1985, 86
Zimmerman, Bonnie, San Diego SU, 1980
Zimmerman, Larry, USD, 1985
Zimmerman, Roy, Henkel Corp, St. Paul, 1982
Zimolzak, Chester, Glassboro SC, 1979, 84, 85
Zipes, Jack D., U Wisc-Milwaukee, 1974, 83
Zito, George, Syracuse U, 1984
Zolberg, Vera L., Purdue, 1979
Zone, Ray, USC, 1983
Zrilich, Franz, BGSU, 1979, 80
Zucker, Jacob, Ok SU, 1983
Zulandt, George, Oh SU, 1973
Zung, Thomas T.K., AIA, Architects Inc., 1971
Zwink, Tim, NW Ok SU, 1983

M